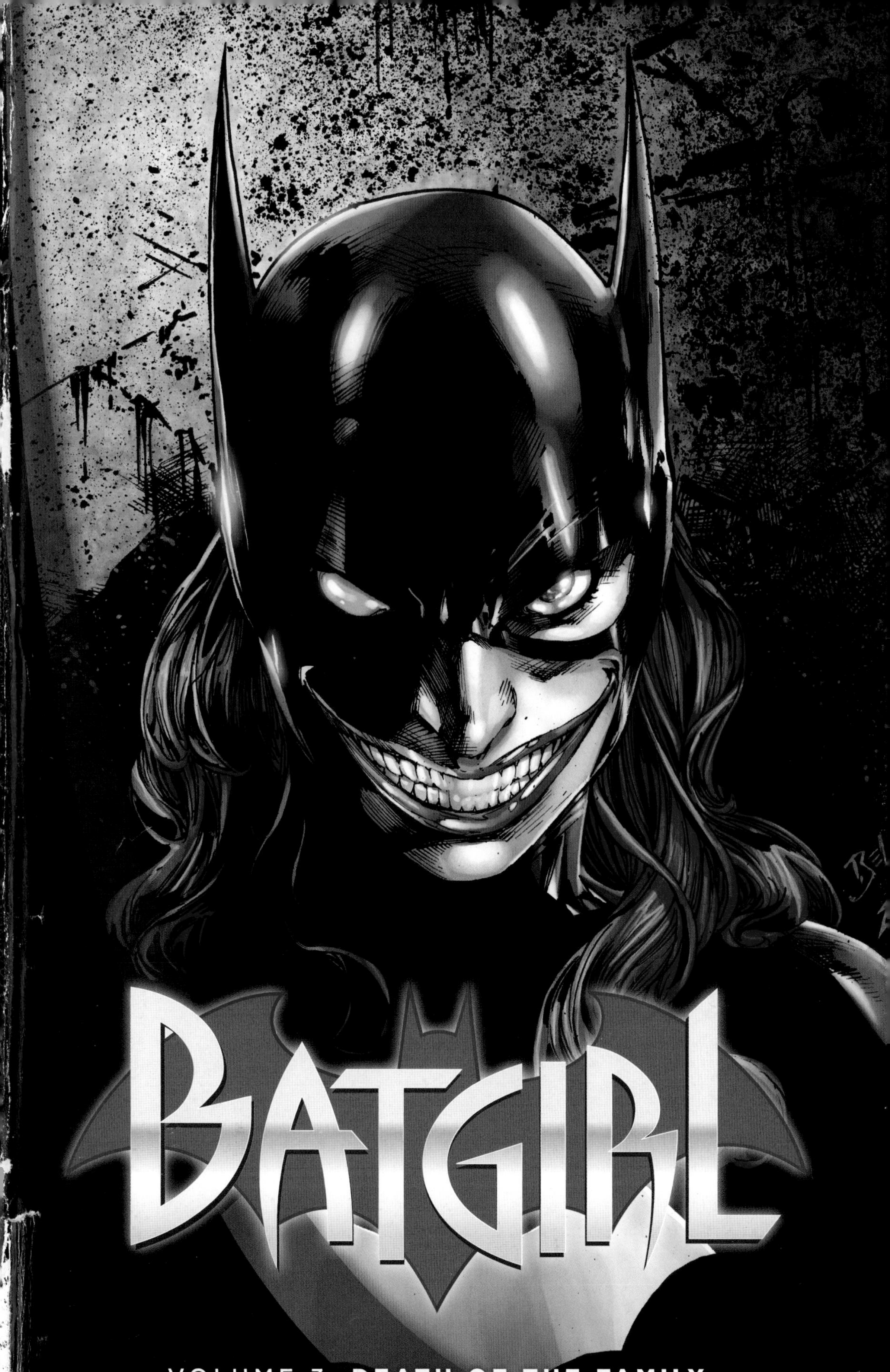
BATGIRL

VOLUME 3 DEATH OF THE FAMILY

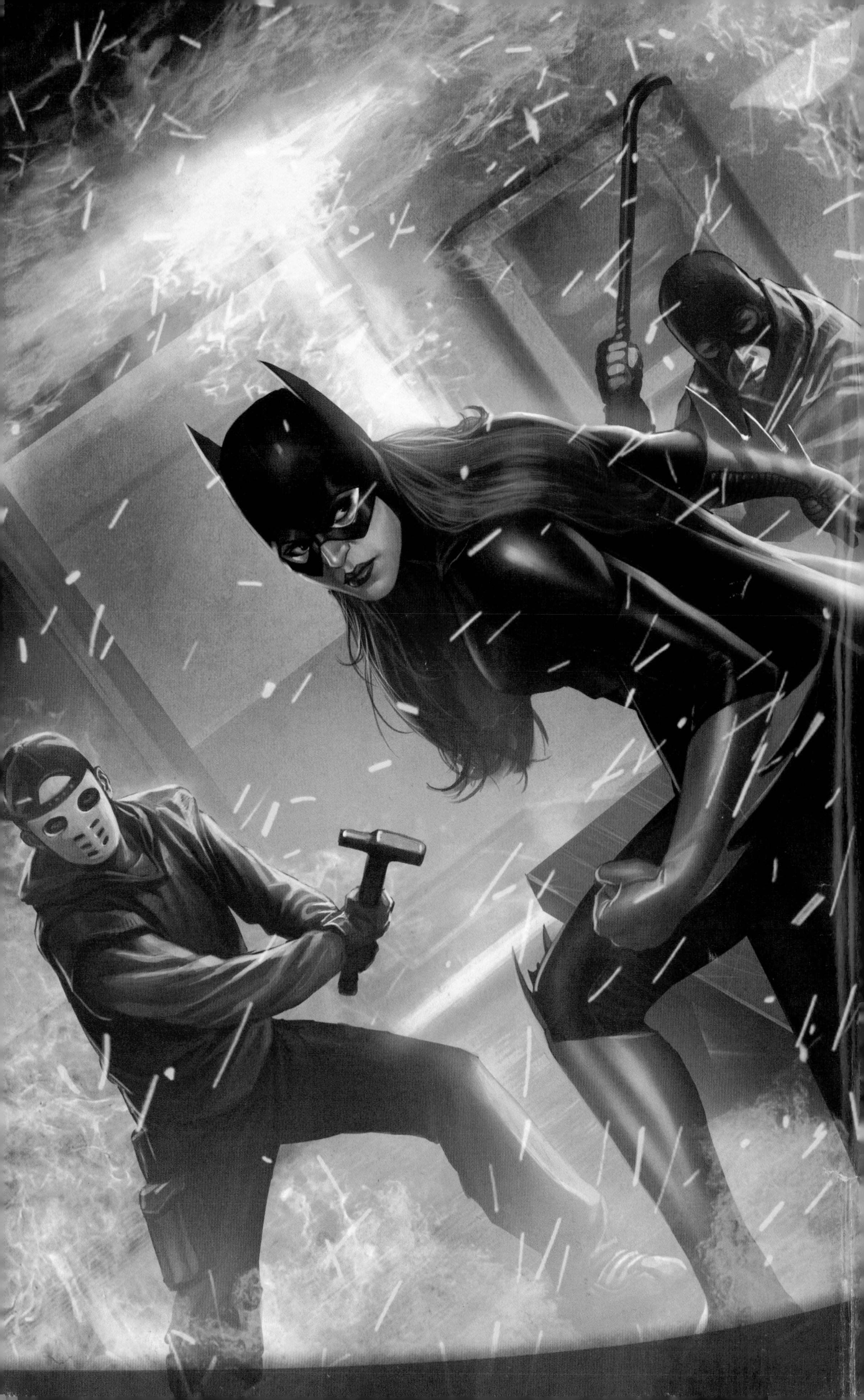

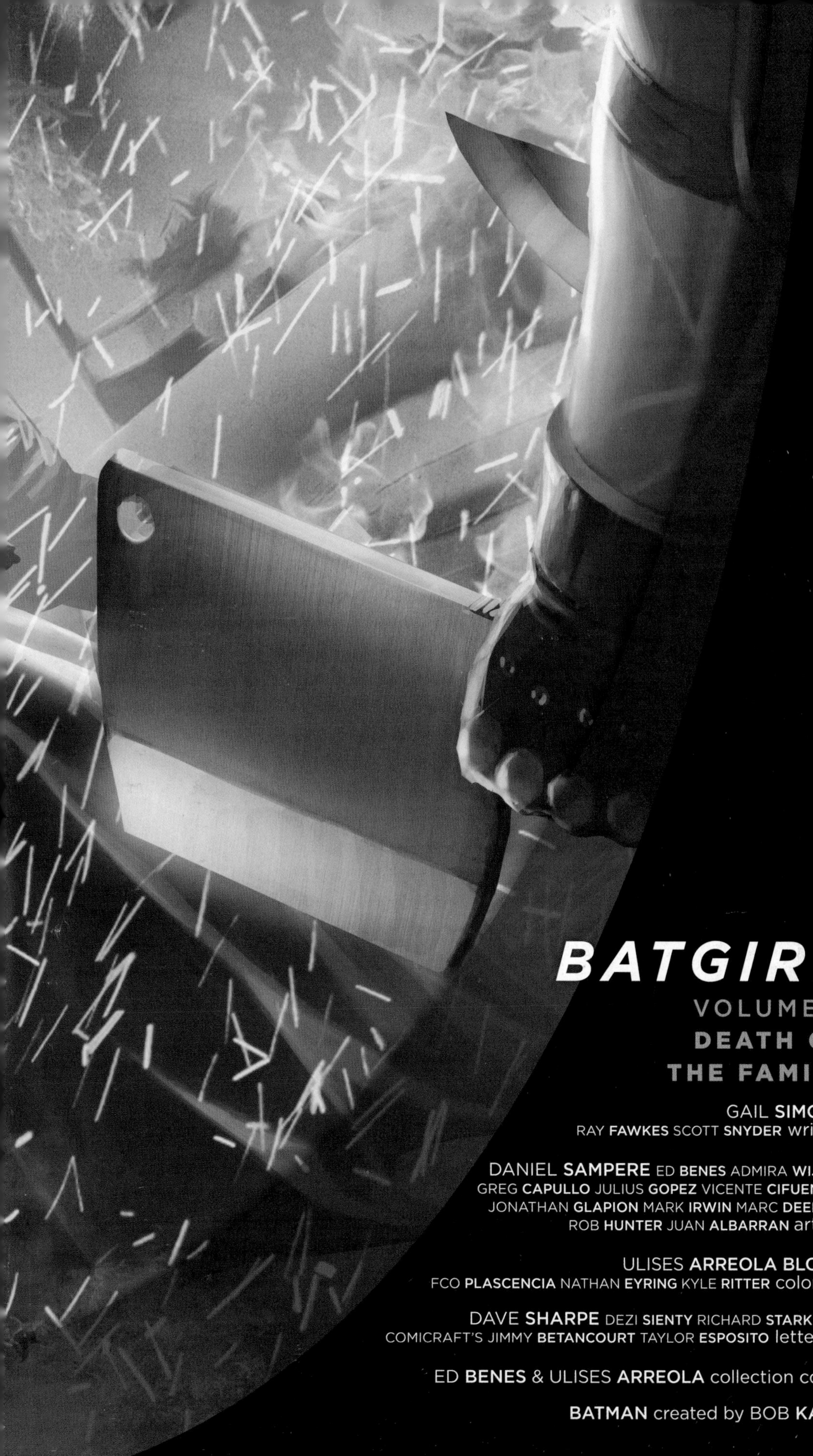

BATGIRL

VOLUME 3
DEATH OF THE FAMILY

GAIL **SIMONE**
RAY **FAWKES** SCOTT **SNYDER** writers

DANIEL **SAMPERE** ED **BENES** ADMIRA **WIJAYA**
GREG **CAPULLO** JULIUS **GOPEZ** VICENTE **CIFUENTES**
JONATHAN **GLAPION** MARK **IRWIN** MARC **DEERING**
ROB **HUNTER** JUAN **ALBARRAN** artists

ULISES **ARREOLA BLOND**
FCO **PLASCENCIA** NATHAN **EYRING** KYLE **RITTER** colorists

DAVE **SHARPE** DEZI **SIENTY** RICHARD **STARKINGS**
COMICRAFT'S JIMMY **BETANCOURT** TAYLOR **ESPOSITO** letterers

ED **BENES** & ULISES **ARREOLA** collection cover

BATMAN created by BOB **KANE**

BRIAN CUNNINGHAM KATIE KUBERT BRIAN SMITH MIKE MARTS EDDIE BERGANZA Editors – Original Series
DARREN SHAN Assistant Editor – Original Series ROBIN WILDMAN Editor
ROBBIN BROSTERMAN Design Director – Books ROBBIE BIEDERMAN Publication Design

BOB HARRAS SENIOR VP – Editor-in-Chief, DC Comics

DIANE NELSON President DAN DIDIO and JIM LEE Co-Publishers
GEOFF JOHNS Chief Creative Officer
JOHN ROOD Executive VP – Sales, Marketing and Business Development
AMY GENKINS Senior VP – Business and Legal Affairs NAIRI GARDINER Senior VP – Finance
JEFF BOISON VP – Publishing Planning MARK CHIARELLO VP – Art Direction and Design
JOHN CUNNINGHAM VP – Marketing TERRI CUNNINGHAM VP – Editorial Administration
ALISON GILL Senior VP – Manufacturing and Operations HANK KANALZ Senior VP – Vertigo and Integrated Publishing
JAY KOGAN VP – Business and Legal Affairs, Publishing JACK MAHAN VP – Business Affairs, Talent
NICK NAPOLITANO VP – Manufacturing Administration SUE POHJA VP – Book Sales
COURTNEY SIMMONS Senior VP – Publicity BOB WAYNE Senior VP – Sales

BATGIRL VOLUME 3: DEATH OF THE FAMILY

DC Comics, 1700 Broadway, New York, NY 10019
A Warner Bros. Entertainment Company.
Printed by RR Donnelley, Salem, VA, USA. 9/20/13. First Printing.

HC ISBN: 978-1-4012-4259-6
SC ISBN: 978-1-4012-4628-0

SUSTAINABLE FORESTRY INITIATIVE

Certified Chain of Custody
At Least 20% Certified Forest Content
www.sfiprogram.org
SFI-01042
APPLIES TO TEXT STOCK ONLY

Library of Congress Cataloging-in-Publication Data

Simone, Gail.
Batgirl. Volume 3, Death of the family / Gail Simone, Ed Benes.
pages cm
"Originally published in single magazine form as Batgirl 14-19, Batgirl Annual 1, Batman 17, Young Romance 1."
ISBN 978-1-4012-4259-6
1. Graphic novels. I. Benes, Ed. II. Title. III. Title: Death of the family.
PN6728.B358S58 2013
741.5'973—dc23

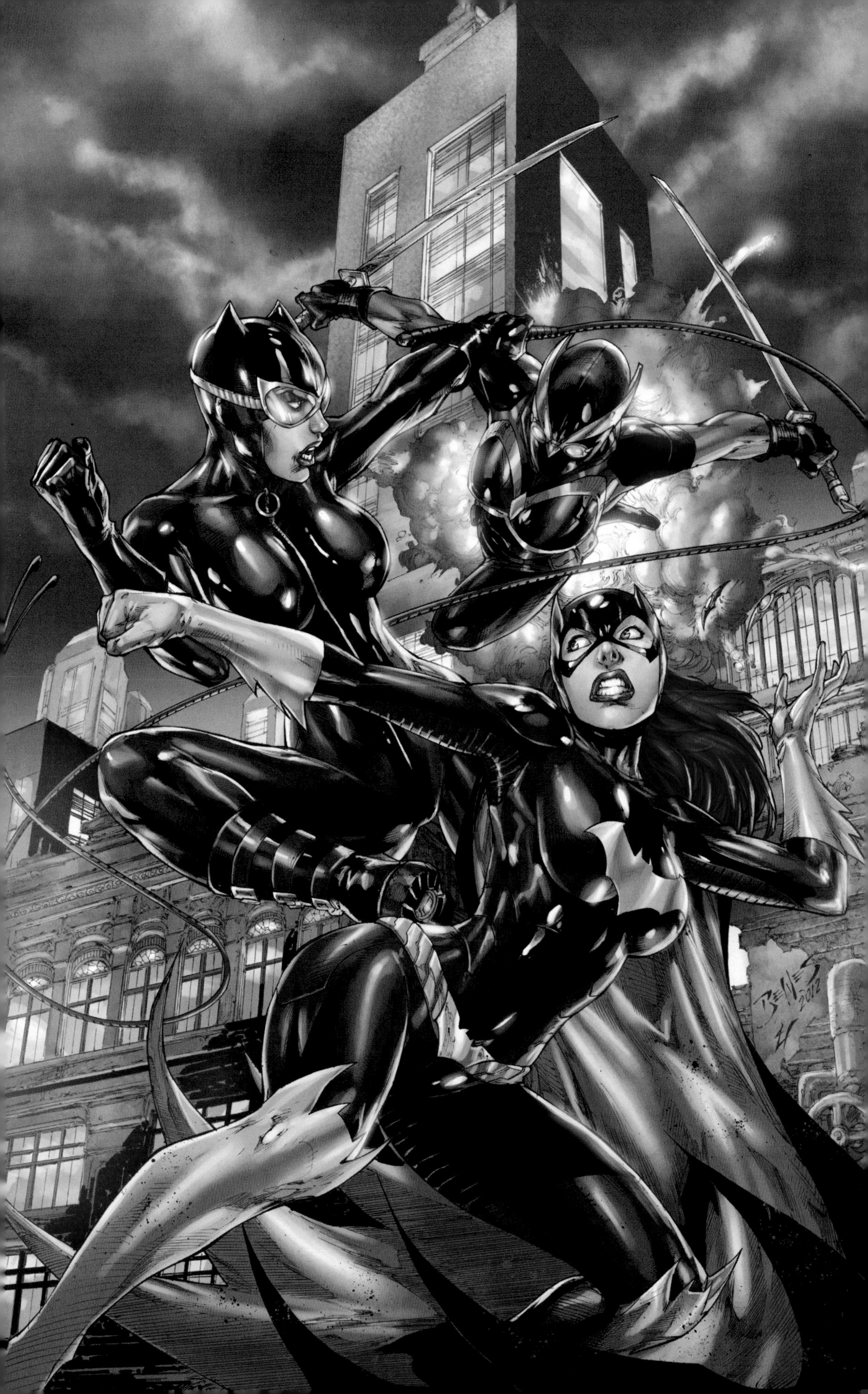

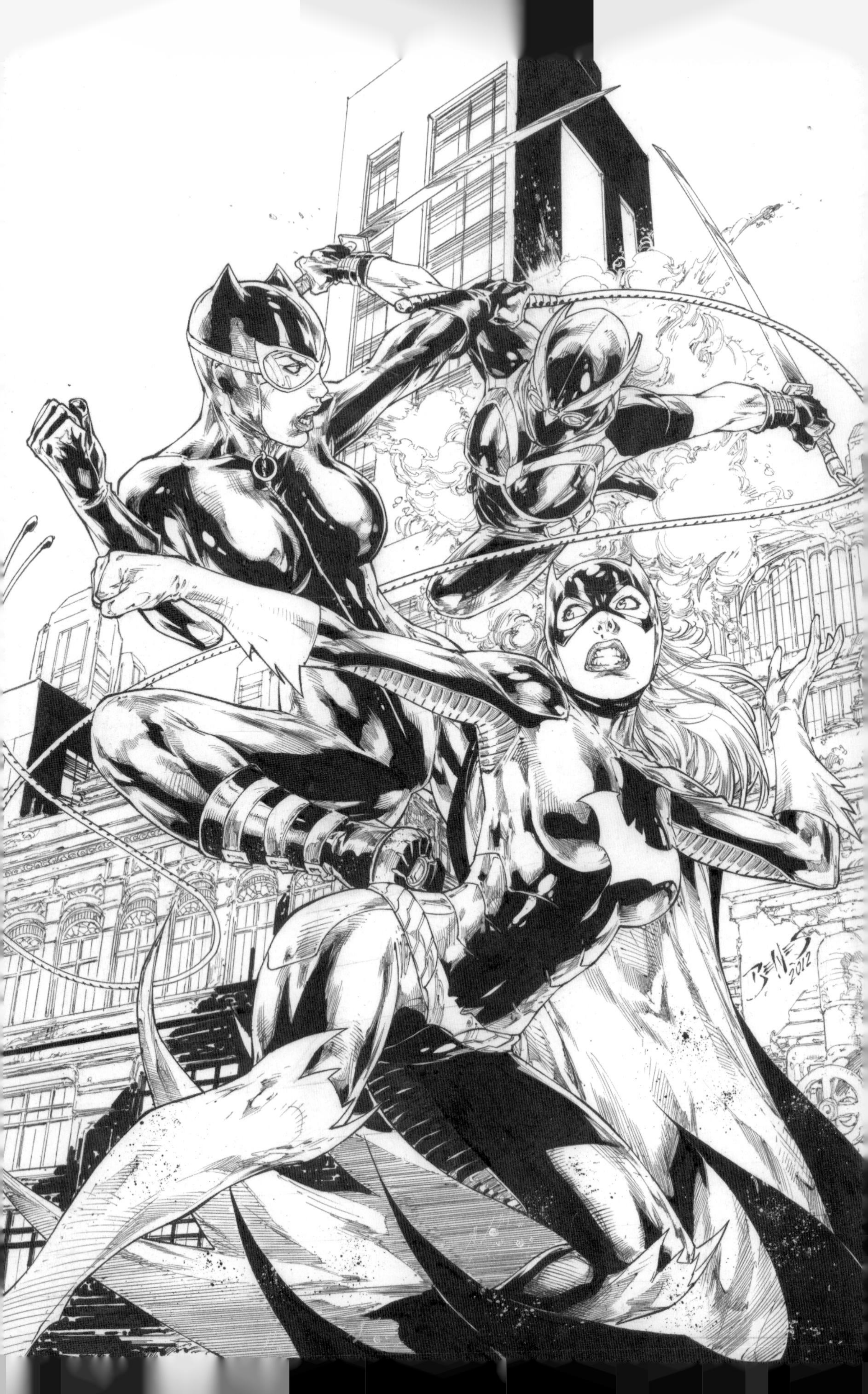

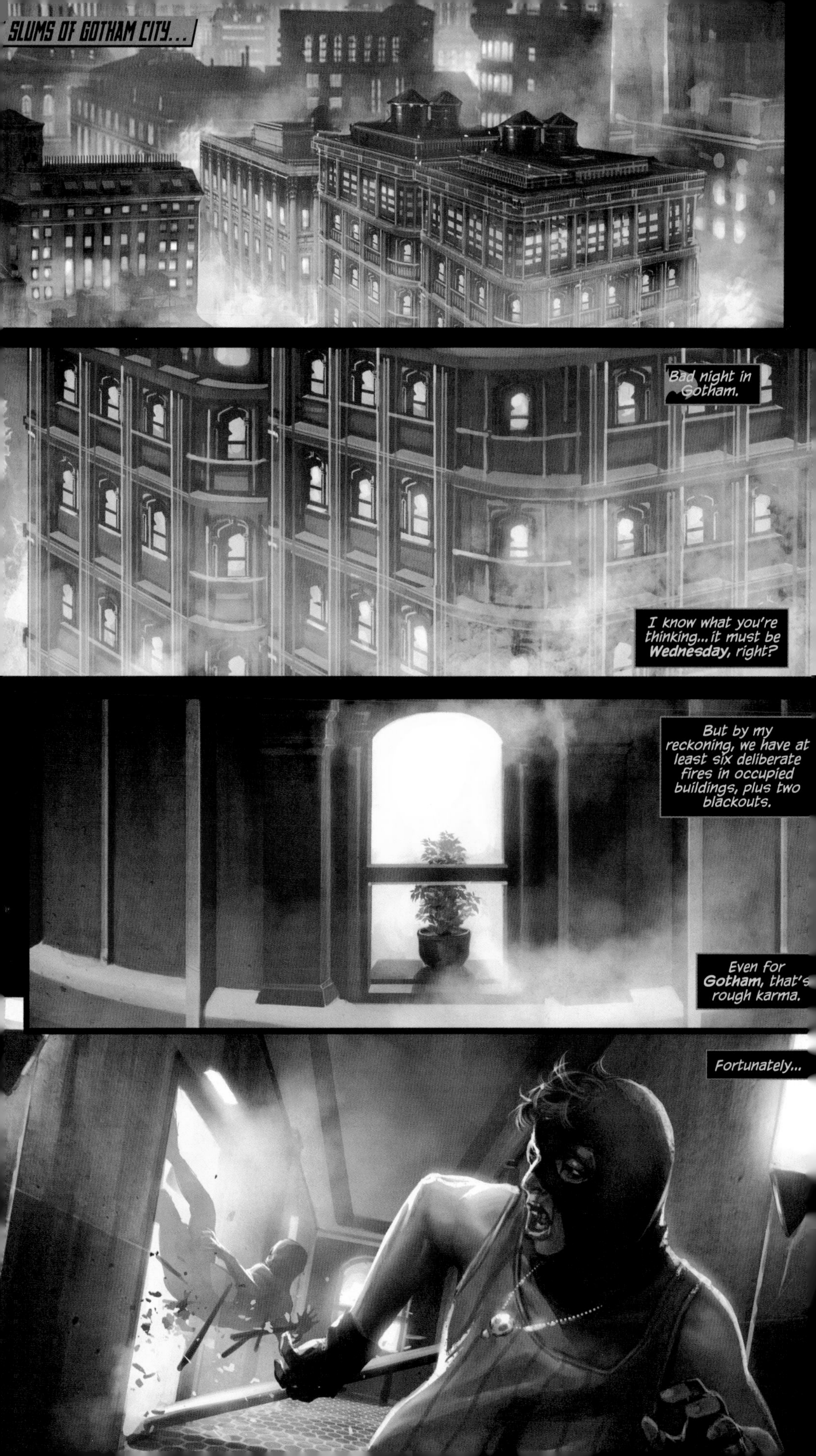
SLUMS OF GOTHAM CITY...
Bad night in Gotham.
I know what you're thinking... it must be Wednesday, right?
But by my reckoning, we have at least six deliberate fires in occupied buildings, plus two blackouts.
Even for Gotham, that's rough karma.
Fortunately...

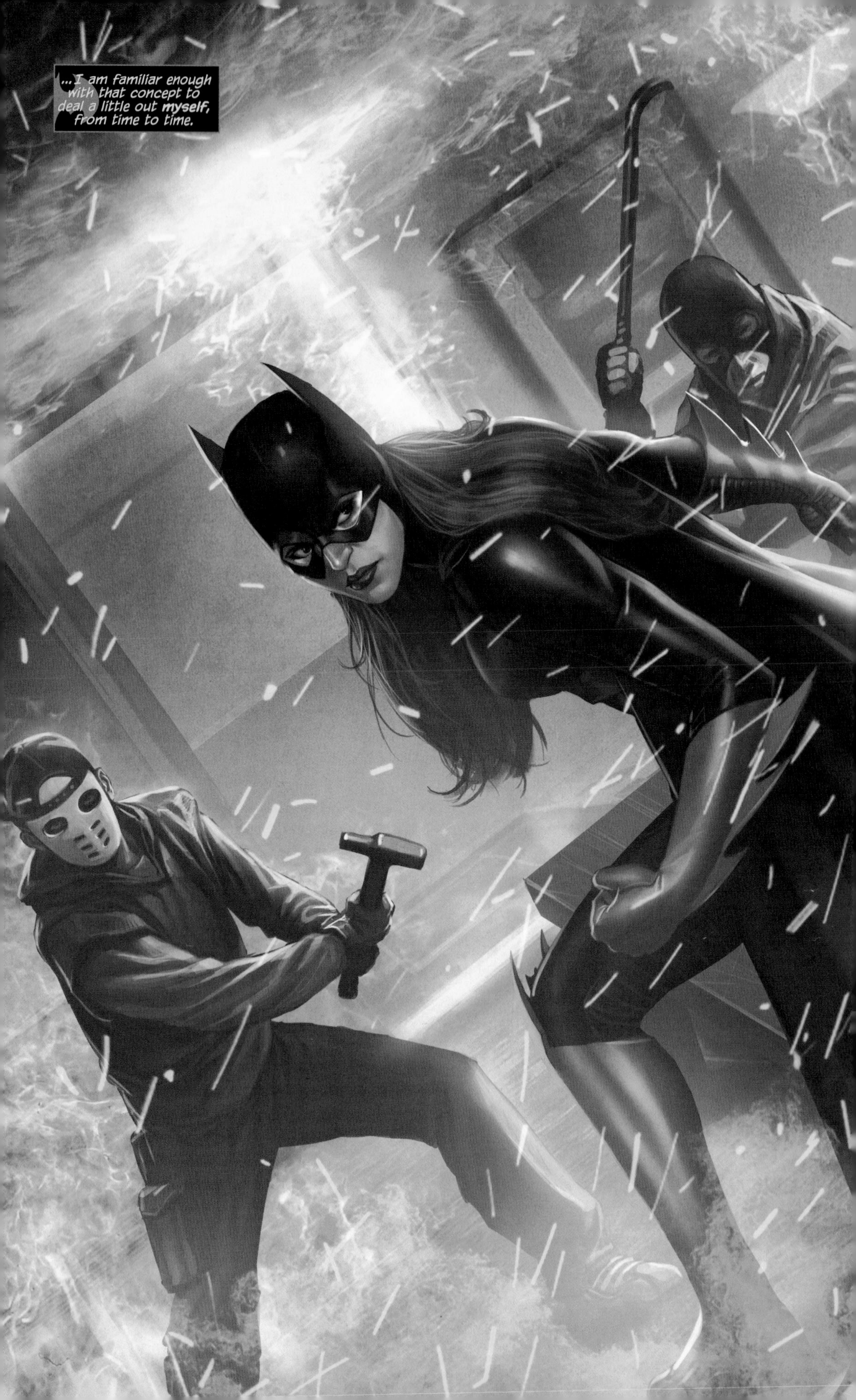
...I am familiar enough with that concept to deal a little out myself, from time to time.

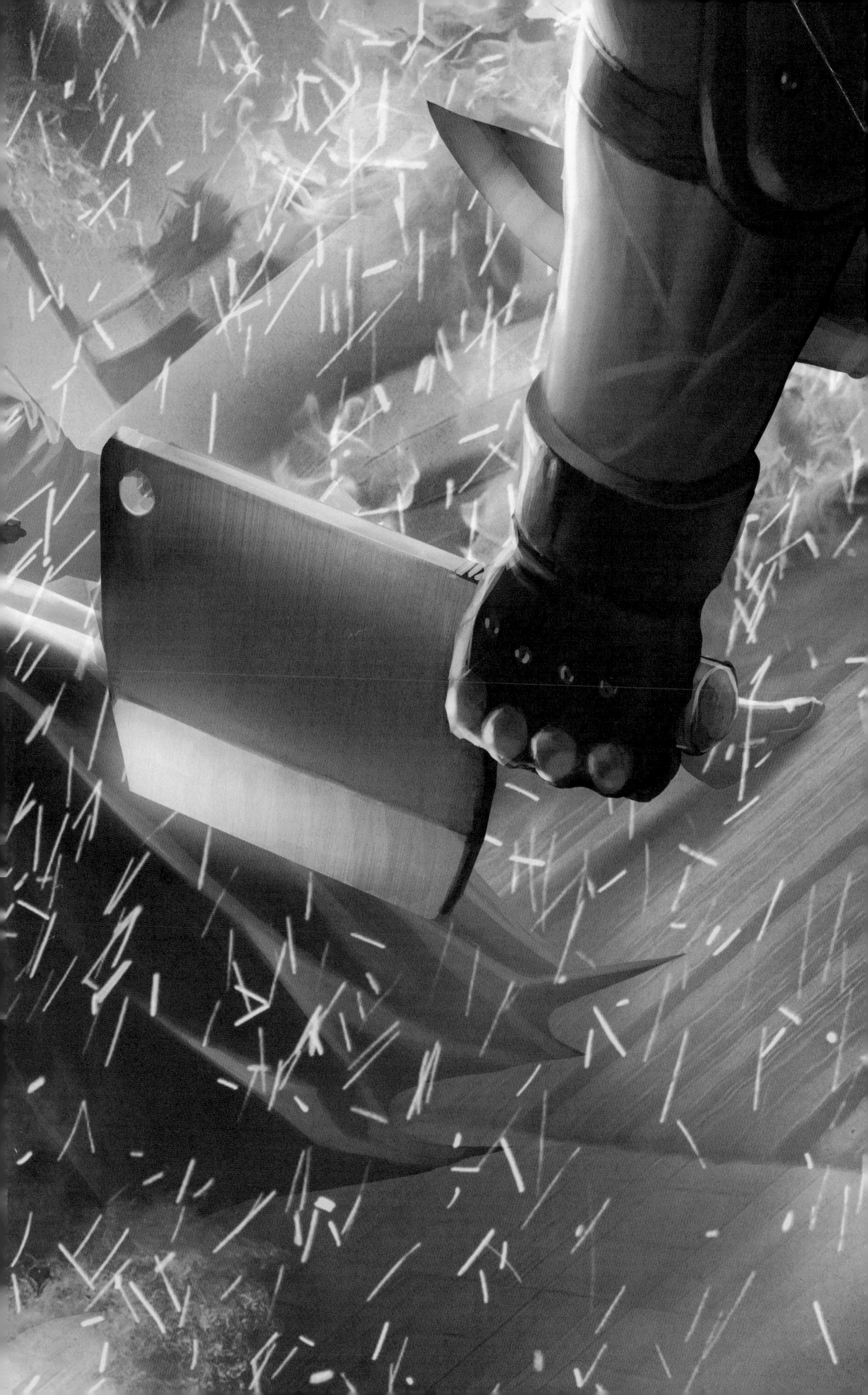

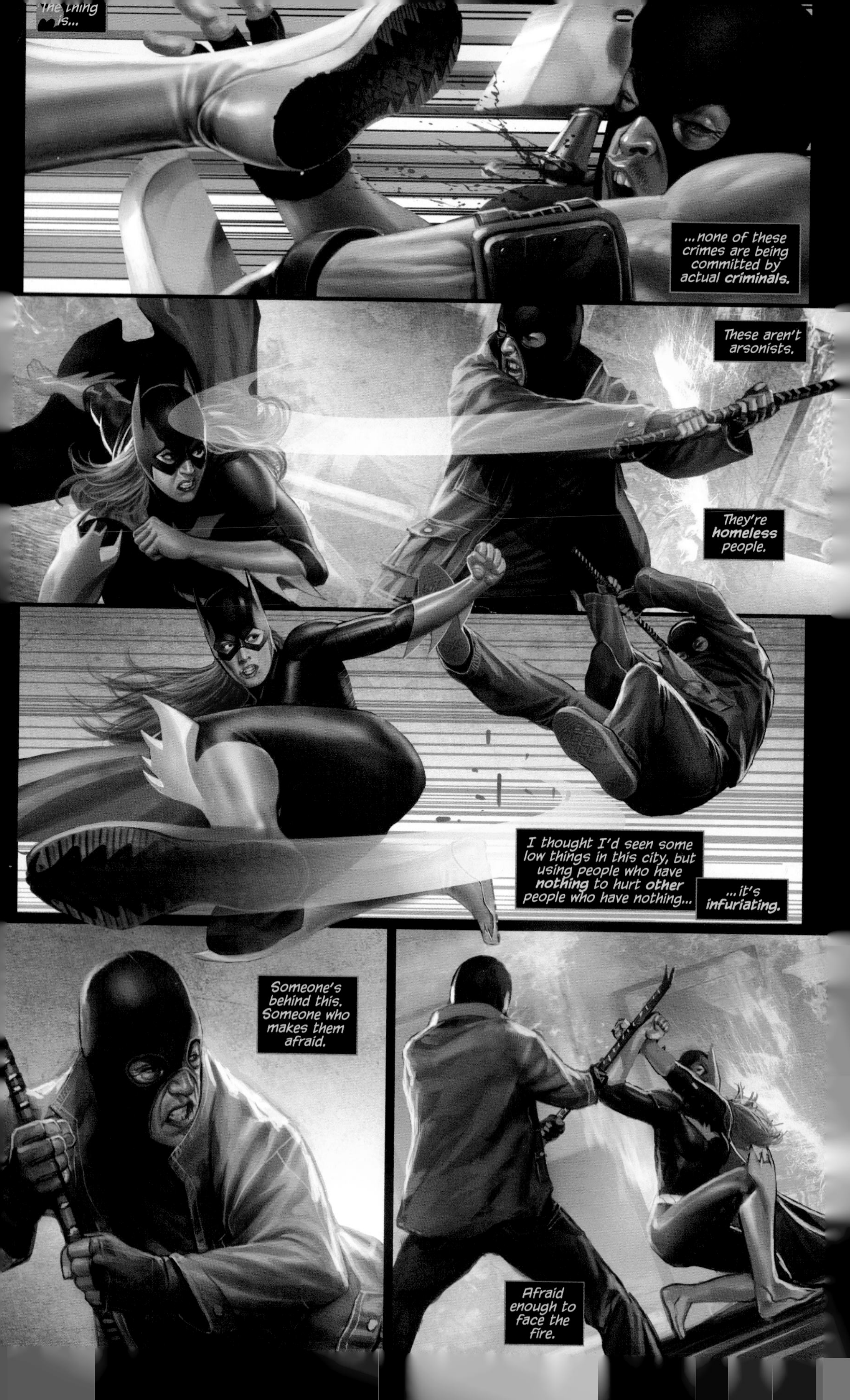
The thing is...
...none of these crimes are being committed by actual criminals.
These aren't arsonists.
They're homeless people.
I thought I'd seen some low things in this city, but using people who have nothing to hurt other people who have nothing...
...it's infuriating.
Someone's behind this. Someone who makes them afraid.
Afraid enough to face the fire.

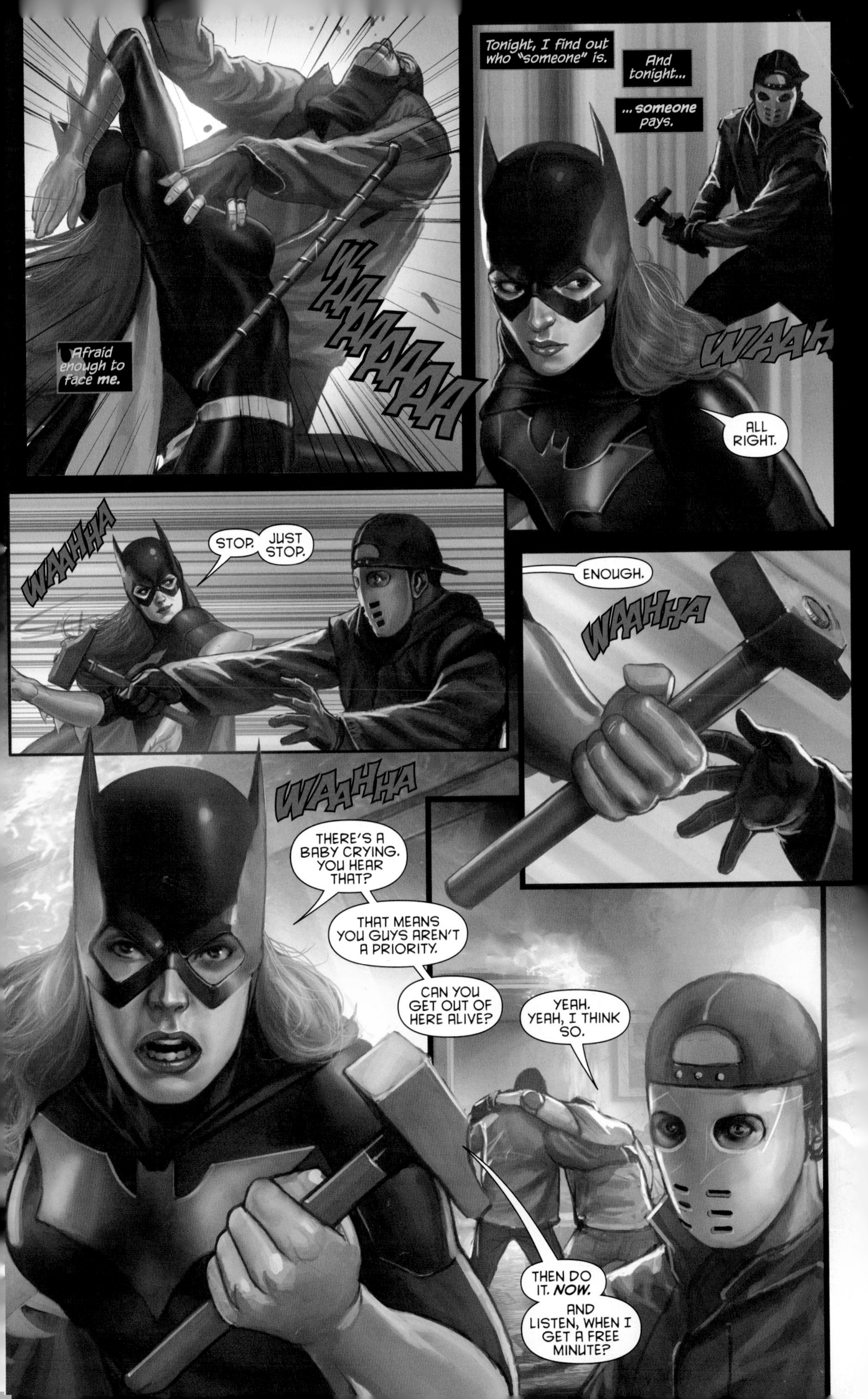
Afraid enough to face me.
WAAAAAAAAA
Tonight, I find out who "someone" is.
And tonight...
...someone pays.
WAAH
ALL RIGHT.
WAAHHA
STOP. JUST STOP.
ENOUGH.
WAAHHA
WAAHHA
THERE'S A BABY CRYING. YOU HEAR THAT?
THAT MEANS YOU GUYS AREN'T A PRIORITY.
CAN YOU GET OUT OF HERE ALIVE?
YEAH. YEAH, I THINK SO.
THEN DO IT. NOW.
AND LISTEN, WHEN I GET A FREE MINUTE?

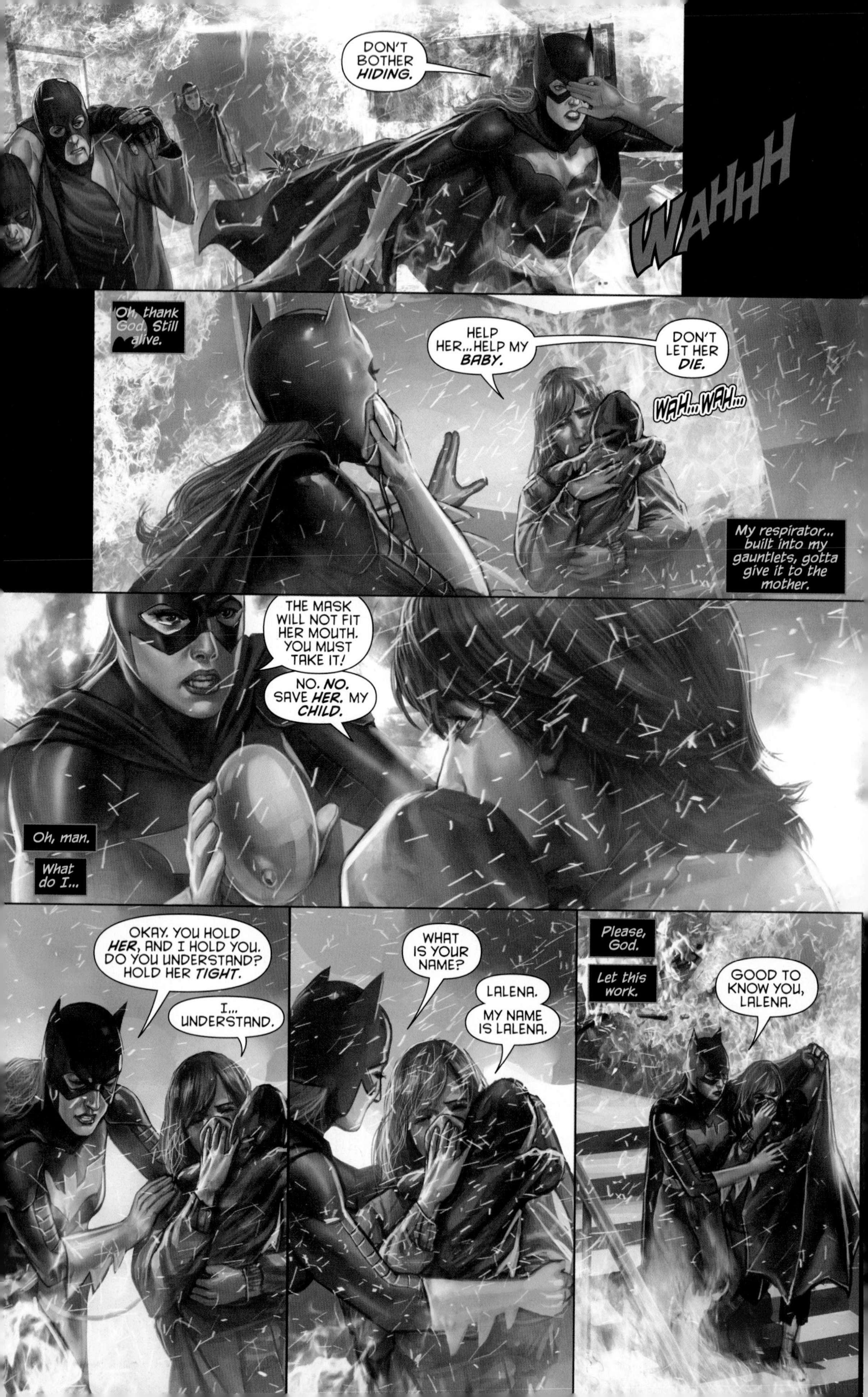
DON'T BOTHER *HIDING.*
WAHHH
Oh, thank God. Still alive.
HELP HER...HELP MY *BABY.*
DON'T LET HER *DIE.*
WAH...WAH...
My respirator... built into my gauntlets, gotta give it to the mother.
THE MASK WILL NOT FIT HER MOUTH. YOU MUST TAKE IT!
NO. *NO.* SAVE *HER.* MY *CHILD.*
Oh, man.
What do I...
OKAY. YOU HOLD *HER*, AND I HOLD YOU. DO YOU UNDERSTAND? HOLD HER *TIGHT.*
I... UNDERSTAND.
WHAT IS YOUR NAME?
LALENA.
MY NAME IS LALENA.
Please, God.
Let this work.
GOOD TO KNOW YOU, LALENA.

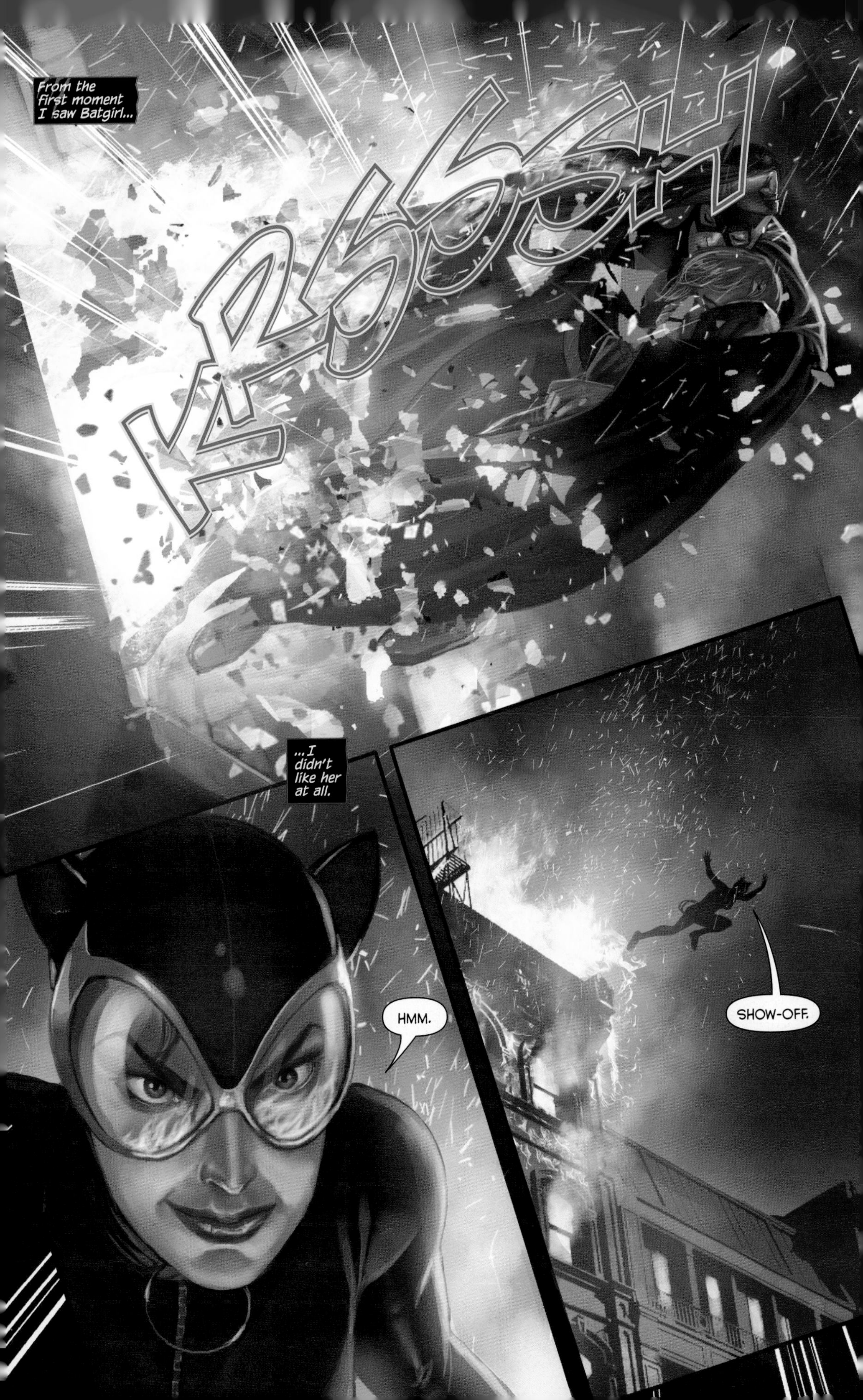
From the first moment I saw Batgirl...
KRBOOM
...I didn't like her at all.
HMM.
SHOW-OFF.

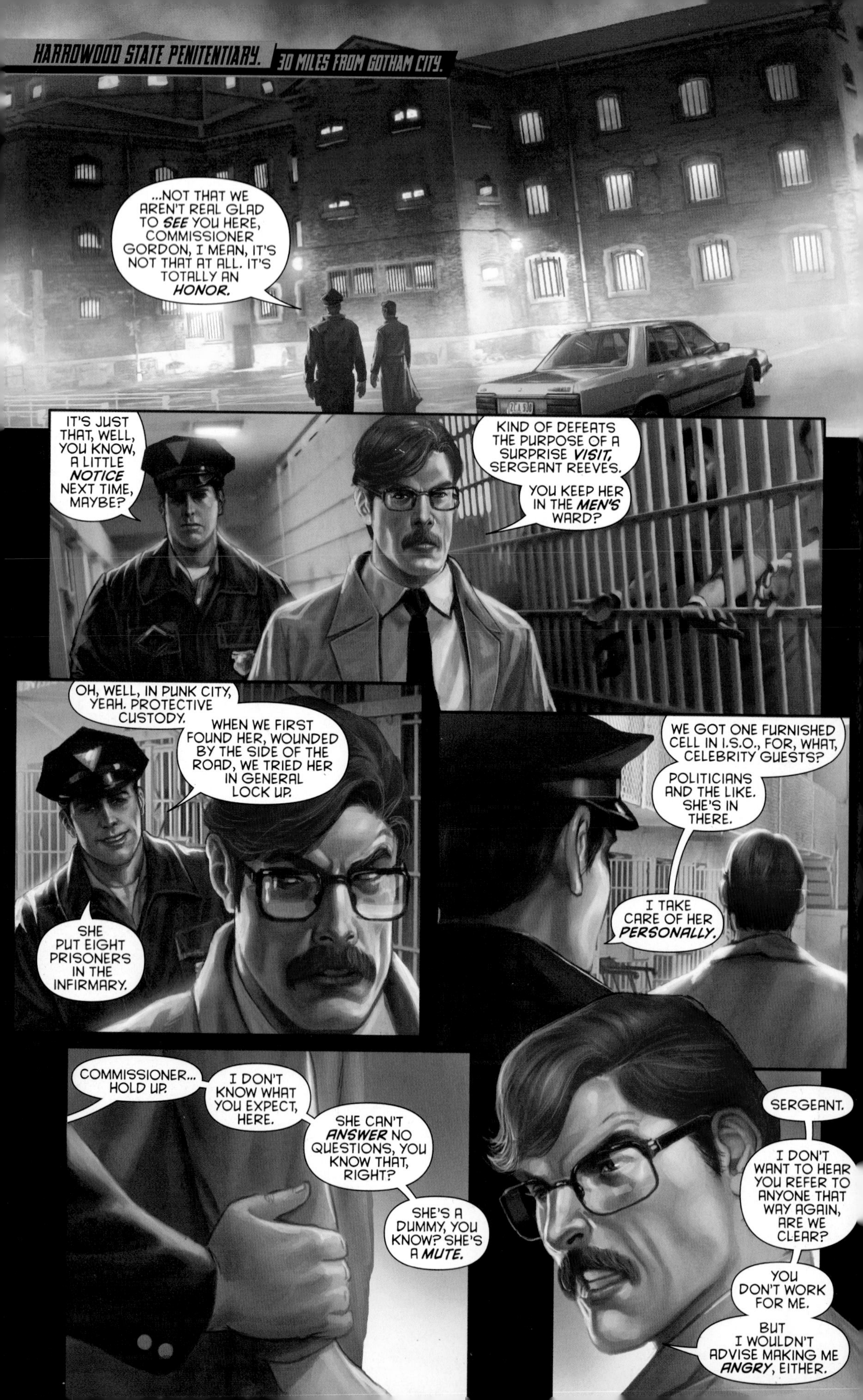
HARROWOOD STATE PENITENTIARY.
30 MILES FROM GOTHAM CITY.
...NOT THAT WE AREN'T REAL GLAD TO SEE YOU HERE, COMMISSIONER GORDON, I MEAN, IT'S NOT THAT AT ALL. IT'S TOTALLY AN HONOR.
IT'S JUST THAT, WELL, YOU KNOW, A LITTLE NOTICE NEXT TIME, MAYBE?
KIND OF DEFEATS THE PURPOSE OF A SURPRISE VISIT, SERGEANT REEVES.
YOU KEEP HER IN THE MEN'S WARD?
OH, WELL, IN PUNK CITY, YEAH. PROTECTIVE CUSTODY.
WHEN WE FIRST FOUND HER, WOUNDED BY THE SIDE OF THE ROAD, WE TRIED HER IN GENERAL LOCK UP.
SHE PUT EIGHT PRISONERS IN THE INFIRMARY.
WE GOT ONE FURNISHED CELL IN I.S.O., FOR, WHAT, CELEBRITY GUESTS?
POLITICIANS AND THE LIKE. SHE'S IN THERE.
I TAKE CARE OF HER PERSONALLY.
COMMISSIONER... HOLD UP.
I DON'T KNOW WHAT YOU EXPECT, HERE.
SHE CAN'T ANSWER NO QUESTIONS, YOU KNOW THAT, RIGHT?
SHE'S A DUMMY, YOU KNOW? SHE'S A MUTE.
SERGEANT.
I DON'T WANT TO HEAR YOU REFER TO ANYONE THAT WAY AGAIN, ARE WE CLEAR?
YOU DON'T WORK FOR ME.
BUT I WOULDN'T ADVISE MAKING ME ANGRY, EITHER.

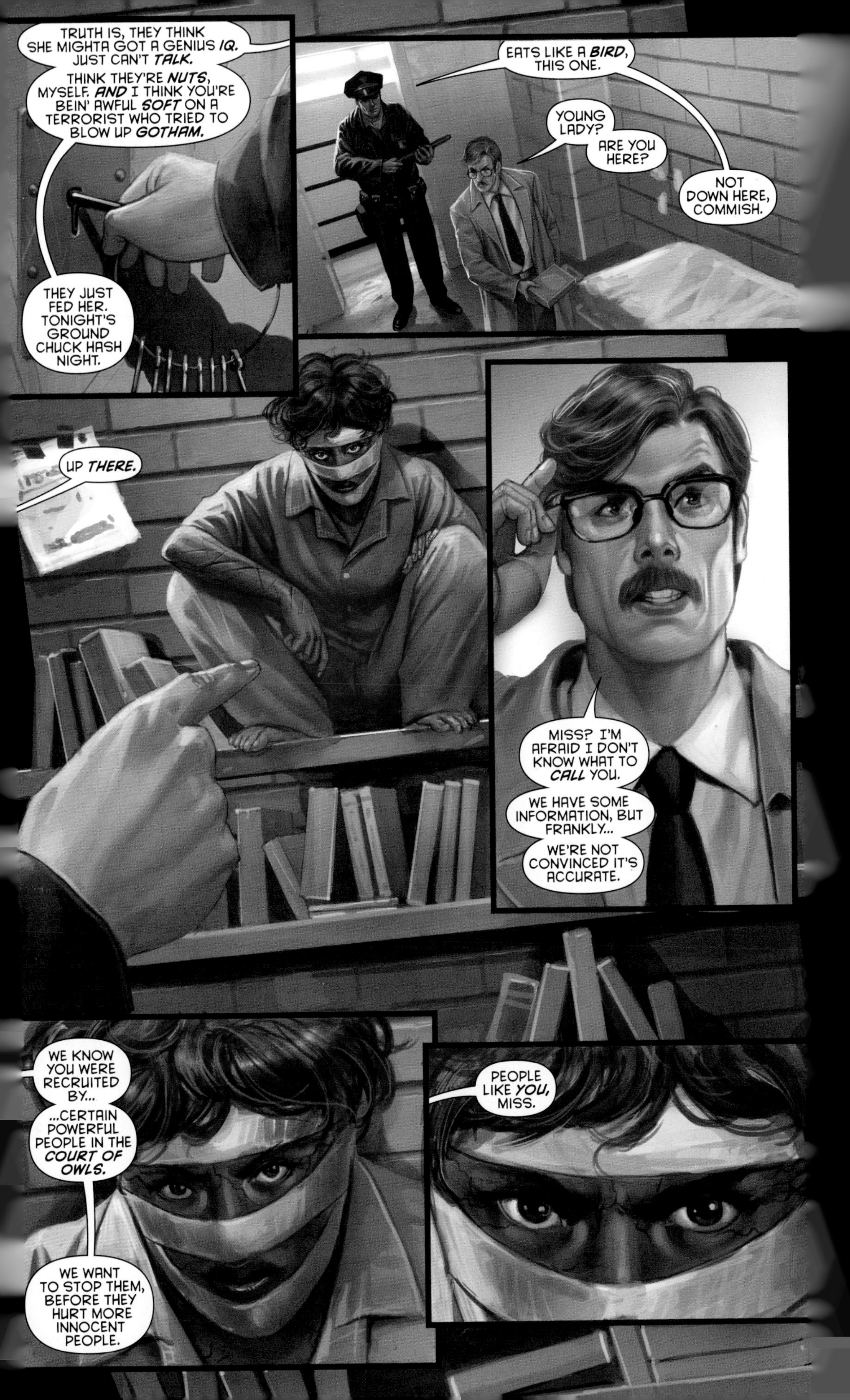
TRUTH IS, THEY THINK SHE MIGHTA GOT A GENIUS *IQ.* JUST CAN'T *TALK.*
THINK THEY'RE *NUTS*, MYSELF. *AND* I THINK YOU'RE BEIN' AWFUL *SOFT* ON A TERRORIST WHO TRIED TO BLOW UP *GOTHAM.*
THEY JUST FED HER. TONIGHT'S GROUND CHUCK HASH NIGHT.
EATS LIKE A *BIRD*, THIS ONE.
YOUNG LADY?
ARE YOU HERE?
NOT DOWN HERE, COMMISH.
UP *THERE.*
MISS? I'M AFRAID I DON'T KNOW WHAT TO *CALL* YOU.
WE HAVE SOME INFORMATION, BUT FRANKLY...
WE'RE NOT CONVINCED IT'S ACCURATE.
WE KNOW YOU WERE RECRUITED BY...
...CERTAIN POWERFUL PEOPLE IN THE *COURT OF OWLS.*
WE WANT TO STOP THEM, BEFORE THEY HURT MORE INNOCENT PEOPLE.
PEOPLE LIKE *YOU,* MISS.

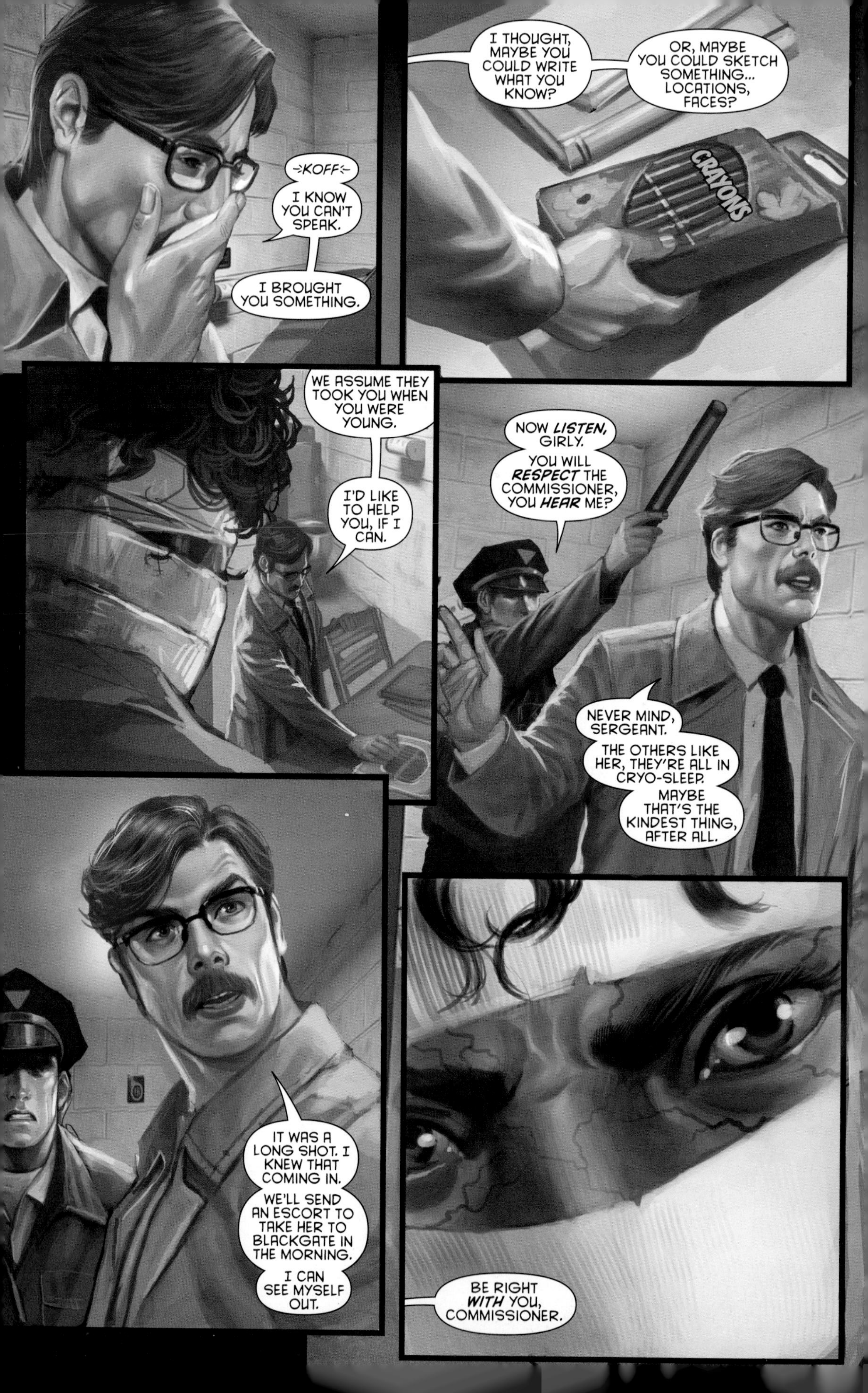
-KOFF-
I KNOW YOU CAN'T SPEAK.
I BROUGHT YOU SOMETHING.
I THOUGHT, MAYBE YOU COULD WRITE WHAT YOU KNOW?
OR, MAYBE YOU COULD SKETCH SOMETHING... LOCATIONS, FACES?
CRAYONS
WE ASSUME THEY TOOK YOU WHEN YOU WERE YOUNG.
I'D LIKE TO HELP YOU, IF I CAN.
NOW LISTEN, GIRLY.
YOU WILL RESPECT THE COMMISSIONER, YOU HEAR ME?
NEVER MIND, SERGEANT.
THE OTHERS LIKE HER, THEY'RE ALL IN CRYO-SLEEP.
MAYBE THAT'S THE KINDEST THING, AFTER ALL.
IT WAS A LONG SHOT. I KNEW THAT COMING IN.
WE'LL SEND AN ESCORT TO TAKE HER TO BLACKGATE IN THE MORNING.
I CAN SEE MYSELF OUT.
BE RIGHT WITH YOU, COMMISSIONER.

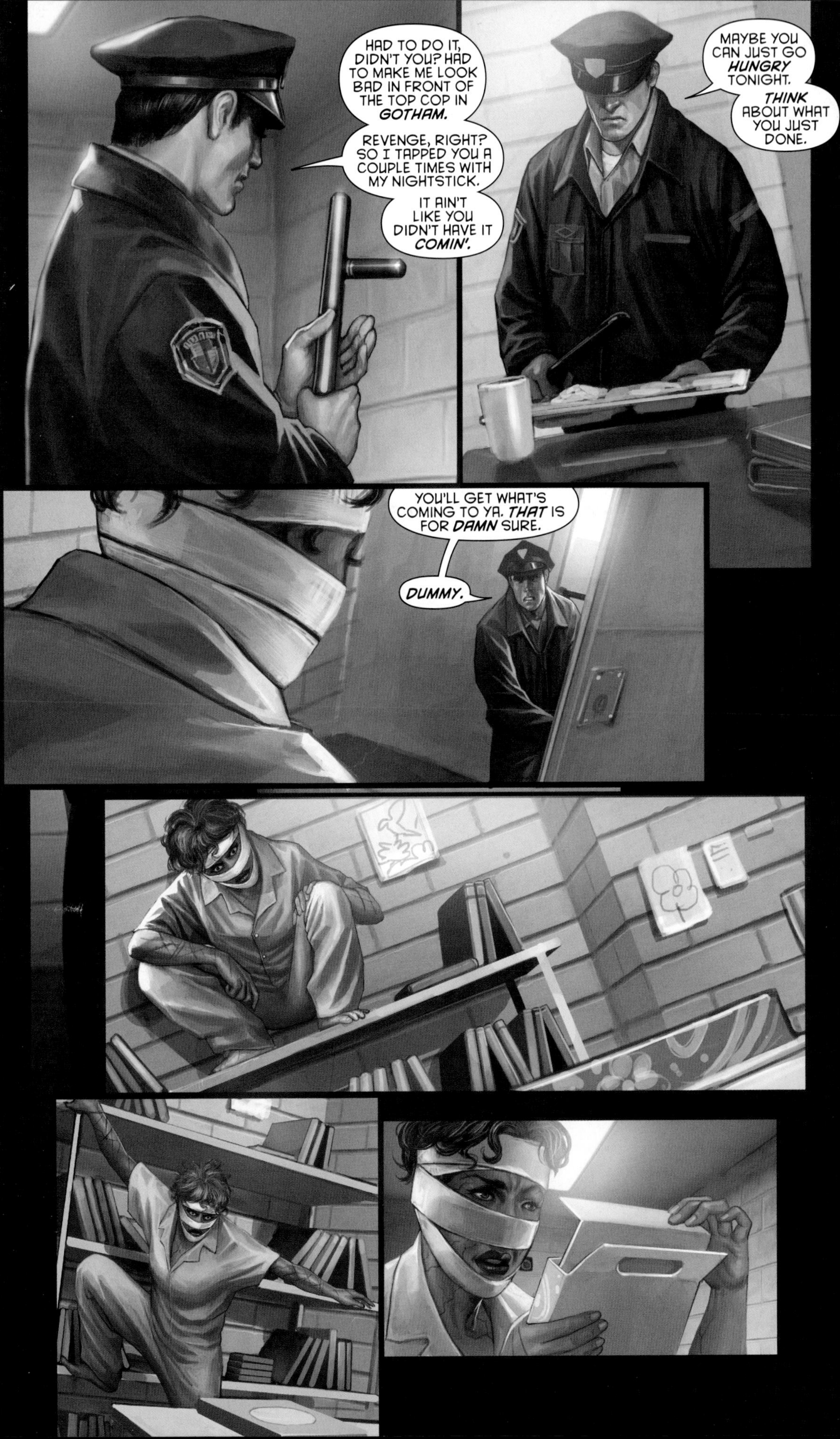
HAD TO DO IT, DIDN'T YOU? HAD TO MAKE ME LOOK BAD IN FRONT OF THE TOP COP IN GOTHAM.
REVENGE, RIGHT? SO I TAPPED YOU A COUPLE TIMES WITH MY NIGHTSTICK.
IT AIN'T LIKE YOU DIDN'T HAVE IT COMIN'.
MAYBE YOU CAN JUST GO HUNGRY TONIGHT.
THINK ABOUT WHAT YOU JUST DONE.
YOU'LL GET WHAT'S COMING TO YA. THAT IS FOR DAMN SURE.
DUMMY.

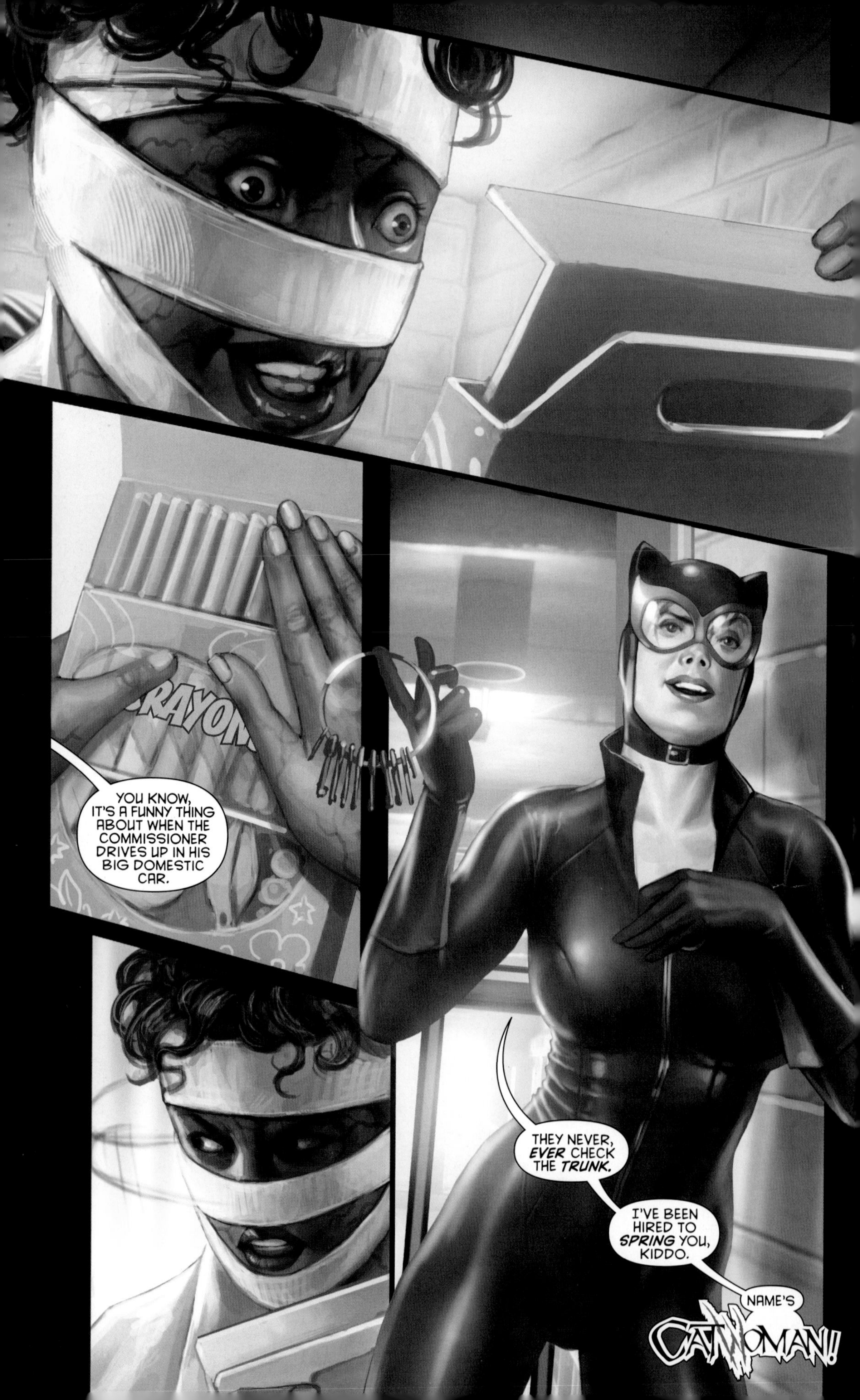
CRAYONS
YOU KNOW, IT'S A FUNNY THING ABOUT WHEN THE COMMISSIONER DRIVES UP IN HIS BIG DOMESTIC CAR.
THEY NEVER, *EVER* CHECK THE *TRUNK.*
I'VE BEEN HIRED TO *SPRING* YOU, KIDDO.
NAME'S
CATWOMAN!

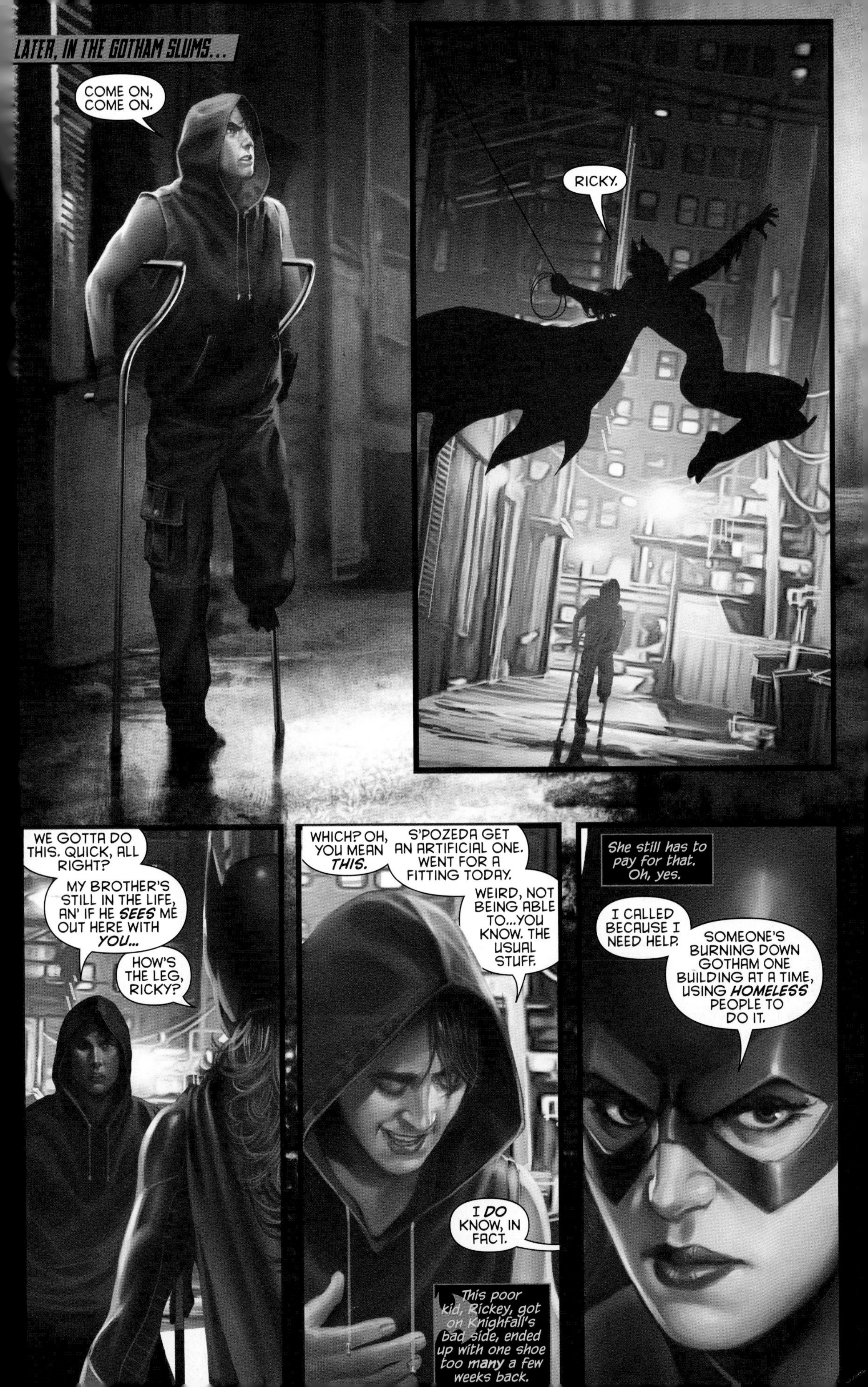
LATER, IN THE GOTHAM SLUMS...
COME ON, COME ON.
RICKY.
WE GOTTA DO THIS. QUICK, ALL RIGHT?
MY BROTHER'S STILL IN THE LIFE, AN' IF HE SEES ME OUT HERE WITH YOU...
HOW'S THE LEG, RICKY?
WHICH? OH, YOU MEAN THIS.
S'POZEDA GET AN ARTIFICIAL ONE. WENT FOR A FITTING TODAY.
WEIRD, NOT BEING ABLE TO...YOU KNOW. THE USUAL STUFF.
I DO KNOW, IN FACT.
This poor kid, Rickey, got on Knighfall's bad side, ended up with one shoe too many a few weeks back.
She still has to pay for that. Oh, yes.
I CALLED BECAUSE I NEED HELP.
SOMEONE'S BURNING DOWN GOTHAM ONE BUILDING AT A TIME, USING HOMELESS PEOPLE TO DO IT.

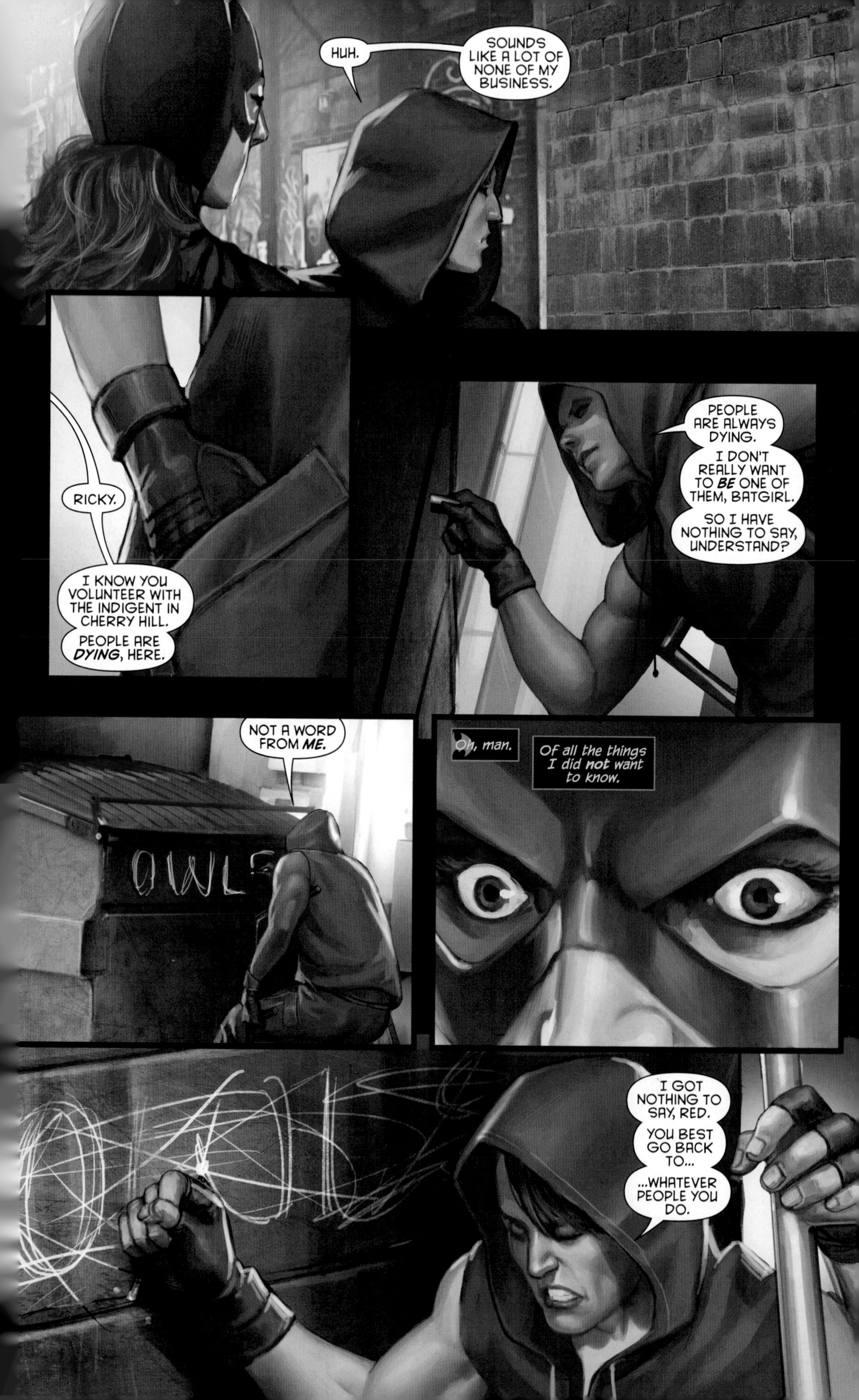
HUH.
SOUNDS LIKE A LOT OF NONE OF MY BUSINESS.
RICKY.
I KNOW YOU VOLUNTEER WITH THE INDIGENT IN CHERRY HILL.
PEOPLE ARE DYING, HERE.
PEOPLE ARE ALWAYS DYING.
I DON'T REALLY WANT TO BE ONE OF THEM, BATGIRL.
SO I HAVE NOTHING TO SAY, UNDERSTAND?
NOT A WORD FROM ME.
OWL
Oh, man.
Of all the things I did not want to know.
I GOT NOTHING TO SAY, RED.
YOU BEST GO BACK TO...
...WHATEVER PEOPLE YOU DO.

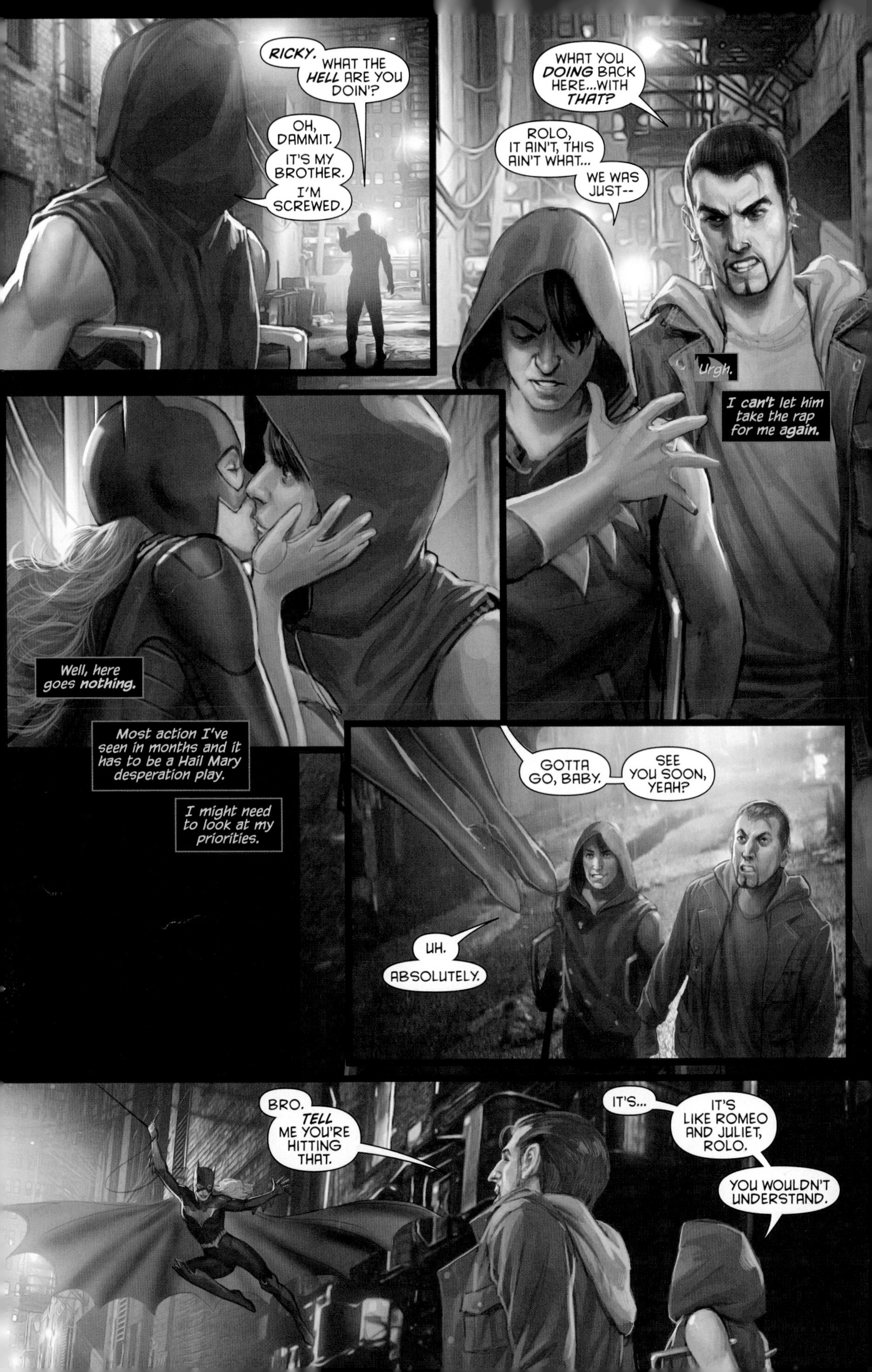
RICKY. WHAT THE HELL ARE YOU DOIN'?
OH, DAMMIT.
IT'S MY BROTHER.
I'M SCREWED.
WHAT YOU DOING BACK HERE...WITH THAT?
ROLO, IT AIN'T, THIS AIN'T WHAT...
WE WAS JUST--
Urgh.
I can't let him take the rap for me again.
Well, here goes nothing.
Most action I've seen in months and it has to be a Hail Mary desperation play.
I might need to look at my priorities.
GOTTA GO, BABY.
SEE YOU SOON, YEAH?
UH.
ABSOLUTELY.
BRO. TELL ME YOU'RE HITTING THAT.
IT'S...
IT'S LIKE ROMEO AND JULIET, ROLO.
YOU WOULDN'T UNDERSTAND.

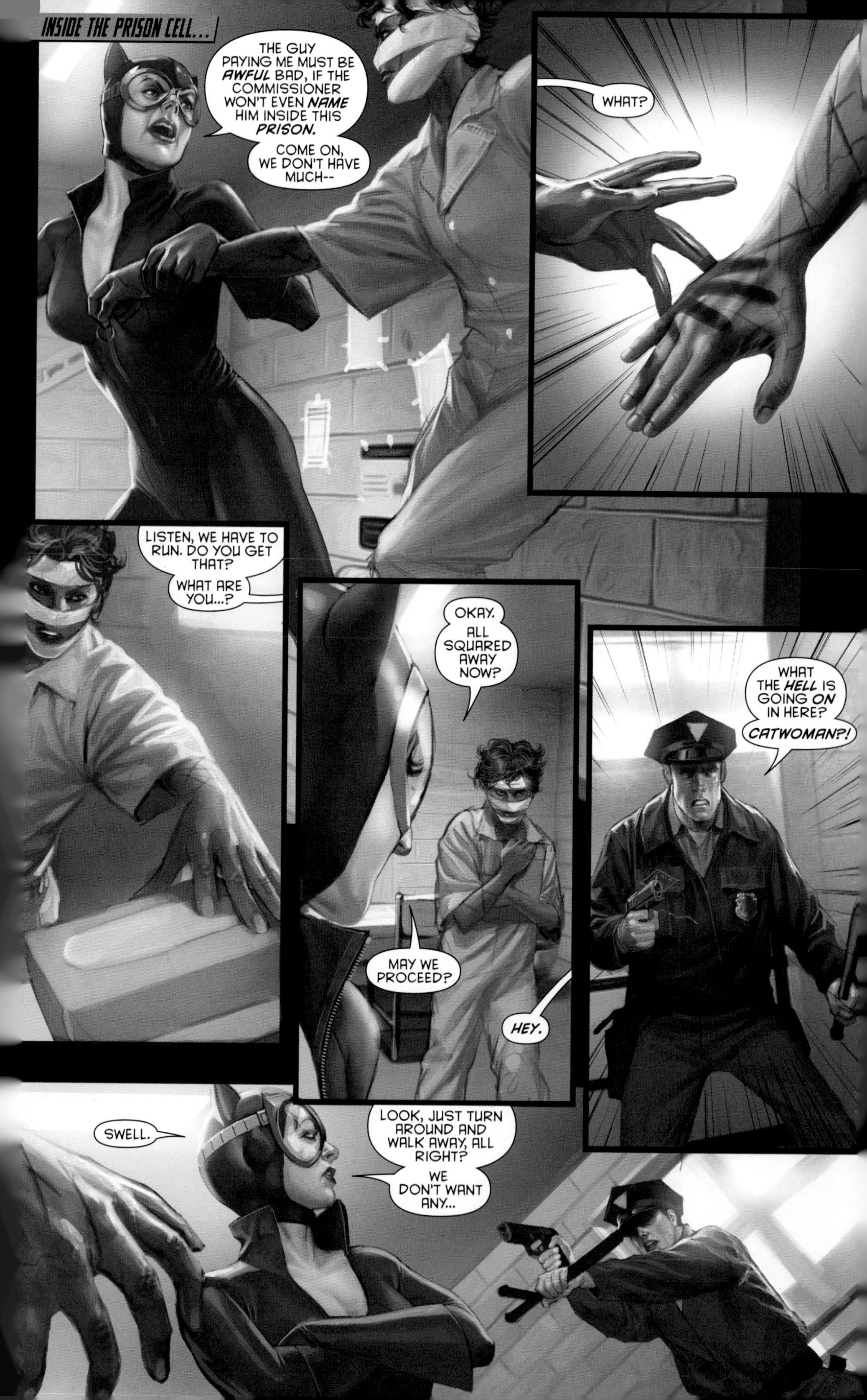
INSIDE THE PRISON CELL...
THE GUY PAYING ME MUST BE AWFUL BAD, IF THE COMMISSIONER WON'T EVEN NAME HIM INSIDE THIS PRISON.
COME ON, WE DON'T HAVE MUCH--
WHAT?
LISTEN, WE HAVE TO RUN. DO YOU GET THAT?
WHAT ARE YOU...?
OKAY. ALL SQUARED AWAY NOW?
MAY WE PROCEED?
HEY.
WHAT THE HELL IS GOING ON IN HERE?
CATWOMAN?!
SWELL.
LOOK, JUST TURN AROUND AND WALK AWAY, ALL RIGHT?
WE DON'T WANT ANY...

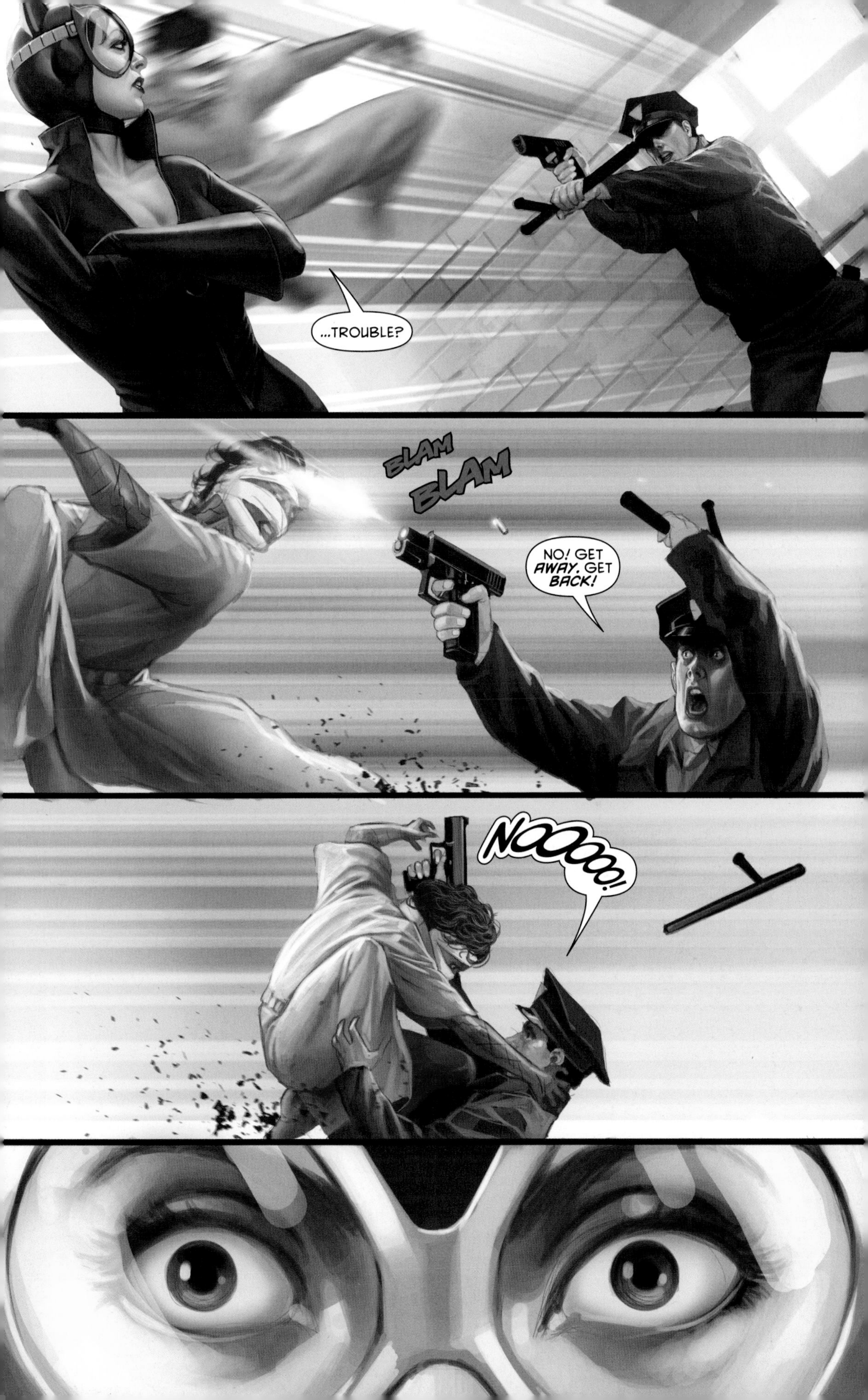
...TROUBLE?
BLAM
BLAM
NO! GET AWAY. GET BACK!
NOOOOO!

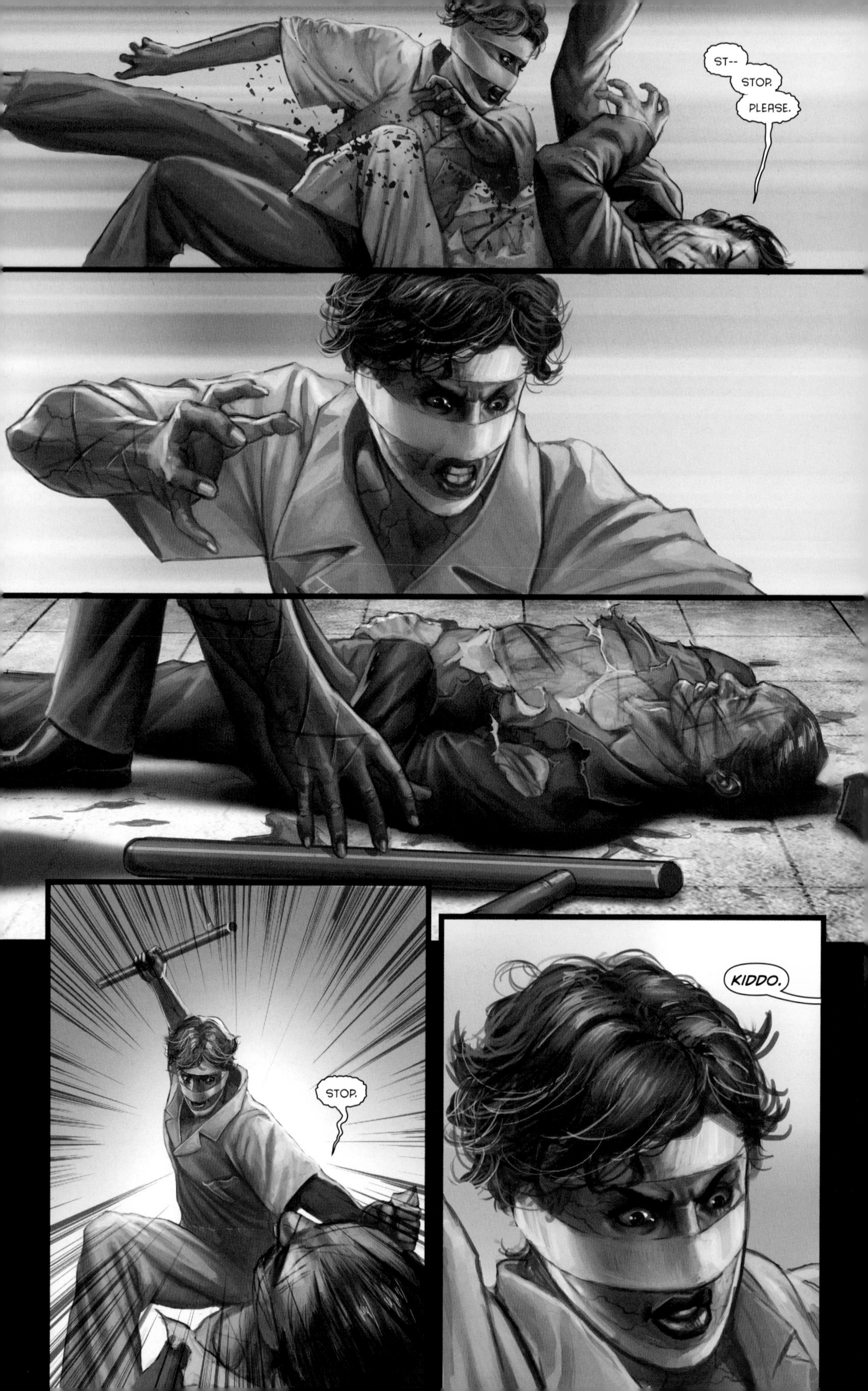
ST--
STOP.
PLEASE.
STOP.
KIDDO.

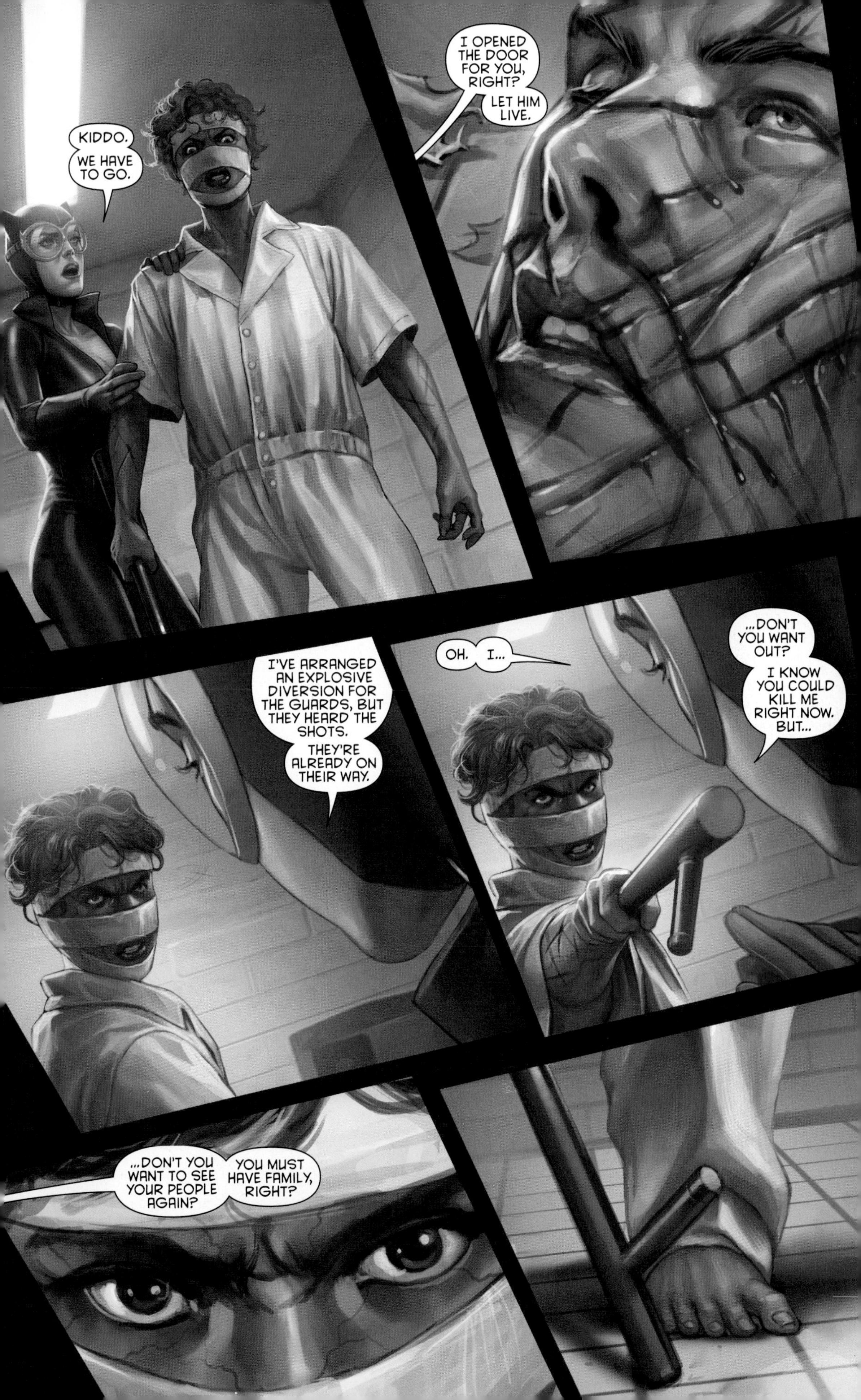
KIDDO.
WE HAVE TO GO.
I OPENED THE DOOR FOR YOU, RIGHT?
LET HIM LIVE.
I'VE ARRANGED AN EXPLOSIVE DIVERSION FOR THE GUARDS, BUT THEY HEARD THE SHOTS.
THEY'RE ALREADY ON THEIR WAY.
OH.
I...
...DON'T YOU WANT OUT?
I KNOW YOU COULD KILL ME RIGHT NOW. BUT...
...DON'T YOU WANT TO SEE YOUR PEOPLE AGAIN?
YOU MUST HAVE FAMILY, RIGHT?

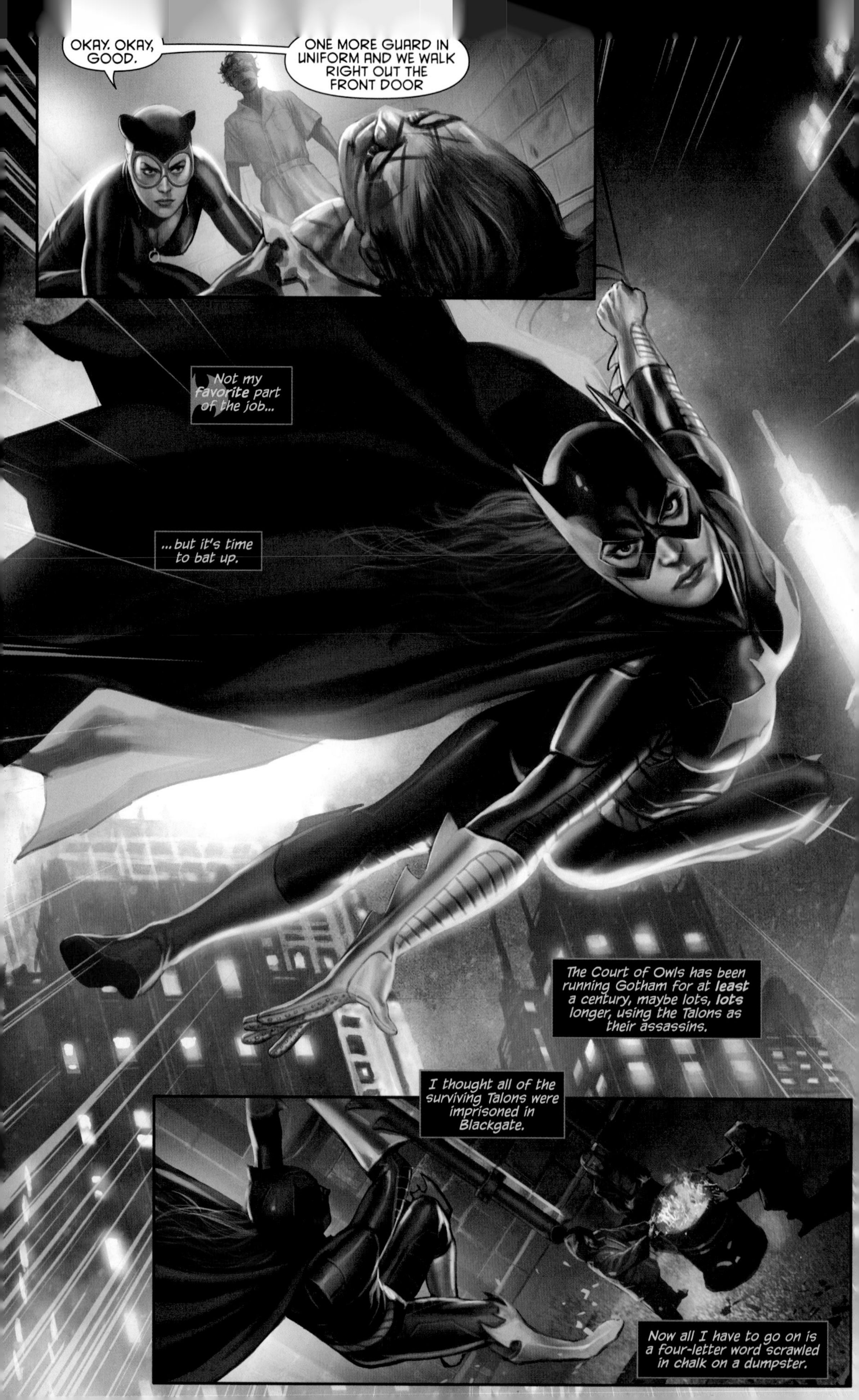
OKAY. OKAY, GOOD.
ONE MORE GUARD IN UNIFORM AND WE WALK RIGHT OUT THE FRONT DOOR
Not my favorite part of the job...
...but it's time to bat up.
The Court of Owls has been running Gotham for at least a century, maybe lots, lots longer, using the Talons as their assassins.
I thought all of the surviving Talons were imprisoned in Blackgate.
Now all I have to go on is a four-letter word scrawled in chalk on a dumpster.

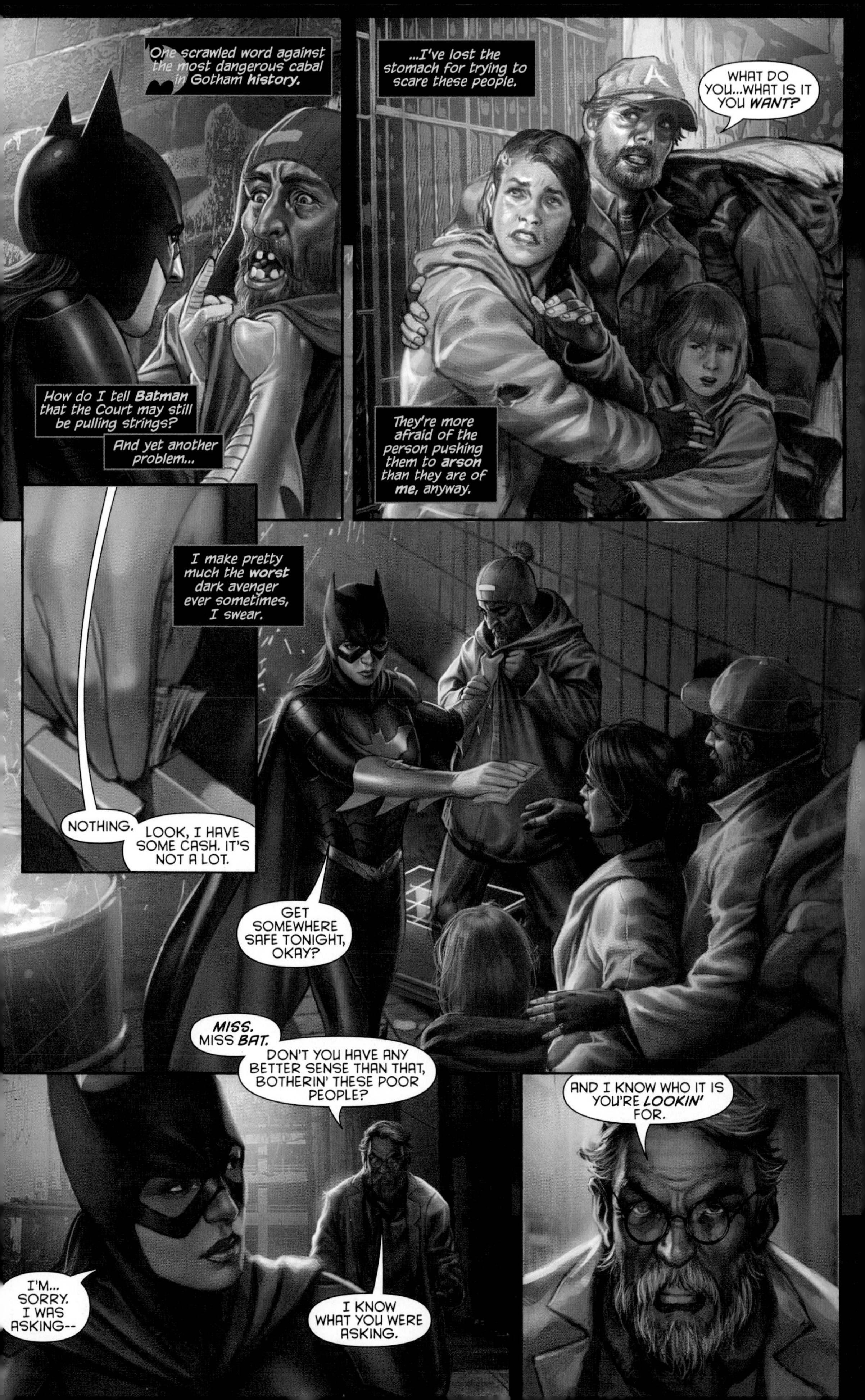
One scrawled word against the most dangerous cabal in Gotham history.
How do I tell Batman that the Court may still be pulling strings?
And yet another problem...
...I've lost the stomach for trying to scare these people.
WHAT DO YOU...WHAT IS IT YOU WANT?
They're more afraid of the person pushing them to arson than they are of me, anyway.
I make pretty much the worst dark avenger ever sometimes, I swear.
NOTHING.
LOOK, I HAVE SOME CASH. IT'S NOT A LOT.
GET SOMEWHERE SAFE TONIGHT, OKAY?
MISS. MISS BAT.
DON'T YOU HAVE ANY BETTER SENSE THAN THAT, BOTHERIN' THESE POOR PEOPLE?
I'M... SORRY. I WAS ASKING--
I KNOW WHAT YOU WERE ASKING.
AND I KNOW WHO IT IS YOU'RE LOOKIN' FOR.

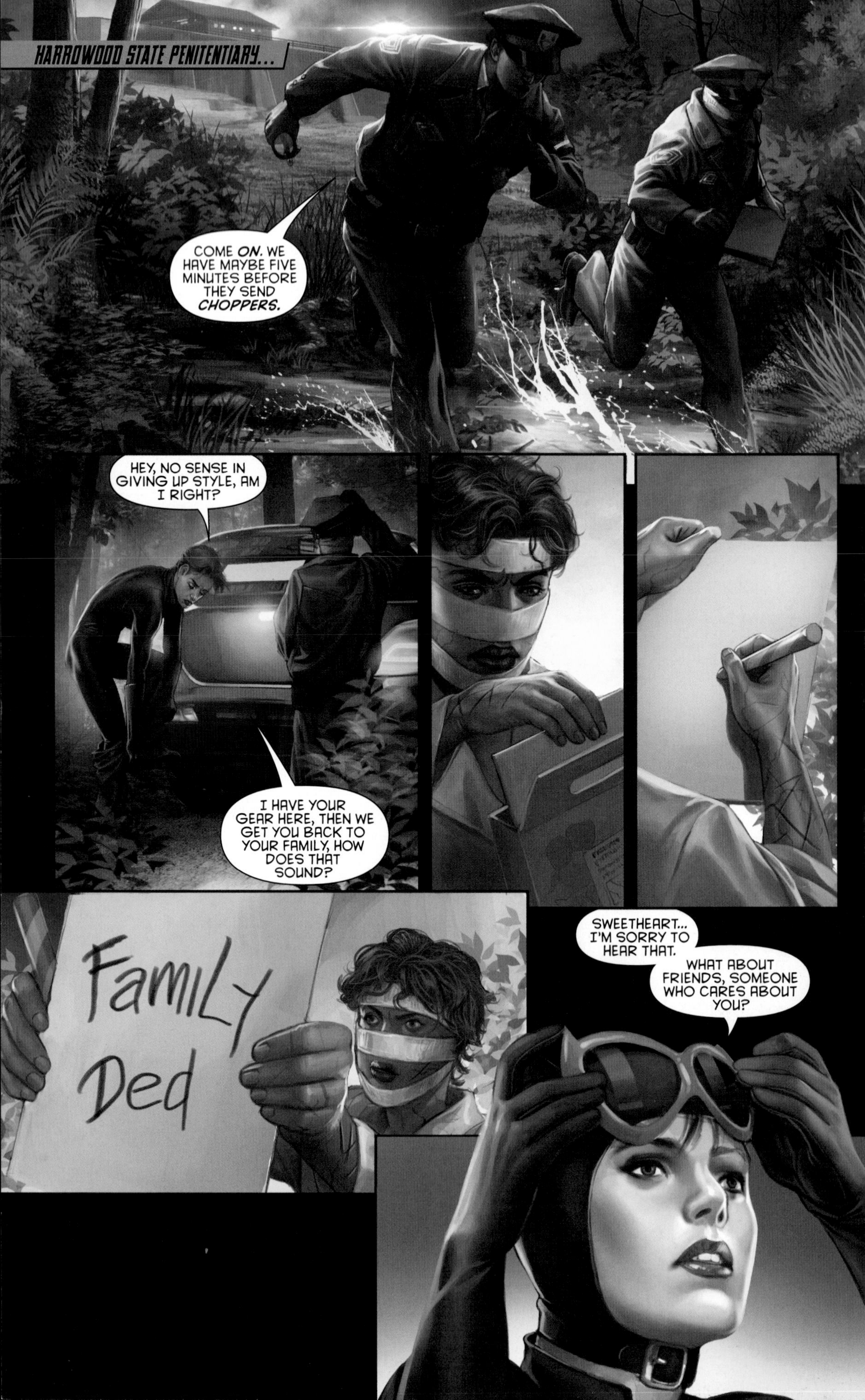
HARROWOOD STATE PENITENTIARY...
COME ON. WE HAVE MAYBE FIVE MINUTES BEFORE THEY SEND CHOPPERS.
HEY, NO SENSE IN GIVING UP STYLE, AM I RIGHT?
I HAVE YOUR GEAR HERE, THEN WE GET YOU BACK TO YOUR FAMILY, HOW DOES THAT SOUND?
FamiLy Ded
SWEETHEART... I'M SORRY TO HEAR THAT.
WHAT ABOUT FRIENDS, SOMEONE WHO CARES ABOUT YOU?

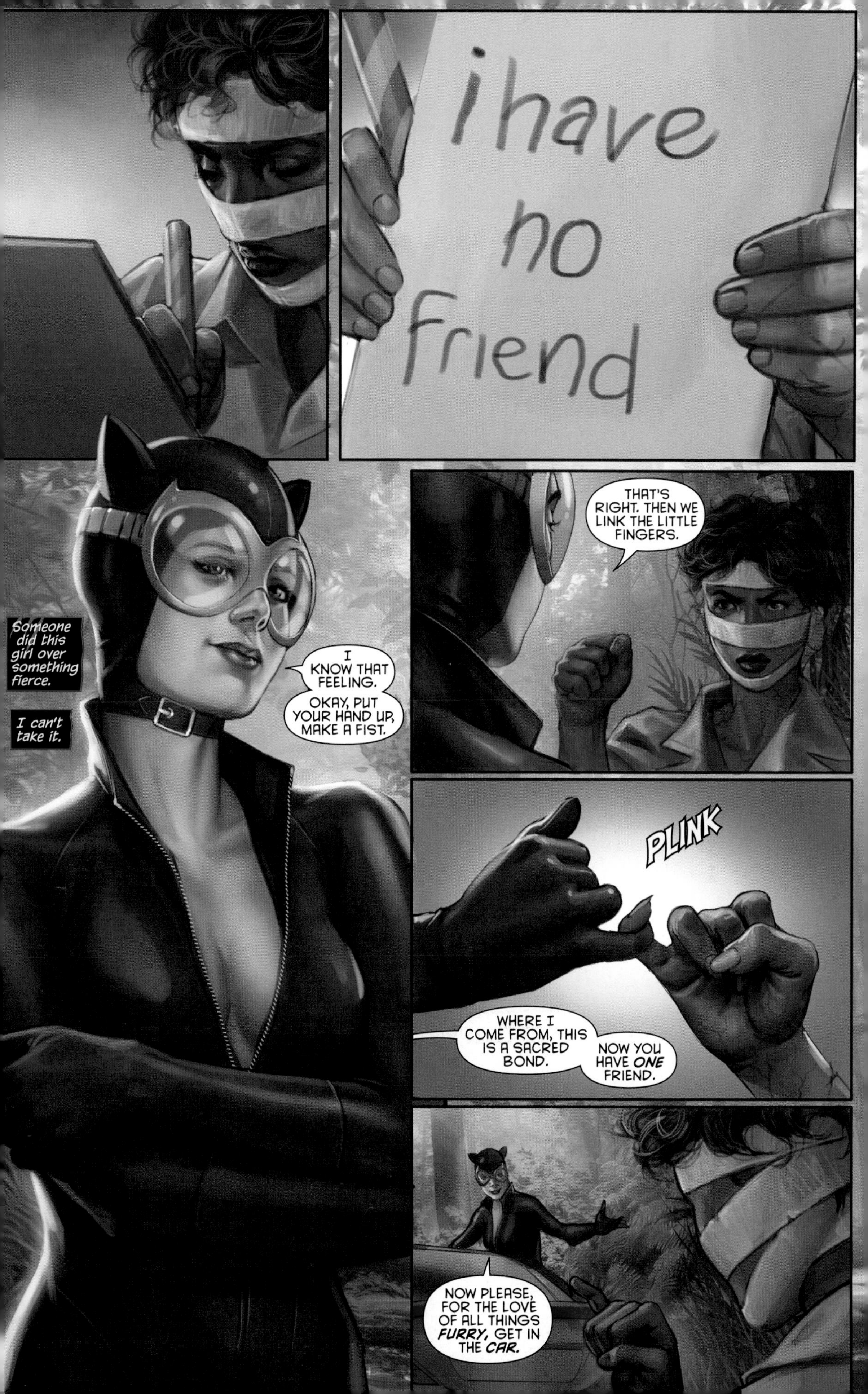

i have no friend
Someone did this girl over something fierce.
I can't take it.
I KNOW THAT FEELING.
OKAY, PUT YOUR HAND UP, MAKE A FIST.
THAT'S RIGHT. THEN WE LINK THE LITTLE FINGERS.
PLINK
WHERE I COME FROM, THIS IS A SACRED BOND.
NOW YOU HAVE *ONE* FRIEND.
NOW PLEASE, FOR THE LOVE OF ALL THINGS ***FURRY,*** GET IN THE ***CAR.***

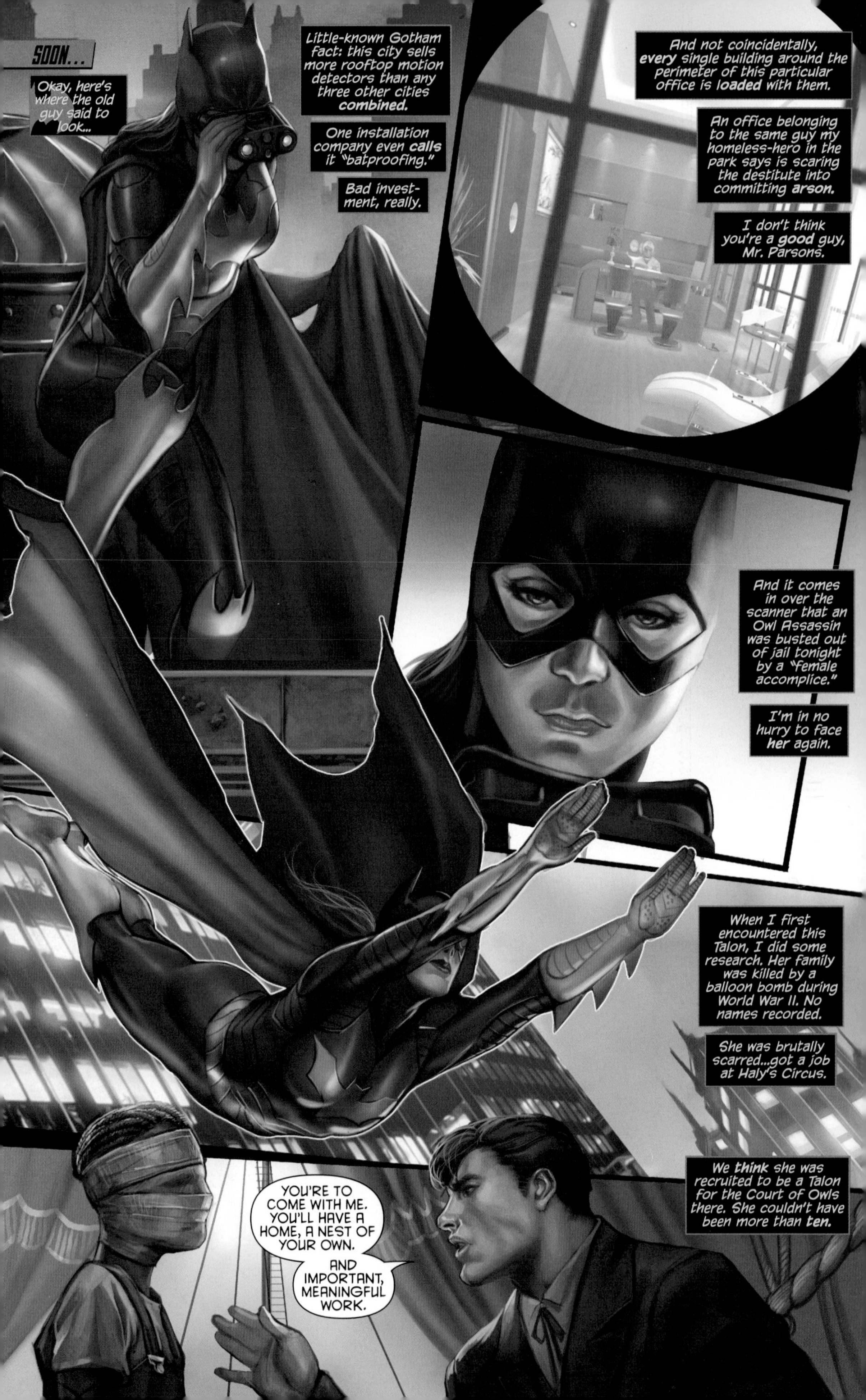
SOON...
Okay, here's where the old guy said to look...
Little-known Gotham fact: this city sells more rooftop motion detectors than any three other cities **combined.**
One installation company even **calls** it "batproofing."
Bad invest-ment, really.
And not coincidentally, **every** single building around the perimeter of this particular office is **loaded** with them.
An office belonging to the same guy my homeless-hero in the park says is scaring the destitute into committing **arson.**
I don't think you're a **good** guy, Mr. Parsons.
And it comes in over the scanner that an Owl Assassin was busted out of jail tonight by a "female accomplice."
I'm in no hurry to face **her** again.
When I first encountered this Talon, I did some research. Her family was killed by a balloon bomb during World War II. No names recorded.
She was brutally scarred...got a job at Haly's Circus.
We **think** she was recruited to be a Talon for the Court of Owls there. She couldn't have been more than **ten.**
YOU'RE TO COME WITH ME. YOU'LL HAVE A HOME, A NEST OF YOUR OWN.
AND IMPORTANT, MEANINGFUL WORK.

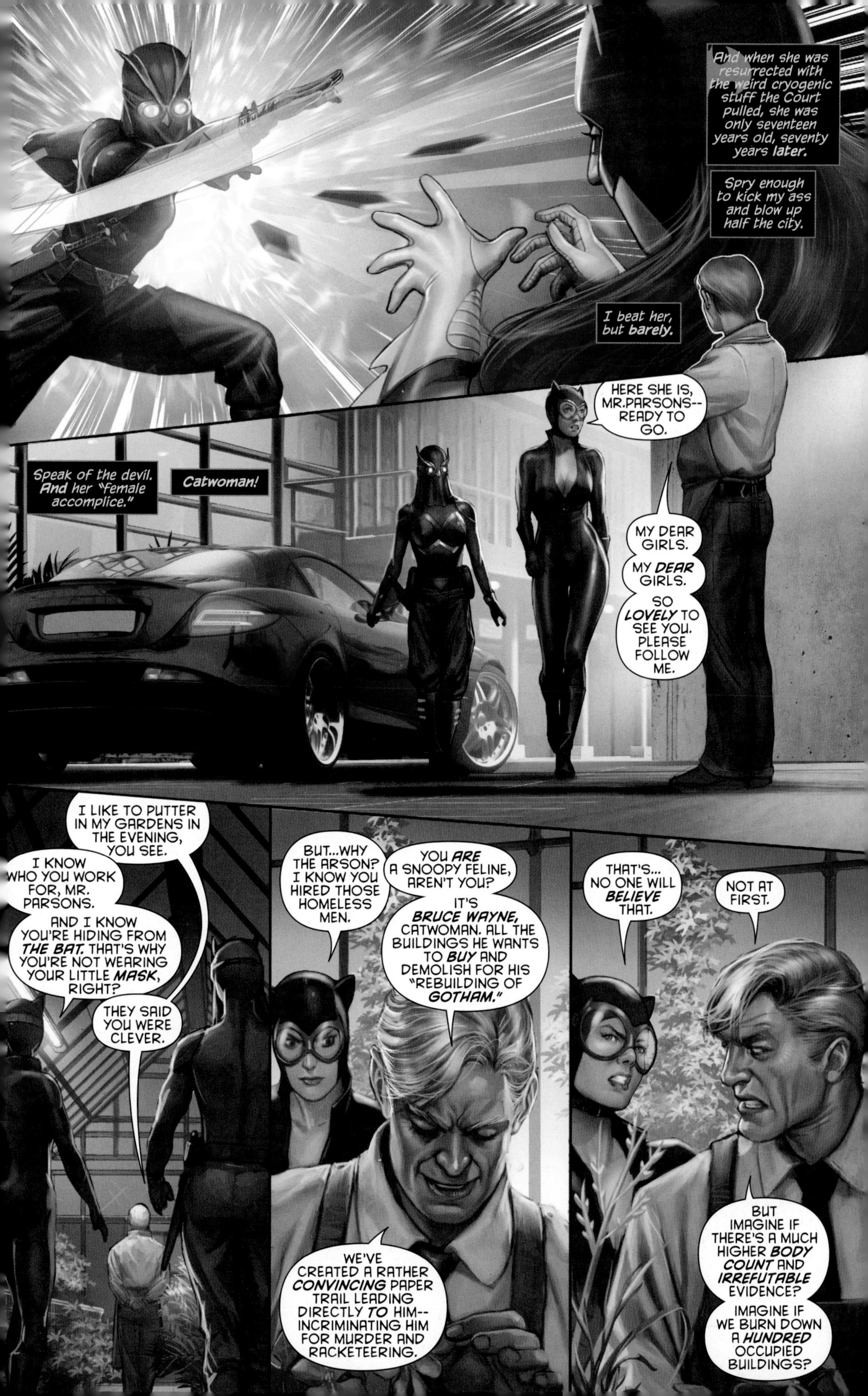
And when she was resurrected with the weird cryogenic stuff the Court pulled, she was only seventeen years old, seventy years later.
Spry enough to kick my ass and blow up half the city.
I beat her, but barely.
HERE SHE IS, MR.PARSONS-- READY TO GO.
Speak of the devil. And her "female accomplice."
Catwoman!
MY DEAR GIRLS.
MY DEAR GIRLS.
SO LOVELY TO SEE YOU. PLEASE FOLLOW ME.
I LIKE TO PUTTER IN MY GARDENS IN THE EVENING, YOU SEE.
I KNOW WHO YOU WORK FOR, MR. PARSONS.
AND I KNOW YOU'RE HIDING FROM THE BAT. THAT'S WHY YOU'RE NOT WEARING YOUR LITTLE MASK, RIGHT?
THEY SAID YOU WERE CLEVER.
BUT...WHY THE ARSON? I KNOW YOU HIRED THOSE HOMELESS MEN.
YOU ARE A SNOOPY FELINE, AREN'T YOU?
IT'S BRUCE WAYNE, CATWOMAN. ALL THE BUILDINGS HE WANTS TO BUY AND DEMOLISH FOR HIS "REBUILDING OF GOTHAM."
WE'VE CREATED A RATHER CONVINCING PAPER TRAIL LEADING DIRECTLY TO HIM-- INCRIMINATING HIM FOR MURDER AND RACKETEERING.
THAT'S... NO ONE WILL BELIEVE THAT.
NOT AT FIRST.
BUT IMAGINE IF THERE'S A MUCH HIGHER BODY COUNT AND IRREFUTABLE EVIDENCE?
IMAGINE IF WE BURN DOWN A HUNDRED OCCUPIED BUILDINGS?

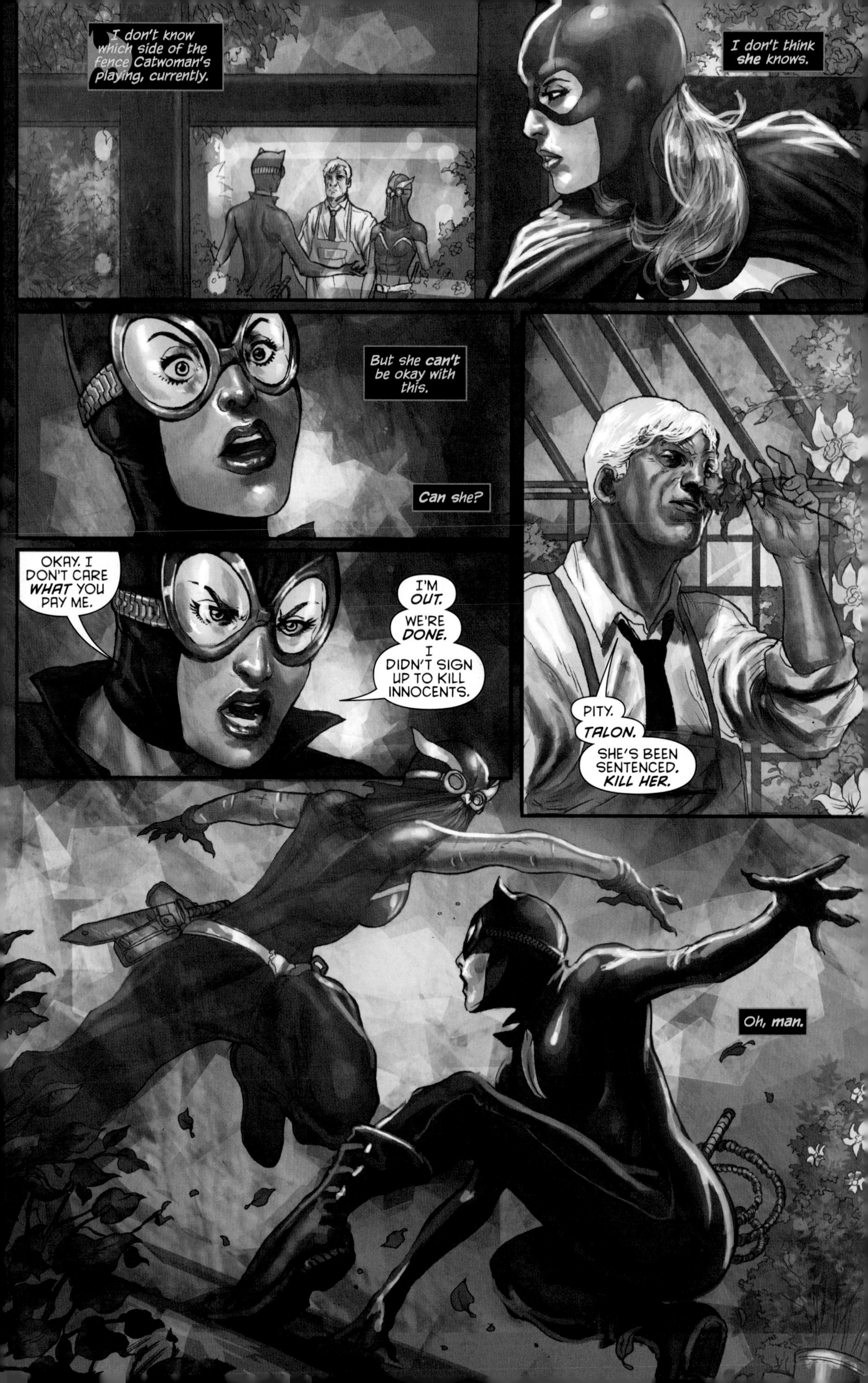
I don't know which side of the fence Catwoman's playing, currently.
I don't think she knows.
But she can't be okay with this.
Can she?
OKAY. I DON'T CARE WHAT YOU PAY ME.
I'M OUT.
WE'RE DONE.
I DIDN'T SIGN UP TO KILL INNOCENTS.
PITY.
TALON.
SHE'S BEEN SENTENCED. KILL HER.
Oh, man.

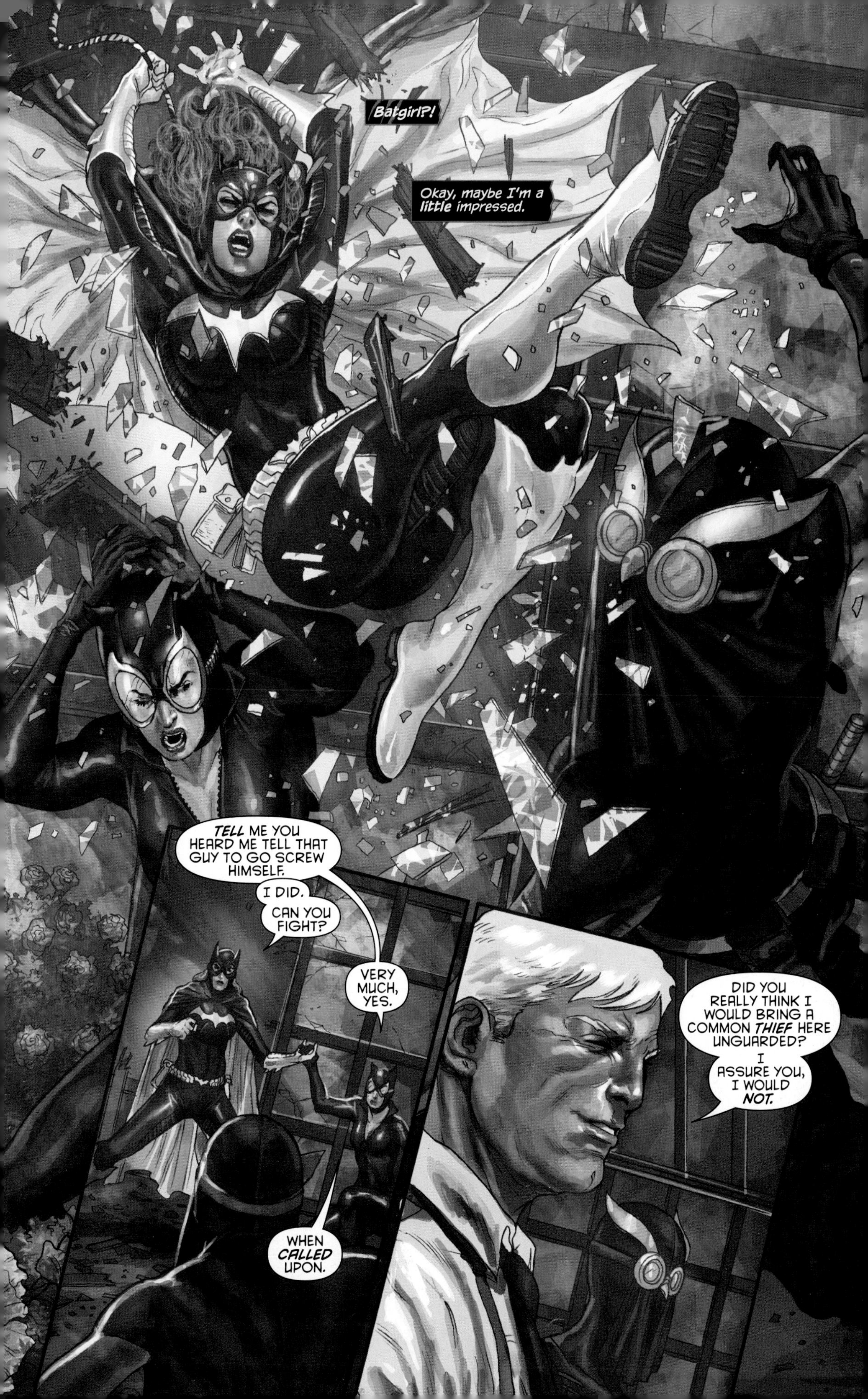
Batgirl?!
Okay, maybe I'm a *little* impressed.
TELL ME YOU HEARD ME TELL THAT GUY TO GO SCREW HIMSELF.
I DID.
CAN YOU FIGHT?
VERY MUCH, YES.
WHEN *CALLED* UPON.
DID YOU REALLY THINK I WOULD BRING A COMMON *THIEF* HERE UNGUARDED?
I ASSURE YOU, I WOULD *NOT.*

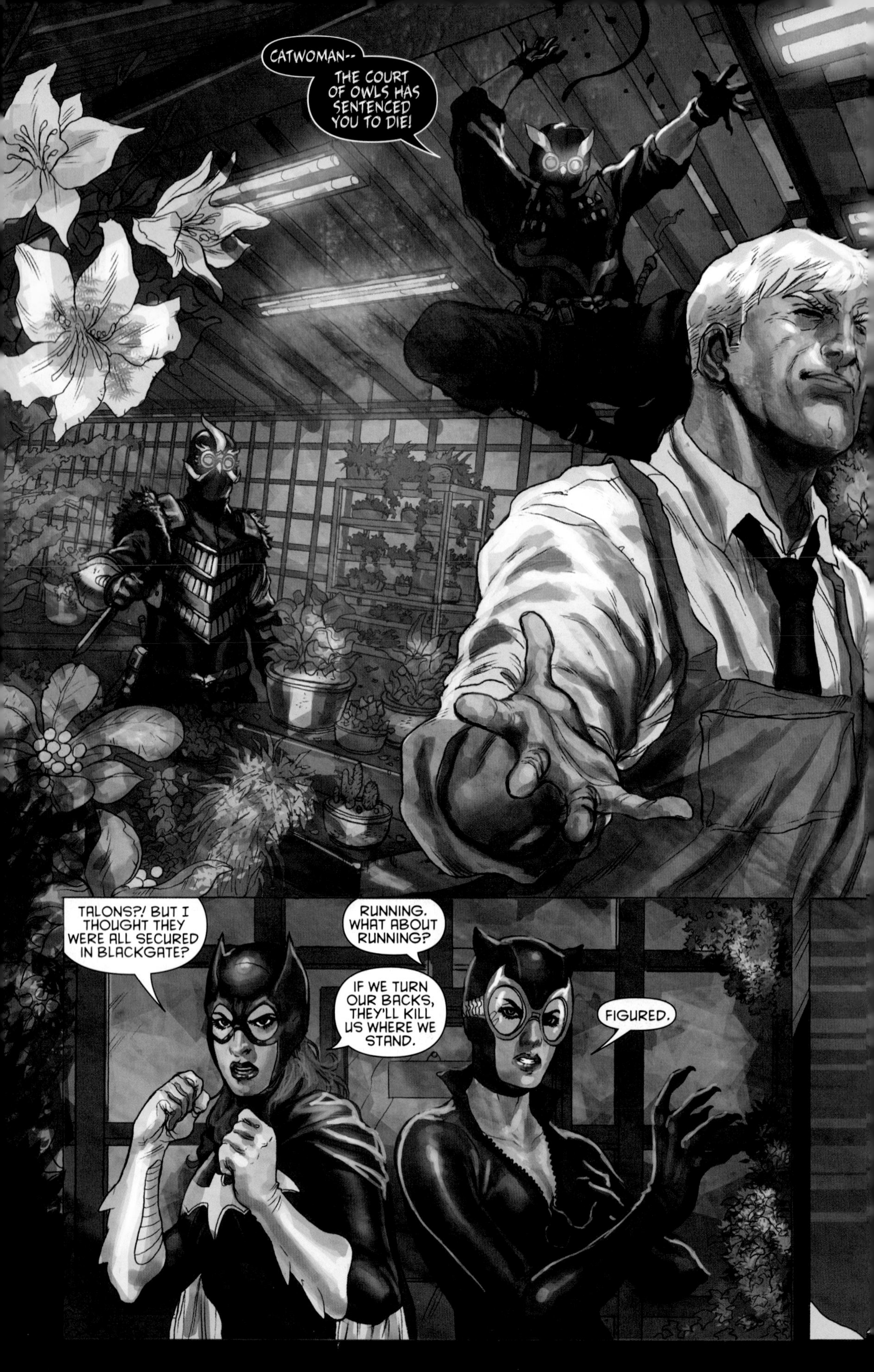
CATWOMAN--
THE COURT OF OWLS HAS SENTENCED YOU TO DIE!
TALONS?! BUT I THOUGHT THEY WERE ALL SECURED IN BLACKGATE?
RUNNING. WHAT ABOUT RUNNING?
IF WE TURN OUR BACKS, THEY'LL KILL US WHERE WE STAND.
FIGURED.

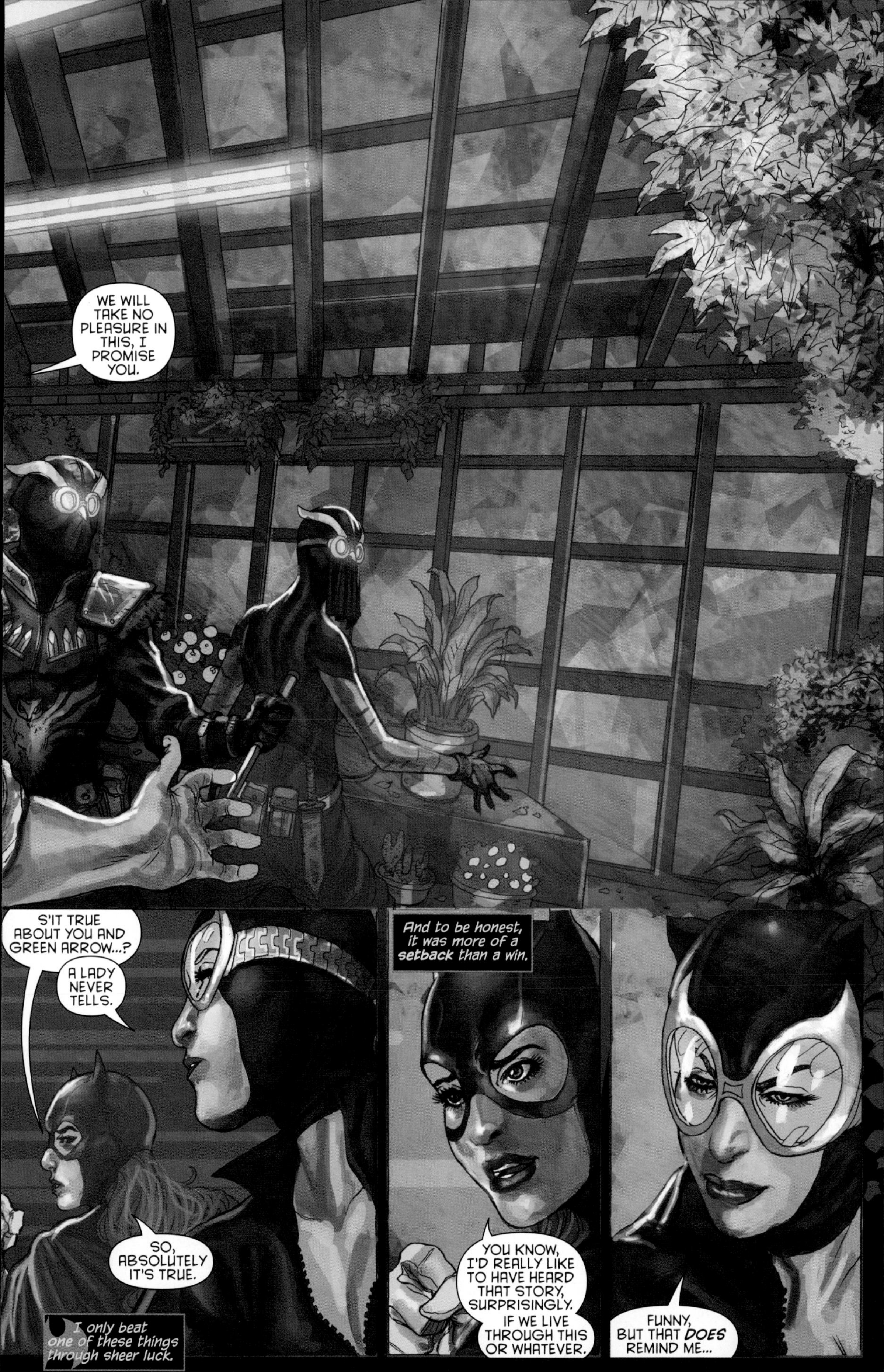
WE WILL TAKE NO PLEASURE IN THIS, I PROMISE YOU.
S'IT TRUE ABOUT YOU AND GREEN ARROW...?
A LADY NEVER TELLS.
SO, ABSOLUTELY IT'S TRUE.
I only beat one of these things through sheer luck.
And to be honest, it was more of a setback than a win.
YOU KNOW, I'D REALLY LIKE TO HAVE HEARD THAT STORY, SURPRISINGLY.
IF WE LIVE THROUGH THIS OR WHATEVER.
FUNNY, BUT THAT DOES REMIND ME...

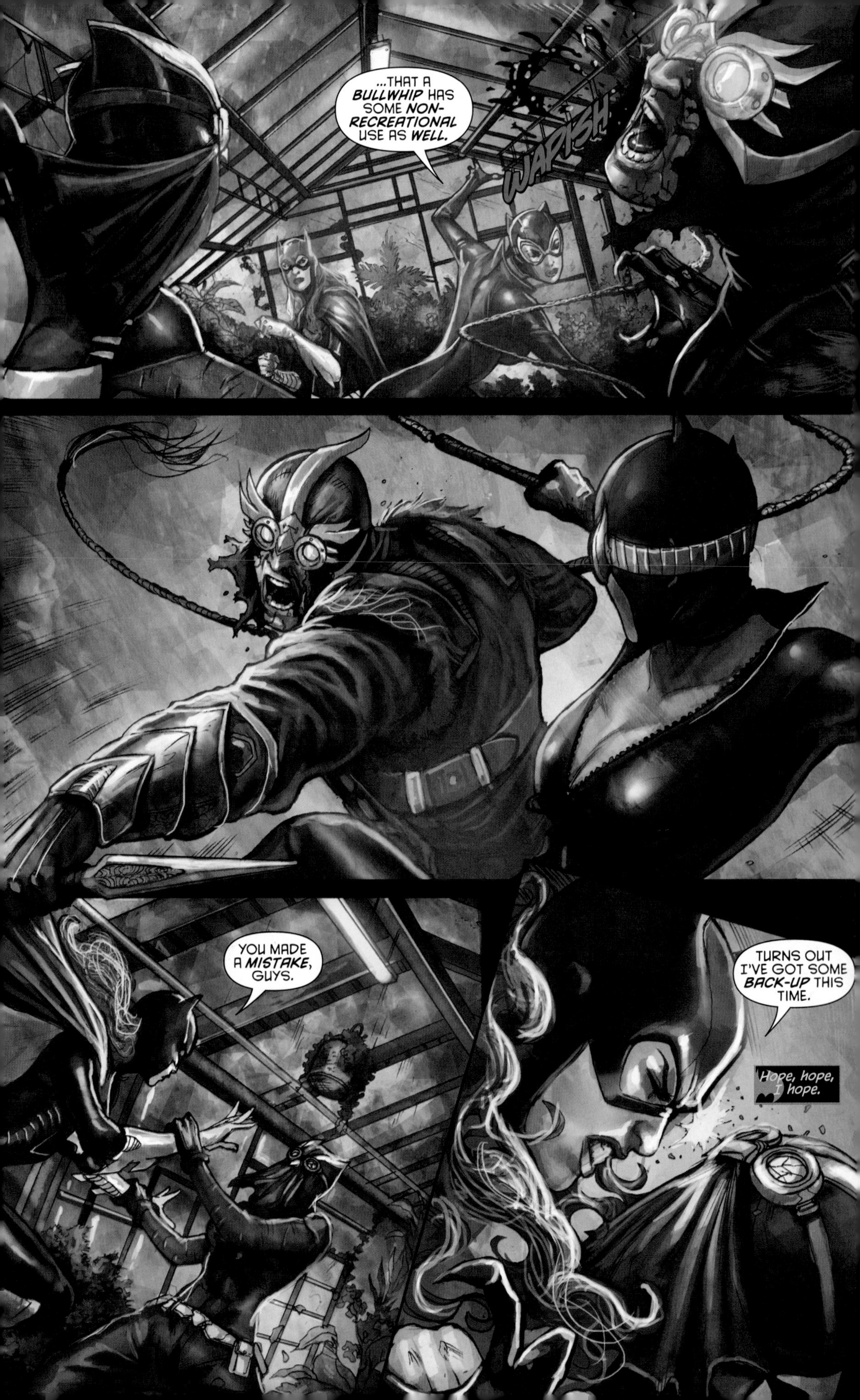
...THAT A BULLWHIP HAS SOME NON-RECREATIONAL USE AS WELL.
WAPISH
YOU MADE A MISTAKE, GUYS.
TURNS OUT I'VE GOT SOME BACK-UP THIS TIME.
Hope, hope, I hope.

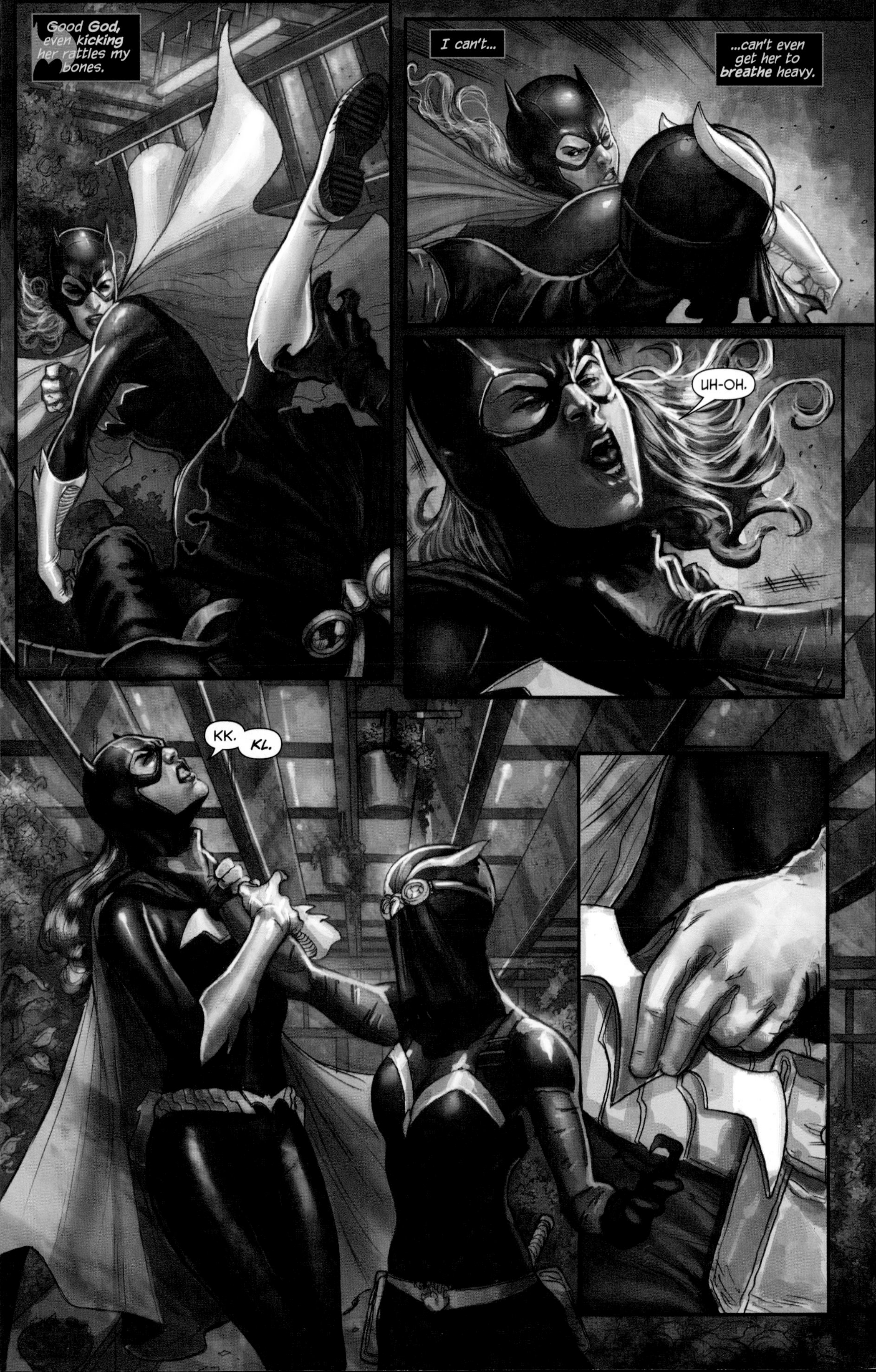
Good God, even kicking her rattles my bones.
I can't...
...can't even get her to breathe heavy.
UH-OH.
KK.
KL.

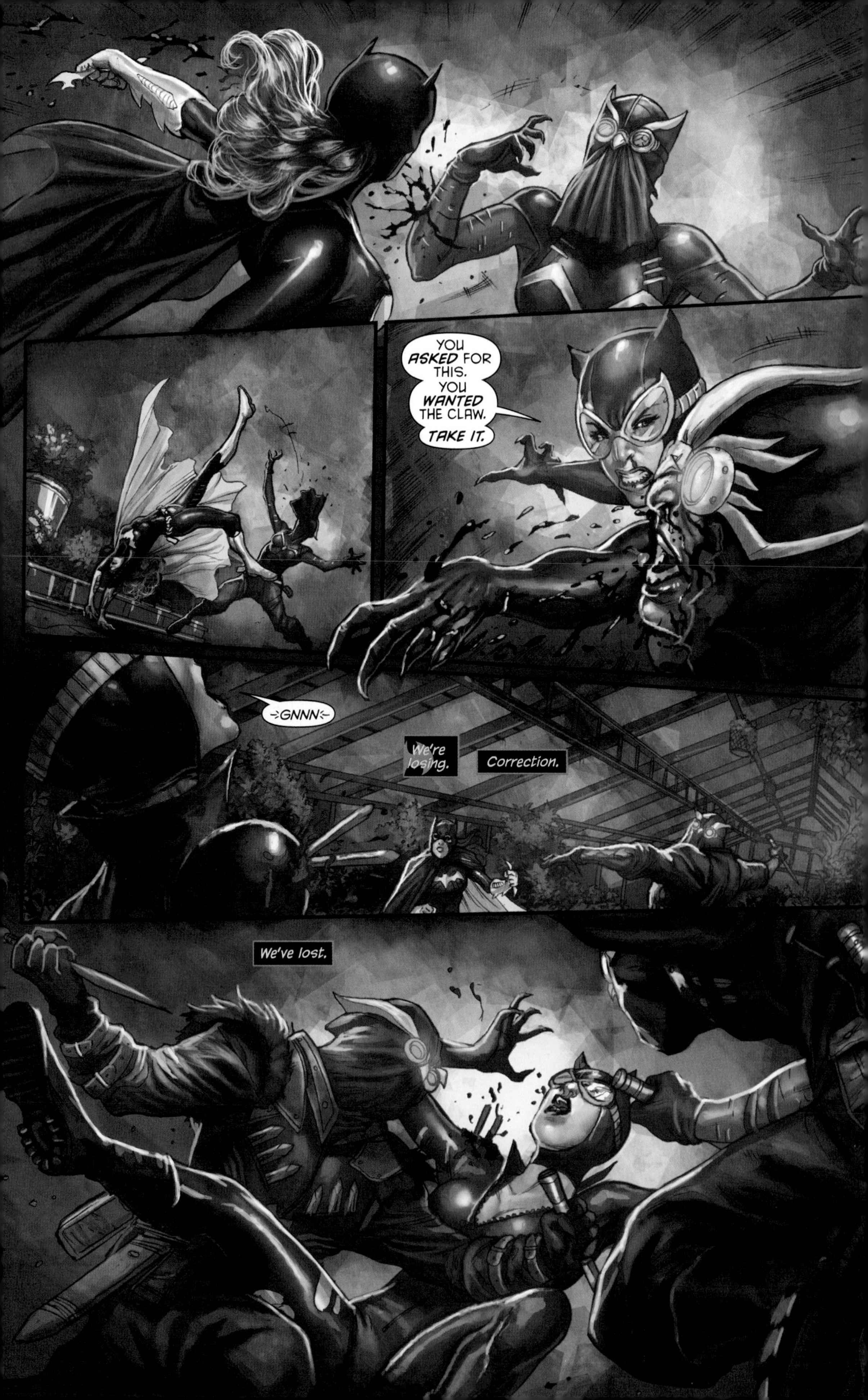
YOU *ASKED* FOR THIS. YOU *WANTED* THE CLAW.
TAKE IT.
–GNNN–
We're losing.
Correction.
We've lost.

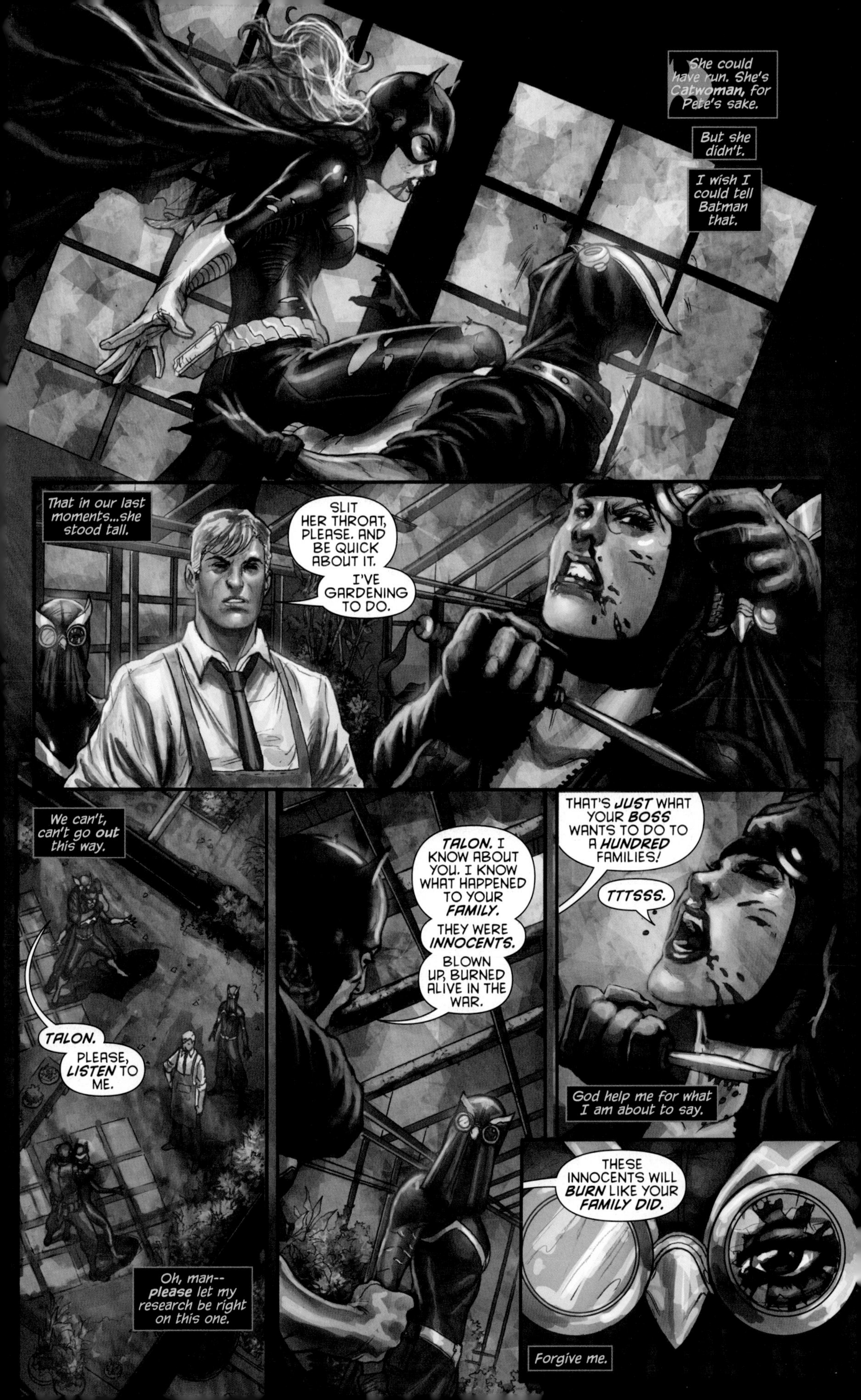
She could have run. She's Catwoman, for Pete's sake.
But she didn't.
I wish I could tell Batman that.
That in our last moments...she stood tall.
SLIT HER THROAT, PLEASE. AND BE QUICK ABOUT IT.
I'VE GARDENING TO DO.
We can't, can't go out this way.
TALON. PLEASE, LISTEN TO ME.
Oh, man-- please let my research be right on this one.
TALON. I KNOW ABOUT YOU. I KNOW WHAT HAPPENED TO YOUR FAMILY.
THEY WERE INNOCENTS.
BLOWN UP, BURNED ALIVE IN THE WAR.
THAT'S JUST WHAT YOUR BOSS WANTS TO DO TO A HUNDRED FAMILIES!
TTTSSS.
God help me for what I am about to say.
THESE INNOCENTS WILL BURN LIKE YOUR FAMILY DID.
Forgive me.

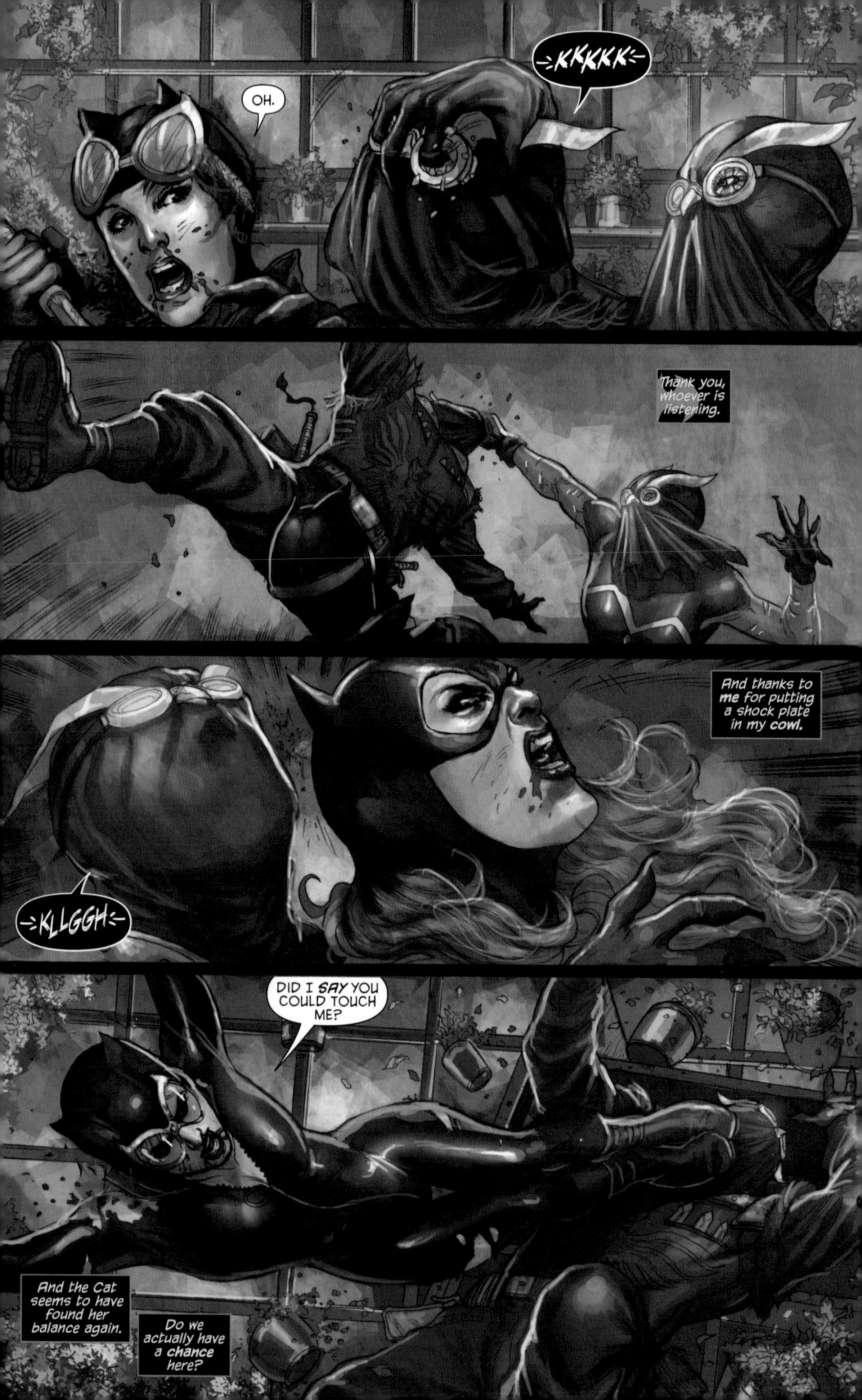
OH.
KKKKK
Thank you, whoever is listening.
And thanks to me for putting a shock plate in my cowl.
KLLGGH
DID I SAY YOU COULD TOUCH ME?
And the Cat seems to have found her balance again.
Do we actually have a chance here?

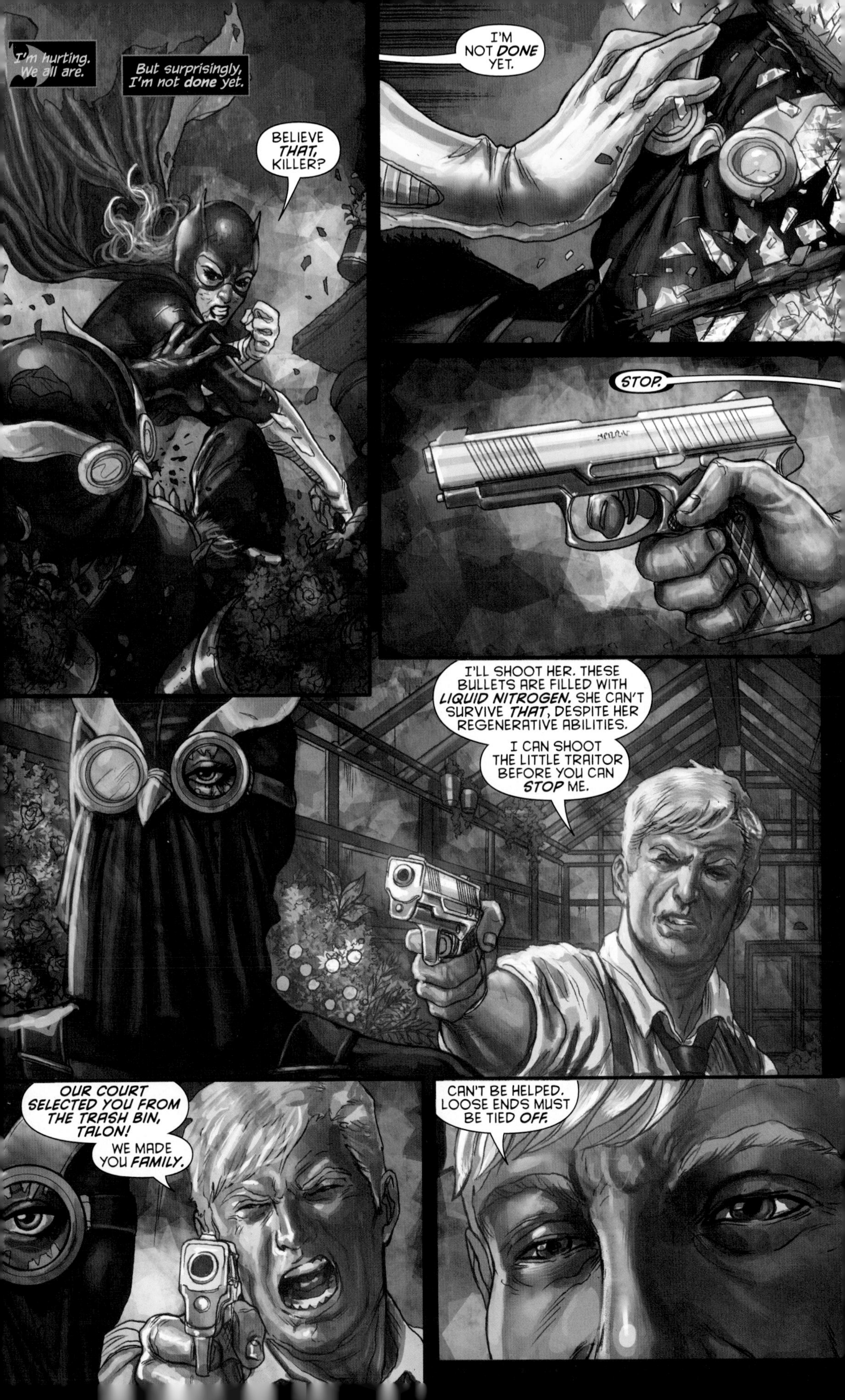

I'm hurting. We all are.
But surprisingly, I'm not done yet.
BELIEVE THAT, KILLER?
I'M NOT DONE YET.
STOP.
I'LL SHOOT HER. THESE BULLETS ARE FILLED WITH LIQUID NITROGEN. SHE CAN'T SURVIVE THAT, DESPITE HER REGENERATIVE ABILITIES.
I CAN SHOOT THE LITTLE TRAITOR BEFORE YOU CAN STOP ME.
OUR COURT SELECTED YOU FROM THE TRASH BIN, TALON!
WE MADE YOU FAMILY.
CAN'T BE HELPED. LOOSE ENDS MUST BE TIED OFF.

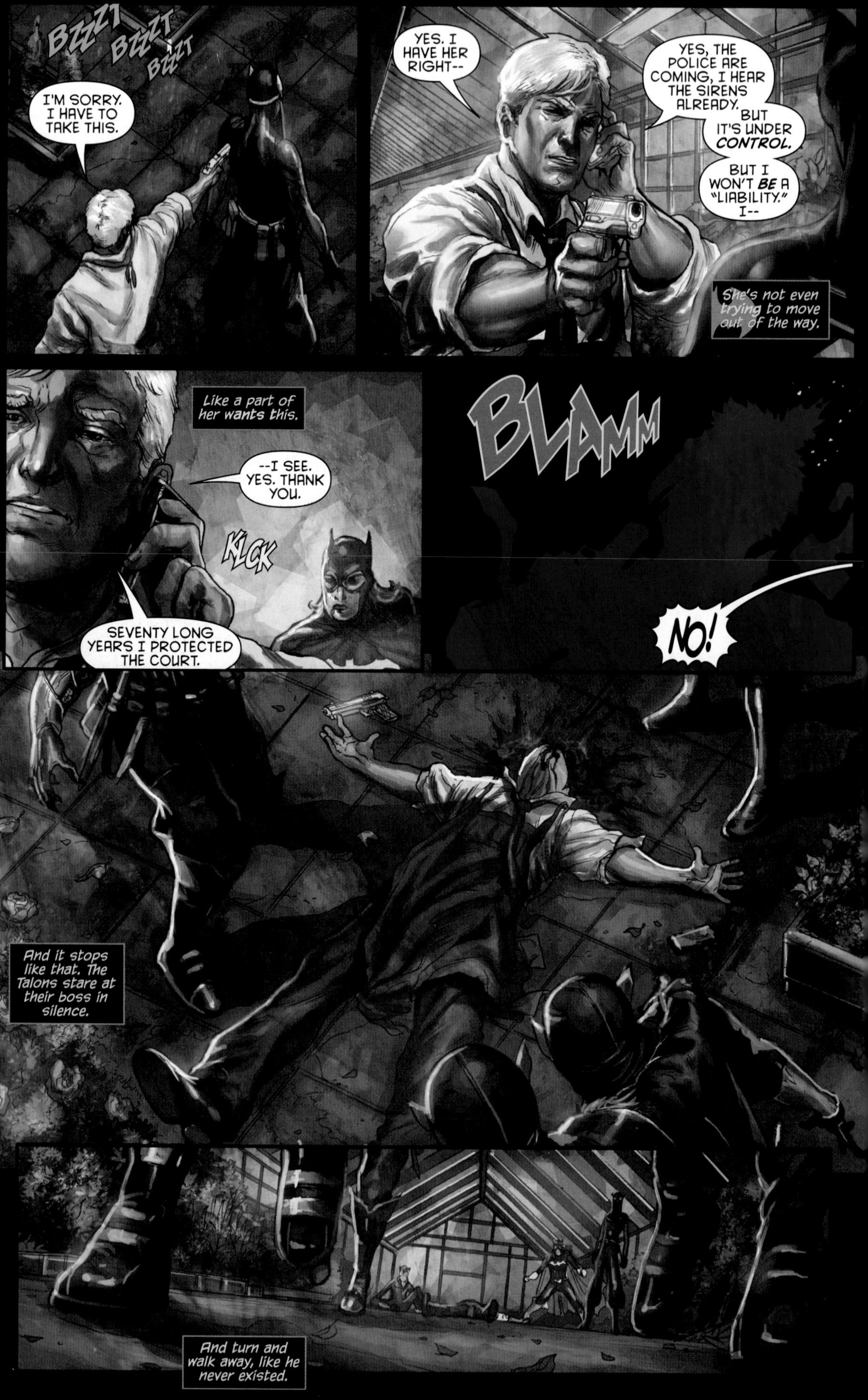
BZZZT BZZZT BZZZT
I'M SORRY. I HAVE TO TAKE THIS.
YES. I HAVE HER RIGHT--
YES, THE POLICE ARE COMING, I HEAR THE SIRENS ALREADY.
BUT IT'S UNDER CONTROL.
BUT I WON'T BE A "LIABILITY." I--
She's not even trying to move out of the way.
Like a part of her wants this.
--I SEE. YES. THANK YOU.
KLCK
SEVENTY LONG YEARS I PROTECTED THE COURT.
BLAMM
NO!
And it stops like that. The Talons stare at their boss in silence.
And turn and walk away, like he never existed.

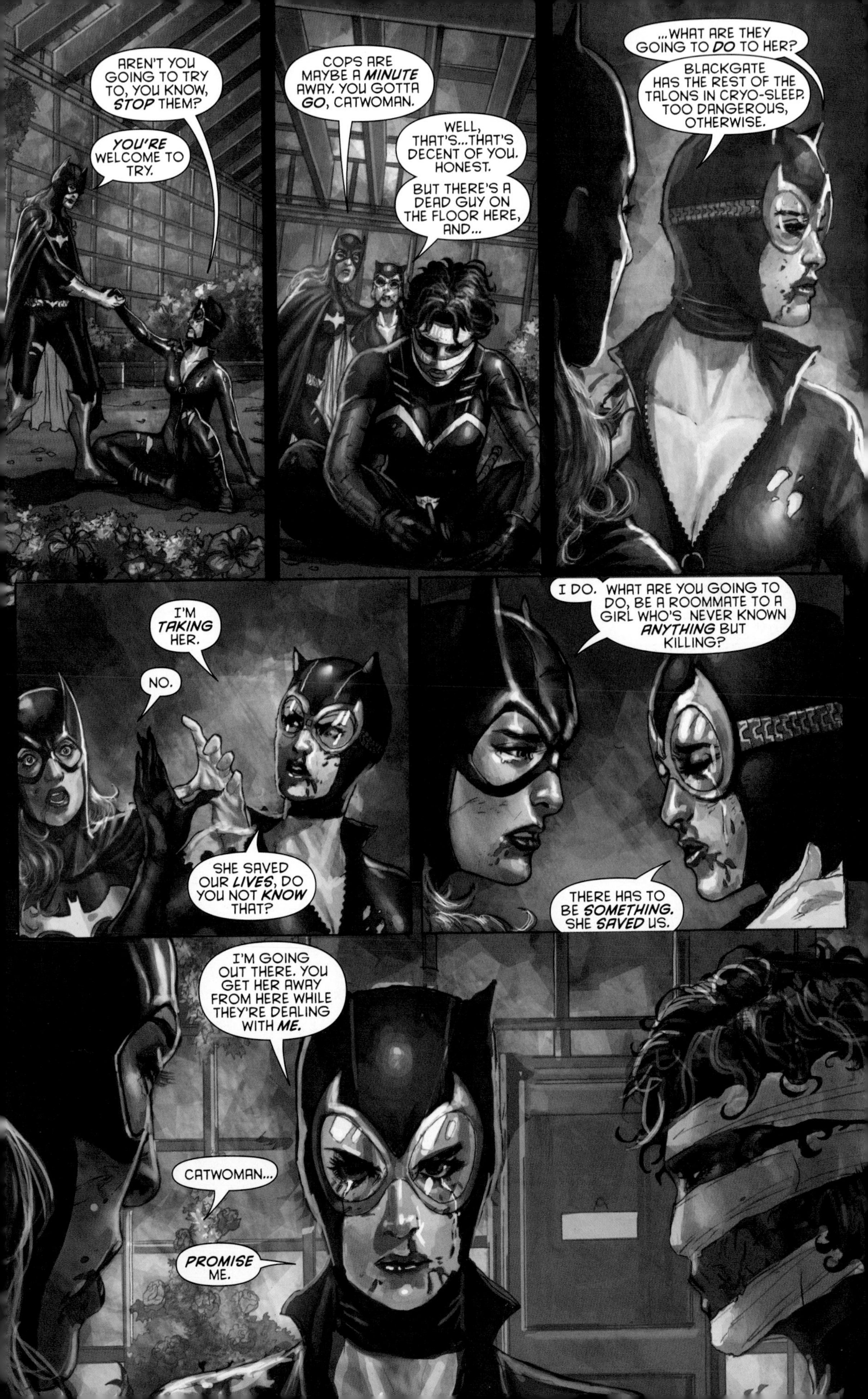
AREN'T YOU GOING TO TRY TO, YOU KNOW, STOP THEM?
YOU'RE WELCOME TO TRY.
COPS ARE MAYBE A MINUTE AWAY. YOU GOTTA GO, CATWOMAN.
WELL, THAT'S...THAT'S DECENT OF YOU. HONEST.
BUT THERE'S A DEAD GUY ON THE FLOOR HERE, AND...
...WHAT ARE THEY GOING TO DO TO HER?
BLACKGATE HAS THE REST OF THE TALONS IN CRYO-SLEEP. TOO DANGEROUS, OTHERWISE.
I'M TAKING HER.
NO.
SHE SAVED OUR LIVES, DO YOU NOT KNOW THAT?
I DO. WHAT ARE YOU GOING TO DO, BE A ROOMMATE TO A GIRL WHO'S NEVER KNOWN ANYTHING BUT KILLING?
THERE HAS TO BE SOMETHING. SHE SAVED US.
I'M GOING OUT THERE. YOU GET HER AWAY FROM HERE WHILE THEY'RE DEALING WITH ME.
CATWOMAN...
PROMISE ME.

OKAY, KIDDO. YOU GO WITH BATGIRL, ALL RIGHT?
I...TRUST HER.
And that's how a bad woman, a thief, a criminal...
...did one of the most heroic things I've ever seen.
WELL? COME AND GET ME, DARLINGS!
COME ON, WE CAN STILL GET OUT THROUGH THE ROOF IF WE GO NOW...
...
I JUST REALIZED YOU ALMOST TOOK MY LIFE AND SAVED MY LIFE IN THE SAME NIGHT, AND I STILL DON'T KNOW WHAT TO CALL YOU.
MY NAME IZ MARY

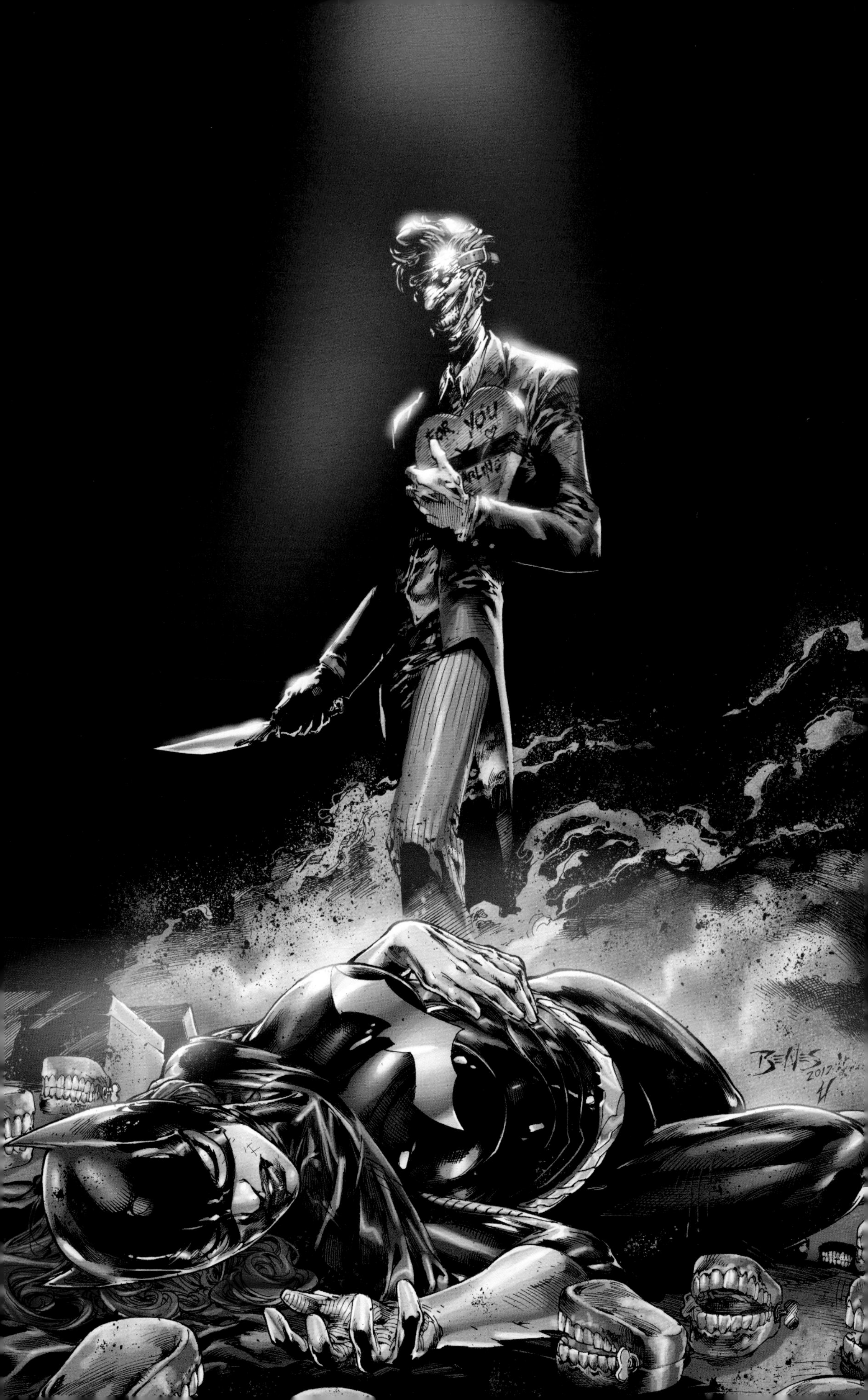
FOR YOU

GAIL SIMONE writer **ED BENES DANIEL SAMPERE** pencillers **VICENTE CIFUENTES MARK IRWIN** inkers
cover by ED BENES & ULISES ARREOLA

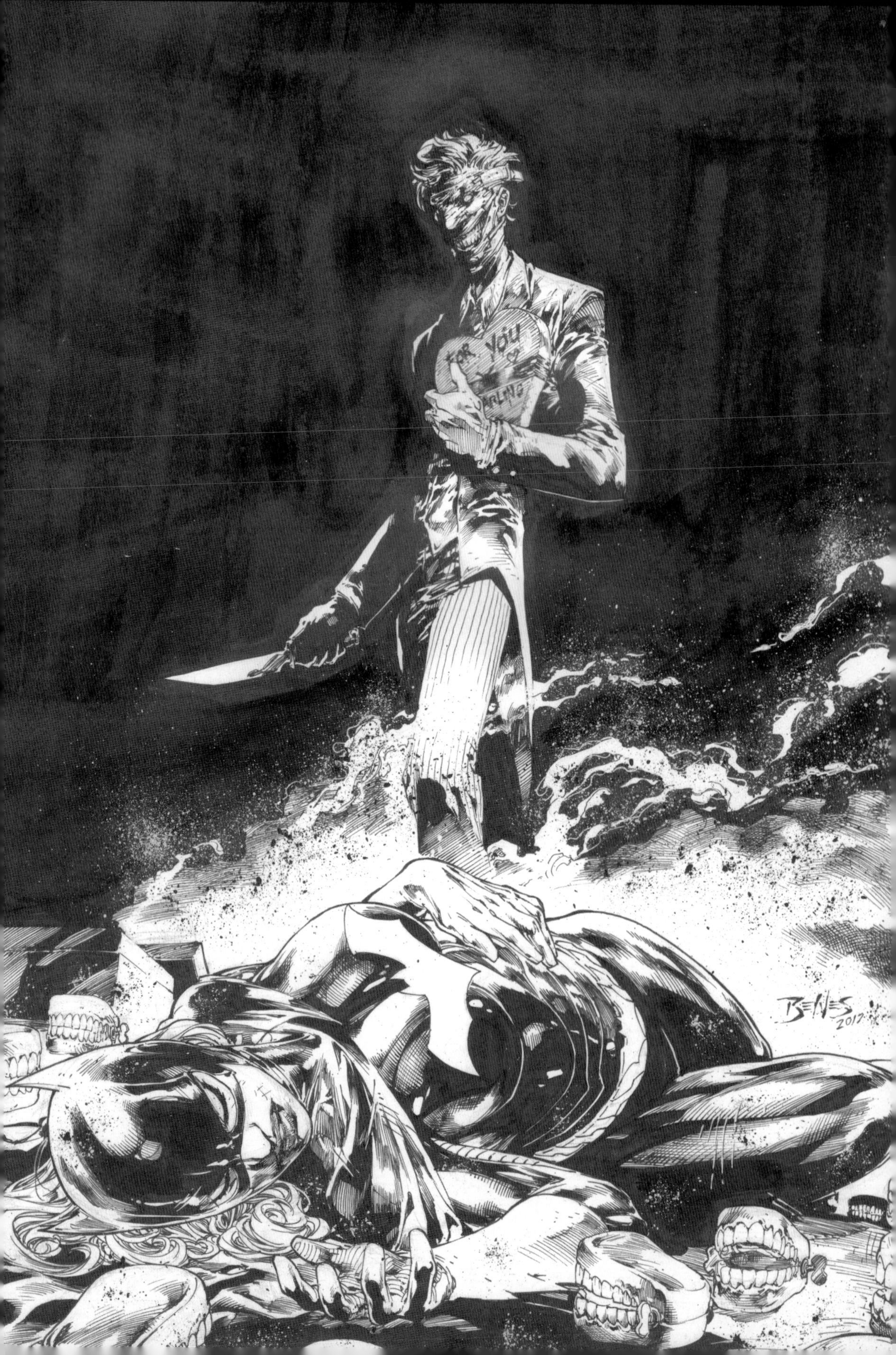
FOR YOU
DARLING
BENES
2012

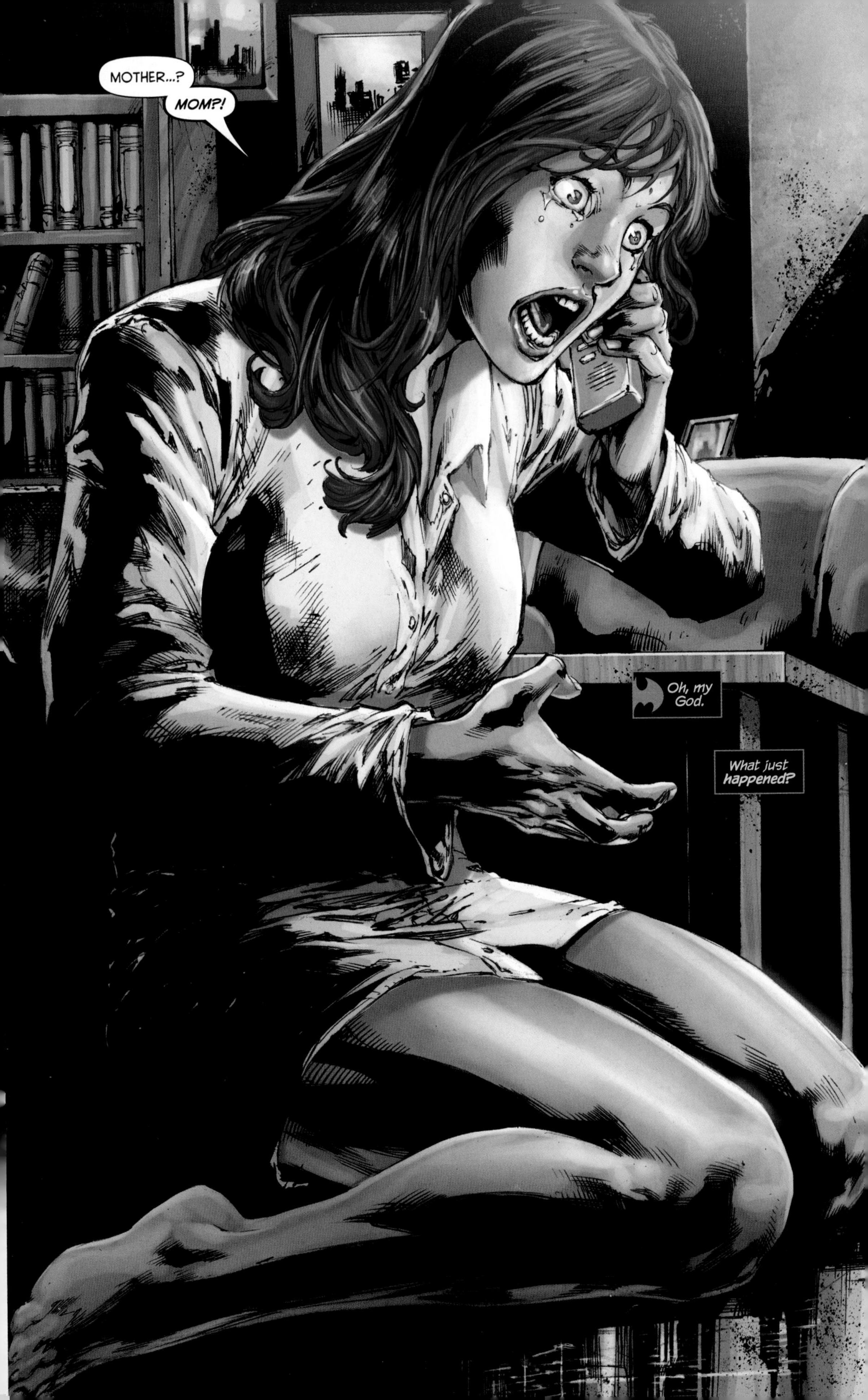
MOTHER...?
MOM?!
Oh, my God.
What just happened?

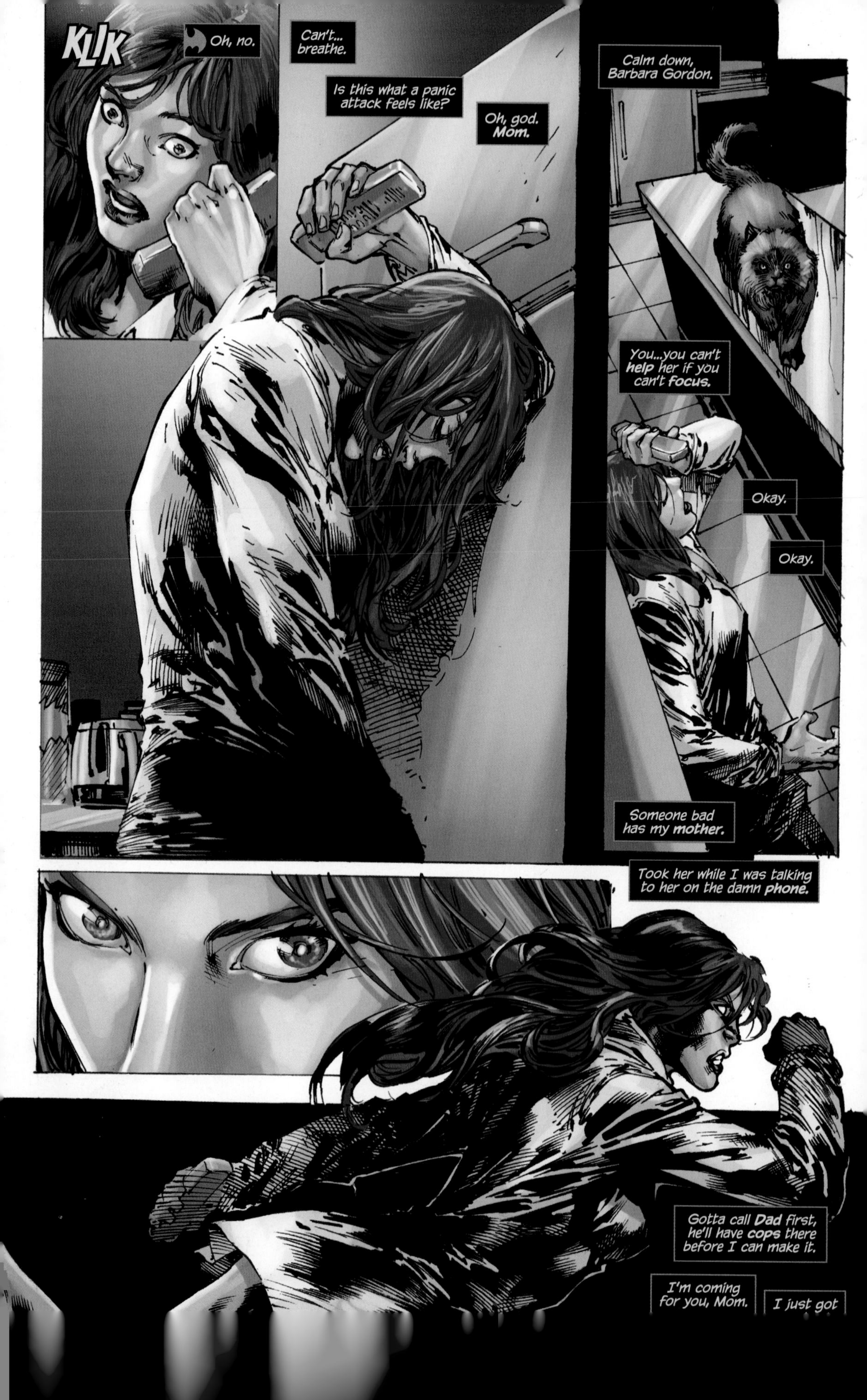

KLIK
Oh, no.
Can't... breathe.
Is this what a panic attack feels like?
Oh, god. Mom.
Calm down, Barbara Gordon.
You...you can't help her if you can't focus.
Okay.
Okay.
Someone bad has my mother.
Took her while I was talking to her on the damn phone.
Gotta call Dad first, he'll have cops there before I can make it.
I'm coming for you, Mom.
I just got

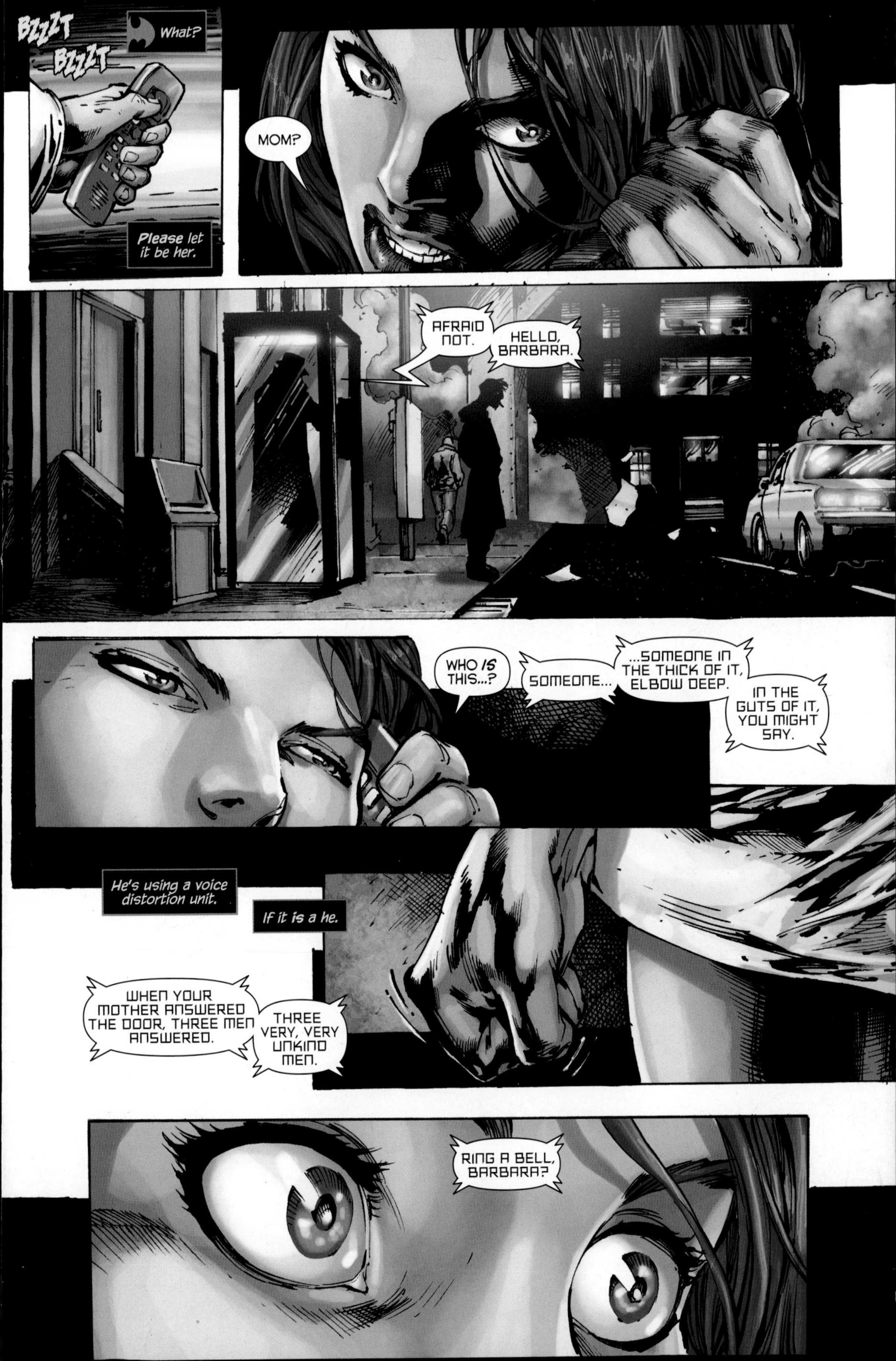
BZZZT
BZZZT
What?
Please let it be her.
MOM?
AFRAID NOT.
HELLO, BARBARA.
WHO IS THIS...?
SOMEONE...
...SOMEONE IN THE THICK OF IT, ELBOW DEEP.
IN THE GUTS OF IT, YOU MIGHT SAY.
He's using a voice distortion unit.
If it is a he.
WHEN YOUR MOTHER ANSWERED THE DOOR, THREE MEN ANSWERED.
THREE VERY, VERY UNKIND MEN.
RING A BELL, BARBARA?

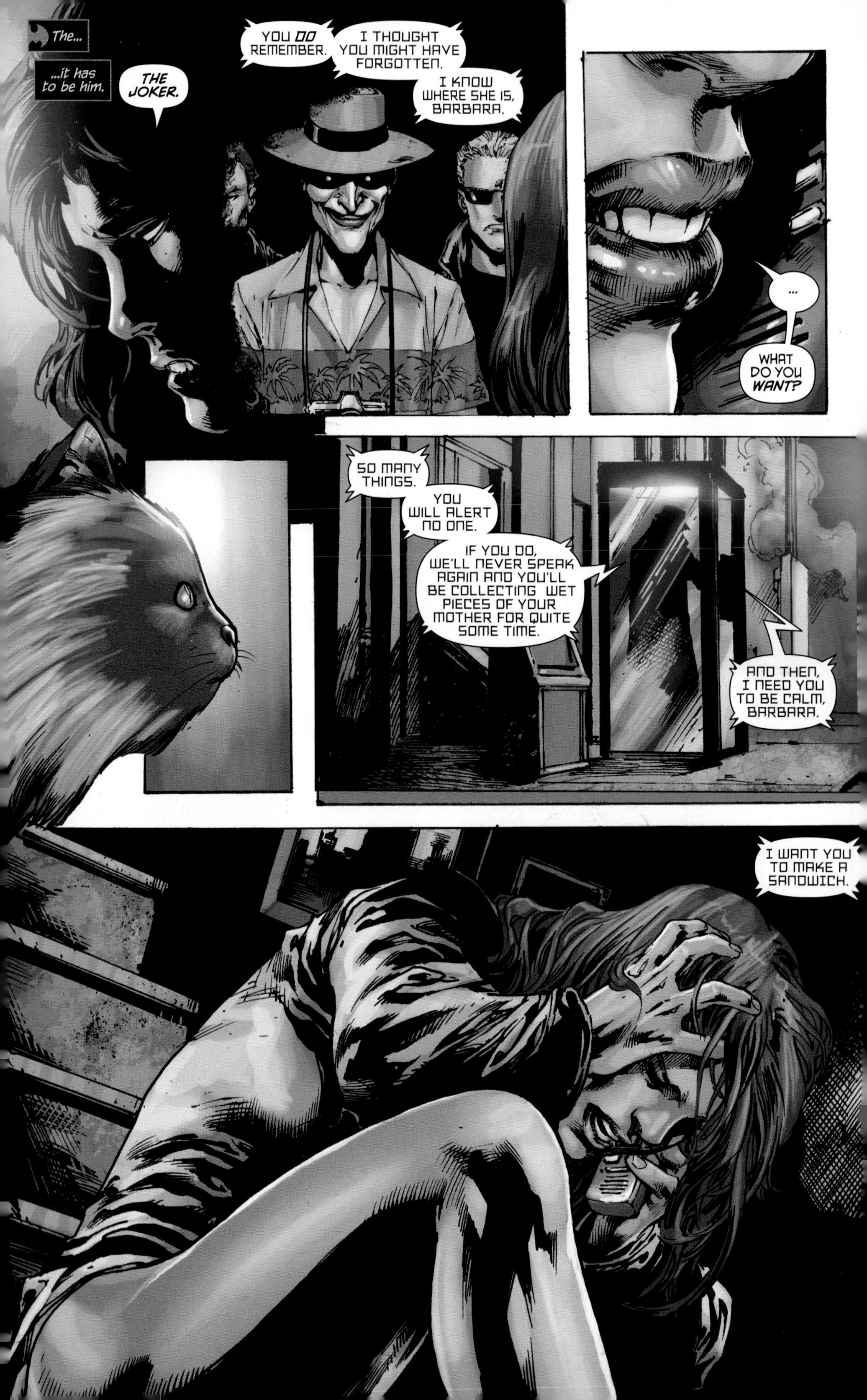
The...
...it has to be him.
THE JOKER.
YOU DO REMEMBER.
I THOUGHT YOU MIGHT HAVE FORGOTTEN.
I KNOW WHERE SHE IS, BARBARA.
...
WHAT DO YOU WANT?
SO MANY THINGS.
YOU WILL ALERT NO ONE.
IF YOU DO, WE'LL NEVER SPEAK AGAIN AND YOU'LL BE COLLECTING WET PIECES OF YOUR MOTHER FOR QUITE SOME TIME.
AND THEN, I NEED YOU TO BE CALM, BARBARA.
I WANT YOU TO MAKE A SANDWICH.

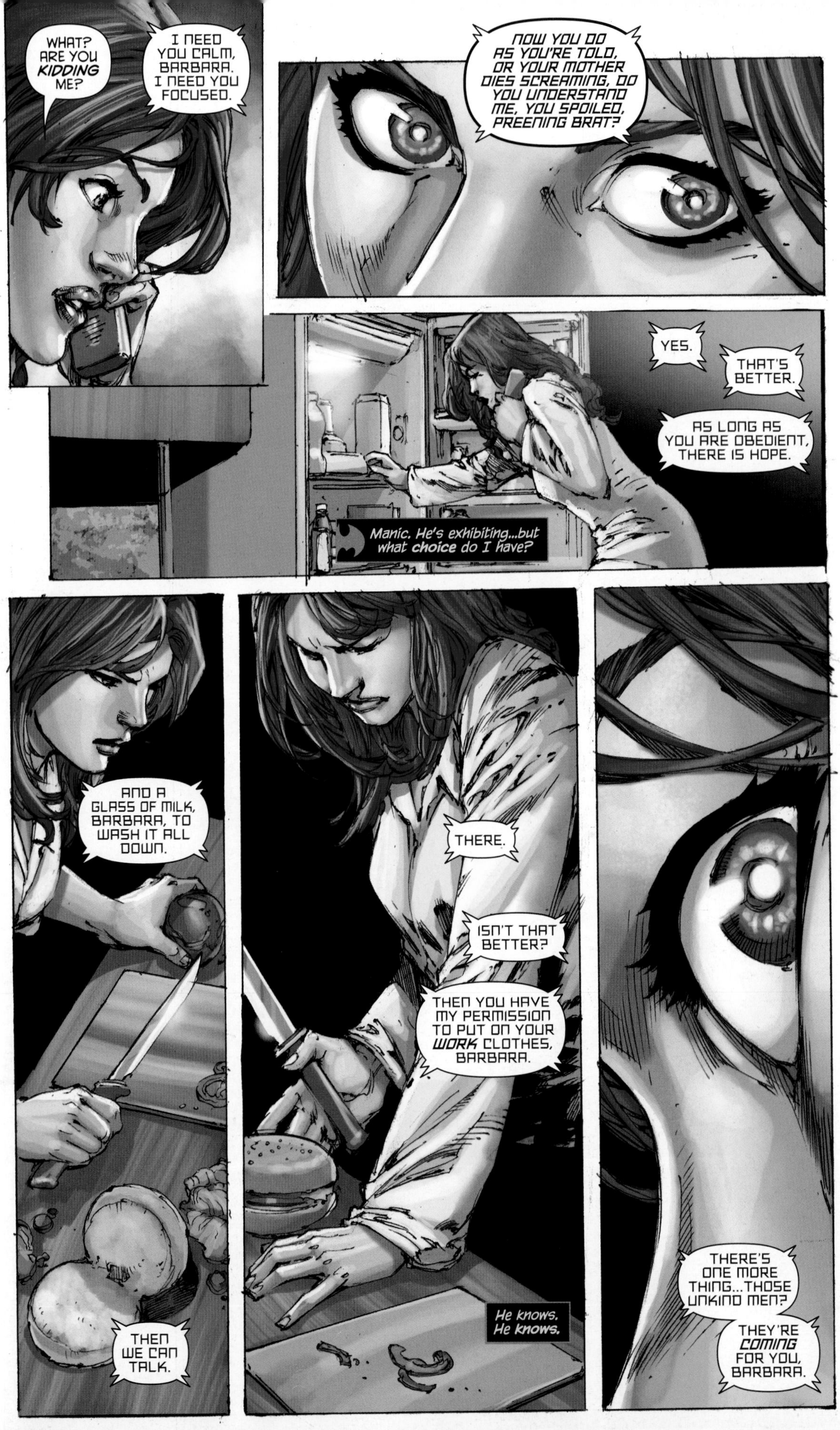
WHAT? ARE YOU KIDDING ME?
I NEED YOU CALM, BARBARA. I NEED YOU FOCUSED.
NOW YOU DO AS YOU'RE TOLD, OR YOUR MOTHER DIES SCREAMING, DO YOU UNDERSTAND ME, YOU SPOILED, PREENING BRAT?
YES.
THAT'S BETTER.
AS LONG AS YOU ARE OBEDIENT, THERE IS HOPE.
Manic. He's exhibiting...but what choice do I have?
AND A GLASS OF MILK, BARBARA, TO WASH IT ALL DOWN.
THEN WE CAN TALK.
THERE.
ISN'T THAT BETTER?
THEN YOU HAVE MY PERMISSION TO PUT ON YOUR WORK CLOTHES, BARBARA.
He knows. He knows.
THERE'S ONE MORE THING...THOSE UNKIND MEN?
THEY'RE COMING FOR YOU, BARBARA.

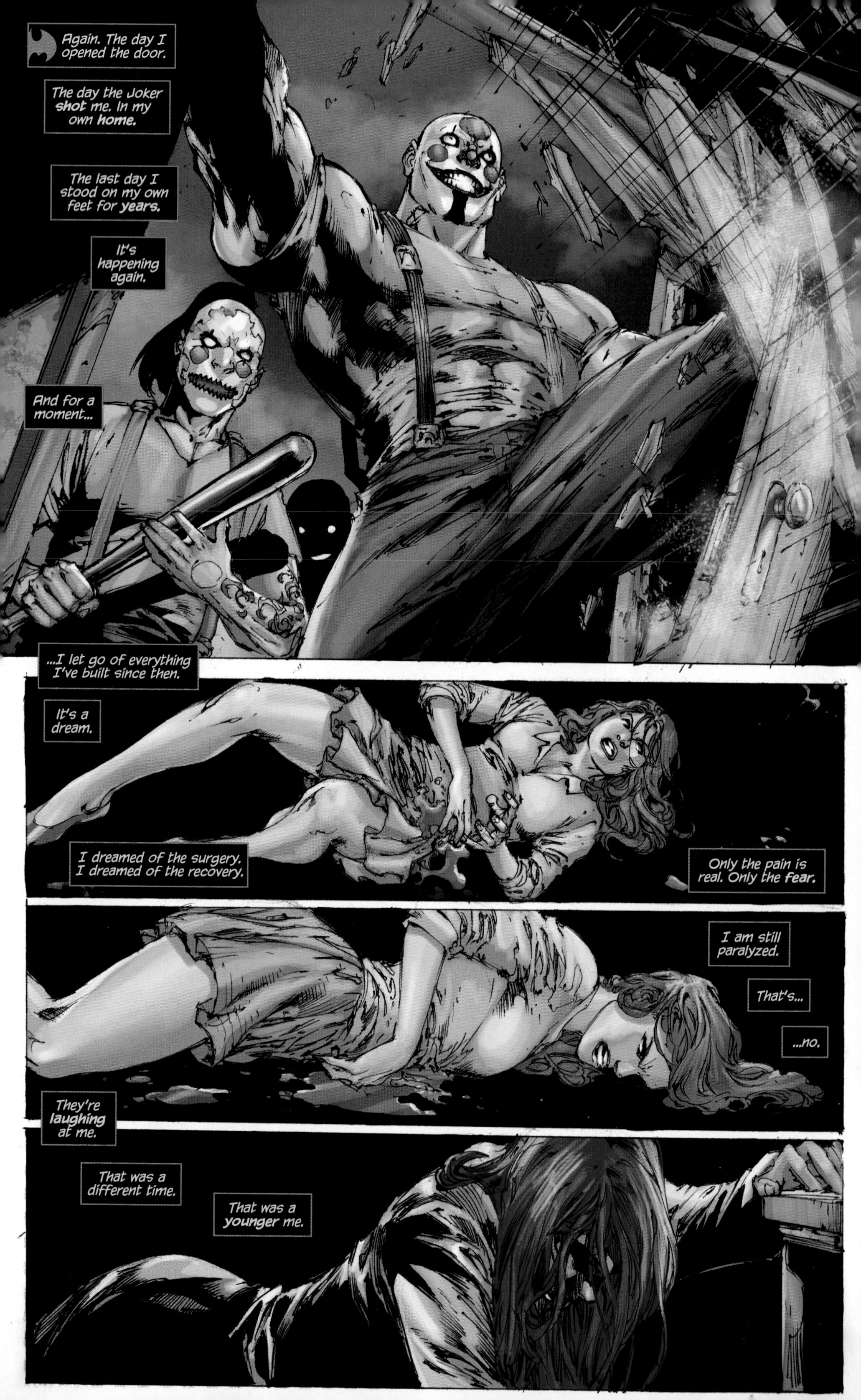
Again. The day I opened the door.
The day the Joker **shot** me. In my own **home.**
The last day I stood on my own feet for **years.**
It's happening again.
And for a moment...
...I let go of everything I've built since then.
It's a dream.
I dreamed of the surgery. I dreamed of the recovery.
Only the pain is real. Only the **fear.**
I am still paralyzed.
That's...
...no.
They're **laughing** at me.
That was a different time.
That was a **younger** me.

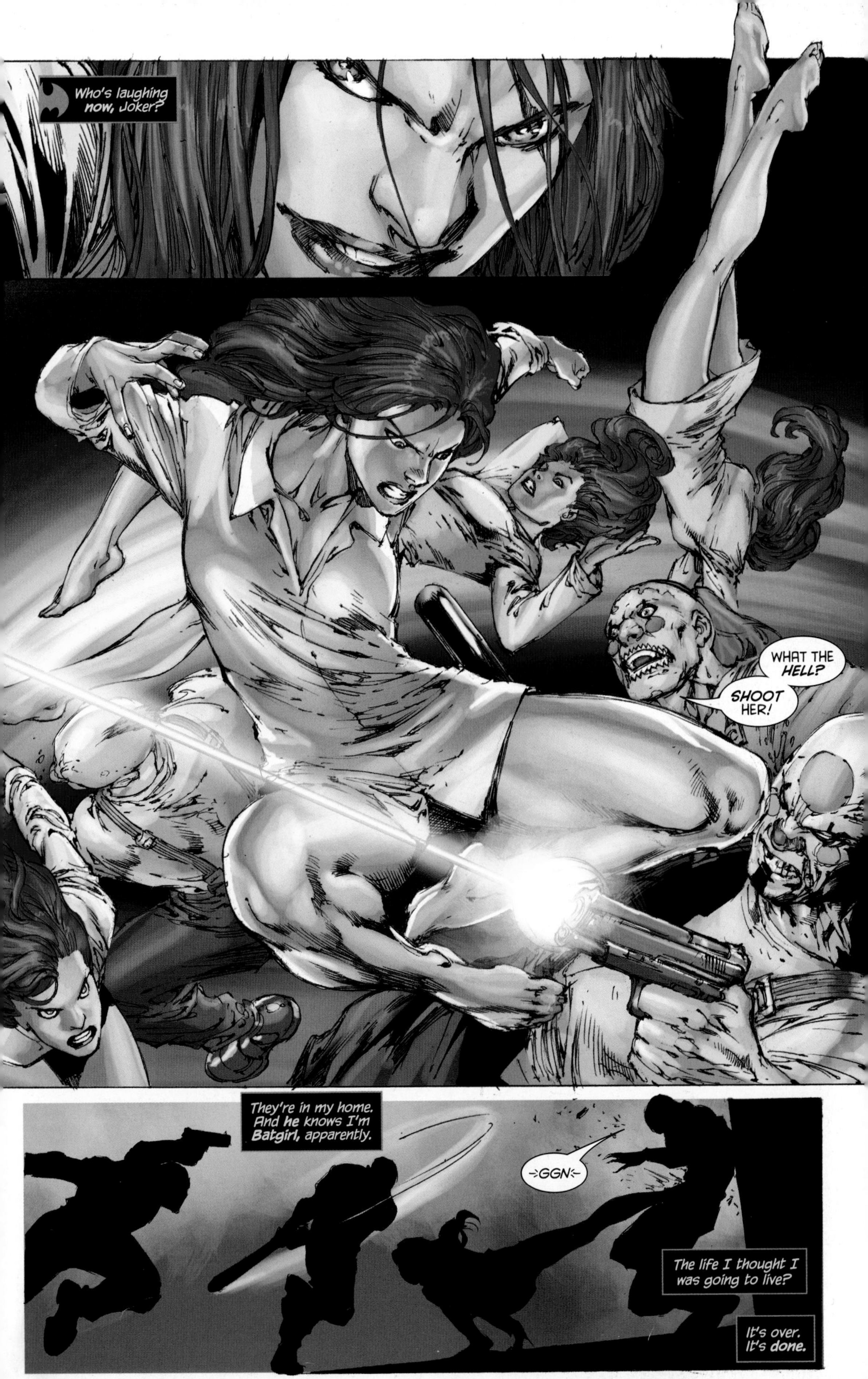
Who's laughing **now**, Joker?
WHAT THE **HELL?**
SHOOT HER!
They're in my home. And **he** knows I'm **Batgirl**, apparently.
-GGN-
The life I thought I was going to live?
It's over. It's **done.**

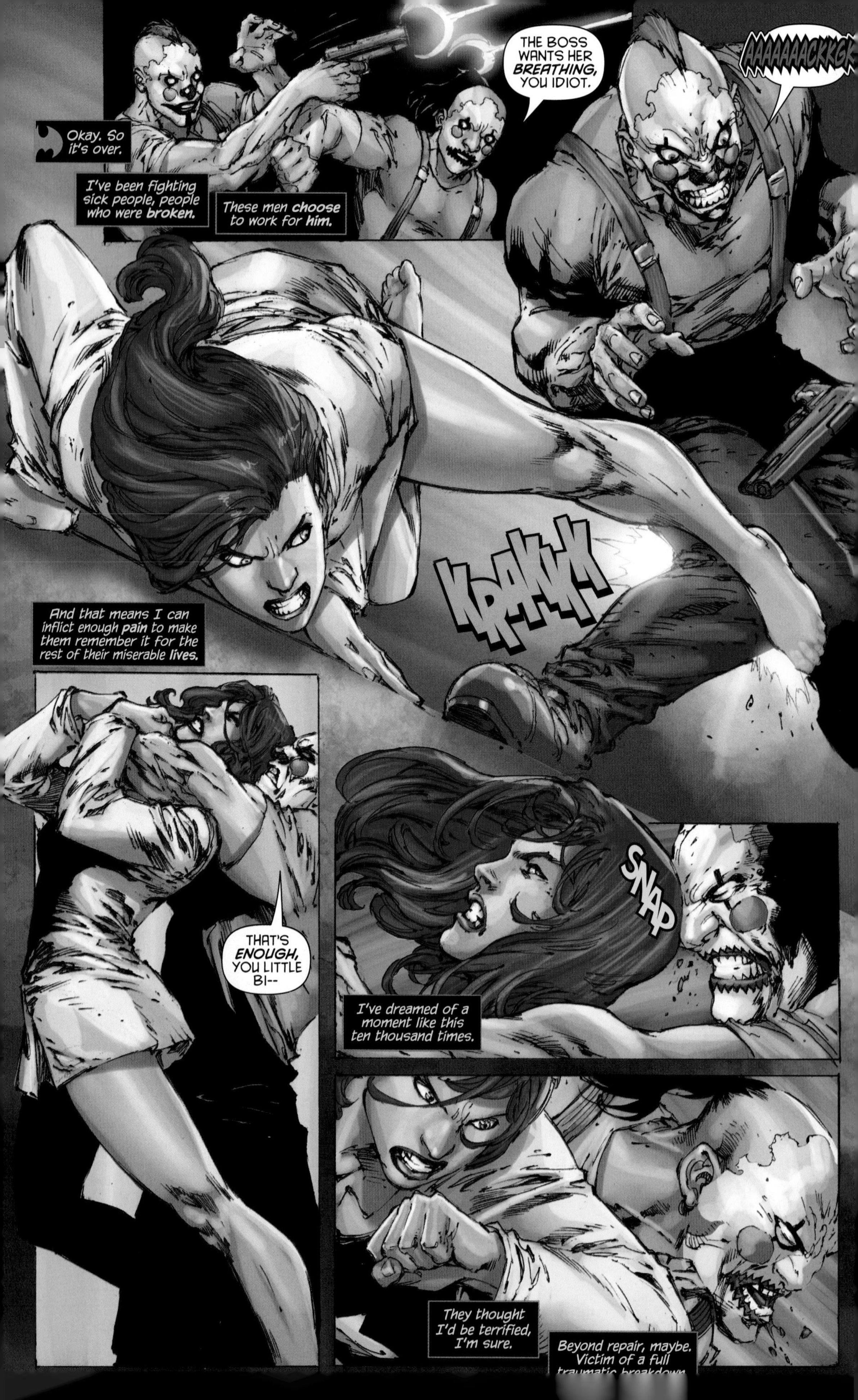

Okay. So it's over.
I've been fighting sick people, people who were broken.
These men choose to work for him.
THE BOSS WANTS HER BREATHING, YOU IDIOT.
AAAAAAACKKGK
KRAKKK
And that means I can inflict enough pain to make them remember it for the rest of their miserable lives.
THAT'S ENOUGH, YOU LITTLE BI--
SNAP
I've dreamed of a moment like this ten thousand times.
They thought I'd be terrified, I'm sure.
Beyond repair, maybe. Victim of a full

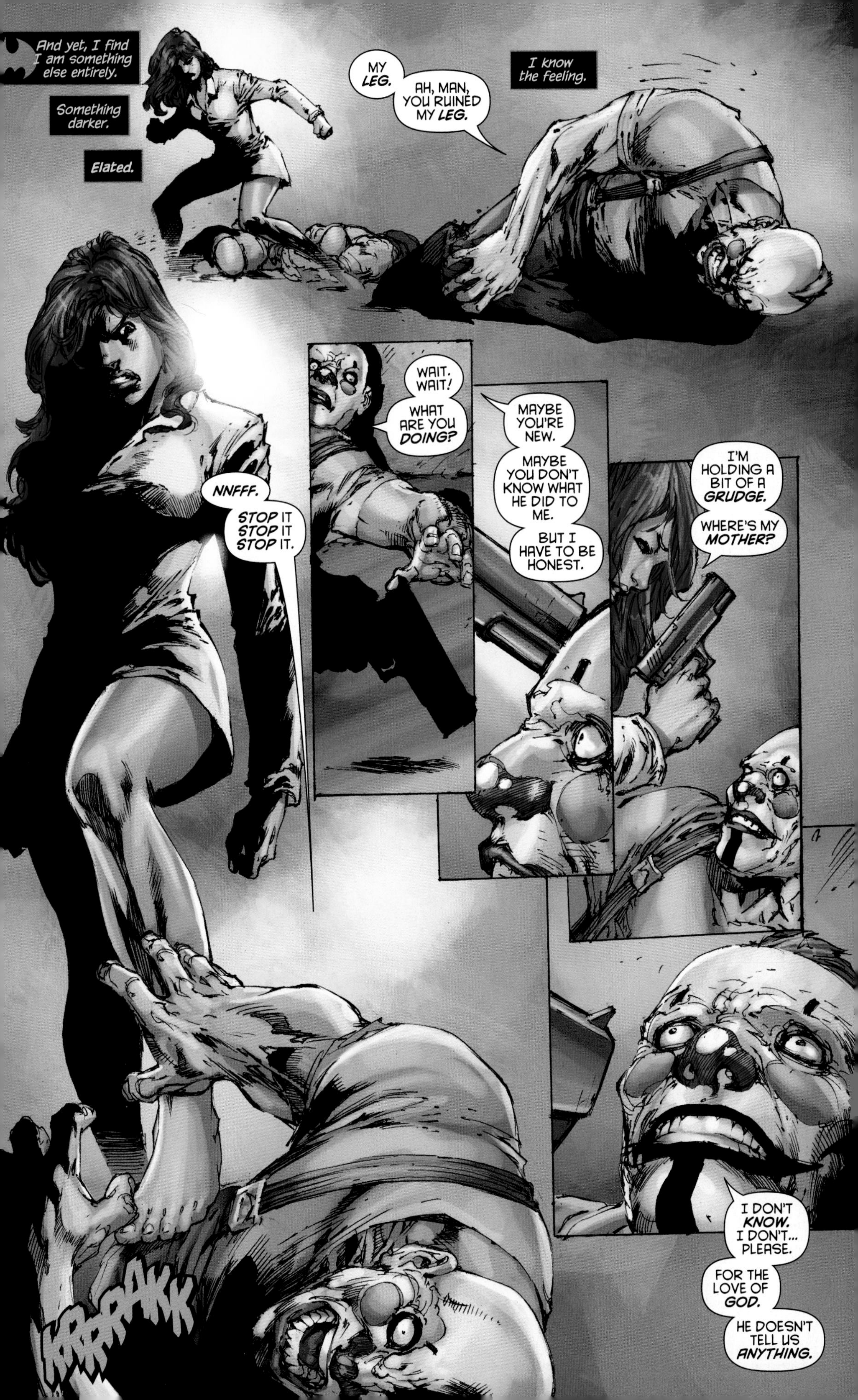
And yet, I find I am something else entirely.
Something darker.
Elated.
MY LEG.
AH, MAN, YOU RUINED MY LEG.
I know the feeling.
NNFFF.
STOP IT STOP IT STOP IT.
WAIT. WAIT!
WHAT ARE YOU DOING?
MAYBE YOU'RE NEW.
MAYBE YOU DON'T KNOW WHAT HE DID TO ME.
BUT I HAVE TO BE HONEST.
I'M HOLDING A BIT OF A GRUDGE.
WHERE'S MY MOTHER?
I DON'T KNOW. I DON'T... PLEASE.
FOR THE LOVE OF GOD.
HE DOESN'T TELL US ANYTHING.
KRRRAKK

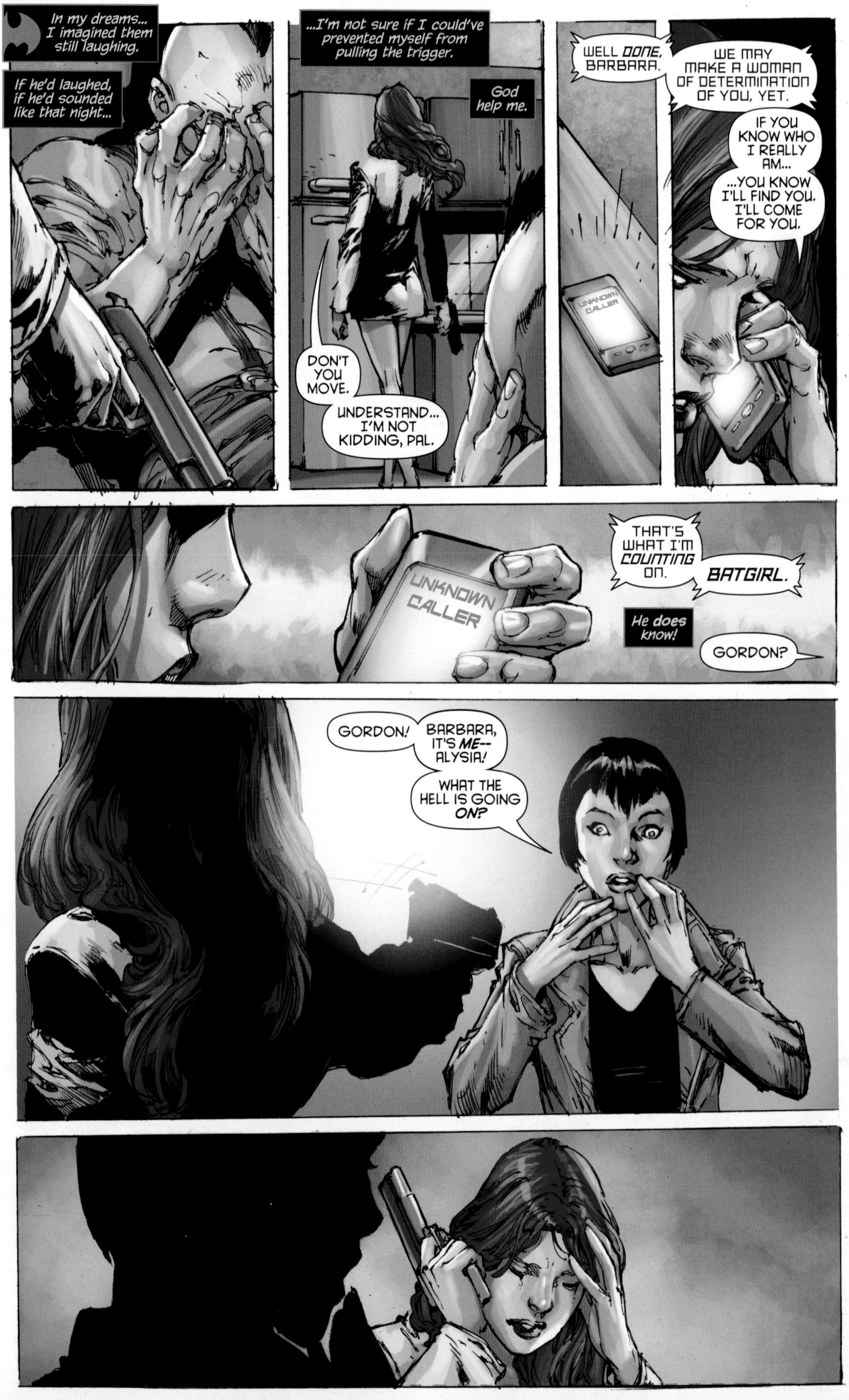
In my dreams... I imagined them still laughing.
If he'd laughed, if he'd sounded like that night...
...I'm not sure if I could've prevented myself from pulling the trigger.
God help me.
DON'T YOU MOVE.
UNDERSTAND... I'M NOT KIDDING, PAL.
UNKNOWN CALLER
WELL DONE, BARBARA.
WE MAY MAKE A WOMAN OF DETERMINATION OF YOU, YET.
IF YOU KNOW WHO I REALLY AM...
...YOU KNOW I'LL FIND YOU. I'LL COME FOR YOU.
UNKNOWN CALLER
THAT'S WHAT I'M COUNTING ON.
BATGIRL.
He does know!
GORDON?
GORDON!
BARBARA, IT'S ME-- ALYSIA!
WHAT THE HELL IS GOING ON?

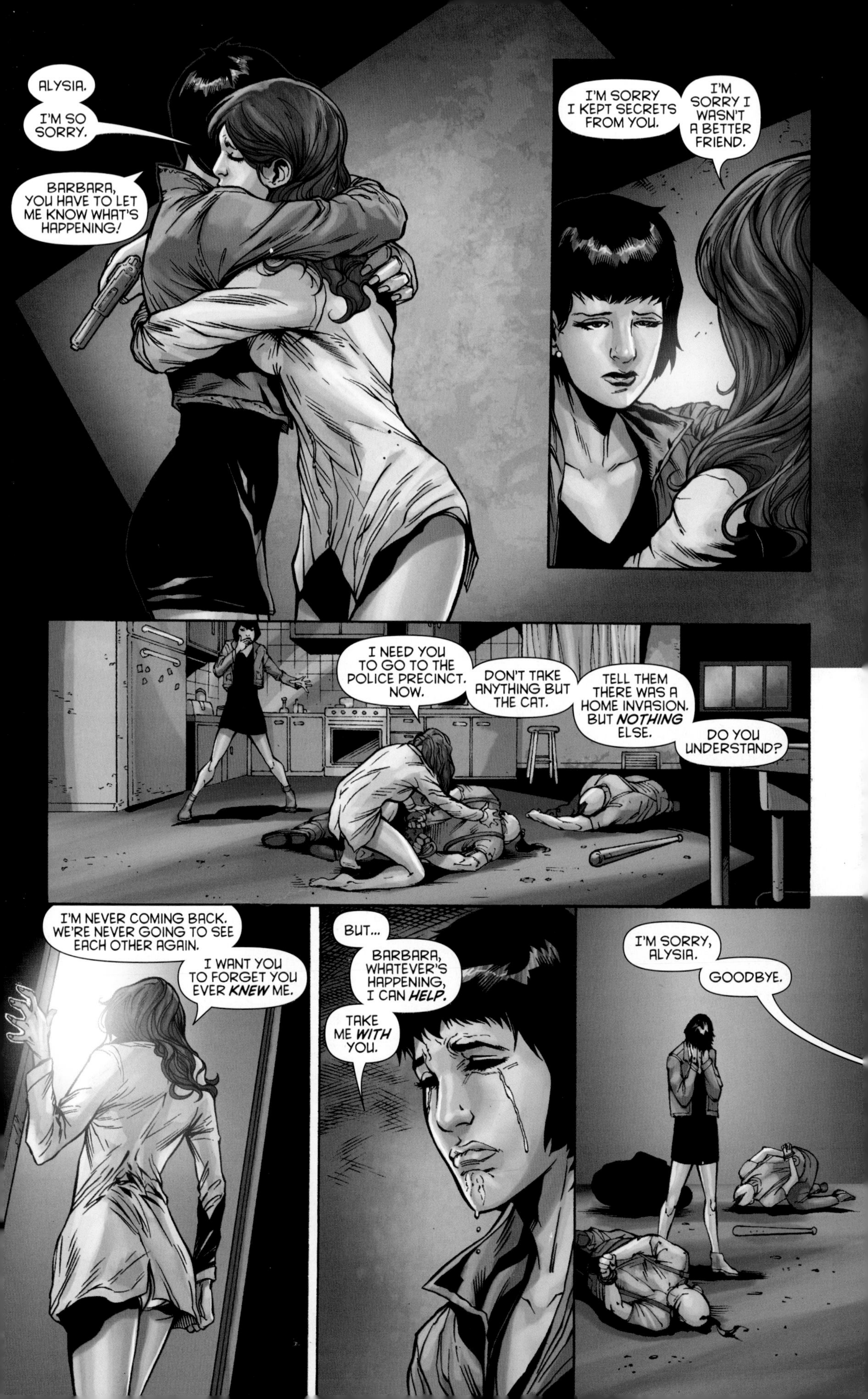
ALYSIA.
I'M SO SORRY.
BARBARA, YOU HAVE TO LET ME KNOW WHAT'S HAPPENING!
I'M SORRY I KEPT SECRETS FROM YOU.
I'M SORRY I WASN'T A BETTER FRIEND.
I NEED YOU TO GO TO THE POLICE PRECINCT. NOW.
DON'T TAKE ANYTHING BUT THE CAT.
TELL THEM THERE WAS A HOME INVASION. BUT NOTHING ELSE.
DO YOU UNDERSTAND?
I'M NEVER COMING BACK. WE'RE NEVER GOING TO SEE EACH OTHER AGAIN.
I WANT YOU TO FORGET YOU EVER KNEW ME.
BUT...
BARBARA, WHATEVER'S HAPPENING, I CAN HELP.
TAKE ME WITH YOU.
I'M SORRY, ALYSIA.
GOODBYE.

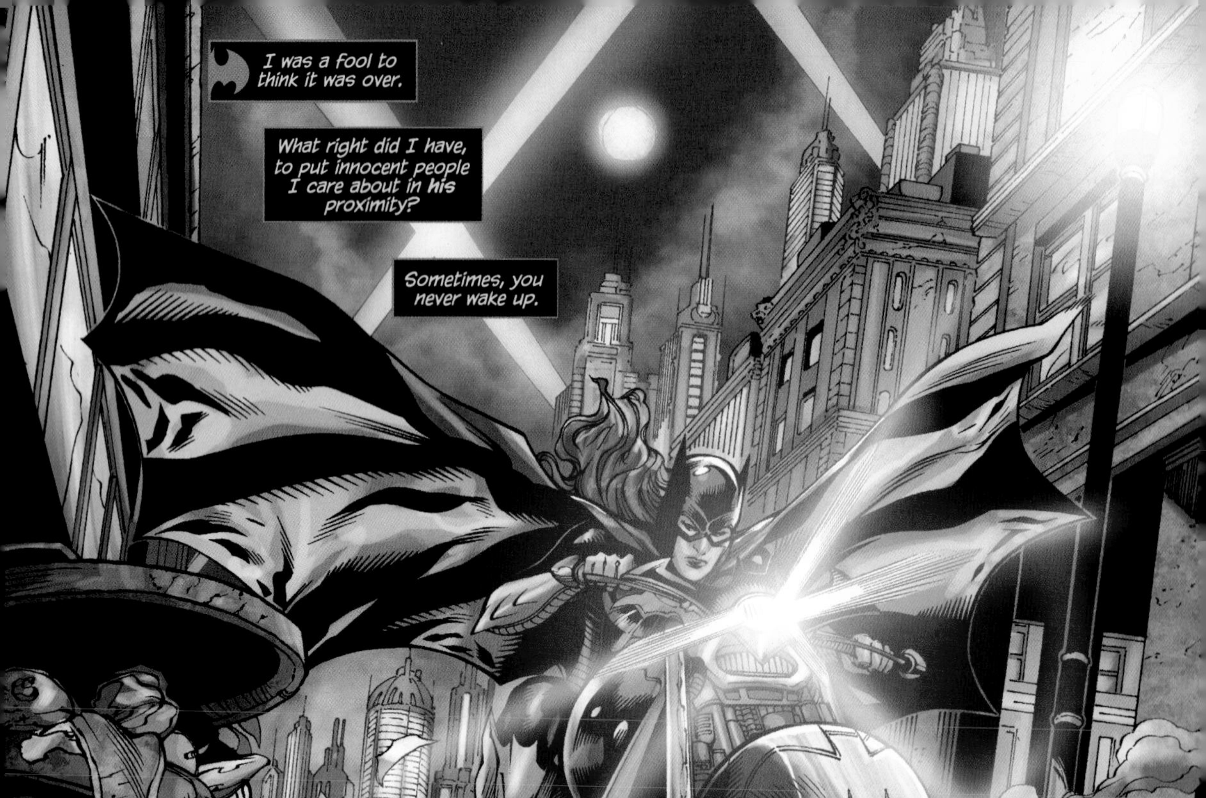
I was a fool to think it was over.
What right did I have, to put innocent people I care about in **his** proximity?
Sometimes, you never wake up.

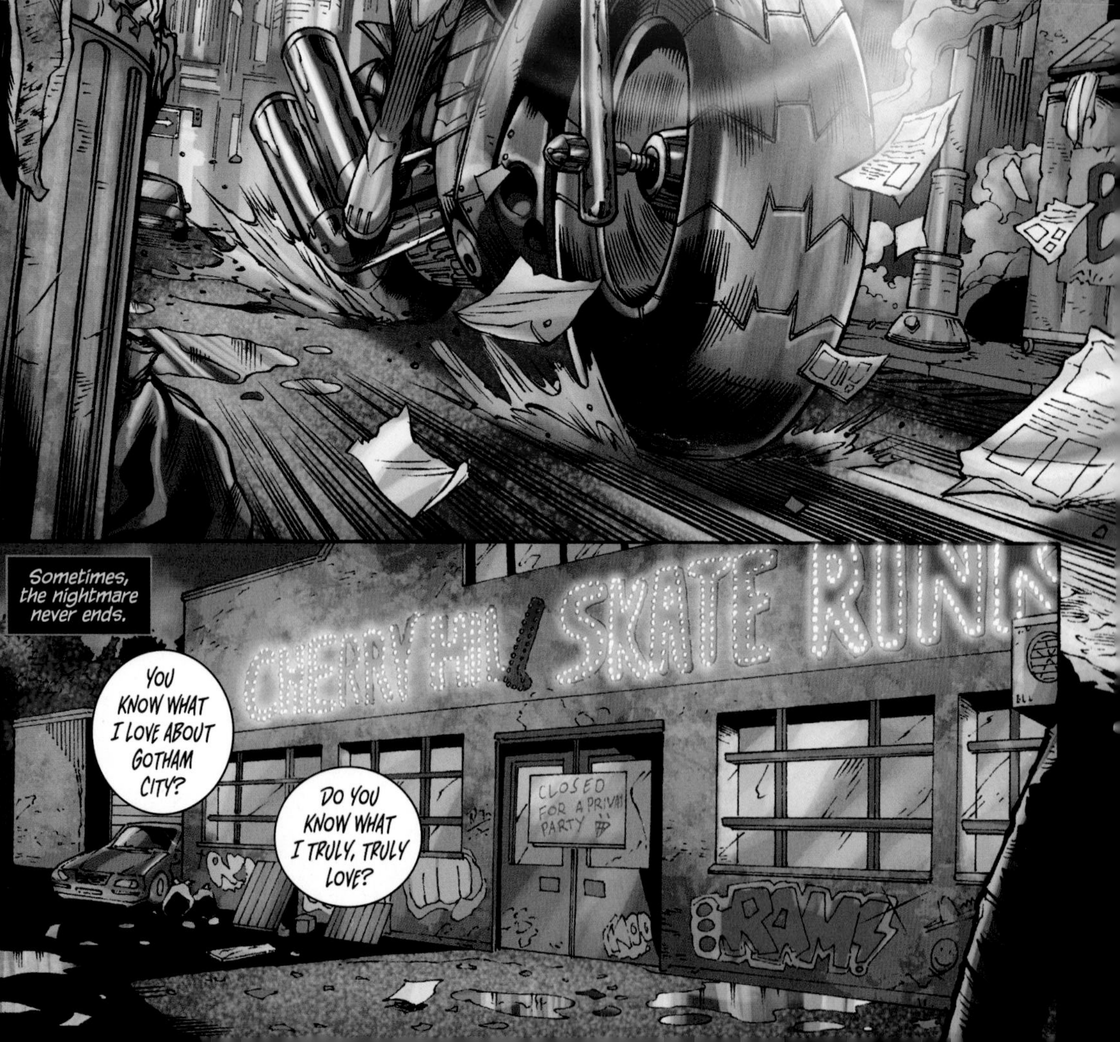
Sometimes, the nightmare never ends.
SKATE RINK
YOU KNOW WHAT I LOVE ABOUT GOTHAM CITY?
DO YOU KNOW WHAT I TRULY, TRULY LOVE?
CLOSED FOR A PRIVA PARTY
RAM!

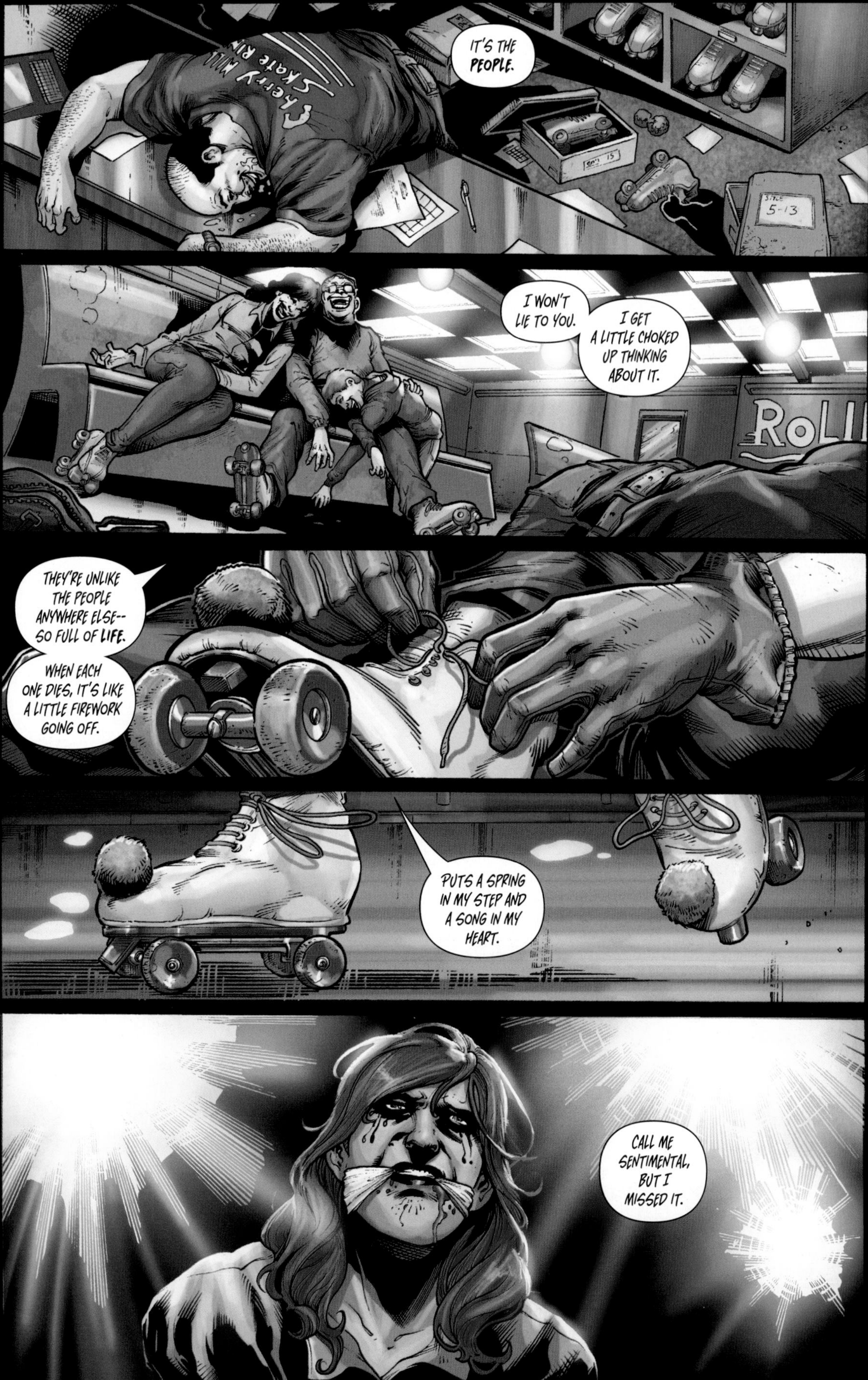
IT'S THE PEOPLE.
CHERRY HILL SKATE RINK
SIZE 15
SIZE 5-13
I WON'T LIE TO YOU.
I GET A LITTLE CHOKED UP THINKING ABOUT IT.
ROLL
THEY'RE UNLIKE THE PEOPLE ANYWHERE ELSE-- SO FULL OF LIFE.
WHEN EACH ONE DIES, IT'S LIKE A LITTLE FIREWORK GOING OFF.
PUTS A SPRING IN MY STEP AND A SONG IN MY HEART.
CALL ME SENTIMENTAL, BUT I MISSED IT.

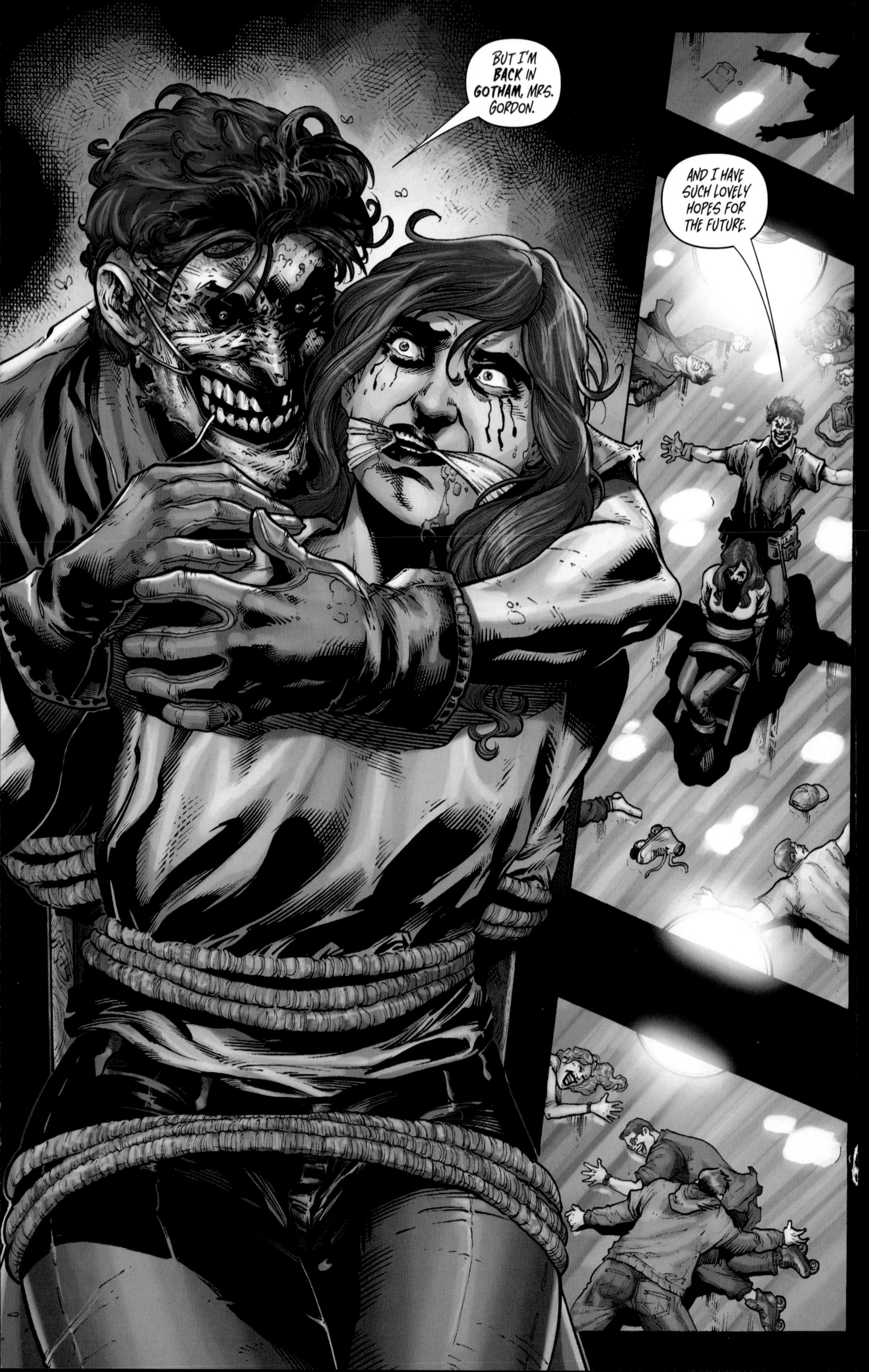
BUT I'M BACK IN GOTHAM, MRS. GORDON.
AND I HAVE SUCH LOVELY HOPES FOR THE FUTURE.

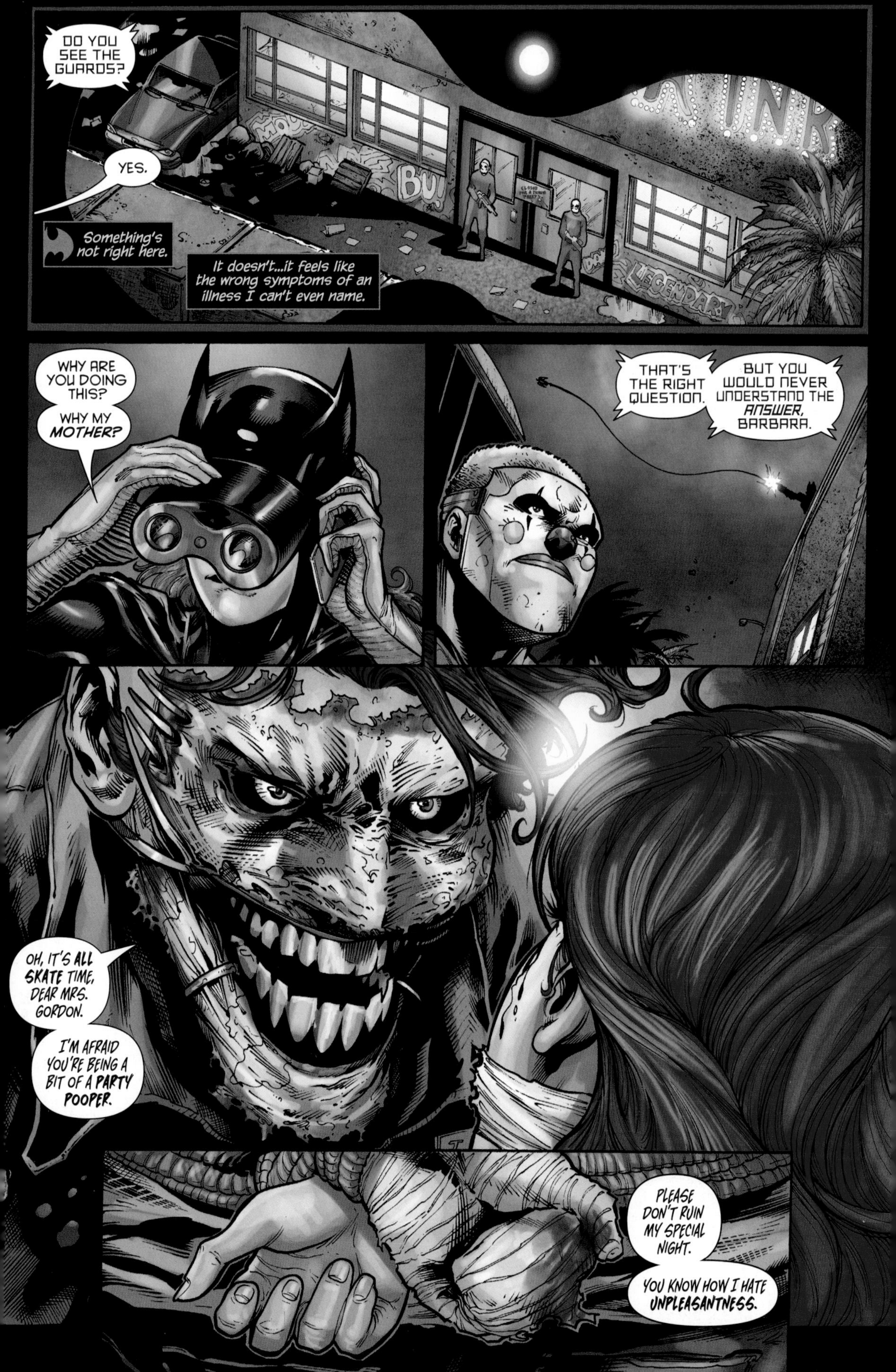

DO YOU SEE THE GUARDS?
YES.
Something's not right here.
It doesn't...it feels like the wrong symptoms of an illness I can't even name.
WHY ARE YOU DOING THIS?
WHY MY MOTHER?
THAT'S THE RIGHT QUESTION.
BUT YOU WOULD NEVER UNDERSTAND THE ANSWER, BARBARA.
OH, IT'S ALL SKATE TIME, DEAR MRS. GORDON.
I'M AFRAID YOU'RE BEING A BIT OF A PARTY POOPER.
PLEASE DON'T RUIN MY SPECIAL NIGHT.
YOU KNOW HOW I HATE UNPLEASANTNESS.

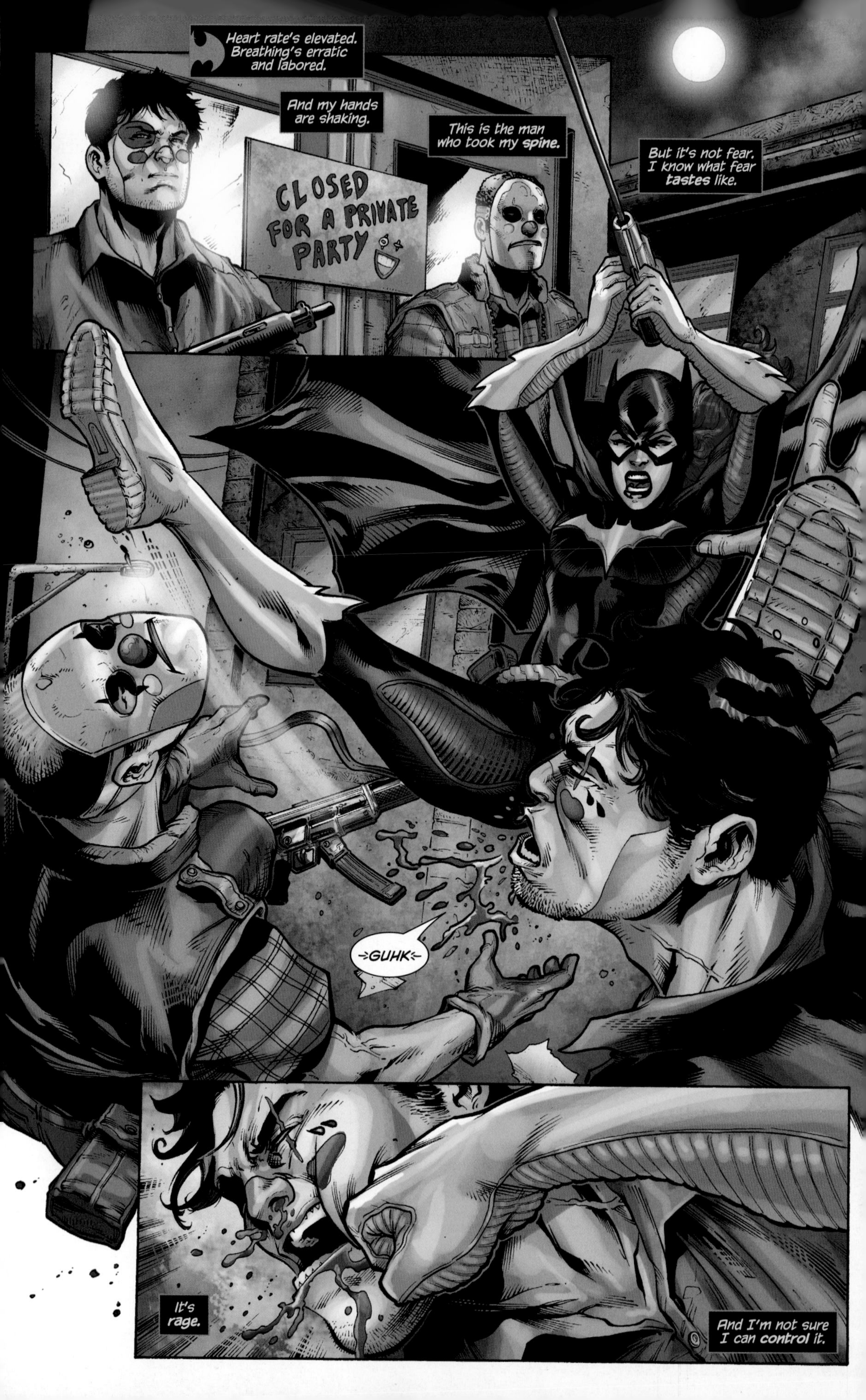

Heart rate's elevated. Breathing's erratic and labored.
And my hands are shaking.
This is the man who took my spine.
But it's not fear. I know what fear tastes like.
CLOSED FOR A PRIVATE PARTY
GUHK
It's rage.
And I'm not sure I can control it.

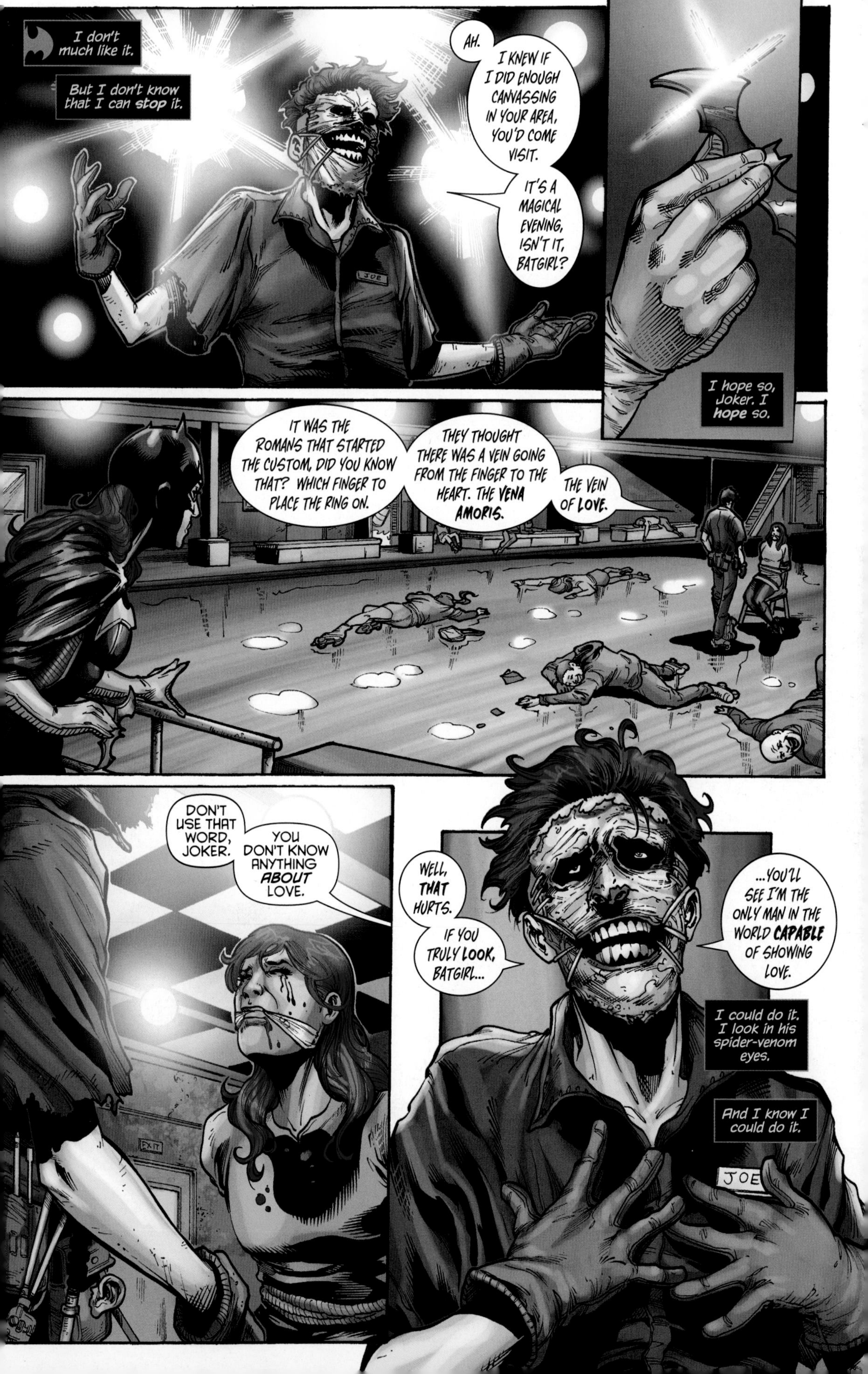

I don't much like it.
But I don't know that I can stop it.
AH.
I KNEW IF I DID ENOUGH CANVASSING IN YOUR AREA, YOU'D COME VISIT.
IT'S A MAGICAL EVENING, ISN'T IT, BATGIRL?
JOE
I hope so, Joker. I hope so.
IT WAS THE ROMANS THAT STARTED THE CUSTOM, DID YOU KNOW THAT? WHICH FINGER TO PLACE THE RING ON.
THEY THOUGHT THERE WAS A VEIN GOING FROM THE FINGER TO THE HEART. THE VENA AMORIS.
THE VEIN OF LOVE.
DON'T USE THAT WORD, JOKER.
YOU DON'T KNOW ANYTHING ABOUT LOVE.
WELL, THAT HURTS.
IF YOU TRULY LOOK, BATGIRL...
...YOU'LL SEE I'M THE ONLY MAN IN THE WORLD CAPABLE OF SHOWING LOVE.
I could do it. I look in his spider-venom eyes.
And I know I could do it.
EXIT
JOE

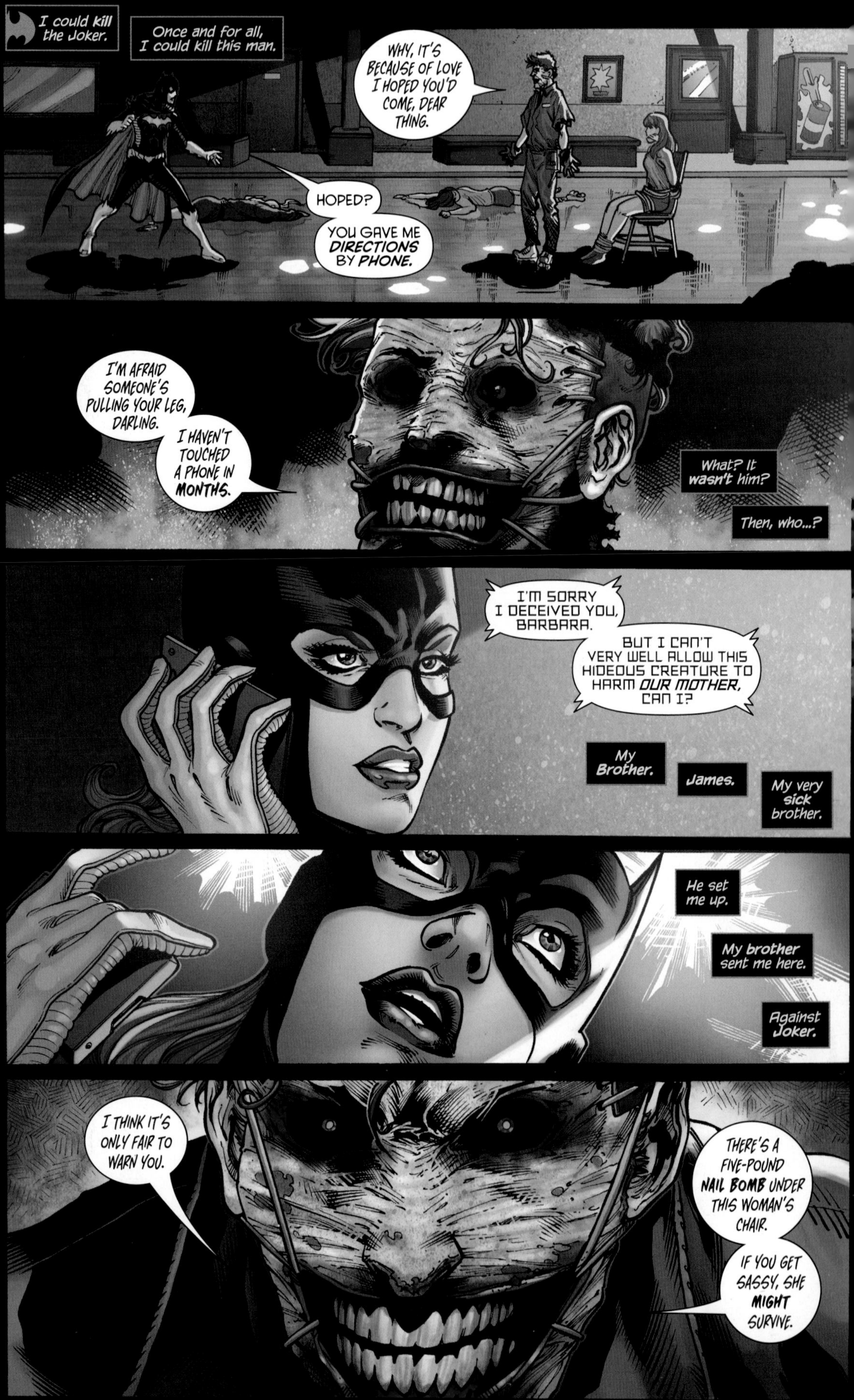
I could **kill** the Joker.
Once and for all, I could kill this man.
WHY, IT'S BECAUSE OF LOVE I HOPED YOU'D COME, DEAR THING.
HOPED?
YOU GAVE ME **DIRECTIONS** BY **PHONE.**
I'M AFRAID SOMEONE'S PULLING YOUR LEG, DARLING.
I HAVEN'T TOUCHED A PHONE IN **MONTHS.**
What? It wasn't him?
Then, who...?
I'M SORRY I DECEIVED YOU, BARBARA.
BUT I CAN'T VERY WELL ALLOW THIS HIDEOUS CREATURE TO HARM ***OUR MOTHER,*** CAN I?
My Brother.
James.
My very **sick** brother.
He set me up.
My brother sent me here.
Against Joker.
I THINK IT'S ONLY FAIR TO WARN YOU.
THERE'S A FIVE-POUND **NAIL BOMB** UNDER THIS WOMAN'S CHAIR.
IF YOU GET SASSY, SHE **MIGHT** SURVIVE.

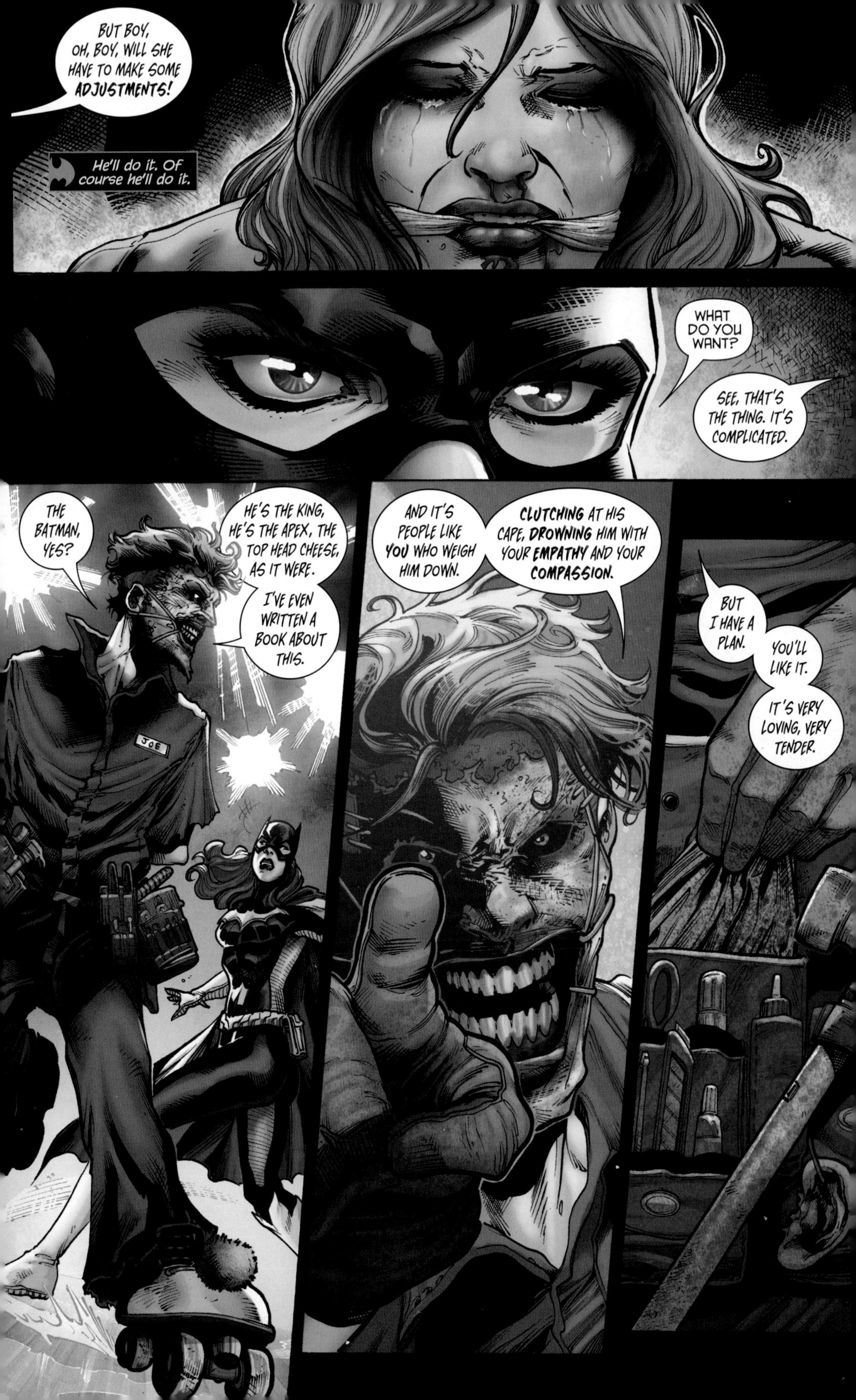
BUT BOY, OH, BOY, WILL SHE HAVE TO MAKE SOME ADJUSTMENTS!
He'll do it. Of course he'll do it.
WHAT DO YOU WANT?
SEE, THAT'S THE THING. IT'S COMPLICATED.
THE BATMAN, YES?
HE'S THE KING, HE'S THE APEX, THE TOP HEAD CHEESE, AS IT WERE.
I'VE EVEN WRITTEN A BOOK ABOUT THIS.
JOE
AND IT'S PEOPLE LIKE YOU WHO WEIGH HIM DOWN.
CLUTCHING AT HIS CAPE, DROWNING HIM WITH YOUR EMPATHY AND YOUR COMPASSION.
BUT I HAVE A PLAN.
YOU'LL LIKE IT.
IT'S VERY LOVING, VERY TENDER.

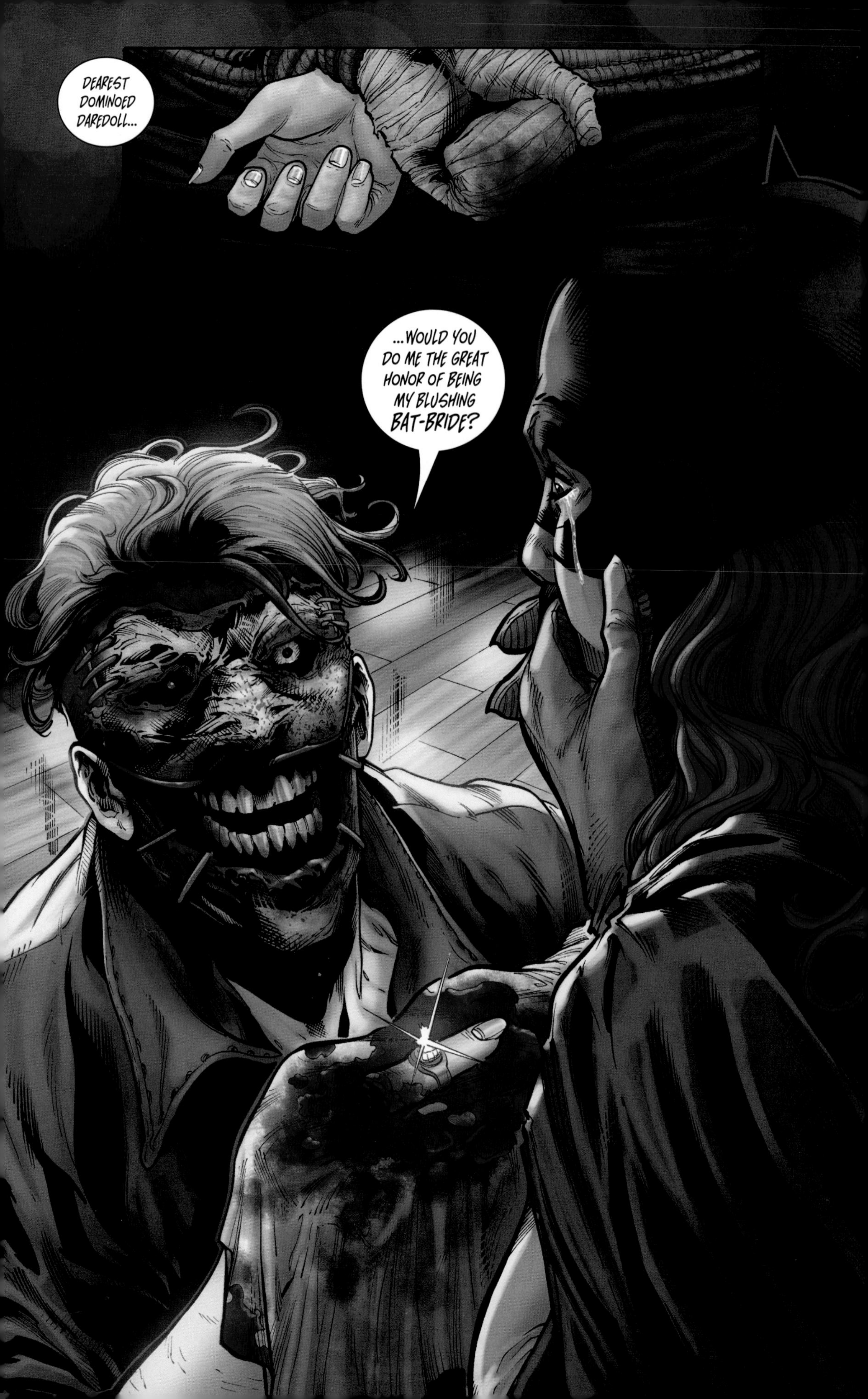
DEAREST DOMINOED DAREDOLL...
...WOULD YOU DO ME THE GREAT HONOR OF BEING MY BLUSHING BAT-BRIDE?

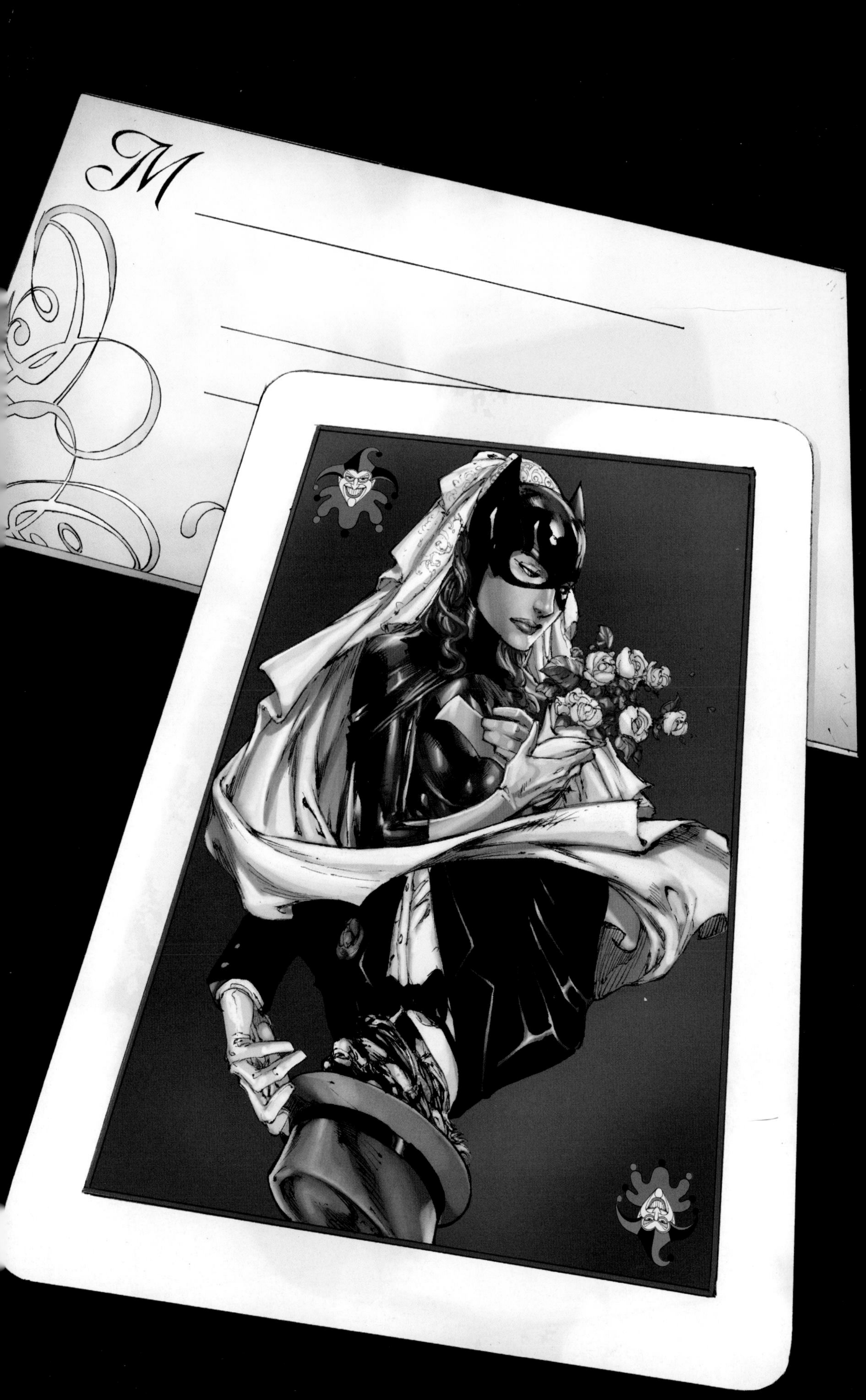
M

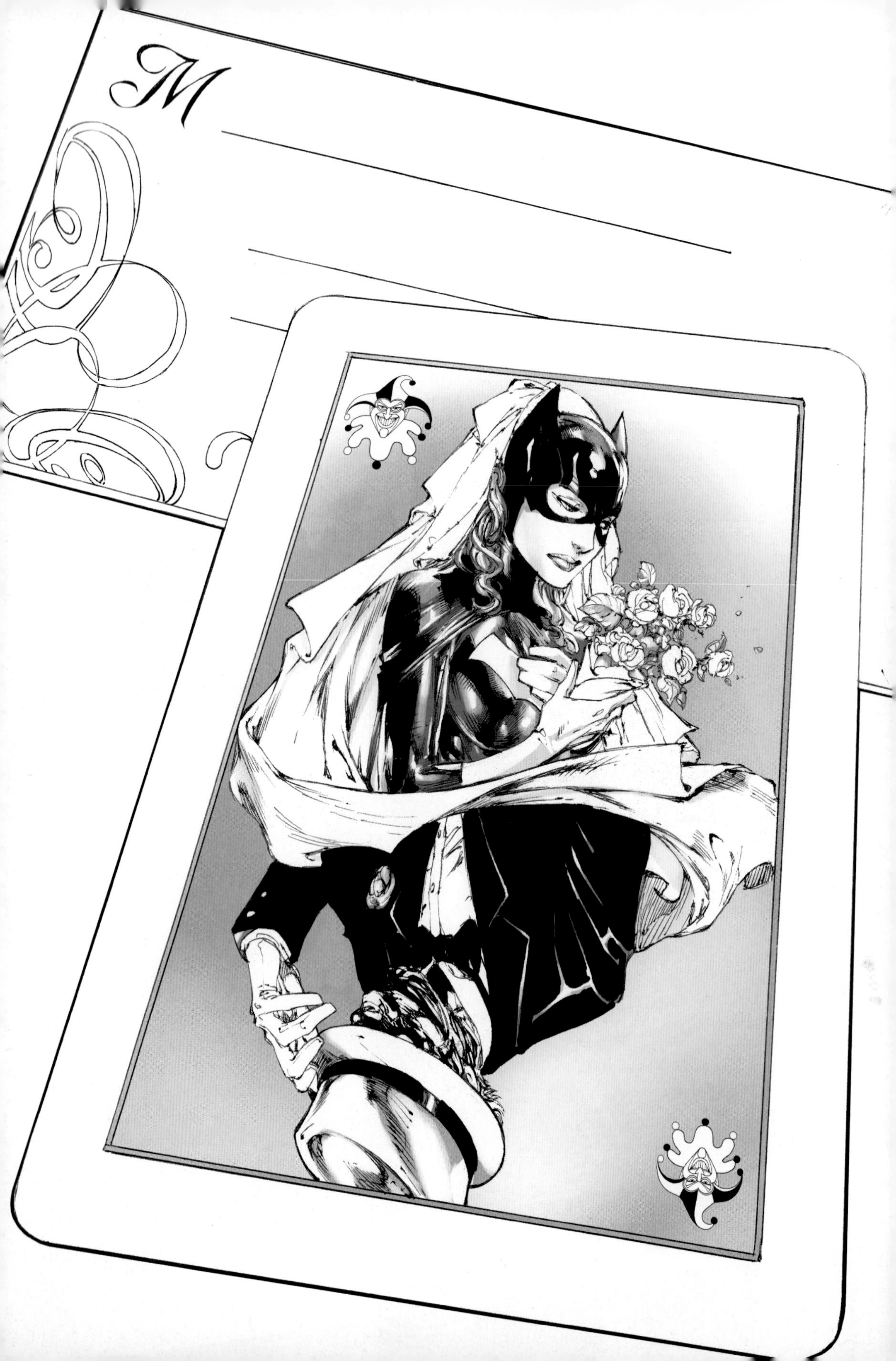
M

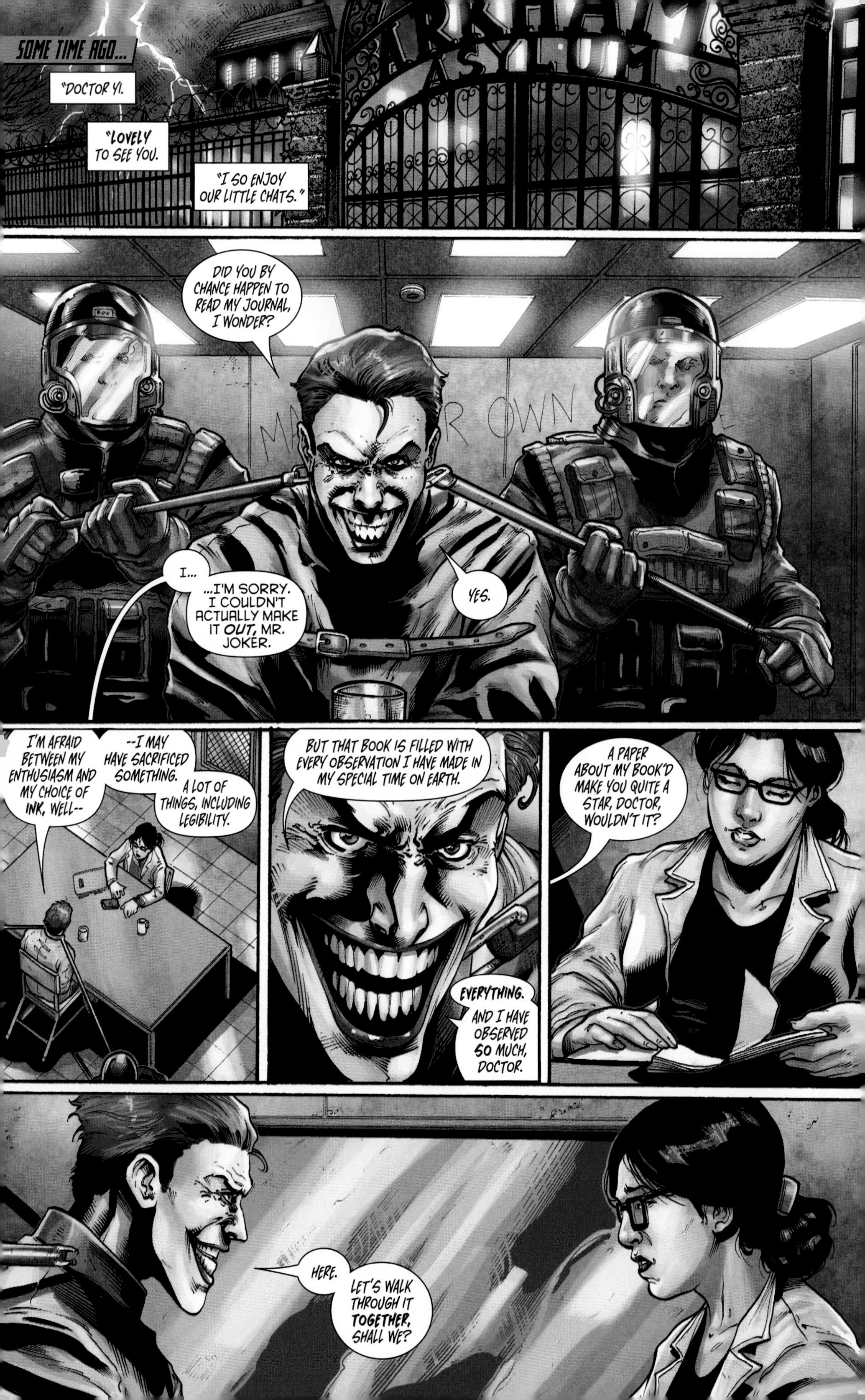
SOME TIME AGO...
"DOCTOR YI.
"LOVELY TO SEE YOU.
"I SO ENJOY OUR LITTLE CHATS."
ARKHAM ASYLUM
DID YOU BY CHANCE HAPPEN TO READ MY JOURNAL, I WONDER?
I...
...I'M SORRY. I COULDN'T ACTUALLY MAKE IT OUT, MR. JOKER.
YES.
I'M AFRAID BETWEEN MY ENTHUSIASM AND MY CHOICE OF INK, WELL--
--I MAY HAVE SACRIFICED SOMETHING.
A LOT OF THINGS, INCLUDING LEGIBILITY.
BUT THAT BOOK IS FILLED WITH EVERY OBSERVATION I HAVE MADE IN MY SPECIAL TIME ON EARTH.
EVERYTHING.
AND I HAVE OBSERVED SO MUCH, DOCTOR.
A PAPER ABOUT MY BOOK'D MAKE YOU QUITE A STAR, DOCTOR, WOULDN'T IT?
HERE.
LET'S WALK THROUGH IT TOGETHER, SHALL WE?

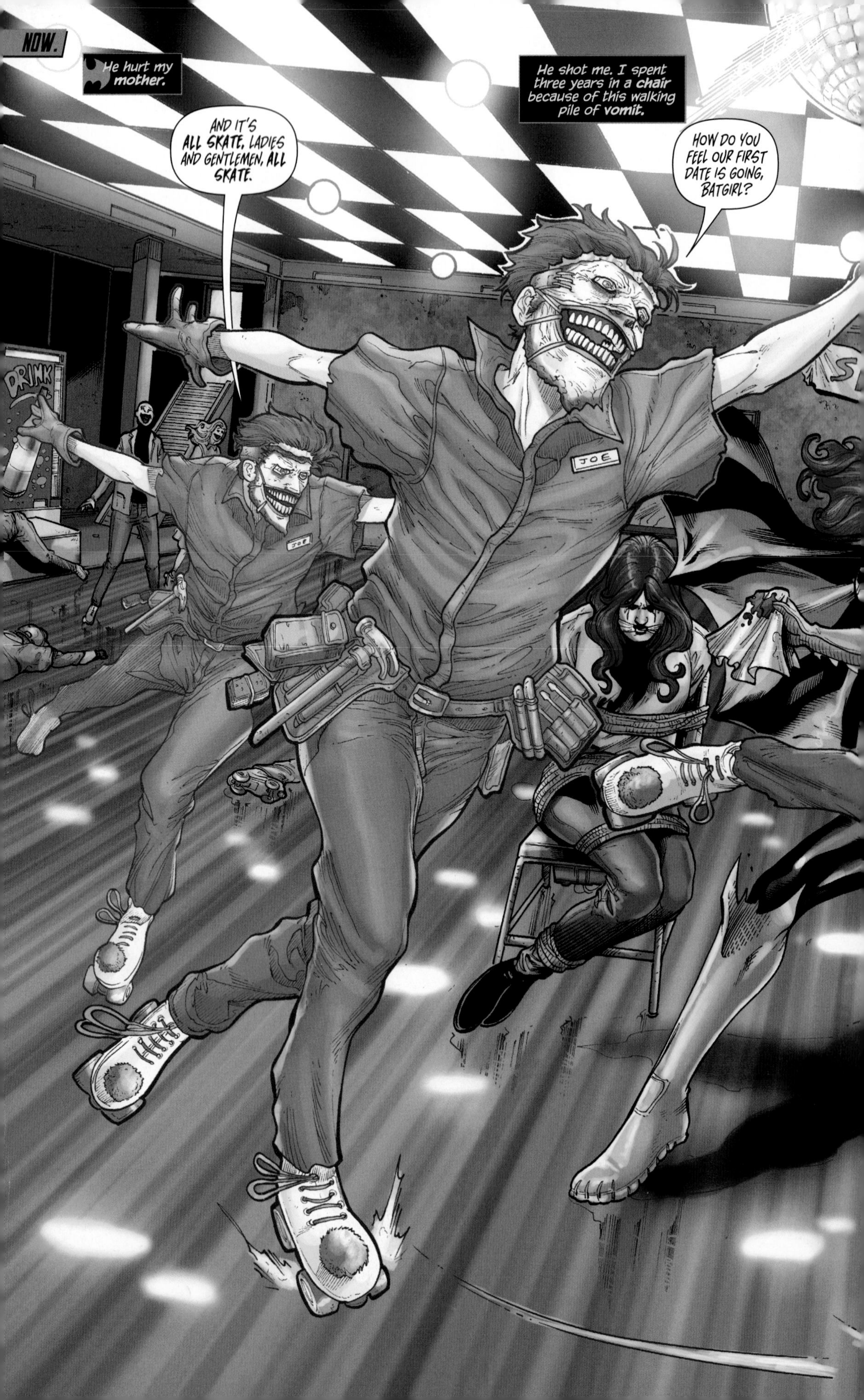
NOW.
He hurt my mother.
AND IT'S ALL SKATE, LADIES AND GENTLEMEN, ALL SKATE.
He shot me. I spent three years in a chair because of this walking pile of vomit.
HOW DO YOU FEEL OUR FIRST DATE IS GOING, BATGIRL?
DRINK
JOE

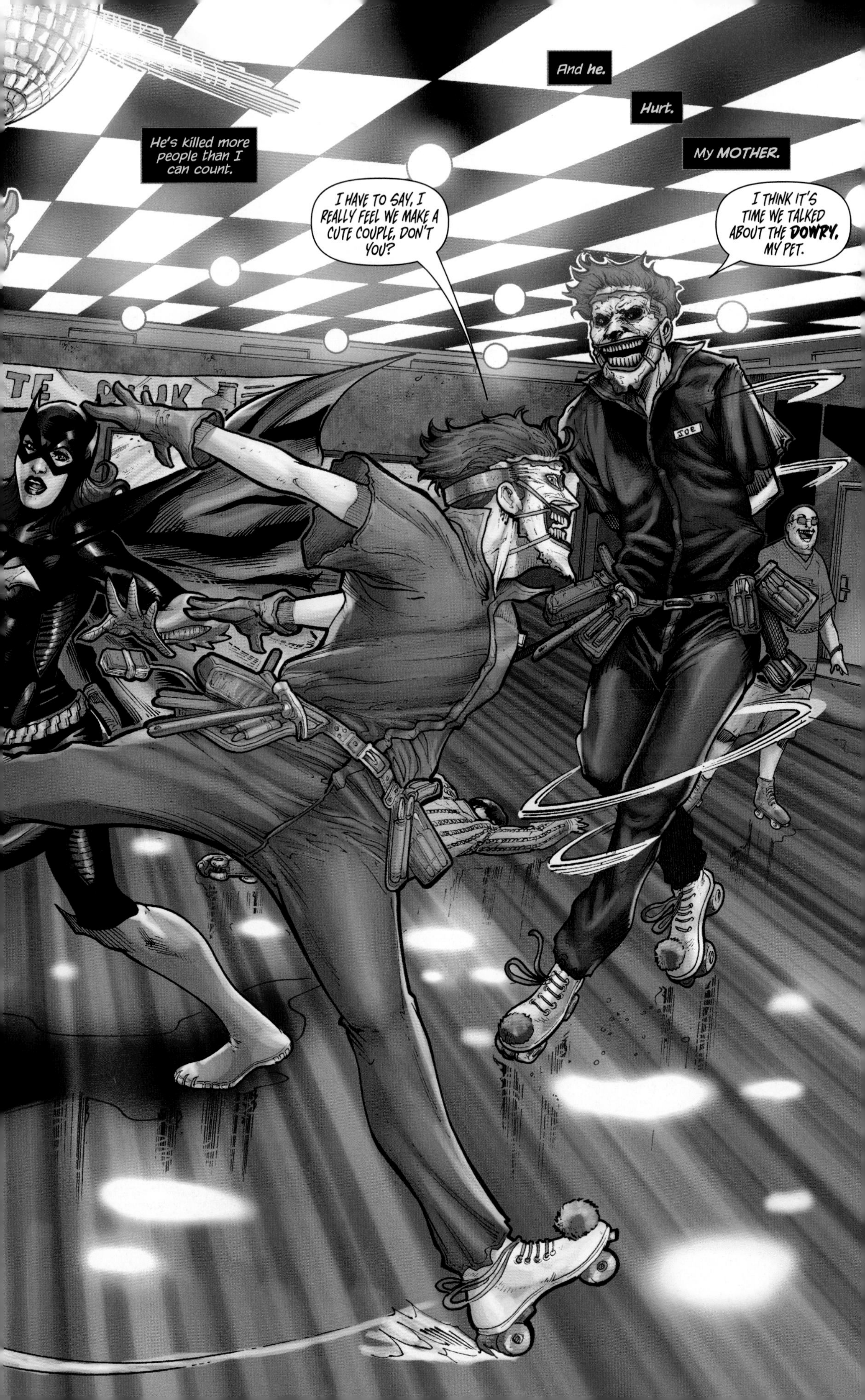
He's killed more people than I can count.
And he.
Hurt.
My MOTHER.
I HAVE TO SAY, I REALLY FEEL WE MAKE A CUTE COUPLE, DON'T YOU?
I THINK IT'S TIME WE TALKED ABOUT THE DOWRY, MY PET.
JOE

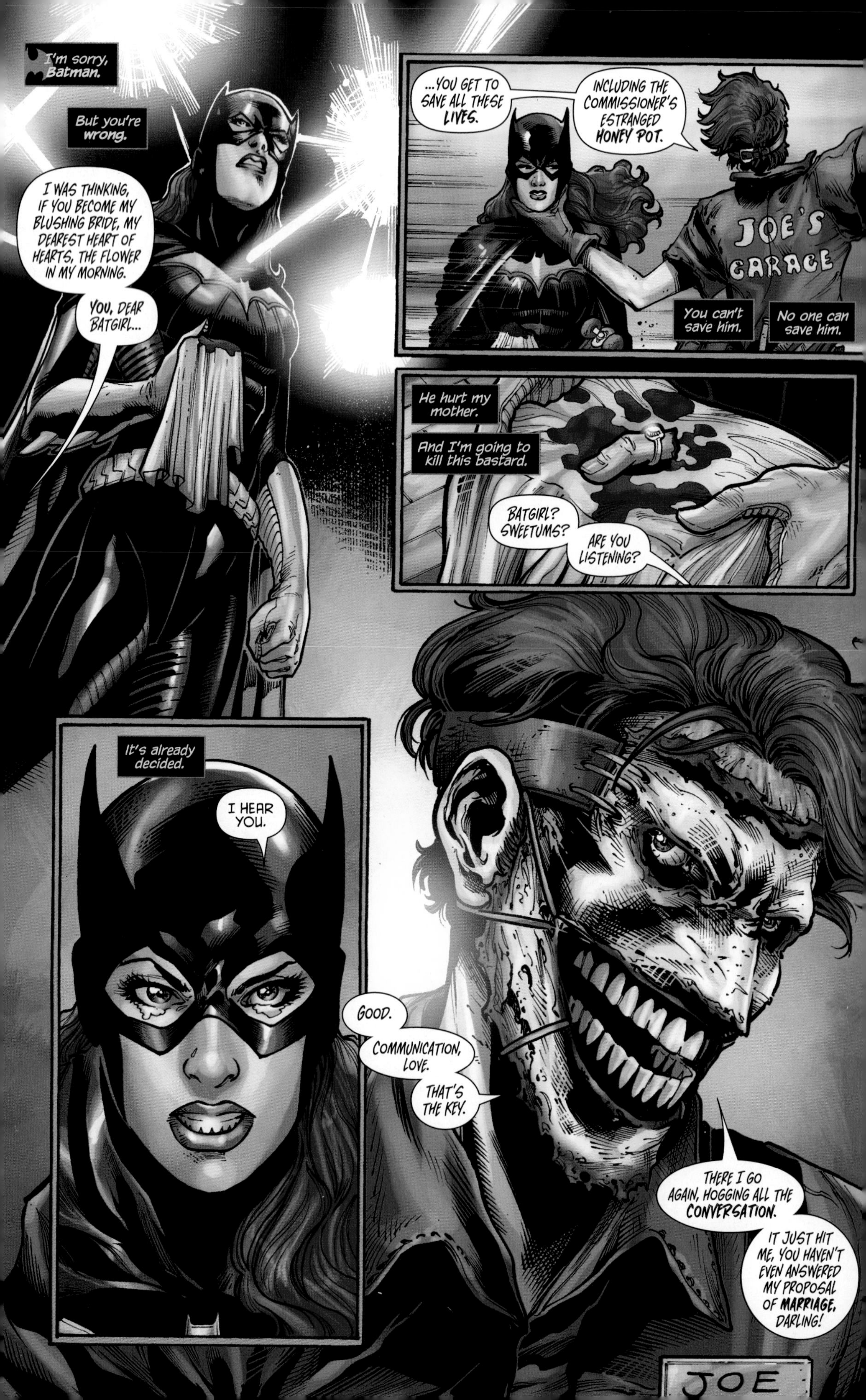
I'm sorry, Batman.
But you're wrong.
I WAS THINKING, IF YOU BECOME MY BLUSHING BRIDE, MY DEAREST HEART OF HEARTS, THE FLOWER IN MY MORNING.
YOU, DEAR BATGIRL...
...YOU GET TO SAVE ALL THESE LIVES.
INCLUDING THE COMMISSIONER'S ESTRANGED HONEY POT.
JOE'S GARAGE
You can't save him.
No one can save him.
He hurt my mother.
And I'm going to kill this bastard.
BATGIRL? SWEETUMS?
ARE YOU LISTENING?
It's already decided.
I HEAR YOU.
GOOD.
COMMUNICATION, LOVE.
THAT'S THE KEY.
THERE I GO AGAIN, HOGGING ALL THE CONVERSATION.
IT JUST HIT ME, YOU HAVEN'T EVEN ANSWERED MY PROPOSAL OF MARRIAGE, DARLING!
JOE

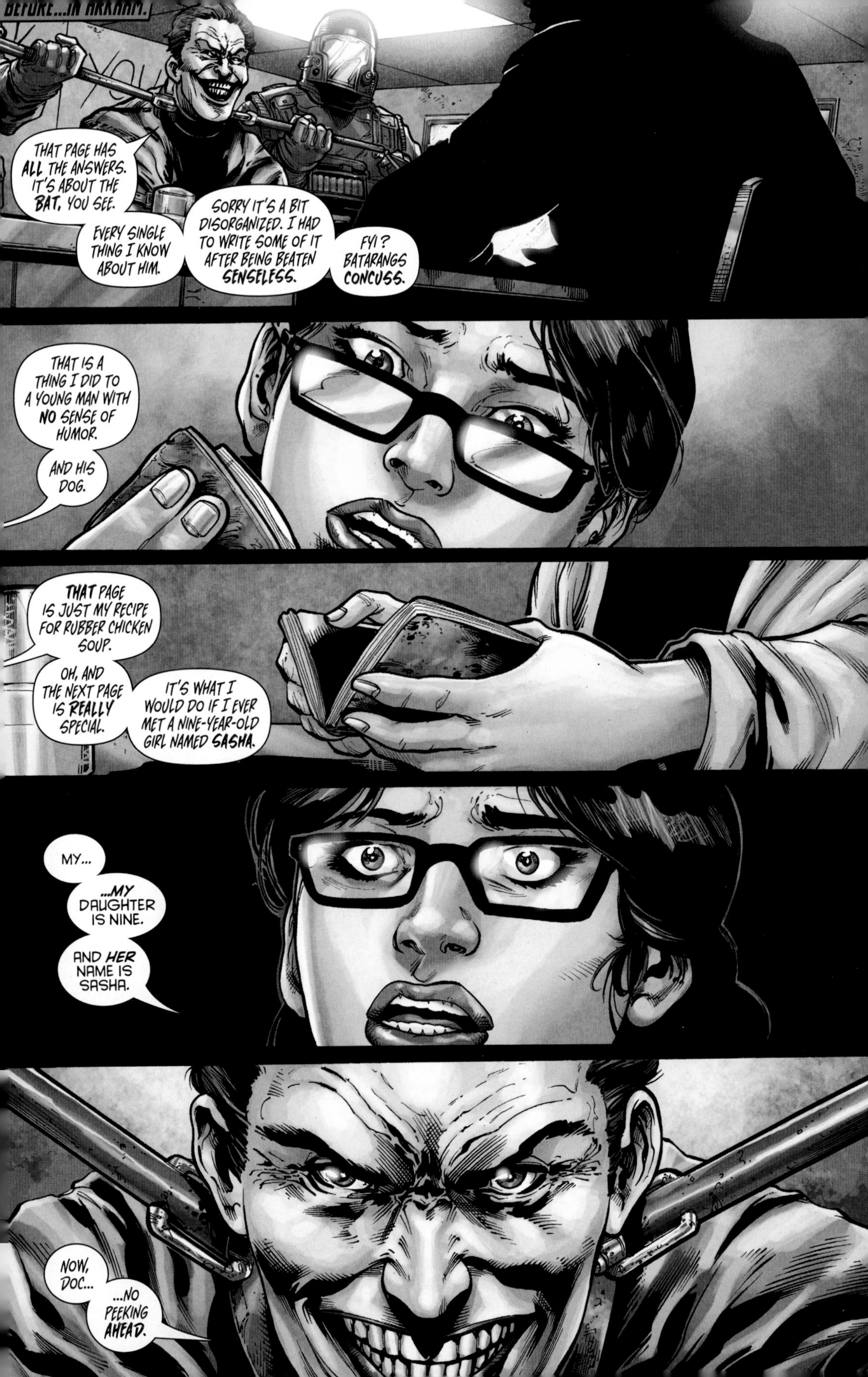
BEFORE...IN ARKHAM.
THAT PAGE HAS ALL THE ANSWERS. IT'S ABOUT THE BAT, YOU SEE.
EVERY SINGLE THING I KNOW ABOUT HIM.
SORRY IT'S A BIT DISORGANIZED. I HAD TO WRITE SOME OF IT AFTER BEING BEATEN SENSELESS.
FYI? BATARANGS CONCUSS.
THAT IS A THING I DID TO A YOUNG MAN WITH NO SENSE OF HUMOR.
AND HIS DOG.
THAT PAGE IS JUST MY RECIPE FOR RUBBER CHICKEN SOUP.
OH, AND THE NEXT PAGE IS REALLY SPECIAL.
IT'S WHAT I WOULD DO IF I EVER MET A NINE-YEAR-OLD GIRL NAMED SASHA.
MY...
...MY DAUGHTER IS NINE.
AND HER NAME IS SASHA.
NOW, DOC...
...NO PEEKING AHEAD.

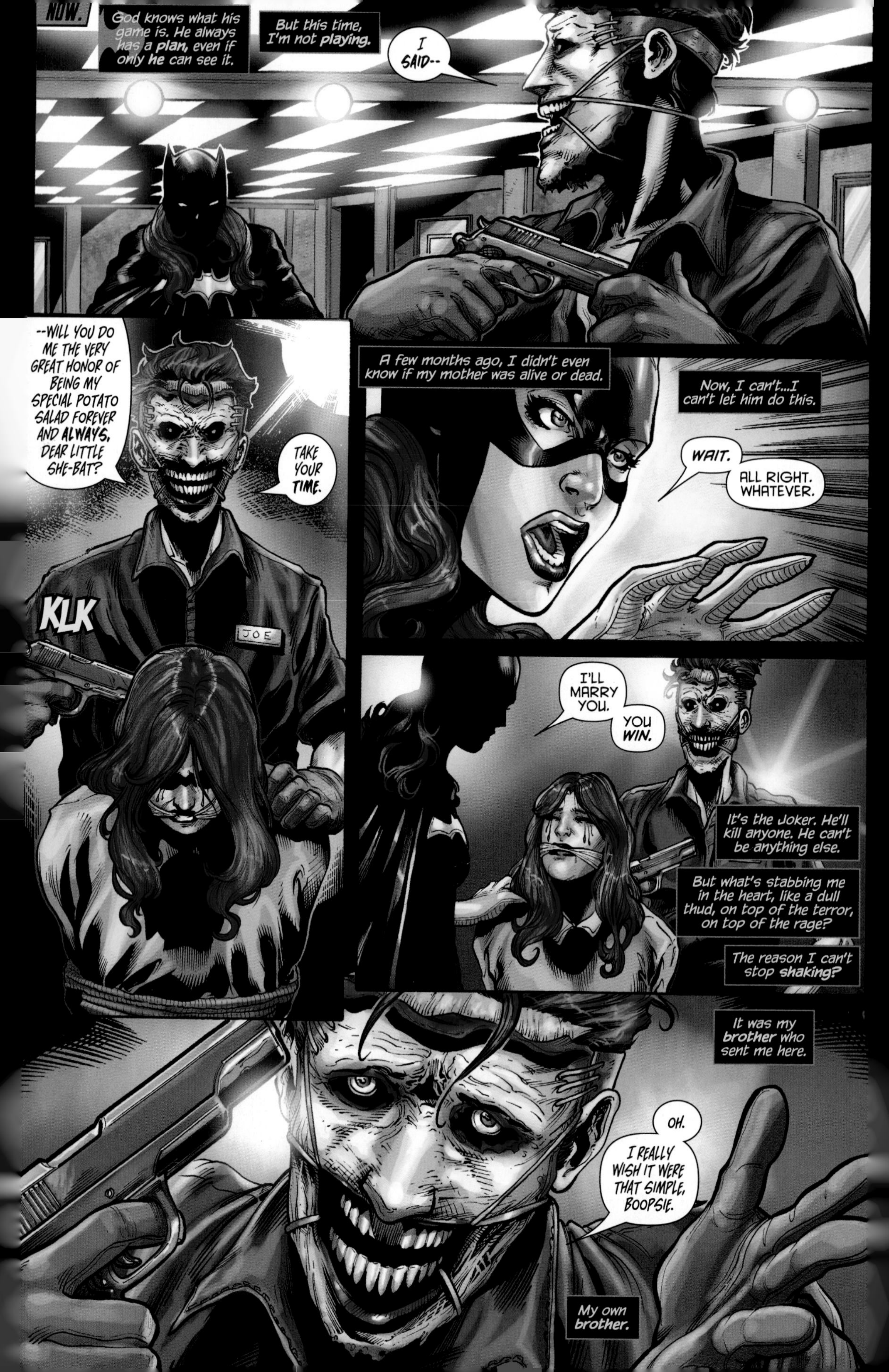
NOW.
God knows what his game is. He always has a plan, even if only he can see it.
But this time, I'm not playing.
I SAID--
--WILL YOU DO ME THE VERY GREAT HONOR OF BEING MY SPECIAL POTATO SALAD FOREVER AND ALWAYS, DEAR LITTLE SHE-BAT?
TAKE YOUR TIME.
KLK
JOE
A few months ago, I didn't even know if my mother was alive or dead.
Now, I can't...I can't let him do this.
WAIT.
ALL RIGHT. WHATEVER.
I'LL MARRY YOU.
YOU WIN.
It's the Joker. He'll kill anyone. He can't be anything else.
But what's stabbing me in the heart, like a dull thud, on top of the terror, on top of the rage?
The reason I can't stop shaking?
It was my brother who sent me here.
OH.
I REALLY WISH IT WERE THAT SIMPLE, BOOPSIE.
My own brother.

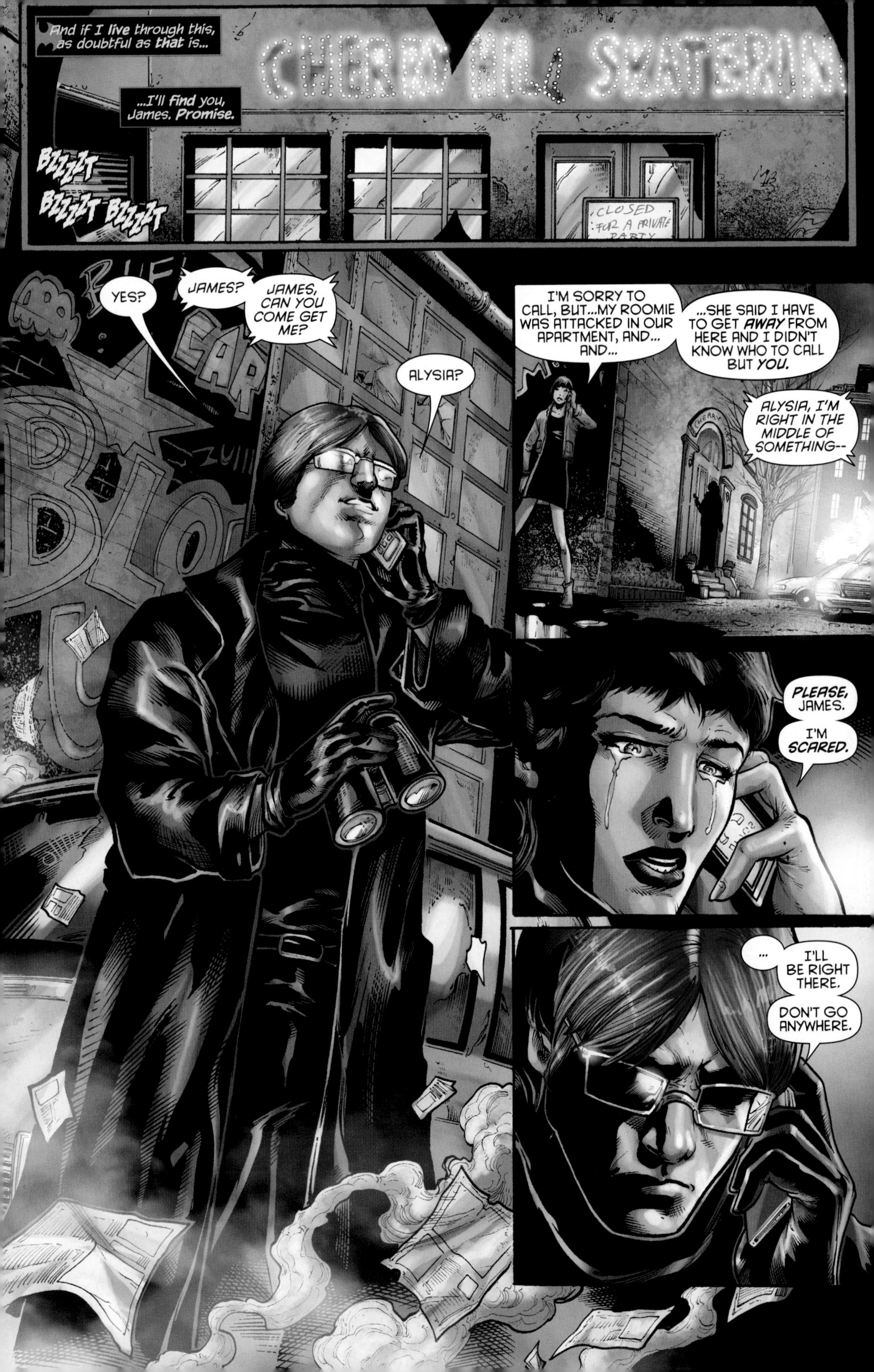
And if I live through this, as doubtful as that is...
...I'll find you, James. Promise.
CHERRY HILL SKATERAMA
BZZZZZT
BZZZZZT BZZZZZT
CLOSED FOR A PRIVATE PARTY
YES?
JAMES?
JAMES, CAN YOU COME GET ME?
ALYSIA?
I'M SORRY TO CALL, BUT...MY ROOMIE WAS ATTACKED IN OUR APARTMENT, AND... AND...
...SHE SAID I HAVE TO GET AWAY FROM HERE AND I DIDN'T KNOW WHO TO CALL BUT YOU.
ALYSIA, I'M RIGHT IN THE MIDDLE OF SOMETHING--
PLEASE, JAMES.
I'M SCARED.
...
I'LL BE RIGHT THERE.
DON'T GO ANYWHERE.

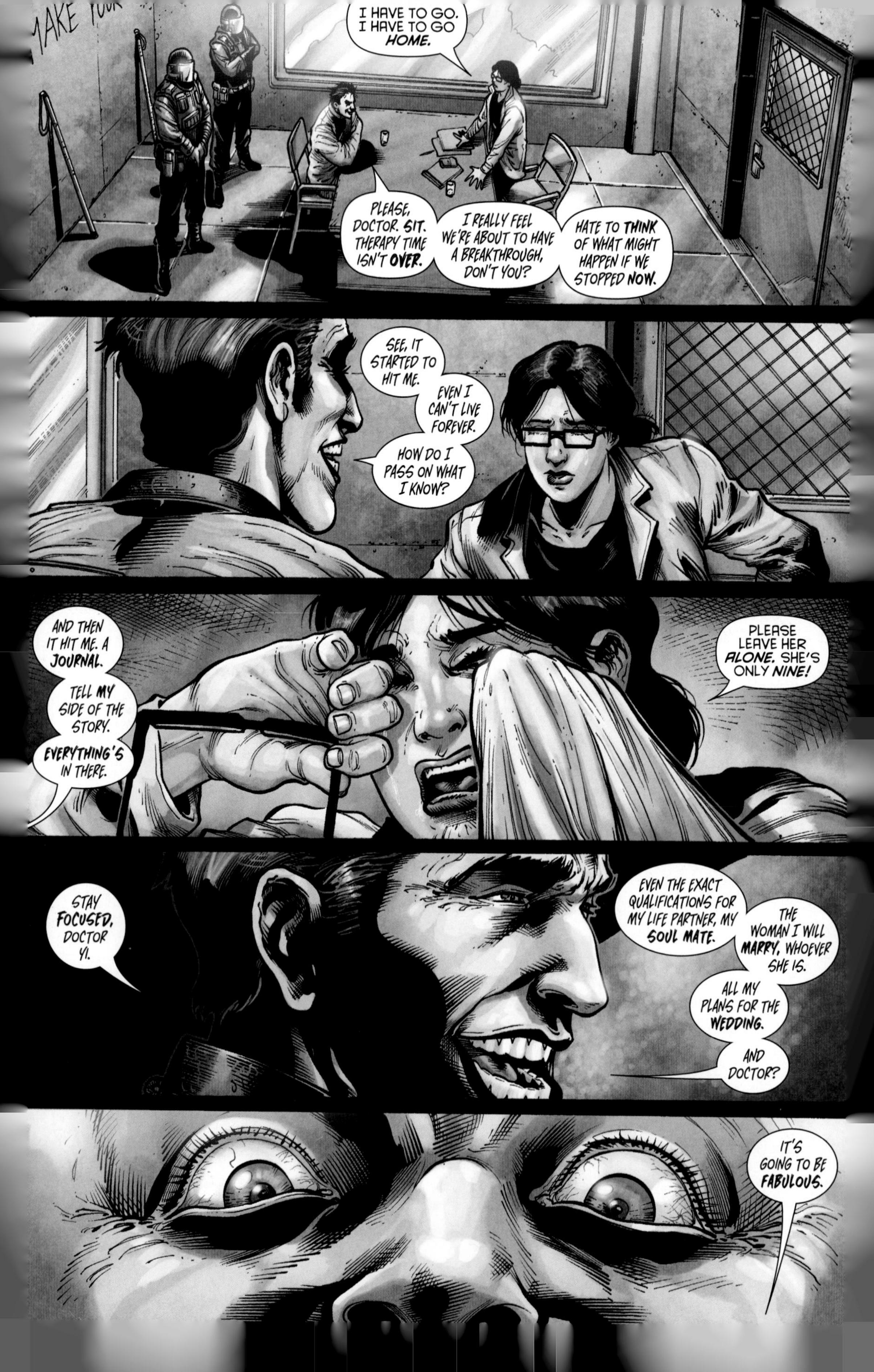

MAKE YOUR
I HAVE TO GO. I HAVE TO GO HOME.
PLEASE, DOCTOR. SIT. THERAPY TIME ISN'T OVER.
I REALLY FEEL WE'RE ABOUT TO HAVE A BREAKTHROUGH, DON'T YOU?
HATE TO THINK OF WHAT MIGHT HAPPEN IF WE STOPPED NOW.
SEE, IT STARTED TO HIT ME.
EVEN I CAN'T LIVE FOREVER.
HOW DO I PASS ON WHAT I KNOW?
AND THEN IT HIT ME. A JOURNAL.
TELL MY SIDE OF THE STORY.
EVERYTHING'S IN THERE.
PLEASE LEAVE HER ALONE. SHE'S ONLY NINE!
STAY FOCUSED, DOCTOR YI.
EVEN THE EXACT QUALIFICATIONS FOR MY LIFE PARTNER, MY SOUL MATE.
THE WOMAN I WILL MARRY, WHOEVER SHE IS.
ALL MY PLANS FOR THE WEDDING.
AND DOCTOR?
IT'S GOING TO BE FABULOUS.

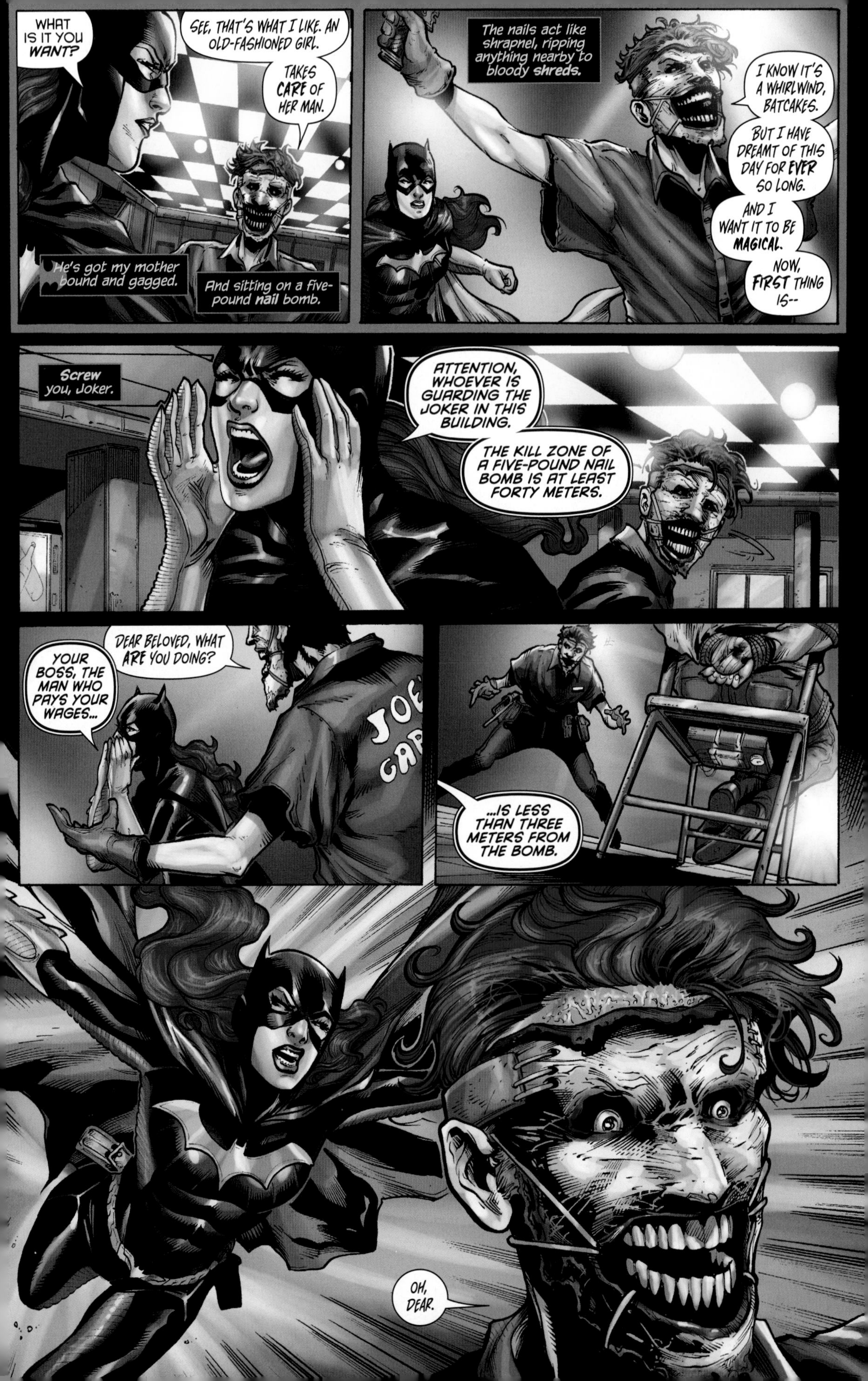
WHAT IS IT YOU WANT?
SEE, THAT'S WHAT I LIKE. AN OLD-FASHIONED GIRL.
TAKES CARE OF HER MAN.
He's got my mother bound and gagged.
And sitting on a five-pound nail bomb.
The nails act like shrapnel, ripping anything nearby to bloody shreds.
I KNOW IT'S A WHIRLWIND, BATCAKES.
BUT I HAVE DREAMT OF THIS DAY FOR EVER SO LONG.
AND I WANT IT TO BE MAGICAL.
NOW, FIRST THING IS--
Screw you, Joker.
ATTENTION, WHOEVER IS GUARDING THE JOKER IN THIS BUILDING.
THE KILL ZONE OF A FIVE-POUND NAIL BOMB IS AT LEAST FORTY METERS.
DEAR BELOVED, WHAT ARE YOU DOING?
YOUR BOSS, THE MAN WHO PAYS YOUR WAGES...
...IS LESS THAN THREE METERS FROM THE BOMB.
OH, DEAR.

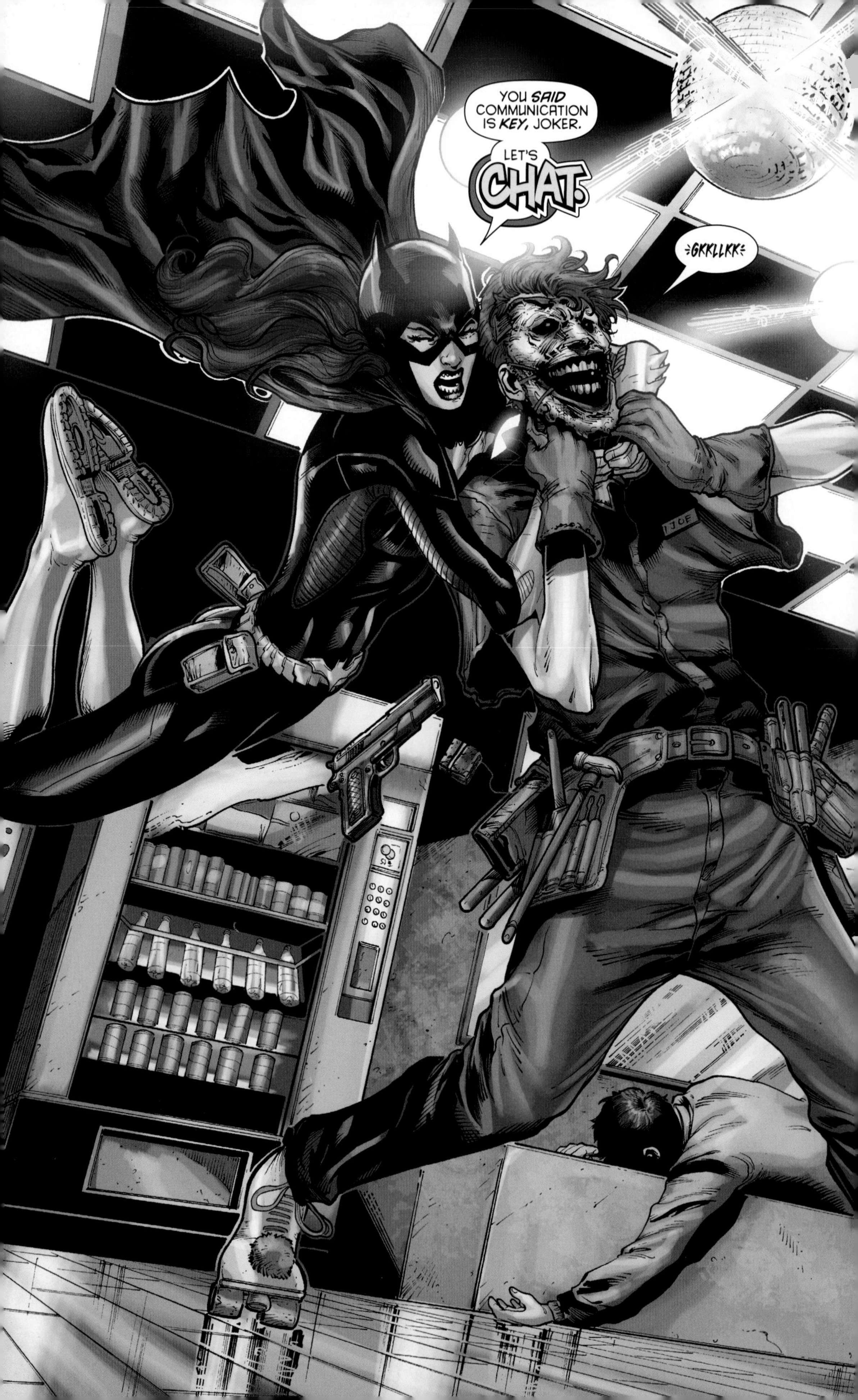
YOU SAID COMMUNICATION IS KEY, JOKER.
LET'S CHAT.
GKKLLKK

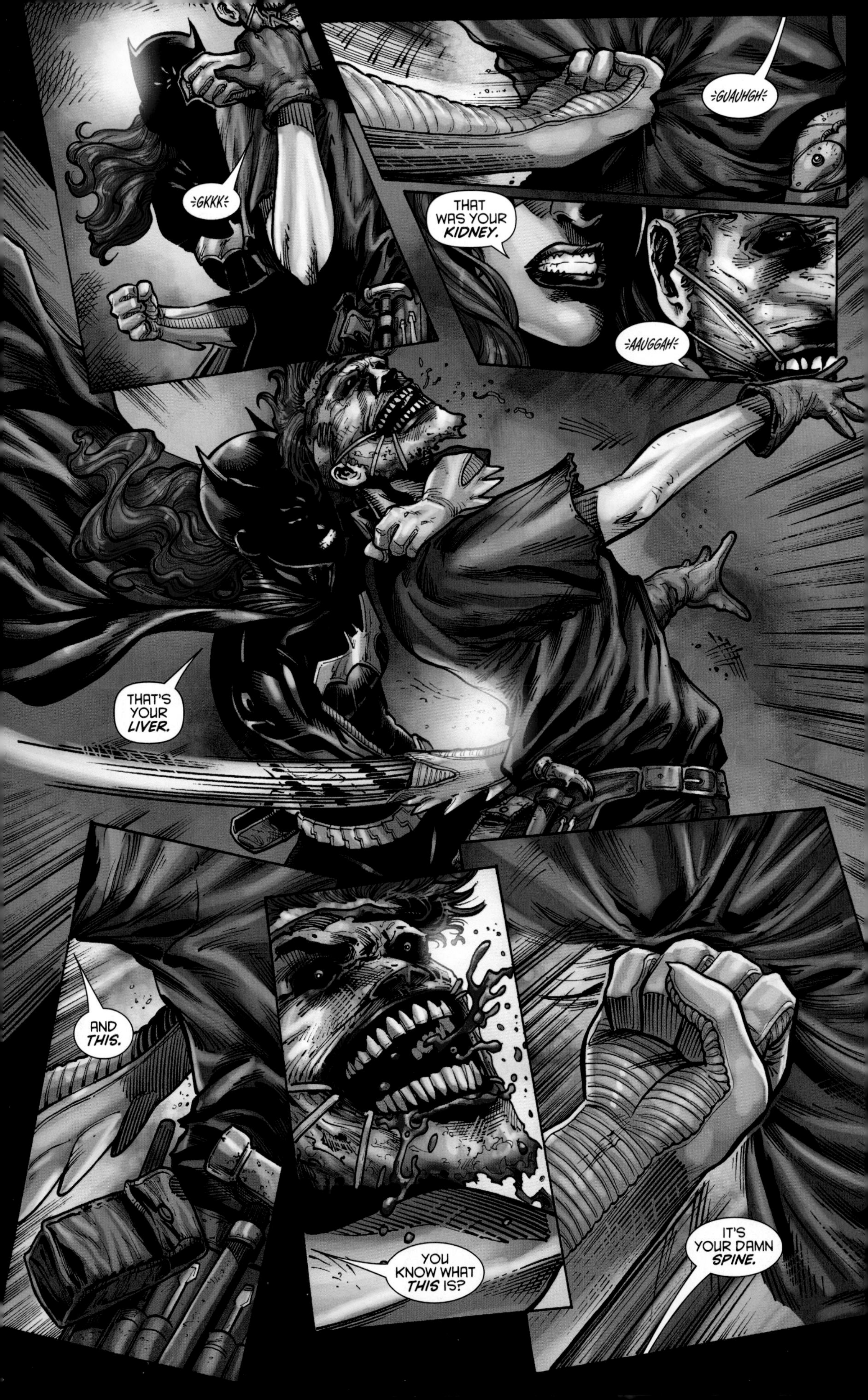
GKKK
GUAUHGH
THAT WAS YOUR KIDNEY.
AAUGGAH
THAT'S YOUR LIVER.
AND THIS.
YOU KNOW WHAT THIS IS?
IT'S YOUR DAMN SPINE.

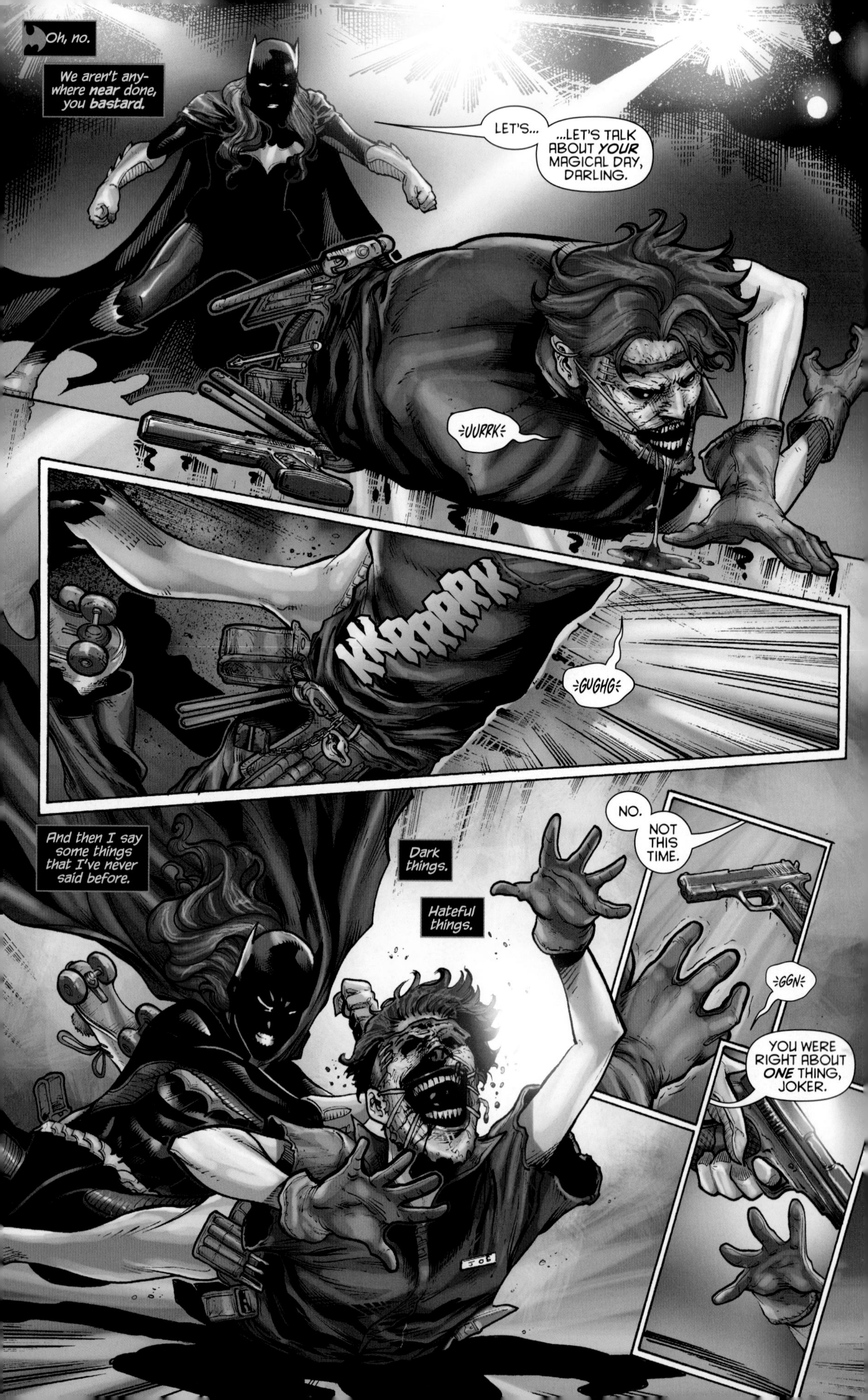
Oh, no.
We aren't any-where near done, you bastard.
LET'S...
...LET'S TALK ABOUT YOUR MAGICAL DAY, DARLING.
UURRK
KKRRRRK
GUGHG
And then I say some things that I've never said before.
Dark things.
Hateful things.
NO.
NOT THIS TIME.
GGN
YOU WERE RIGHT ABOUT ONE THING, JOKER.

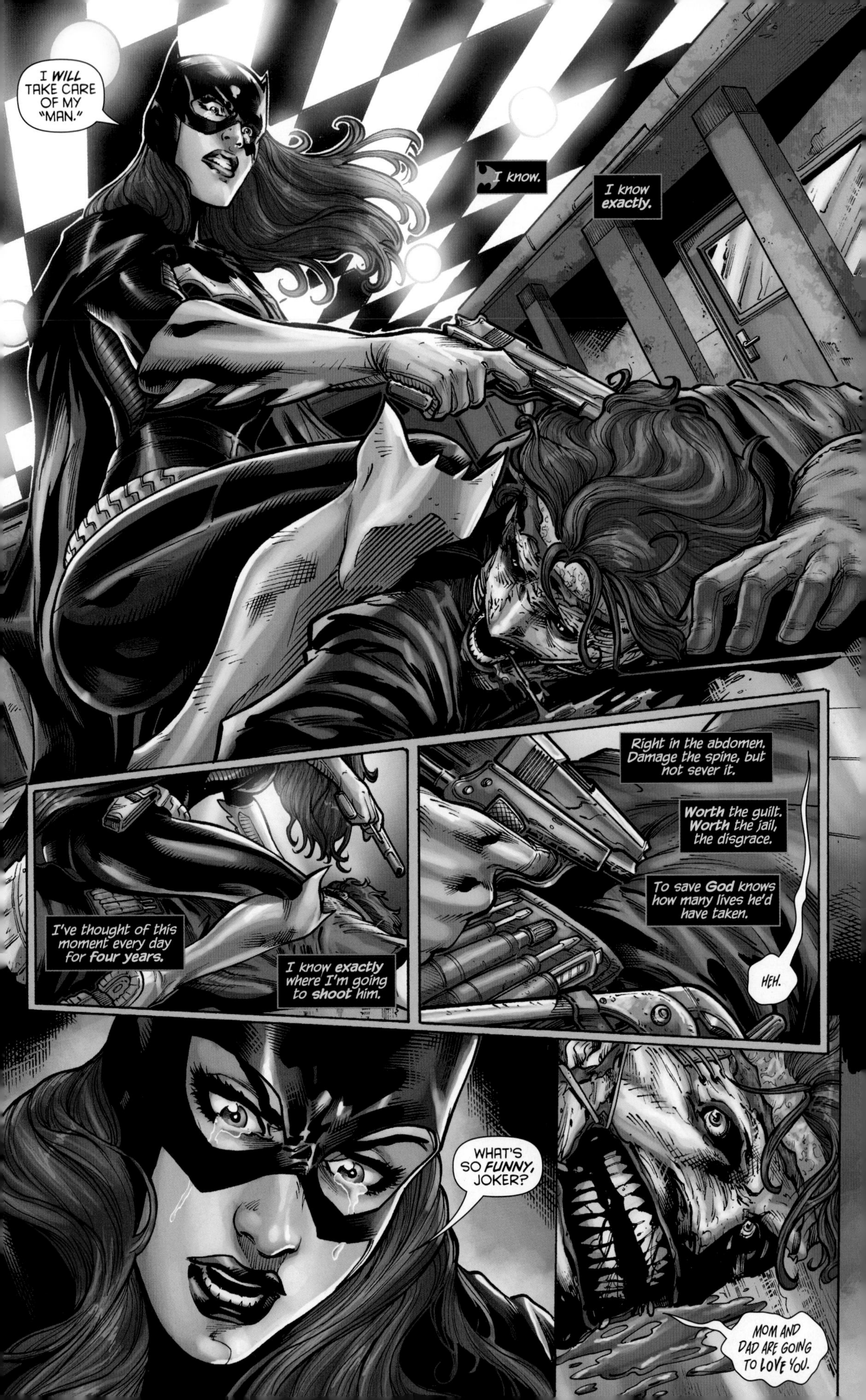

I WILL TAKE CARE OF MY "MAN."
I know.
I know exactly.
I've thought of this moment every day for four years.
I know exactly where I'm going to shoot him.
Right in the abdomen. Damage the spine, but not sever it.
Worth the guilt. Worth the jail, the disgrace.
To save God knows how many lives he'd have taken.
HEH.
WHAT'S SO FUNNY, JOKER?
MOM AND DAD ARE GOING TO LOVE YOU.

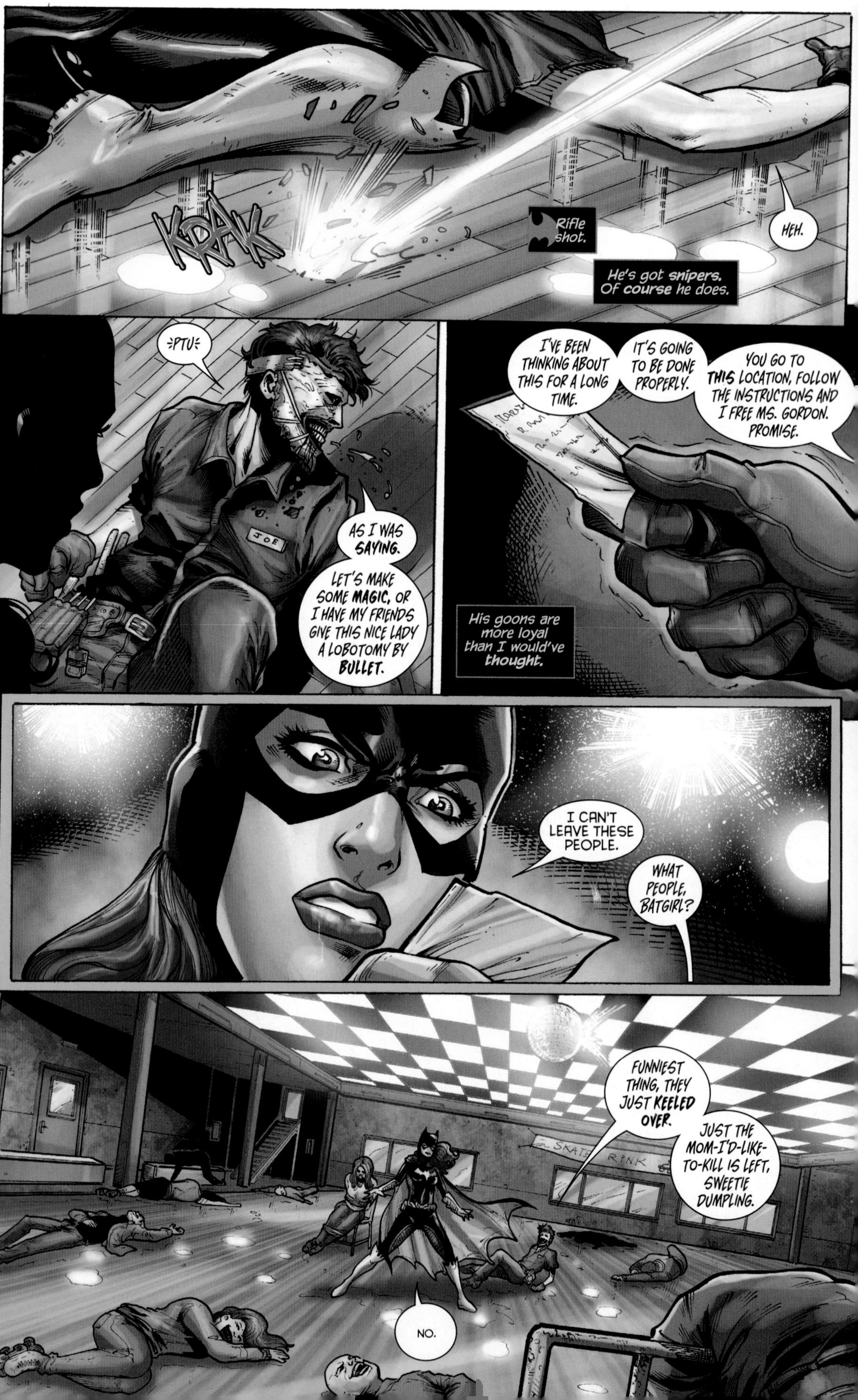
KRAK
Rifle shot.
He's got snipers. Of course he does.
HEH.
PTU
AS I WAS SAYING.
LET'S MAKE SOME MAGIC, OR I HAVE MY FRIENDS GIVE THIS NICE LADY A LOBOTOMY BY BULLET.
I'VE BEEN THINKING ABOUT THIS FOR A LONG TIME.
IT'S GOING TO BE DONE PROPERLY.
YOU GO TO THIS LOCATION, FOLLOW THE INSTRUCTIONS AND I FREE MS. GORDON. PROMISE.
His goons are more loyal than I would've thought.
I CAN'T LEAVE THESE PEOPLE.
WHAT PEOPLE, BATGIRL?
FUNNIEST THING, THEY JUST KEELED OVER.
JUST THE MOM-I'D-LIKE-TO-KILL IS LEFT, SWEETIE DUMPLING.
NO.

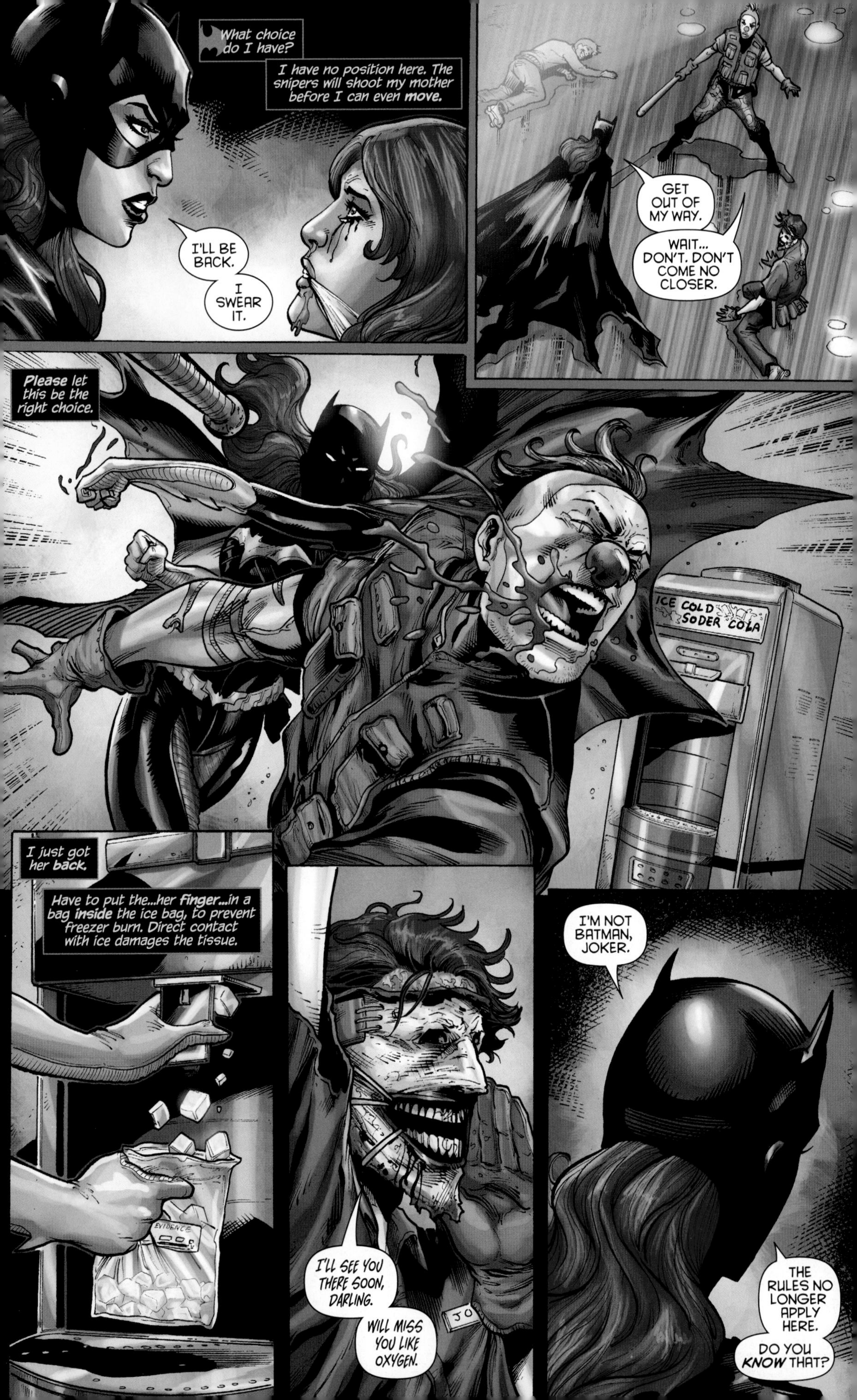
What choice do I have?
I have no position here. The snipers will shoot my mother before I can even move.
I'LL BE BACK.
I SWEAR IT.
GET OUT OF MY WAY.
WAIT... DON'T. DON'T COME NO CLOSER.
Please let this be the right choice.
ICE COLD SODER COLA
I just got her back.
Have to put the...her finger...in a bag inside the ice bag, to prevent freezer burn. Direct contact with ice damages the tissue.
EVIDENCE
I'LL SEE YOU THERE SOON, DARLING.
WILL MISS YOU LIKE OXYGEN.
I'M NOT BATMAN, JOKER.
THE RULES NO LONGER APPLY HERE.
DO YOU KNOW THAT?

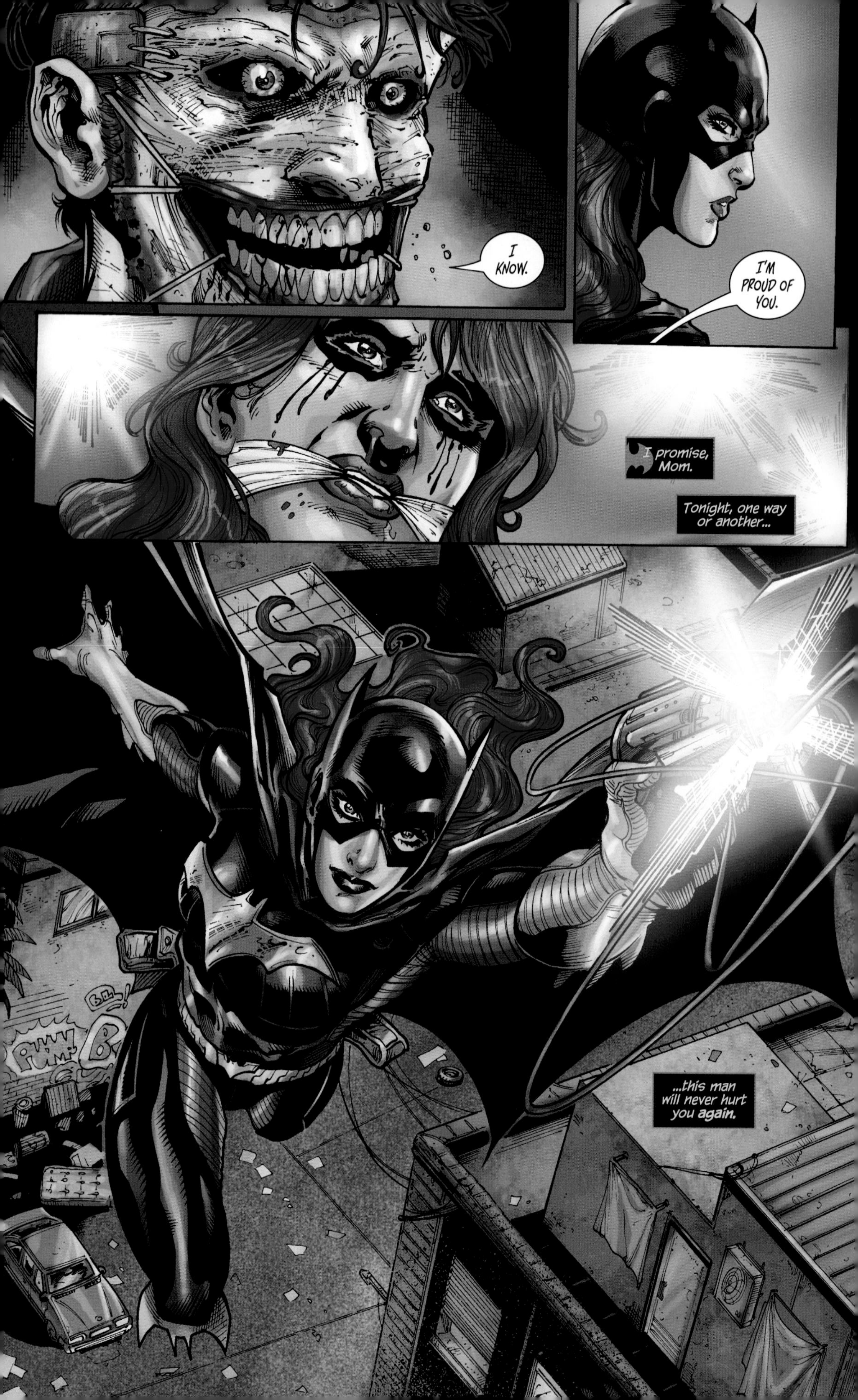
I KNOW.
I'M PROUD OF YOU.
I promise, Mom.
Tonight, one way or another...
...this man will never hurt you again.

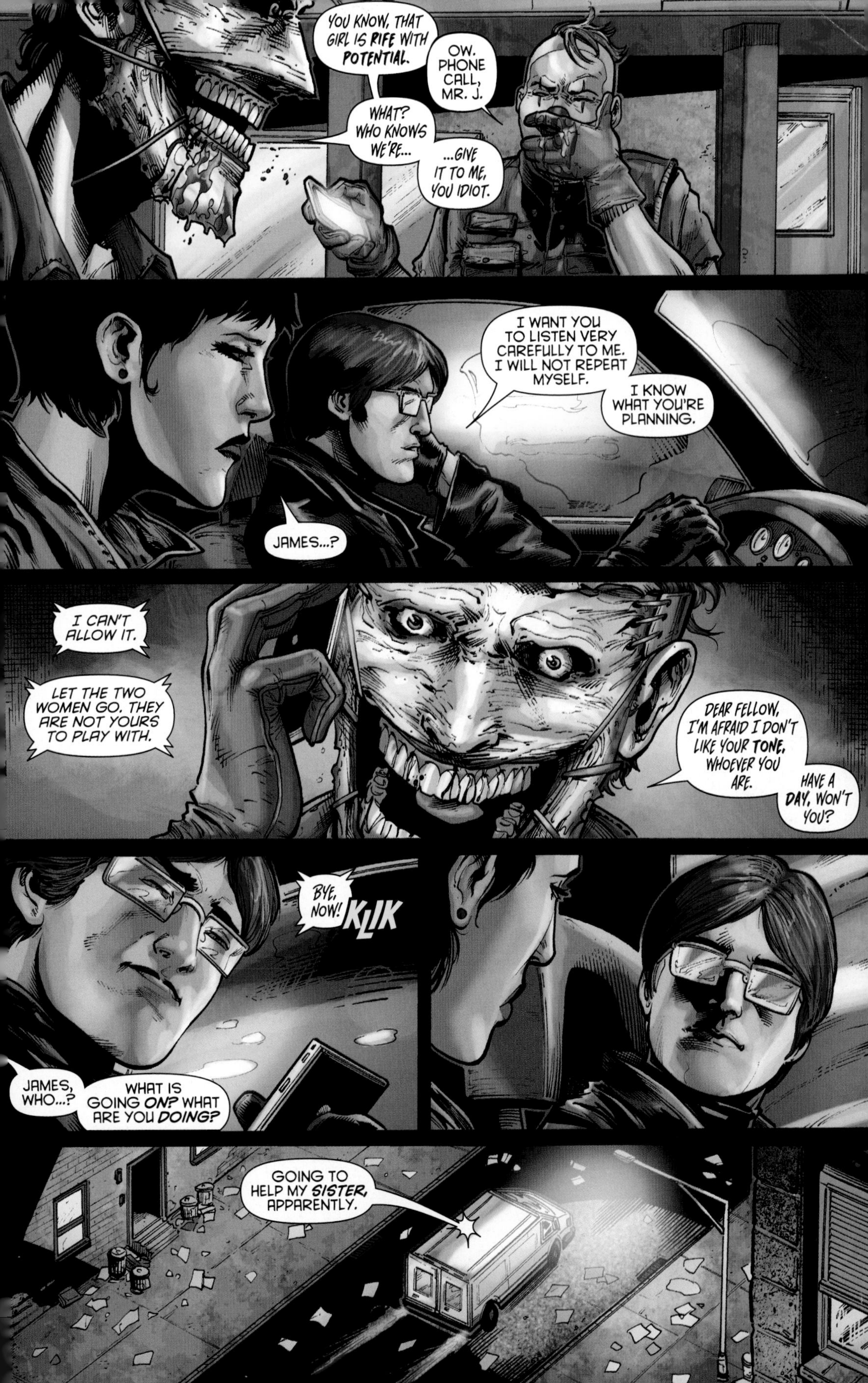
YOU KNOW, THAT GIRL IS RIFE WITH POTENTIAL.
OW. PHONE CALL, MR. J.
WHAT? WHO KNOWS WE'RE...
...GIVE IT TO ME, YOU IDIOT.
I WANT YOU TO LISTEN VERY CAREFULLY TO ME. I WILL NOT REPEAT MYSELF.
I KNOW WHAT YOU'RE PLANNING.
JAMES...?
I CAN'T ALLOW IT.
LET THE TWO WOMEN GO. THEY ARE NOT YOURS TO PLAY WITH.
DEAR FELLOW, I'M AFRAID I DON'T LIKE YOUR TONE, WHOEVER YOU ARE.
HAVE A DAY, WON'T YOU?
BYE, NOW!
KLIK
JAMES, WHO...?
WHAT IS GOING ON? WHAT ARE YOU DOING?
GOING TO HELP MY SISTER, APPARENTLY.

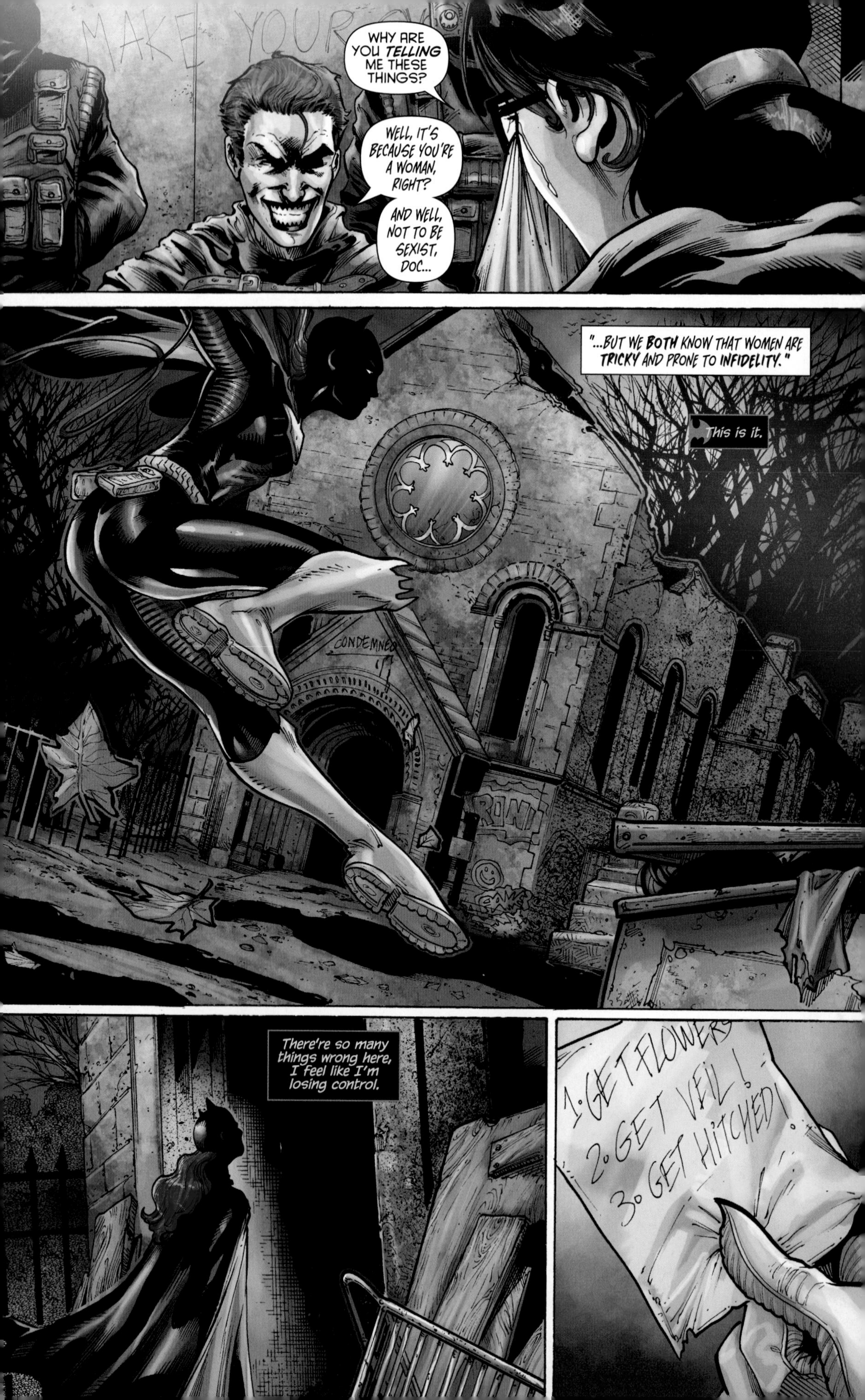

MAKE YOUR
WHY ARE YOU *TELLING* ME THESE THINGS?
WELL, IT'S BECAUSE YOU'RE A WOMAN, RIGHT?
AND WELL, NOT TO BE SEXIST, DOC...
"...BUT WE **BOTH** KNOW THAT WOMEN ARE **TRICKY** AND PRONE TO **INFIDELITY.**"
This is it.
There're so many things wrong here, I feel like I'm losing control.
1. GET FLOWERS
2. GET VEIL!
3. GET HITCHED!

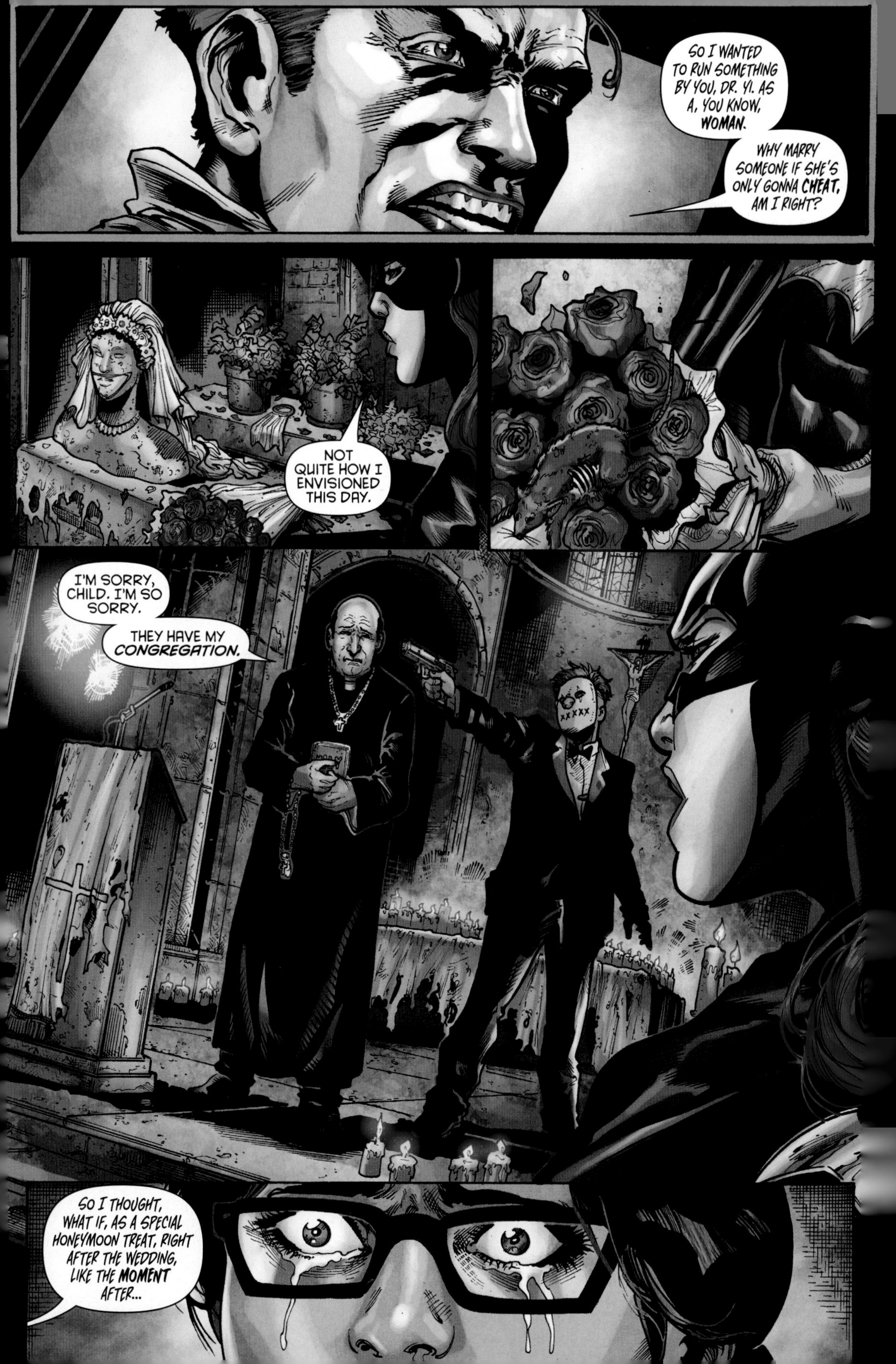
SO I WANTED TO RUN SOMETHING BY YOU, DR. YI. AS A, YOU KNOW, WOMAN.
WHY MARRY SOMEONE IF SHE'S ONLY GONNA CHEAT, AM I RIGHT?
NOT QUITE HOW I ENVISIONED THIS DAY.
I'M SORRY, CHILD. I'M SO SORRY.
THEY HAVE MY CONGREGATION.
SO I THOUGHT, WHAT IF, AS A SPECIAL HONEYMOON TREAT, RIGHT AFTER THE WEDDING, LIKE THE MOMENT AFTER...

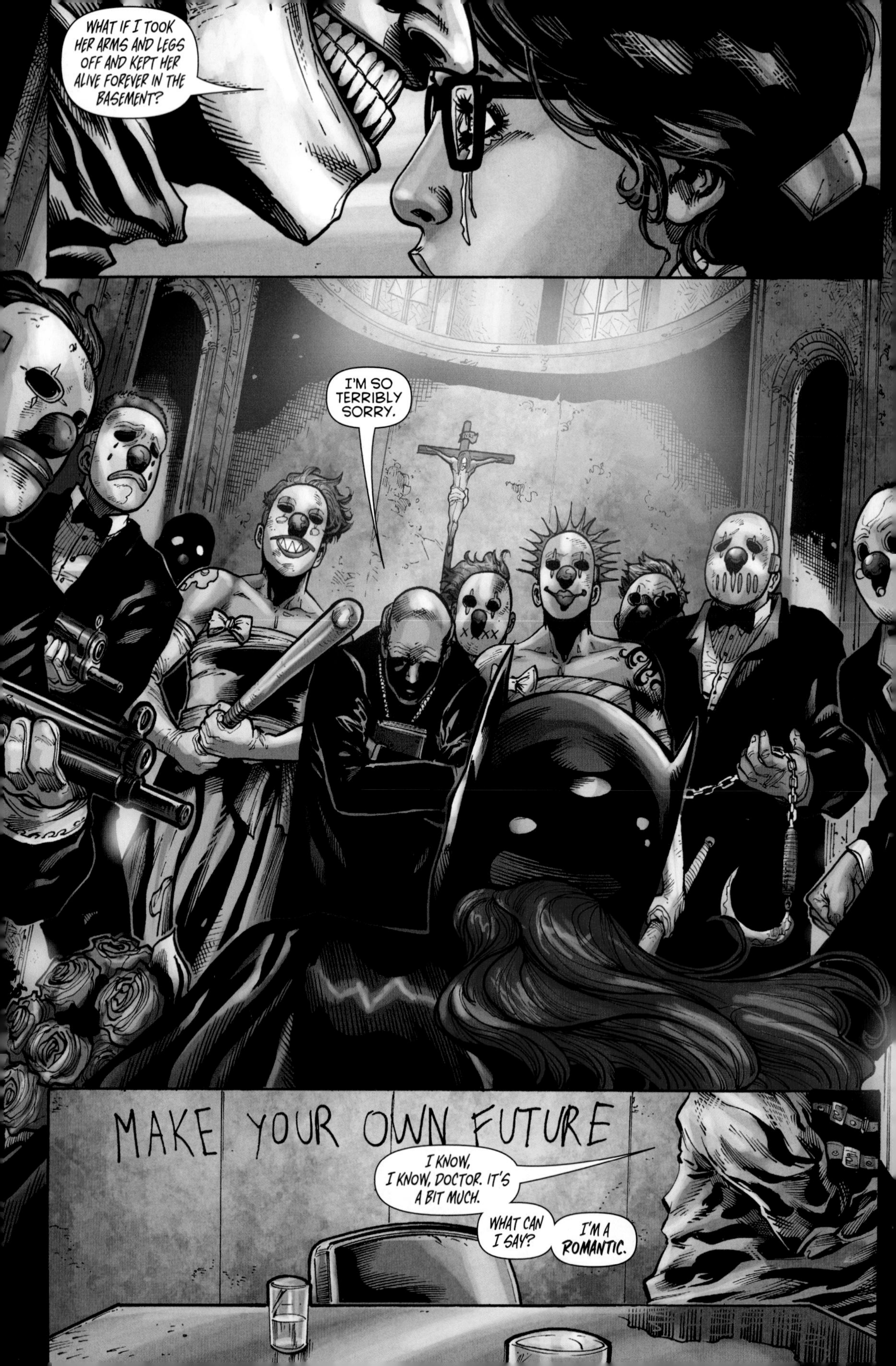
WHAT IF I TOOK HER ARMS AND LEGS OFF AND KEPT HER ALIVE FOREVER IN THE BASEMENT?
I'M SO TERRIBLY SORRY.
MAKE YOUR OWN FUTURE
I KNOW, I KNOW, DOCTOR. IT'S A BIT MUCH.
WHAT CAN I SAY?
I'M A ROMANTIC.

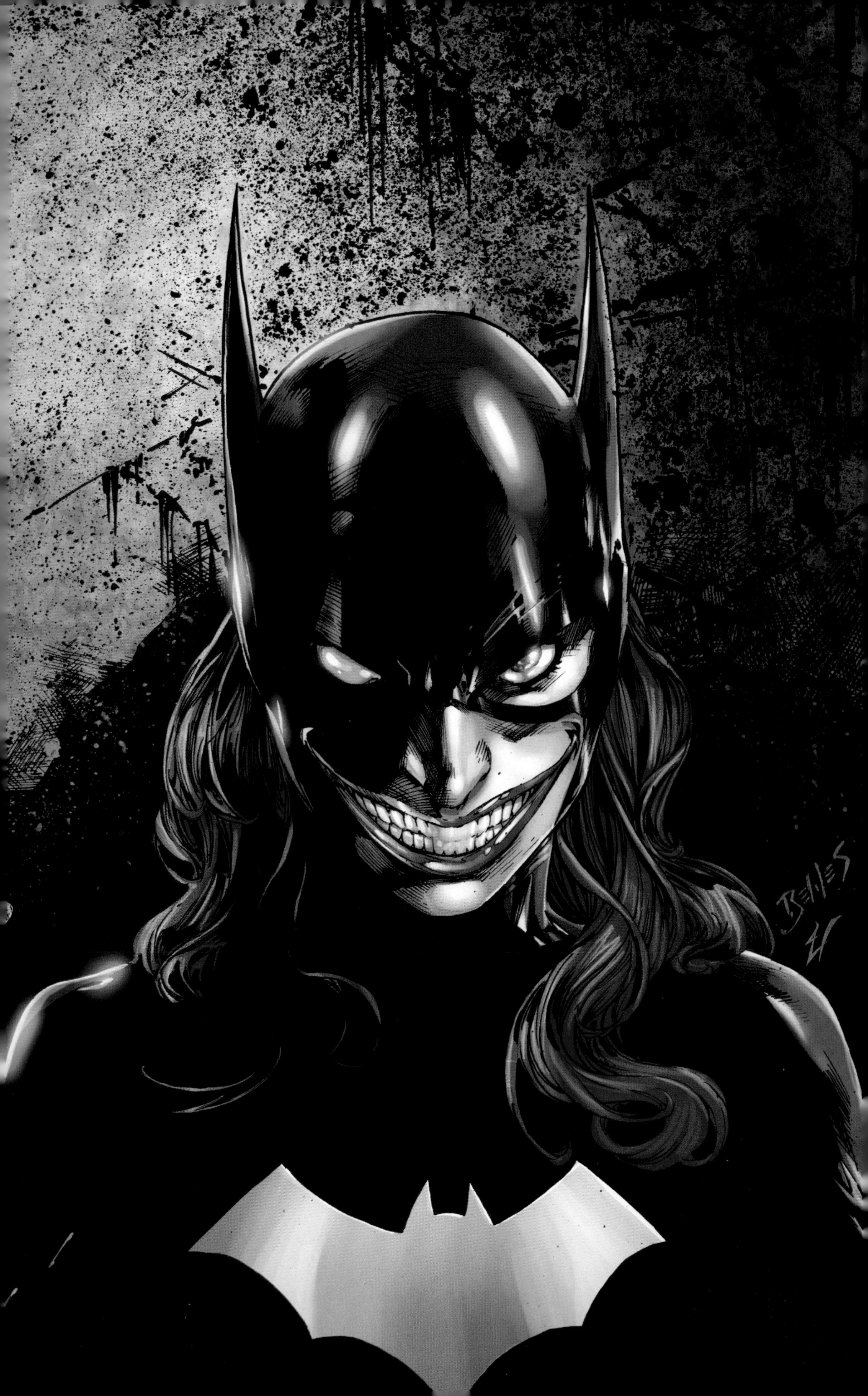

CEREMONY

GAIL SIMONE writer ED BENES DANIEL SAMPERE pencillers VICENTE CIFUENTES ED BENES inkers
cover by ED BENES & ULISES ARREOLA

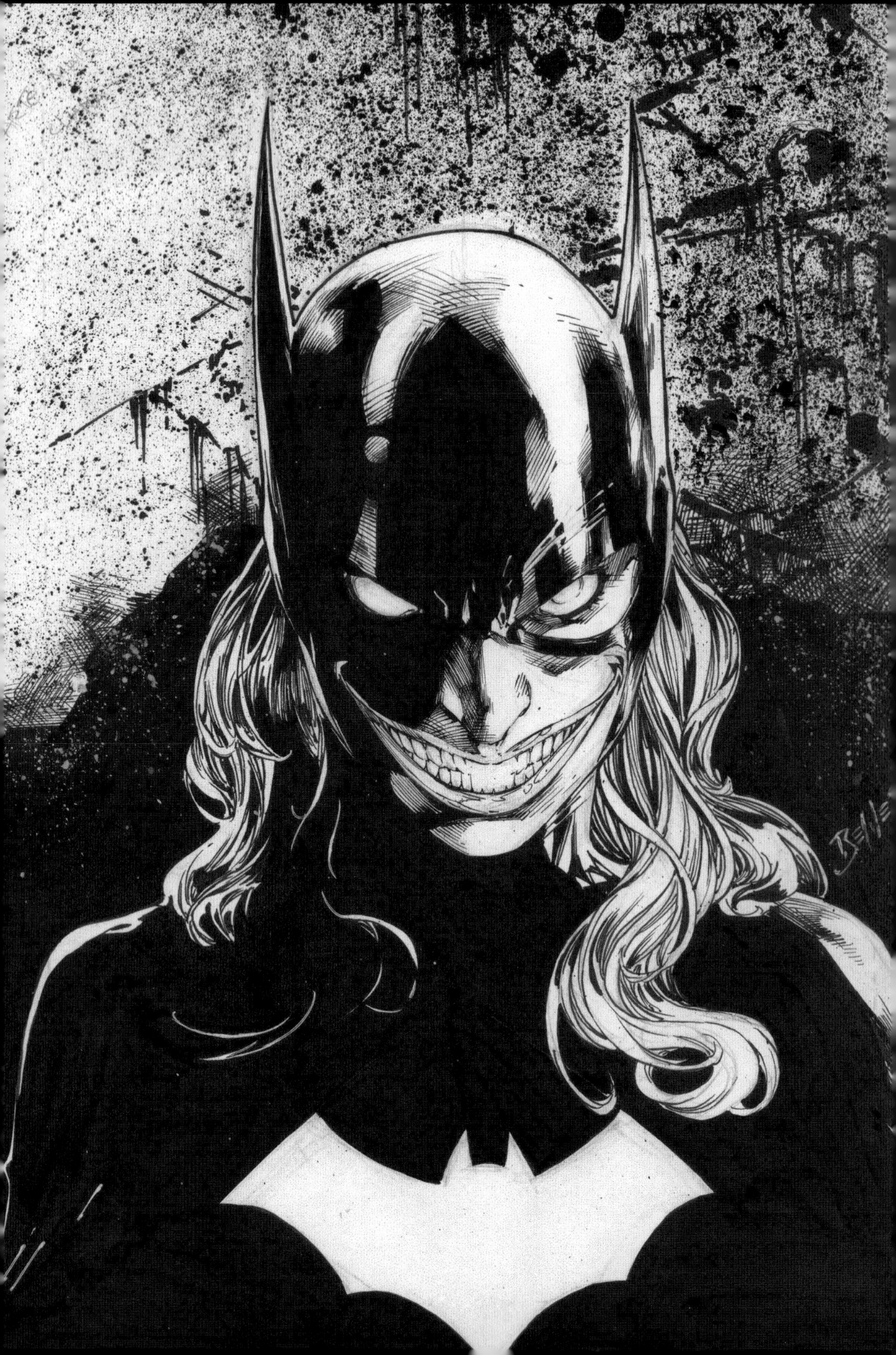

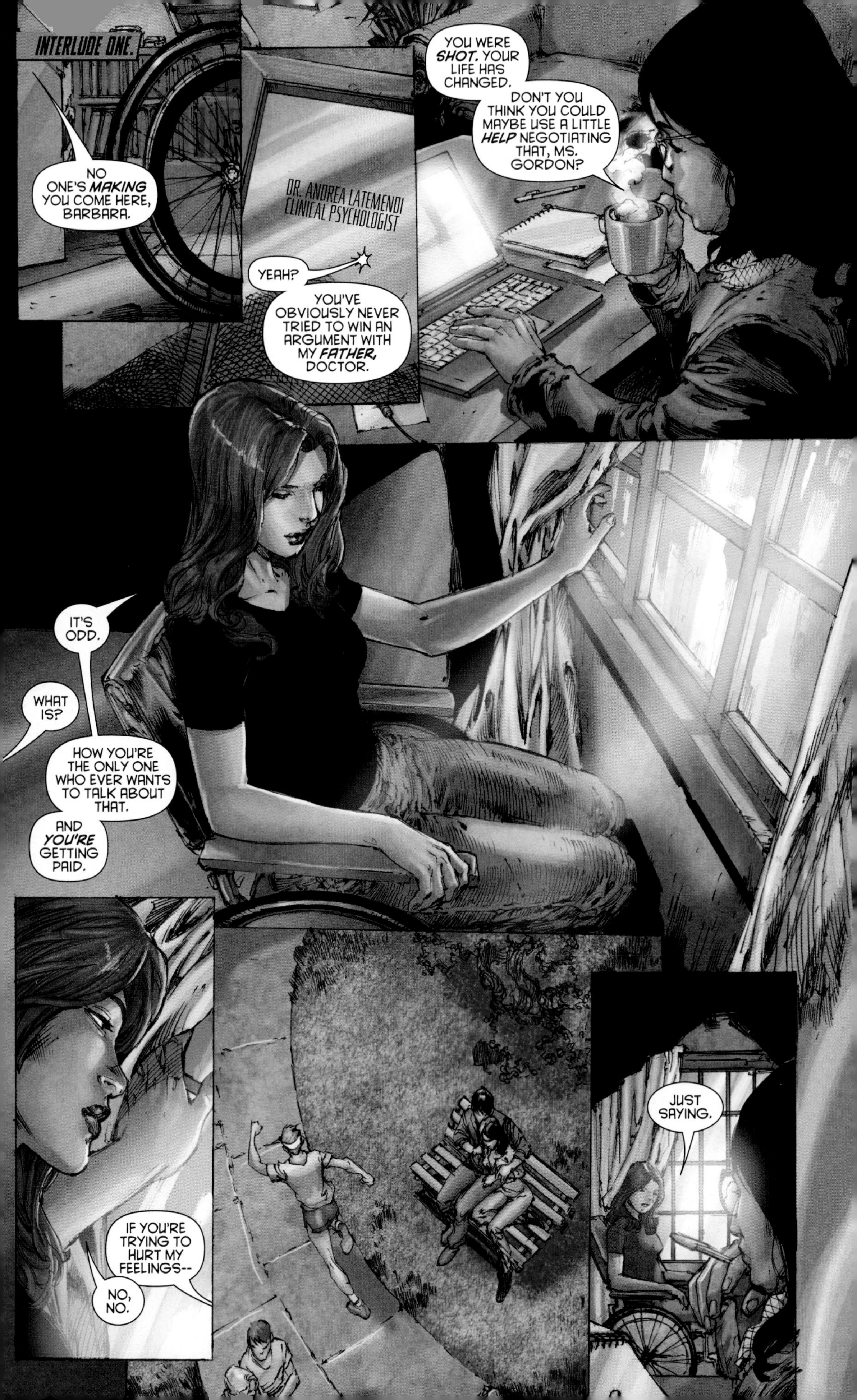
INTERLUDE ONE.
NO ONE'S MAKING YOU COME HERE, BARBARA.
DR. ANDREA LATEMENDI CLINICAL PSYCHOLOGIST
YEAH?
YOU'VE OBVIOUSLY NEVER TRIED TO WIN AN ARGUMENT WITH MY FATHER, DOCTOR.
YOU WERE SHOT. YOUR LIFE HAS CHANGED.
DON'T YOU THINK YOU COULD MAYBE USE A LITTLE HELP NEGOTIATING THAT, MS. GORDON?
IT'S ODD.
WHAT IS?
HOW YOU'RE THE ONLY ONE WHO EVER WANTS TO TALK ABOUT THAT.
AND YOU'RE GETTING PAID.
IF YOU'RE TRYING TO HURT MY FEELINGS--
NO, NO.
JUST SAYING.

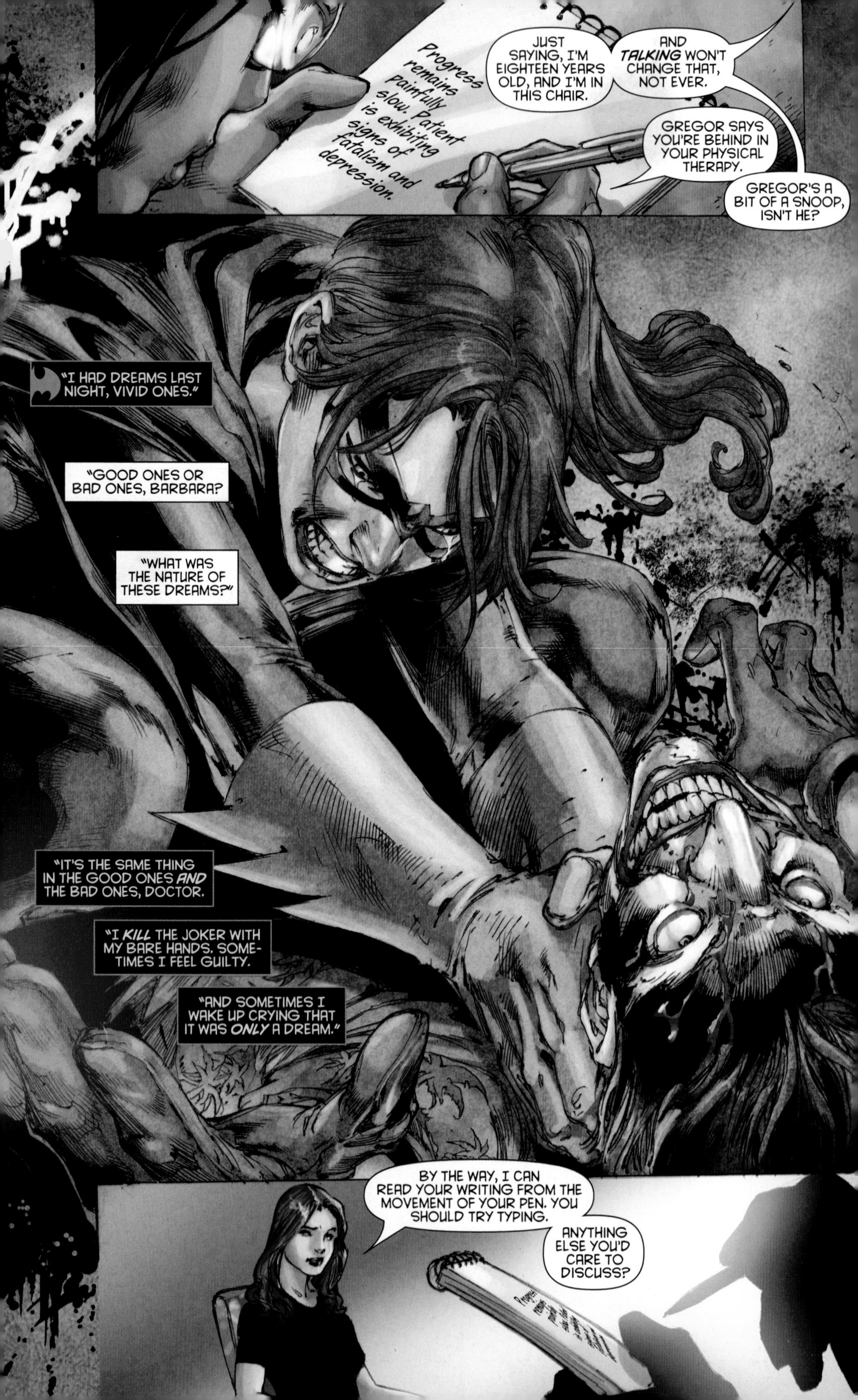

Progress remains painfully slow. Patient is exhibiting signs of fatalism and depression.
JUST SAYING, I'M EIGHTEEN YEARS OLD, AND I'M IN THIS CHAIR.
AND *TALKING* WON'T CHANGE THAT, NOT EVER.
GREGOR SAYS YOU'RE BEHIND IN YOUR PHYSICAL THERAPY.
GREGOR'S A BIT OF A SNOOP, ISN'T HE?
"I HAD DREAMS LAST NIGHT, VIVID ONES."
"GOOD ONES OR BAD ONES, BARBARA?
"WHAT WAS THE NATURE OF THESE DREAMS?"
"IT'S THE SAME THING IN THE GOOD ONES *AND* THE BAD ONES, DOCTOR.
"I *KILL* THE JOKER WITH MY BARE HANDS. SOMETIMES I FEEL GUILTY.
"AND SOMETIMES I WAKE UP CRYING THAT IT WAS *ONLY* A DREAM."
BY THE WAY, I CAN READ YOUR WRITING FROM THE MOVEMENT OF YOUR PEN. YOU SHOULD TRY TYPING.
ANYTHING ELSE YOU'D CARE TO DISCUSS?

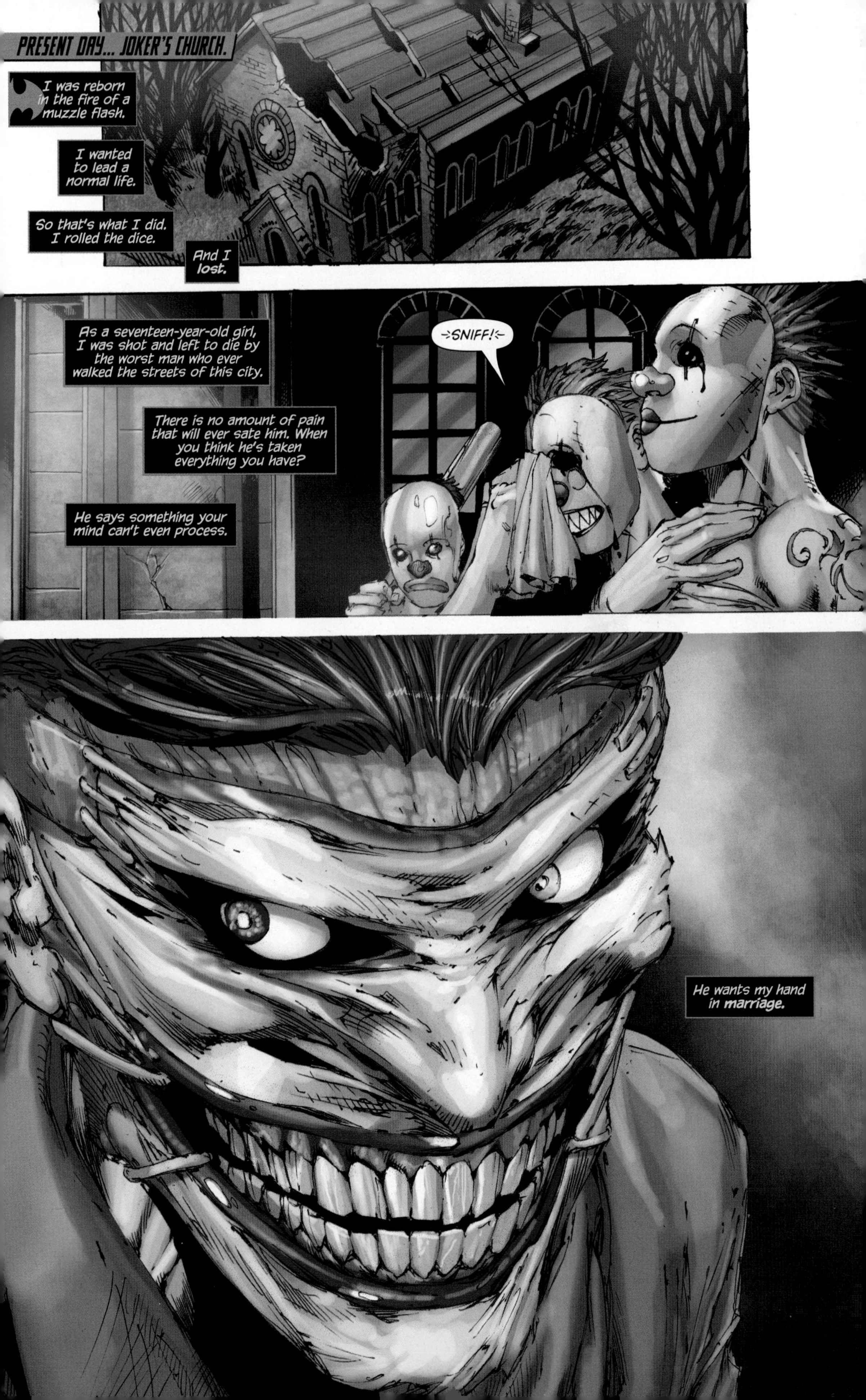

PRESENT DAY... JOKER'S CHURCH.
I was reborn in the fire of a muzzle flash.
I wanted to lead a normal life.
So that's what I did. I rolled the dice.
And I lost.
As a seventeen-year-old girl, I was shot and left to die by the worst man who ever walked the streets of this city.
-SNIFF!-
There is no amount of pain that will ever sate him. When you think he's taken everything you have?
He says something your mind can't even process.
He wants my hand in marriage.

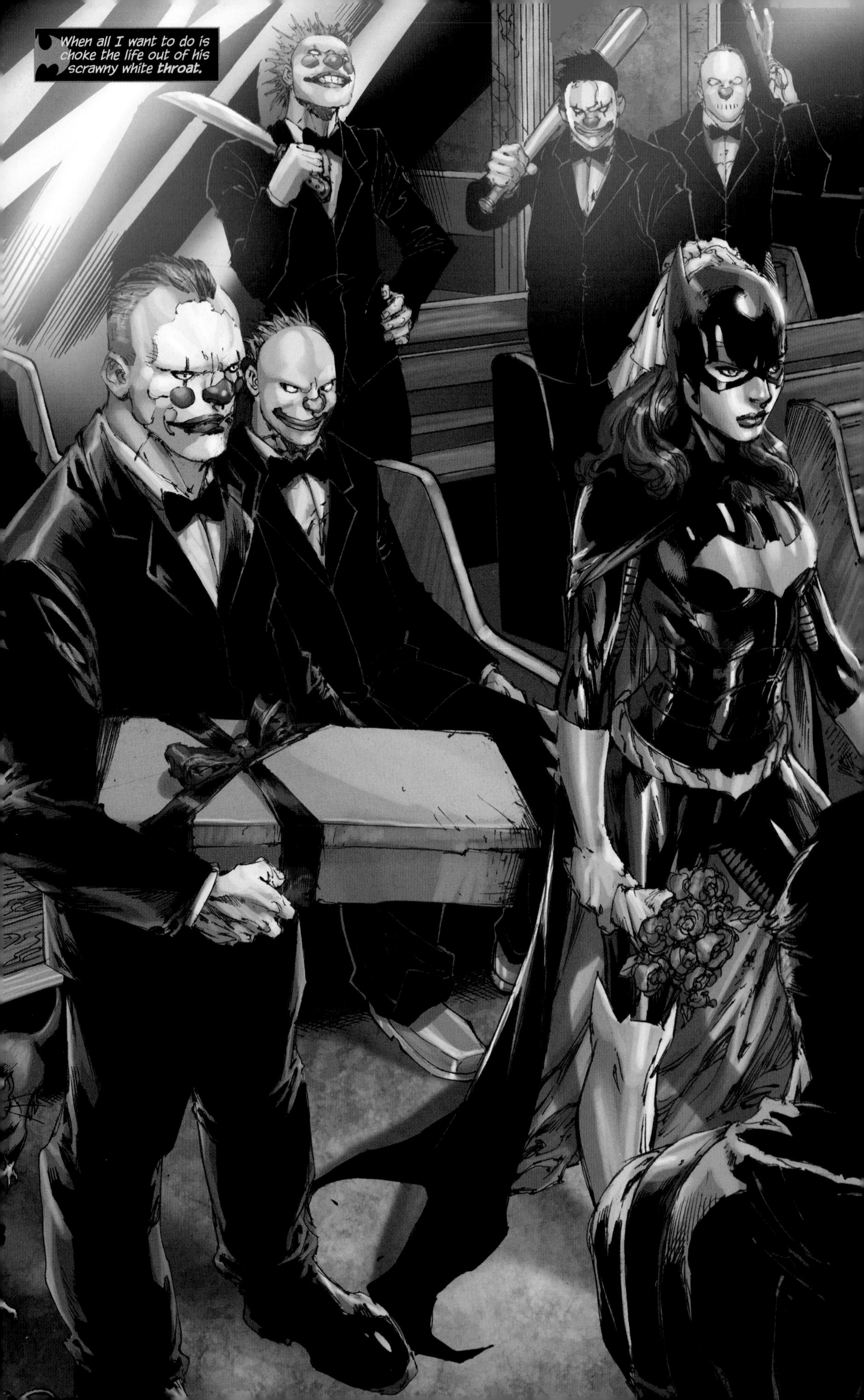
When all I want to do is choke the life out of his scrawny white **throat.**

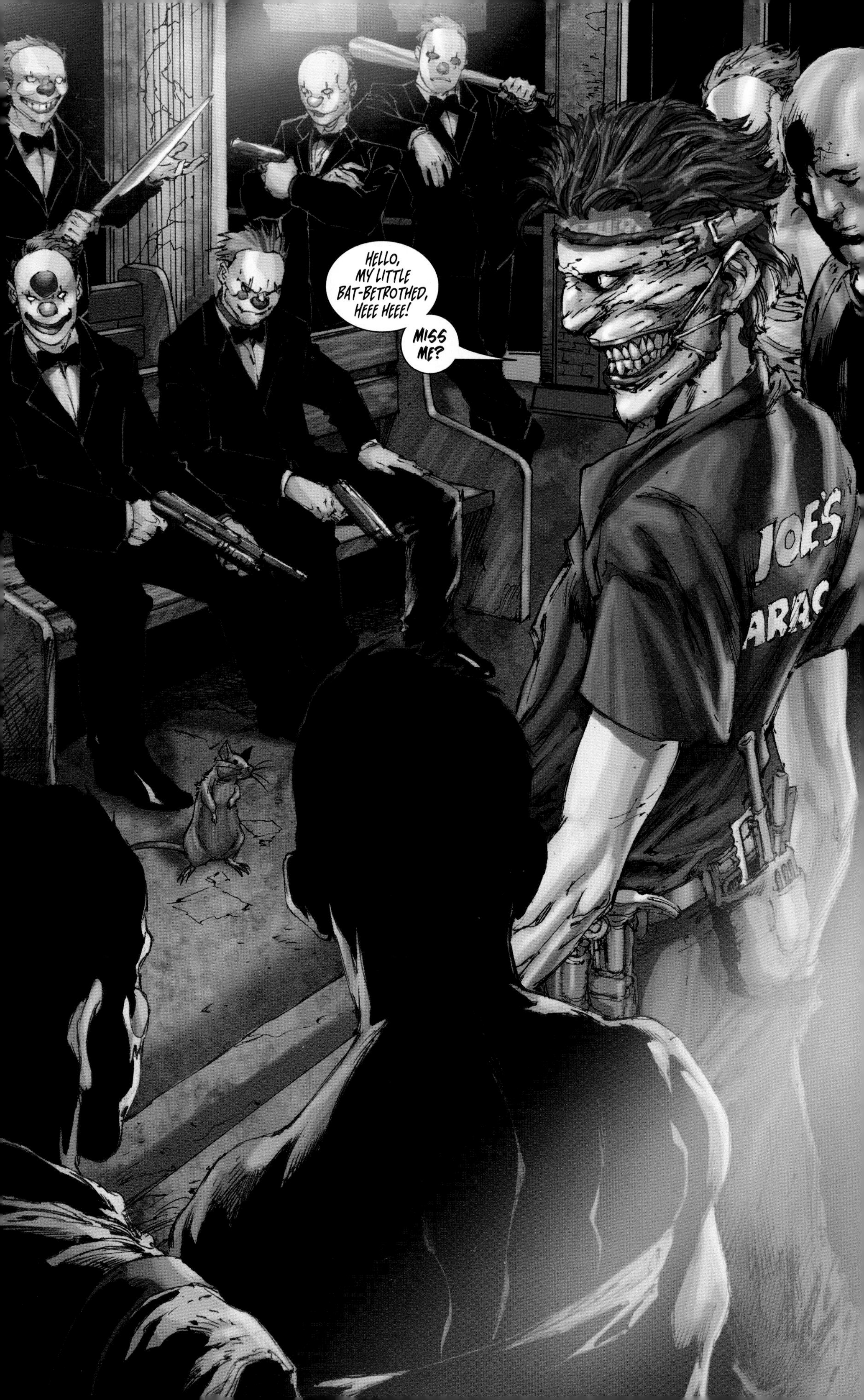
HELLO, MY LITTLE BAT-BETROTHED, HEEE HEEE!
MISS ME?

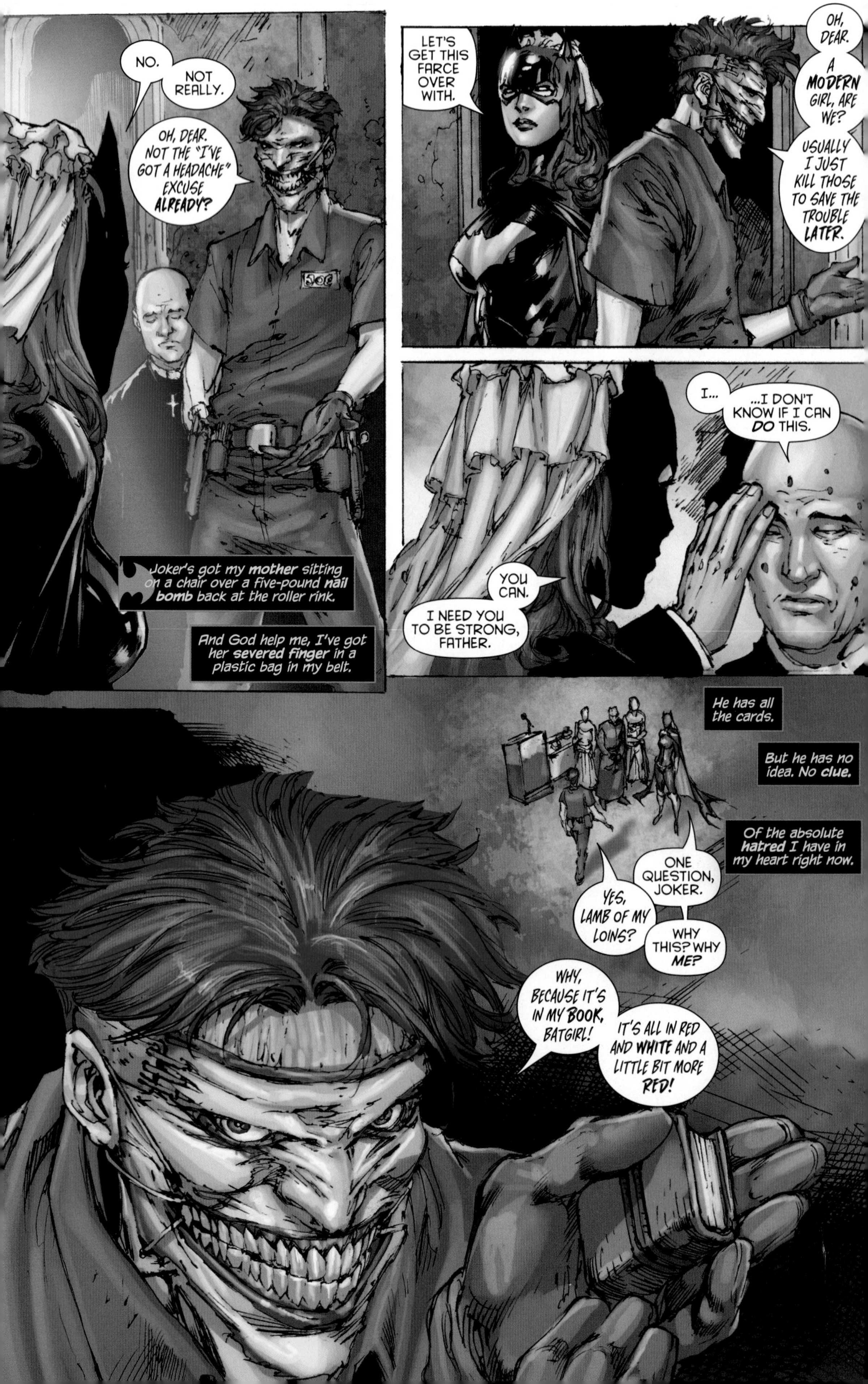
NO.
NOT REALLY.
OH, DEAR. NOT THE "I'VE GOT A HEADACHE" EXCUSE **ALREADY**?
Joker's got my **mother** sitting on a chair over a five-pound **nail bomb** back at the roller rink.
And God help me, I've got her **severed finger** in a plastic bag in my belt.
LET'S GET THIS FARCE OVER WITH.
OH, DEAR.
A **MODERN** GIRL, ARE WE?
USUALLY I JUST KILL THOSE TO SAVE THE TROUBLE **LATER**.
I...
...I DON'T KNOW IF I CAN **DO** THIS.
YOU CAN.
I NEED YOU TO BE STRONG, FATHER.
He has all the cards.
But he has no idea. No **clue**.
Of the absolute **hatred** I have in my heart right now.
ONE QUESTION, JOKER.
YES, LAMB OF MY LOINS?
WHY THIS? WHY **ME**?
WHY, BECAUSE IT'S IN MY **BOOK**, BATGIRL!
IT'S ALL IN RED AND **WHITE** AND A LITTLE BIT MORE **RED**!

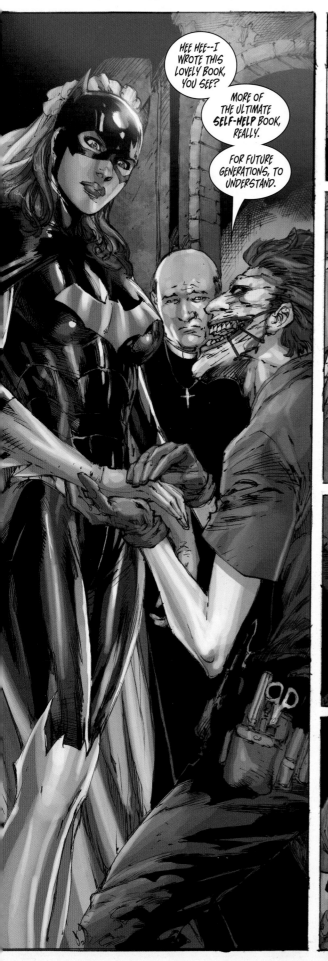

HEE HEE--I WROTE THIS LOVELY BOOK, YOU SEE?

MORE OF THE ULTIMATE *SELF-HELP* BOOK, REALLY.

FOR FUTURE GENERATIONS, TO UNDERSTAND.

TO FOLLOW.

AND *THIS.* THIS IS THE WAY MARRIAGES OF *STATE* HAVE BEEN DONE FOR *CENTURIES.*

ALL RIGHT, SO MAYYYYYYBE THE BRIDE DIDN'T ALWAYS *LOVE* THE GROOM RIGHT AWAY. A *PIFFLE,* I SAY.

BUT THE *BAT.* SEE, HE'S THE KING, AND I'M THE *JESTER.*

DON'T LAUGH, I'M GOING SOMEWHERE WITH THIS.

AND YOU. AND THE *BRATSSS.*

YOU'RE JUST DRAGGING HIM *DOWN.*

YOU A-OKAY, THERE, LEFTY?

→SNFFF←

I ALWAYS CRY AT WEDDINGS, BOSS.

CHIN UP, BIG GUY.

AND SO THE THING, THE THING IS--THE THING TO DO IS...

...TAKE ALL THE PAWNS OFF THE BOARD, MY LITTLE BLACK AND GOLD! HA HA HA HA HA!

YOU CAN'T HONESTLY THINK THIS SHAM *WEDDING* MEANS ANYTHING, CAN YOU?

ON THE CONTRARY, DON'T YOU READ THE PAPERS? SHAM WEDDINGS *ABOUND* FOR A *REASON*, CUDDLEKINS.

BUT YOU MAKE A FAIR POINT.

LEFTY, GRAB THE THING FOR ME, WON'T YOU?

MY PLAN, AND I'VE BEEN WORKING ON THIS FOR SIMPLY EVER...

...IS TO FREE MY DEAR FRIEND THE BAT.

FROM PEOPLE LIKE YOU.

PARASITES. LEECHES. SPIN-OFFS.

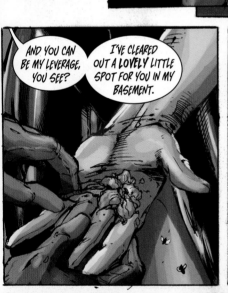

AND YOU CAN BE MY LEVERAGE, YOU SEE?

I'VE CLEARED OUT A *LOVELY* LITTLE SPOT FOR YOU IN MY BASEMENT.

Oh, my God.

What is... what is he on about?

THANK YOU, LEFTY.

ANYHOW, SHE-BAT... YOU JUST *MIGHT* GET NAUGHTY AND TRY TO DO THE OLD *MIDNIGHT DIVORCE* ON ME, RIGHT?

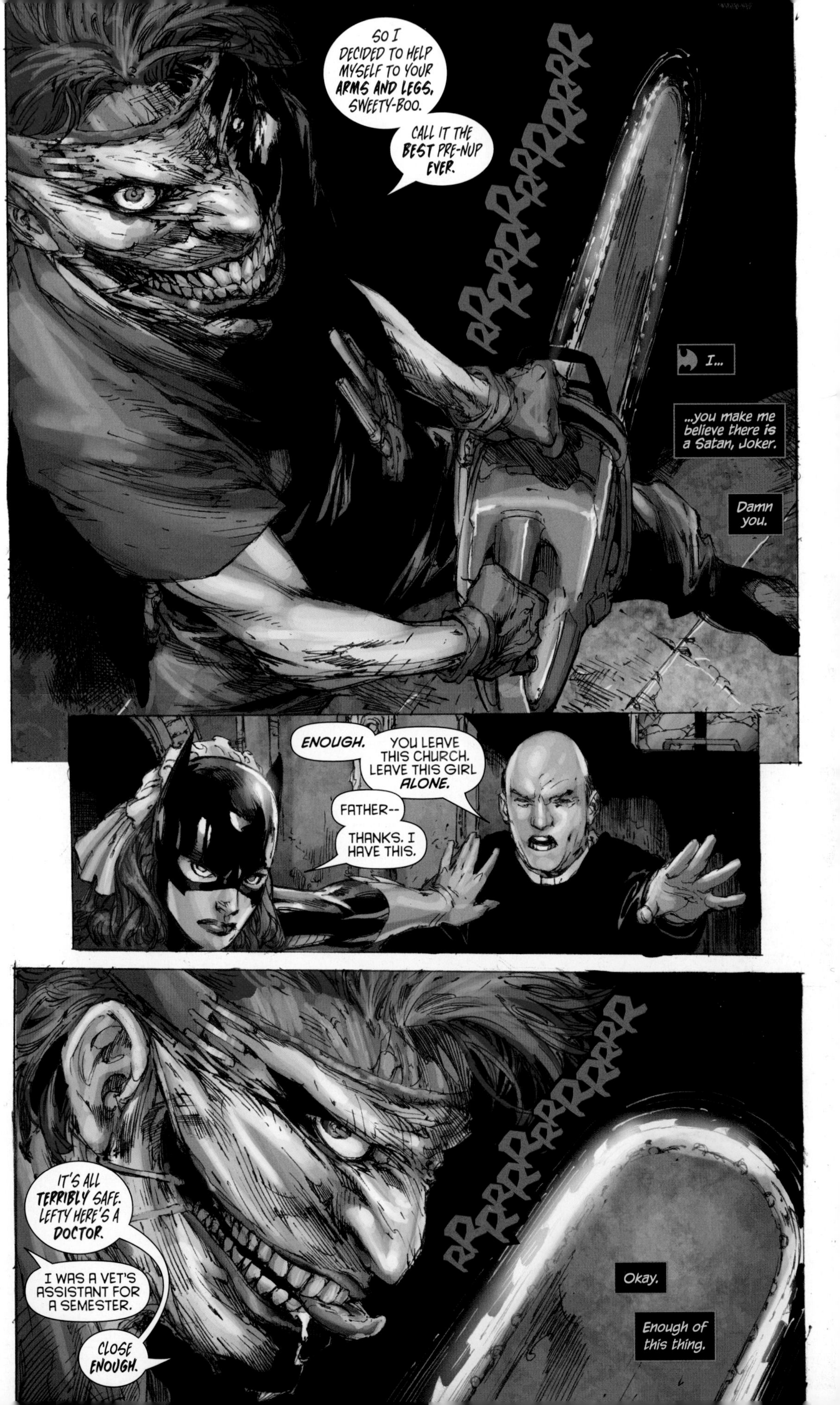

SO I DECIDED TO HELP MYSELF TO YOUR ARMS AND LEGS, SWEETY-BOO.
CALL IT THE BEST PRE-NUP EVER.
RRRRRRRRRRRRRRRRRR
I...
...you make me believe there is a Satan, Joker.
Damn you.
ENOUGH.
YOU LEAVE THIS CHURCH. LEAVE THIS GIRL ALONE.
FATHER--
THANKS. I HAVE THIS.
RRRRRRRRRRRRRRRRR
IT'S ALL TERRIBLY SAFE. LEFTY HERE'S A DOCTOR.
I WAS A VET'S ASSISTANT FOR A SEMESTER.
CLOSE ENOUGH.
Okay.
Enough of this thing.

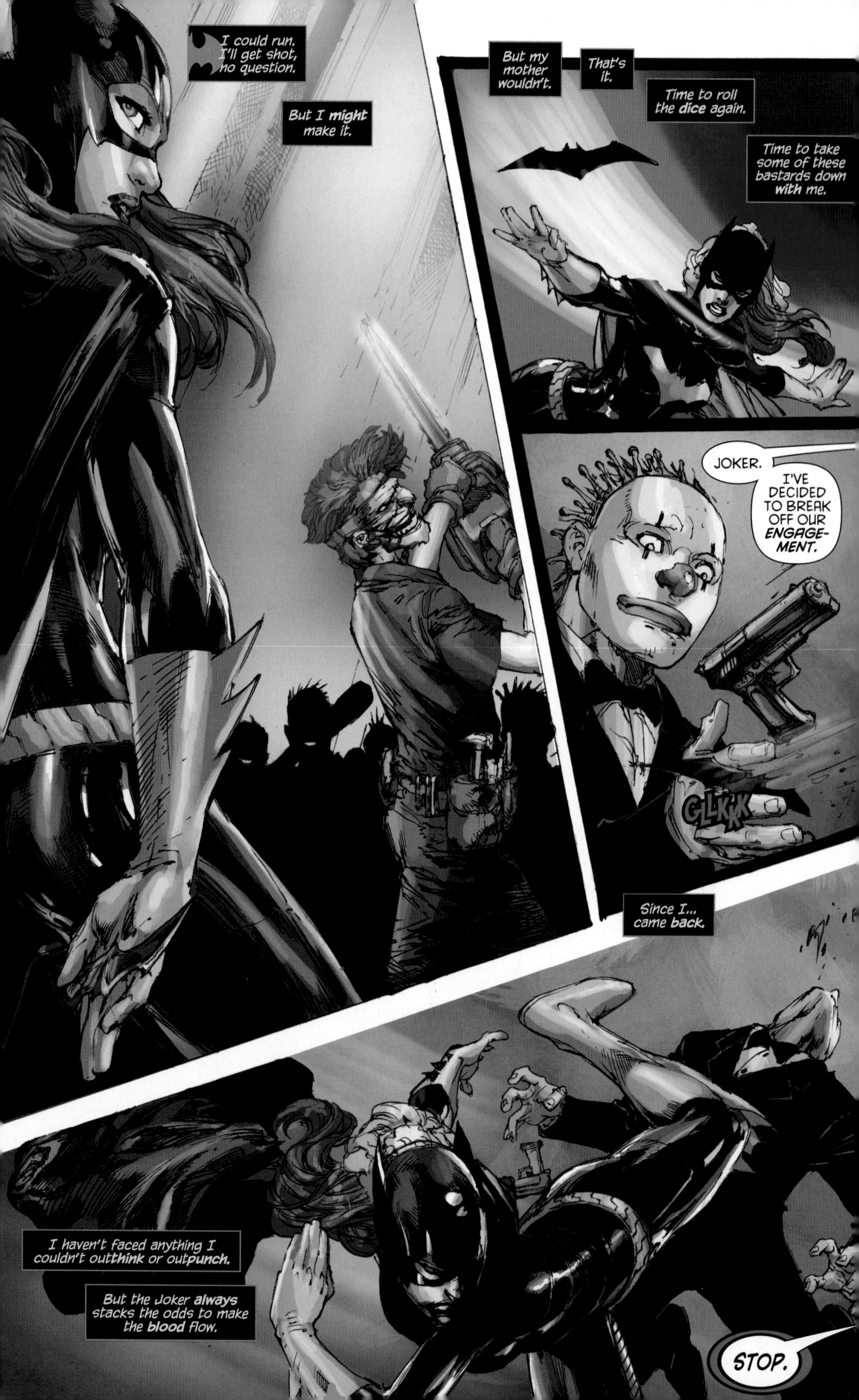
I could run. I'll get shot, no question.
But I might make it.
But my mother wouldn't.
That's it.
Time to roll the dice again.
Time to take some of these bastards down with me.
JOKER.
I'VE DECIDED TO BREAK OFF OUR ENGAGE-MENT.
GLLKKK
Since I... came back.
I haven't faced anything I couldn't outthink or outpunch.
But the Joker always stacks the odds to make the blood flow.
STOP.

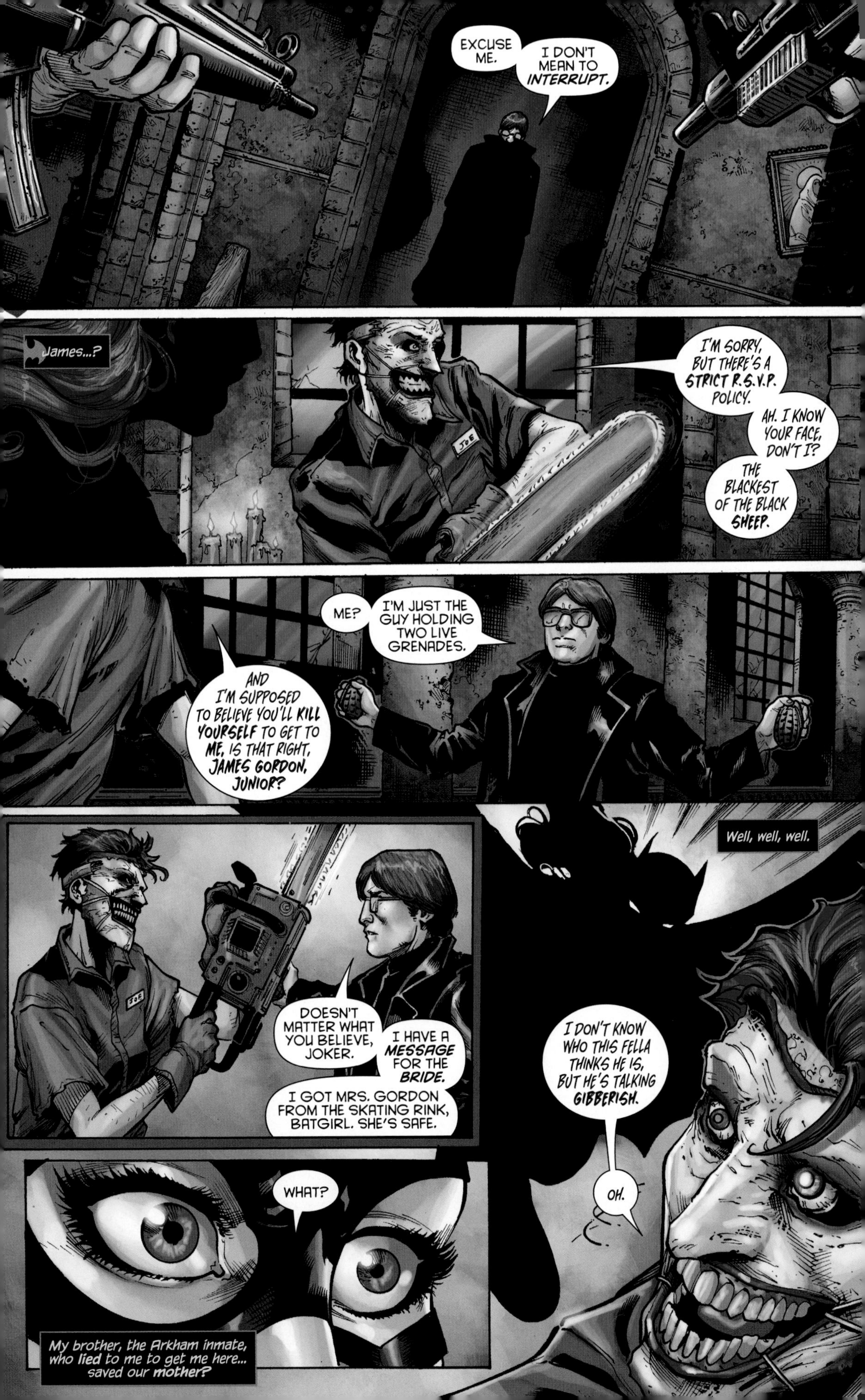
EXCUSE ME.
I DON'T MEAN TO INTERRUPT.
James...?
I'M SORRY, BUT THERE'S A STRICT R.S.V.P. POLICY.
AH. I KNOW YOUR FACE, DON'T I?
THE BLACKEST OF THE BLACK SHEEP.
ME?
I'M JUST THE GUY HOLDING TWO LIVE GRENADES.
AND I'M SUPPOSED TO BELIEVE YOU'LL KILL YOURSELF TO GET TO ME, IS THAT RIGHT, JAMES GORDON, JUNIOR?
DOESN'T MATTER WHAT YOU BELIEVE, JOKER.
I HAVE A MESSAGE FOR THE BRIDE.
I GOT MRS. GORDON FROM THE SKATING RINK, BATGIRL. SHE'S SAFE.
Well, well, well.
I DON'T KNOW WHO THIS FELLA THINKS HE IS, BUT HE'S TALKING GIBBERISH.
WHAT?
OH.
My brother, the Arkham inmate, who lied to me to get me here... saved our mother?

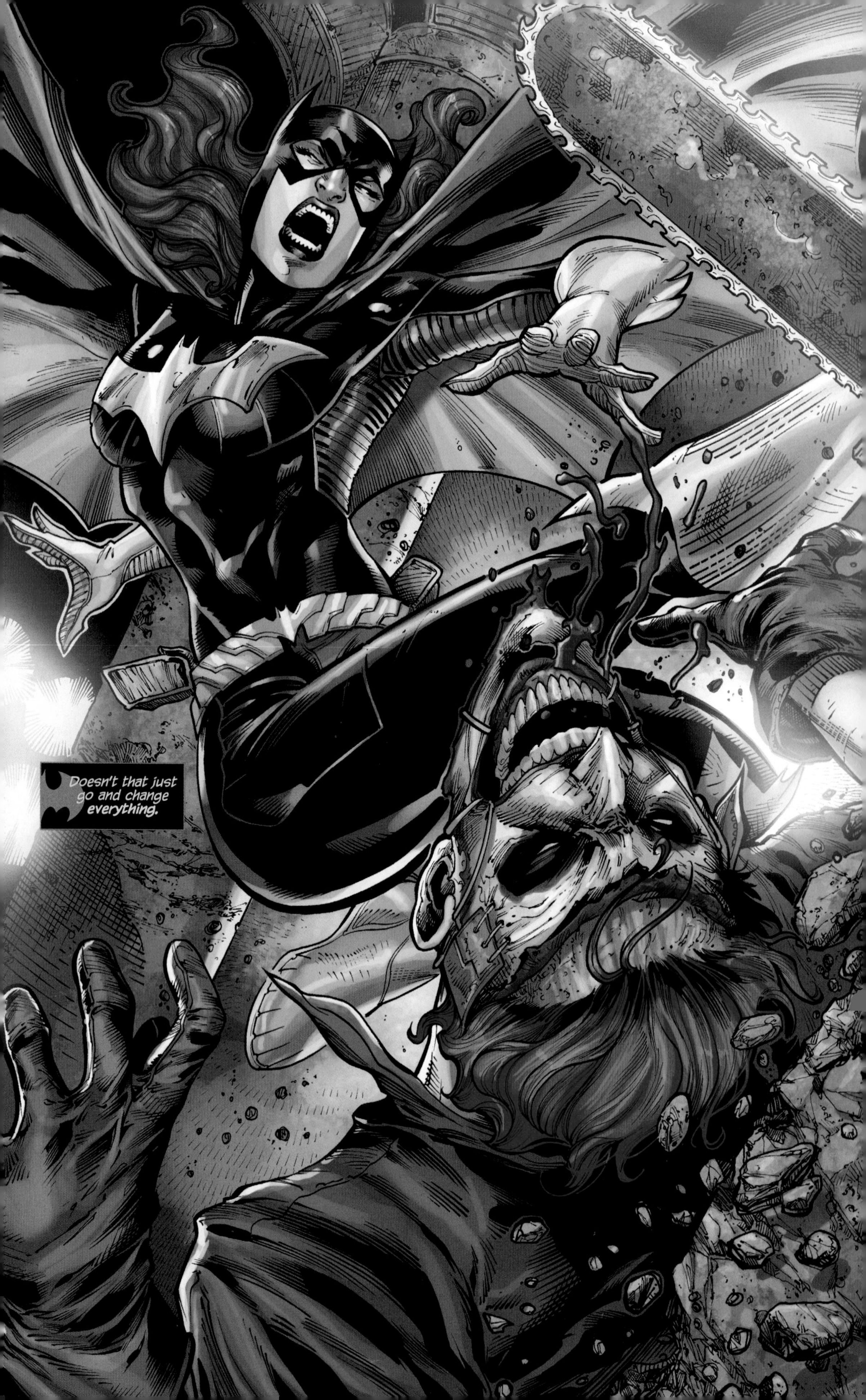
Doesn't that just go and change everything.

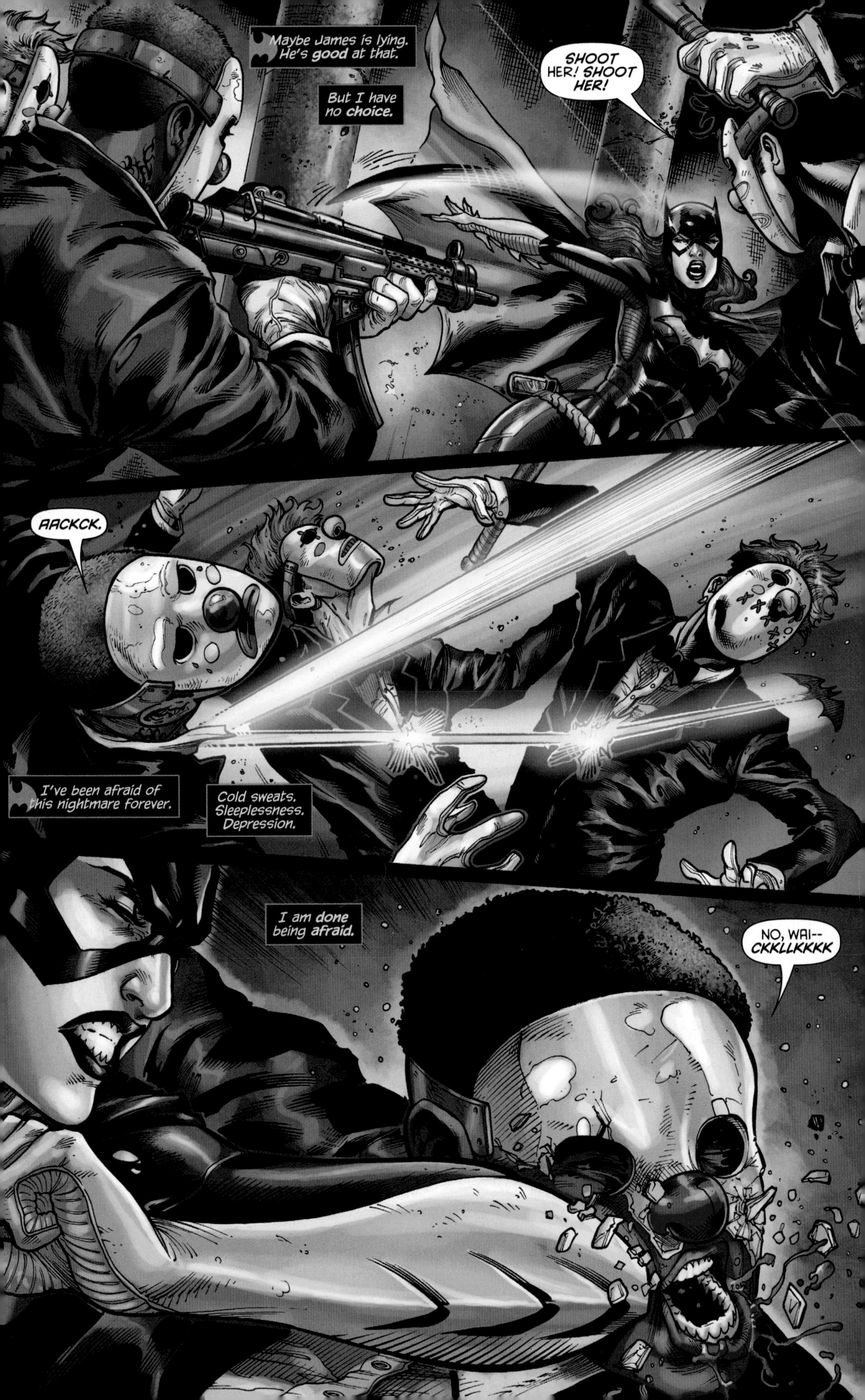

Maybe James is lying. He's good at that.
But I have no choice.
SHOOT HER! SHOOT HER!
AACKCK.
I've been afraid of this nightmare forever.
Cold sweats. Sleeplessness. Depression.
I am done being afraid.
NO, WAI-- CKKLLKKKK

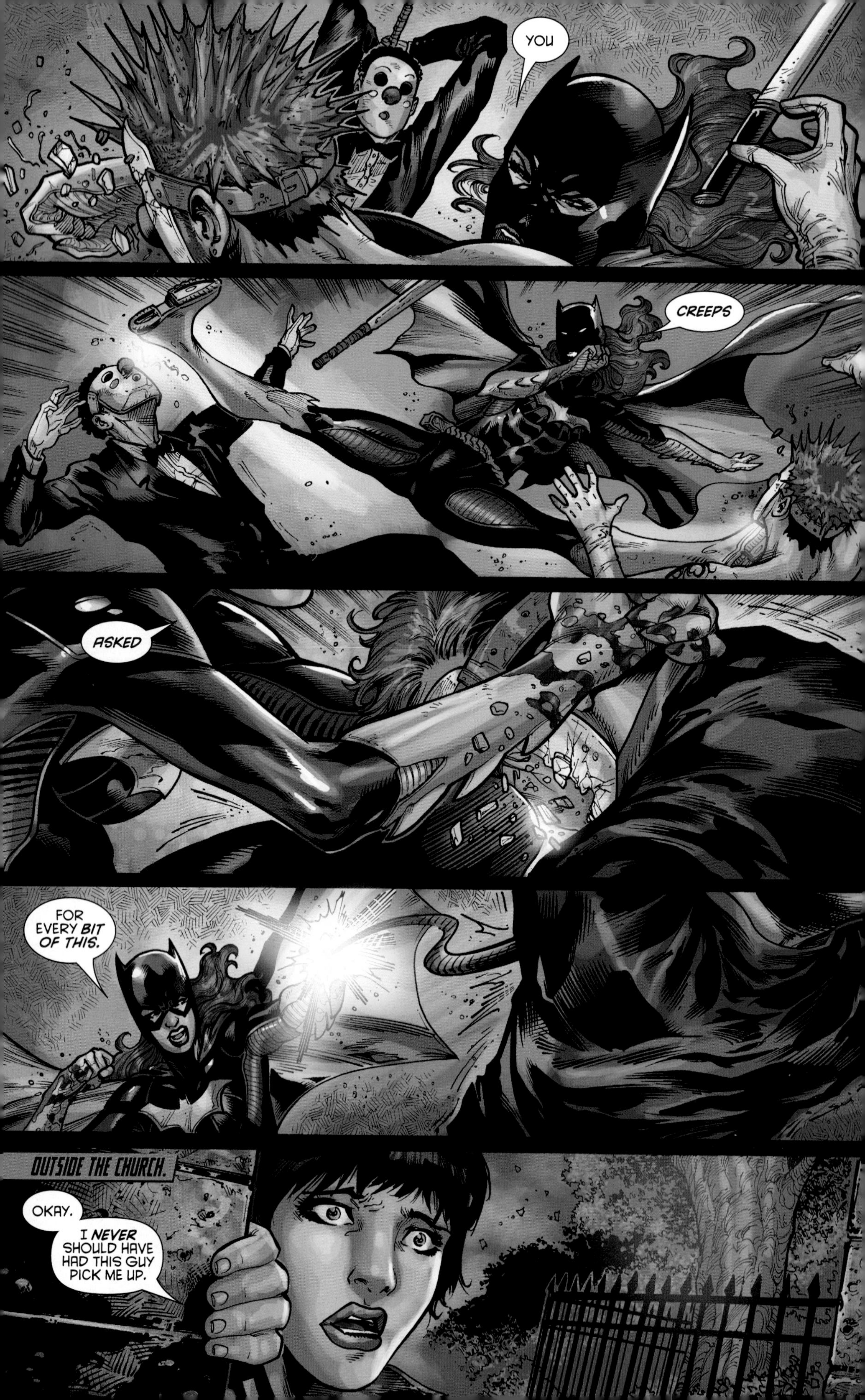
YOU
CREEPS
ASKED
FOR EVERY BIT OF THIS.
OUTSIDE THE CHURCH.
OKAY.
I NEVER SHOULD HAVE HAD THIS GUY PICK ME UP.

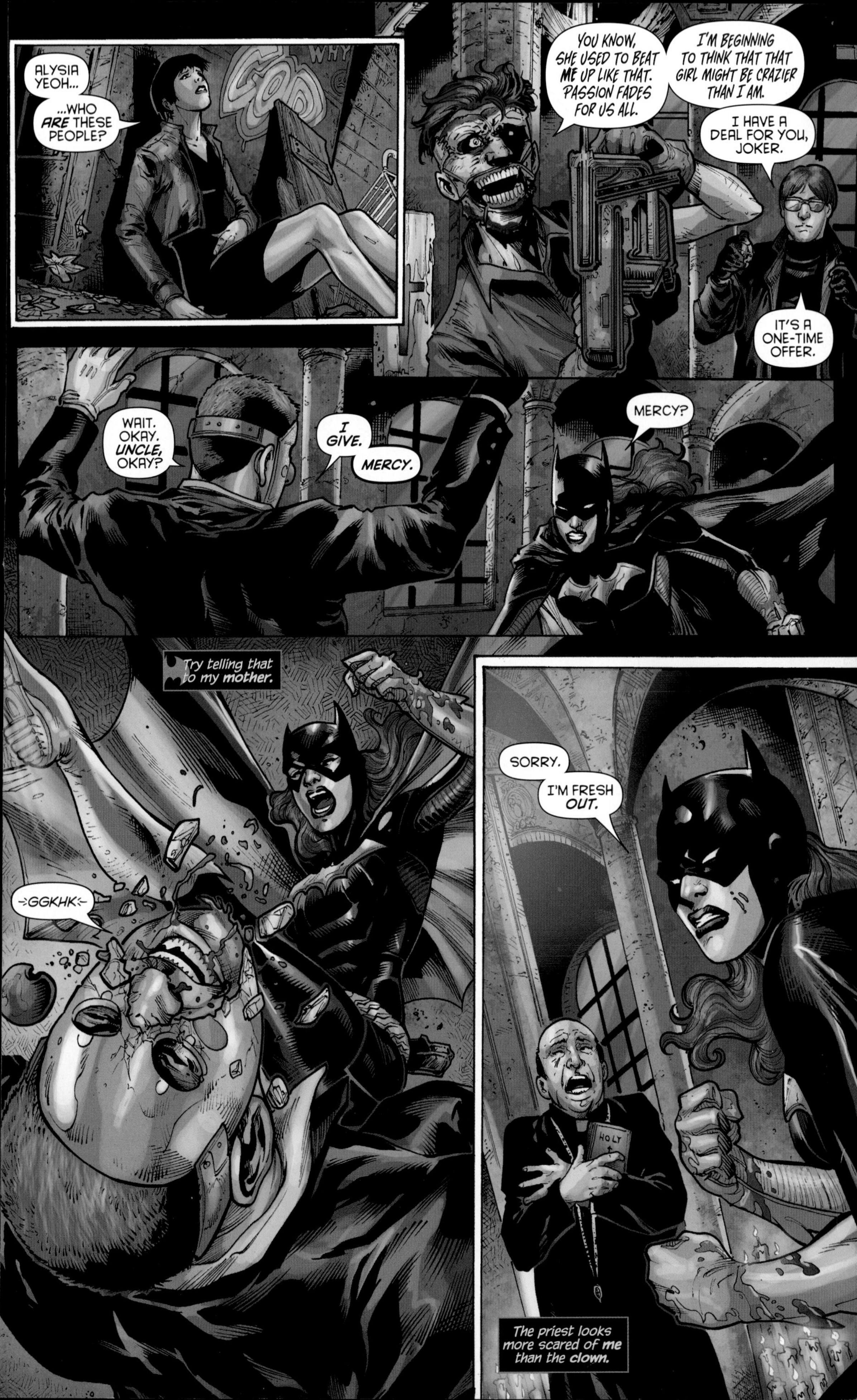
ALYSIA YEOH...
...WHO ARE THESE PEOPLE?
YOU KNOW, SHE USED TO BEAT ME UP LIKE THAT. PASSION FADES FOR US ALL.
I'M BEGINNING TO THINK THAT THAT GIRL MIGHT BE CRAZIER THAN I AM.
I HAVE A DEAL FOR YOU, JOKER.
IT'S A ONE-TIME OFFER.
WAIT. OKAY. UNCLE, OKAY?
I GIVE. MERCY.
MERCY?
Try telling that to my mother.
-GGKHK-
SORRY. I'M FRESH OUT.
HOLY
The priest looks more scared of me than the clown.

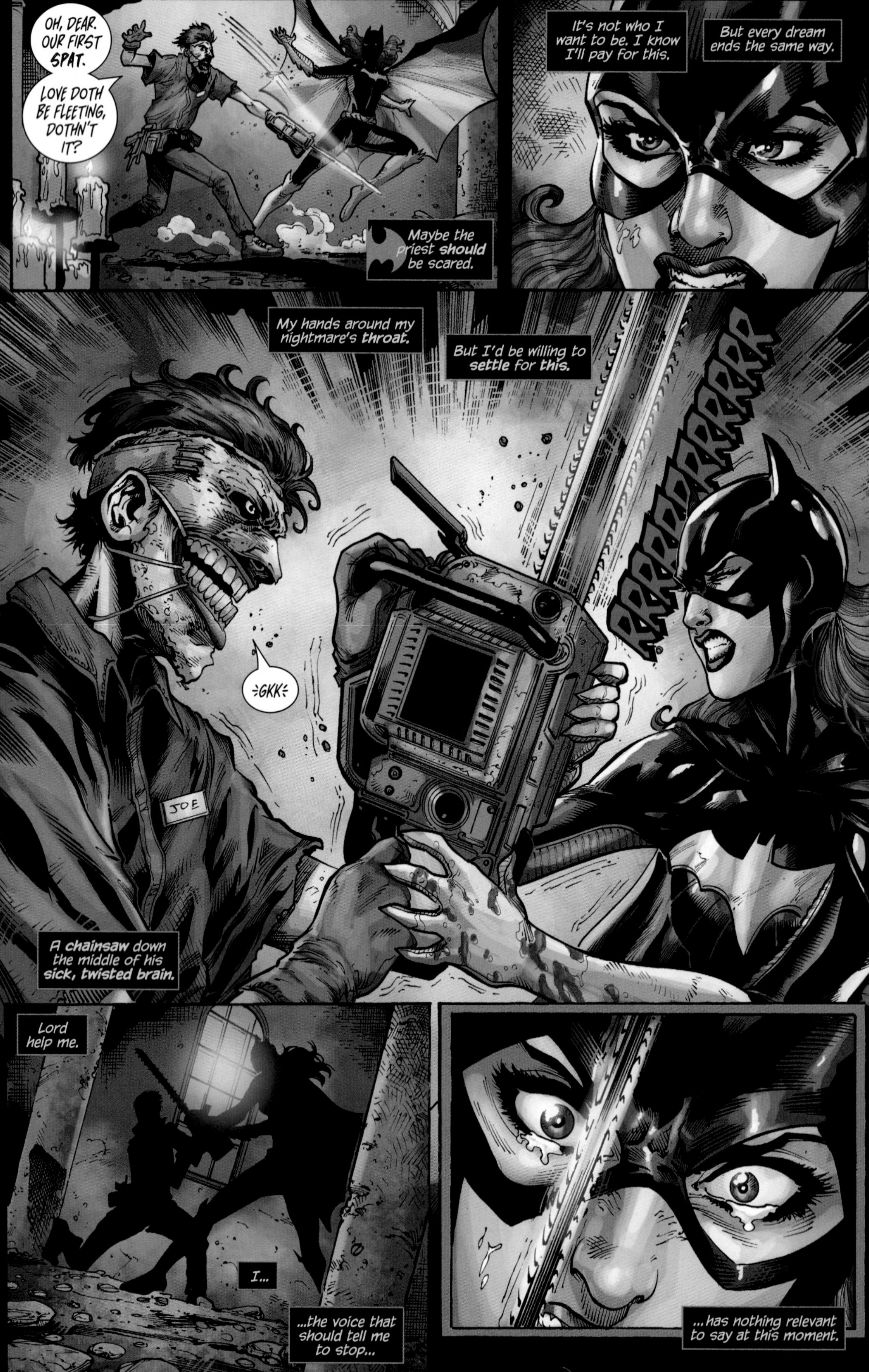
OH, DEAR. OUR FIRST SPAT.
LOVE DOTH BE FLEETING, DOTHN'T IT?
Maybe the priest should be scared.
It's not who I want to be. I know I'll pay for this.
But every dream ends the same way.
My hands around my nightmare's throat.
But I'd be willing to settle for this.
RRRRRRRRRRRRR
GKK
JOE
A chainsaw down the middle of his sick, twisted brain.
Lord help me.
I...
...the voice that should tell me to stop...
...has nothing relevant to say at this moment.

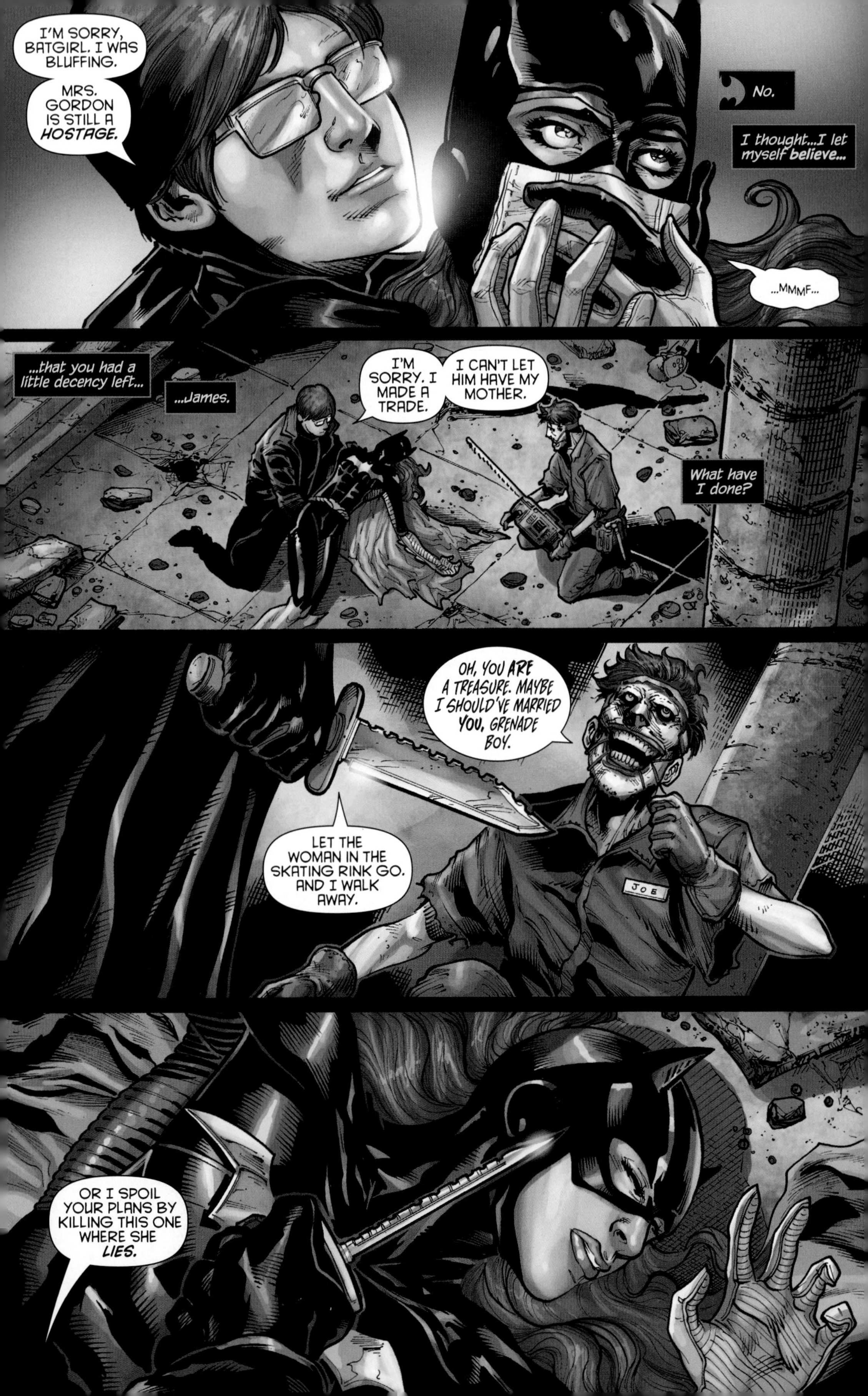
I'M SORRY, BATGIRL. I WAS BLUFFING.
MRS. GORDON IS STILL A *HOSTAGE.*
No.
I thought...I let myself **believe...**
...MMMF...
...that you had a little decency left...
...James.
I'M SORRY. I MADE A TRADE.
I CAN'T LET HIM HAVE MY MOTHER.
What have I done?
OH, YOU **ARE** A TREASURE. MAYBE I SHOULD'VE MARRIED **YOU**, GRENADE BOY.
LET THE WOMAN IN THE SKATING RINK GO. AND I WALK AWAY.
JOE
OR I SPOIL YOUR PLANS BY KILLING THIS ONE WHERE SHE *LIES.*

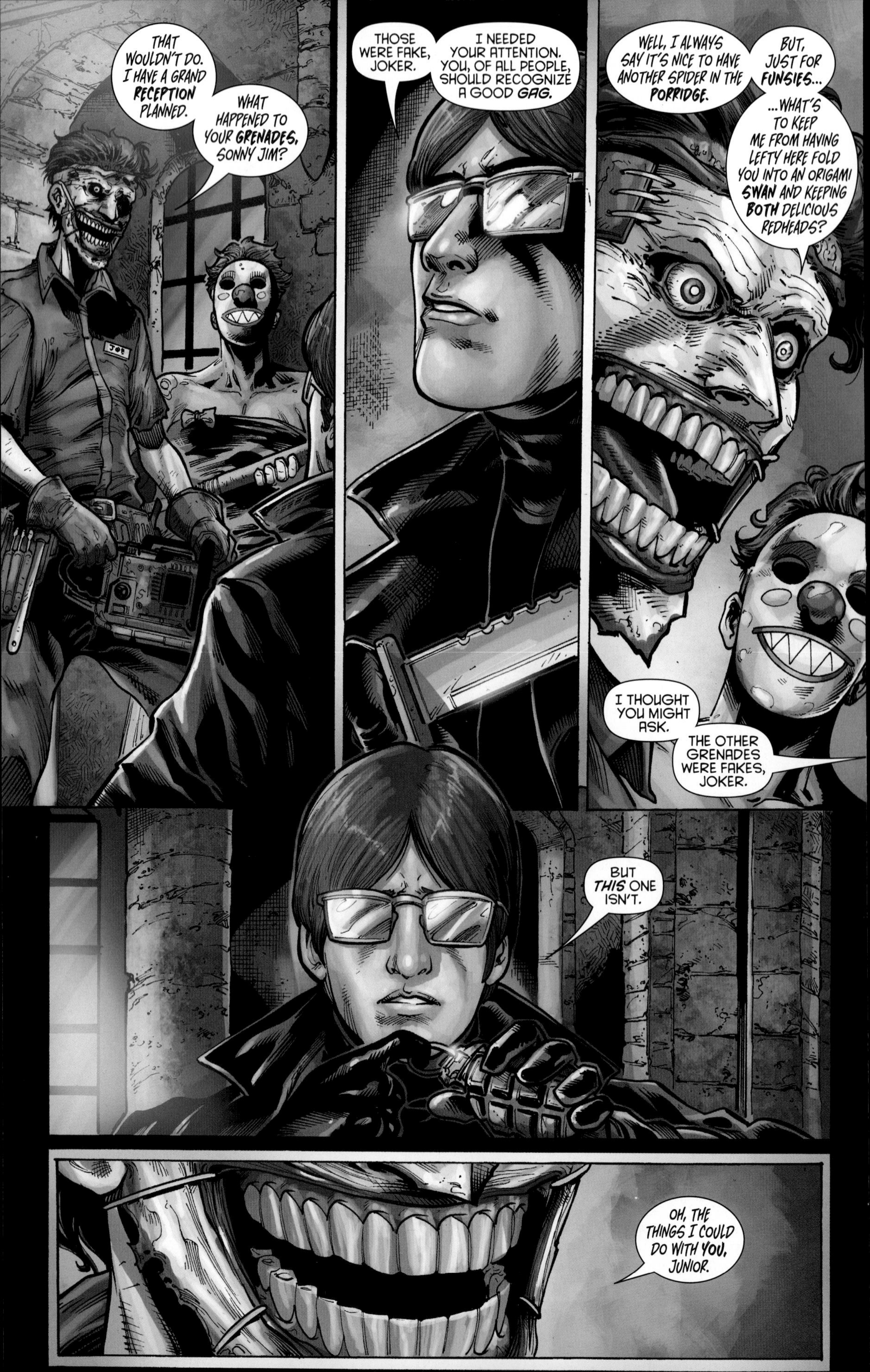
THAT WOULDN'T DO. I HAVE A GRAND RECEPTION PLANNED.
WHAT HAPPENED TO YOUR GRENADES, SONNY JIM?
THOSE WERE FAKE, JOKER.
I NEEDED YOUR ATTENTION. YOU, OF ALL PEOPLE, SHOULD RECOGNIZE A GOOD GAG.
WELL, I ALWAYS SAY IT'S NICE TO HAVE ANOTHER SPIDER IN THE PORRIDGE.
BUT, JUST FOR FUNSIES...
...WHAT'S TO KEEP ME FROM HAVING LEFTY HERE FOLD YOU INTO AN ORIGAMI SWAN AND KEEPING BOTH DELICIOUS REDHEADS?
I THOUGHT YOU MIGHT ASK.
THE OTHER GRENADES WERE FAKES, JOKER.
BUT THIS ONE ISN'T.
OH, THE THINGS I COULD DO WITH YOU, JUNIOR.

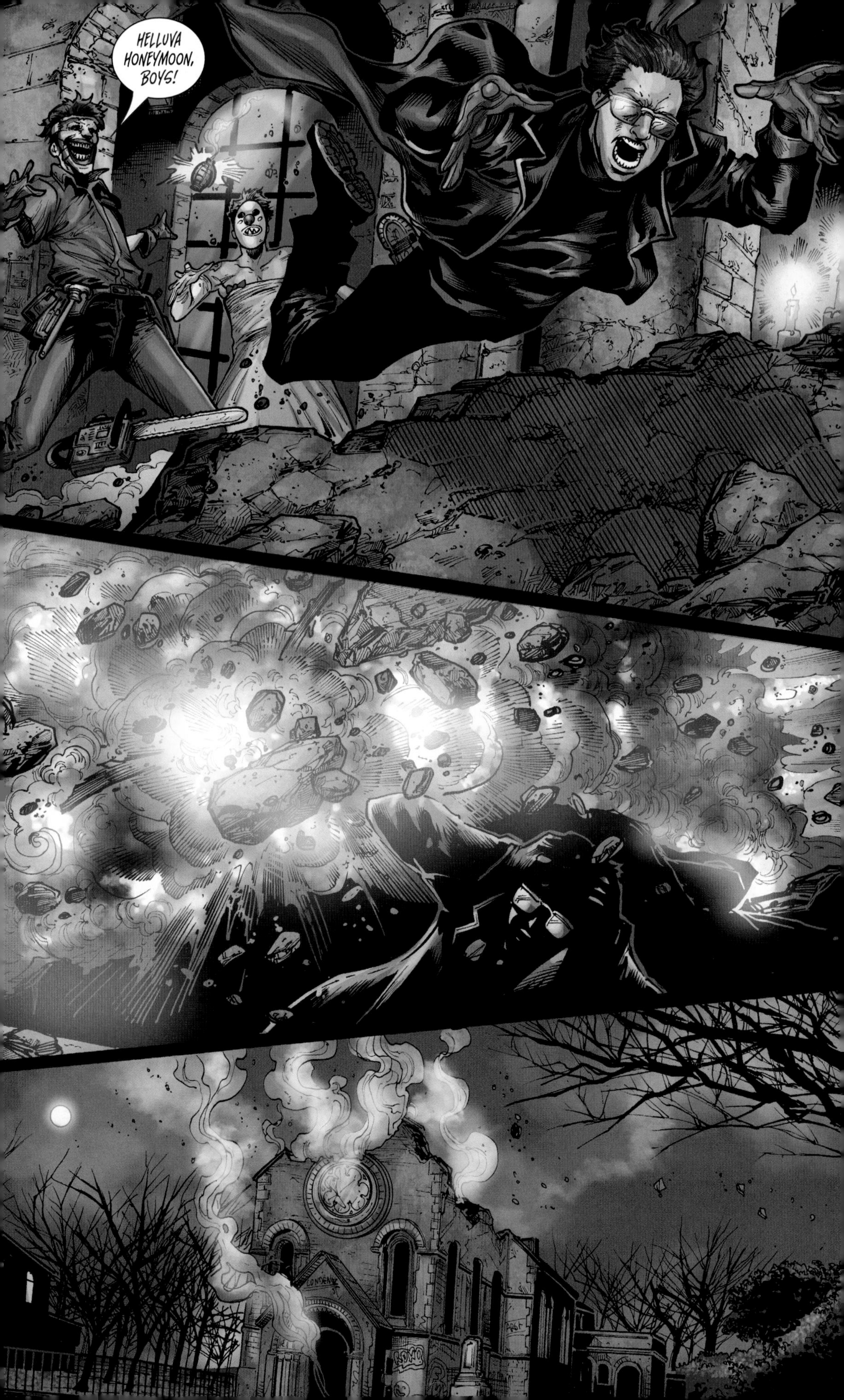
HELLUVA HONEYMOON, BOYS!

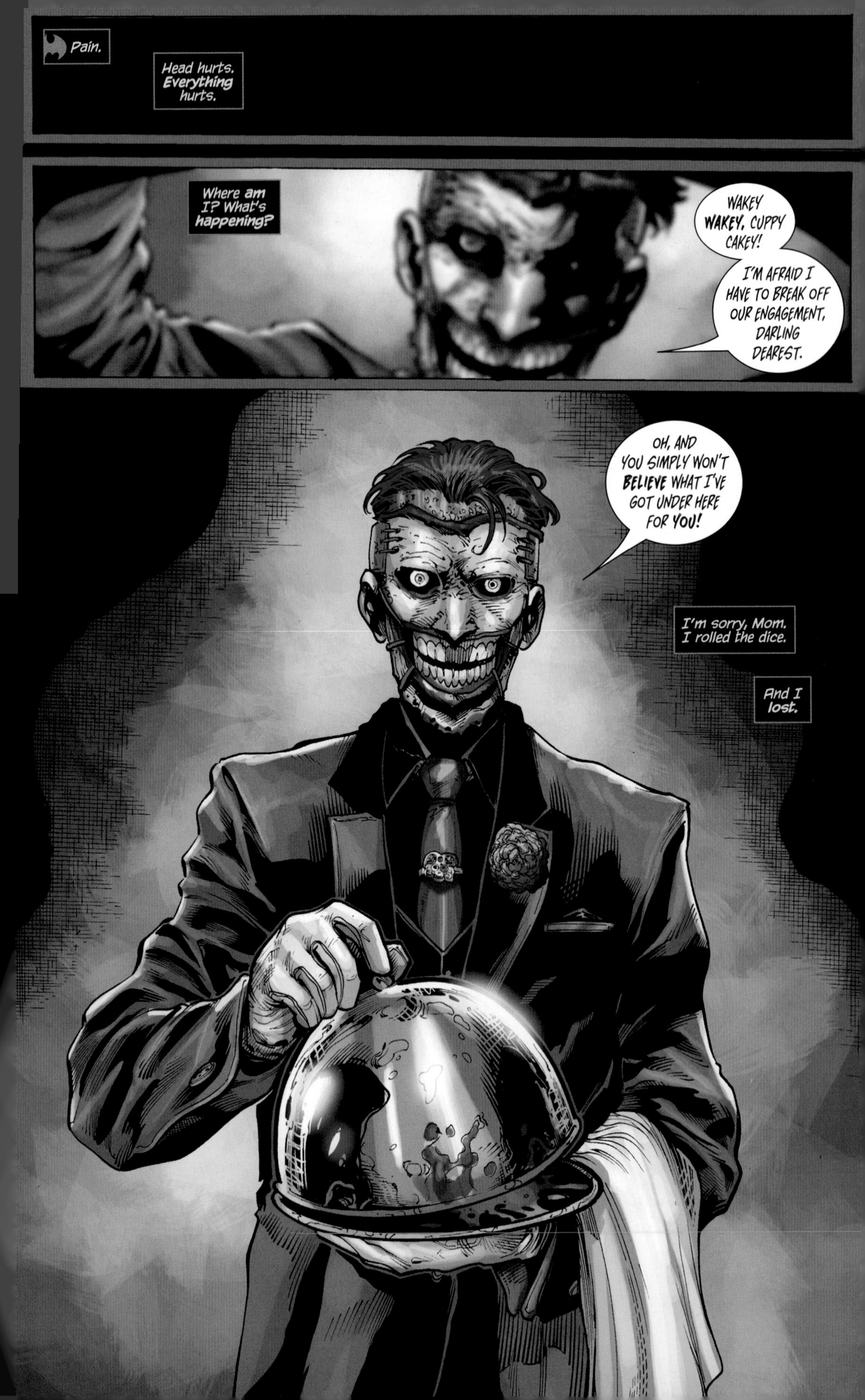
Pain.
Head hurts. Everything hurts.
Where am I? What's happening?
WAKEY WAKEY, CUPPY CAKEY!
I'M AFRAID I HAVE TO BREAK OFF OUR ENGAGEMENT, DARLING DEAREST.
OH, AND YOU SIMPLY WON'T BELIEVE WHAT I'VE GOT UNDER HERE FOR YOU!
I'm sorry, Mom. I rolled the dice.
And I lost.

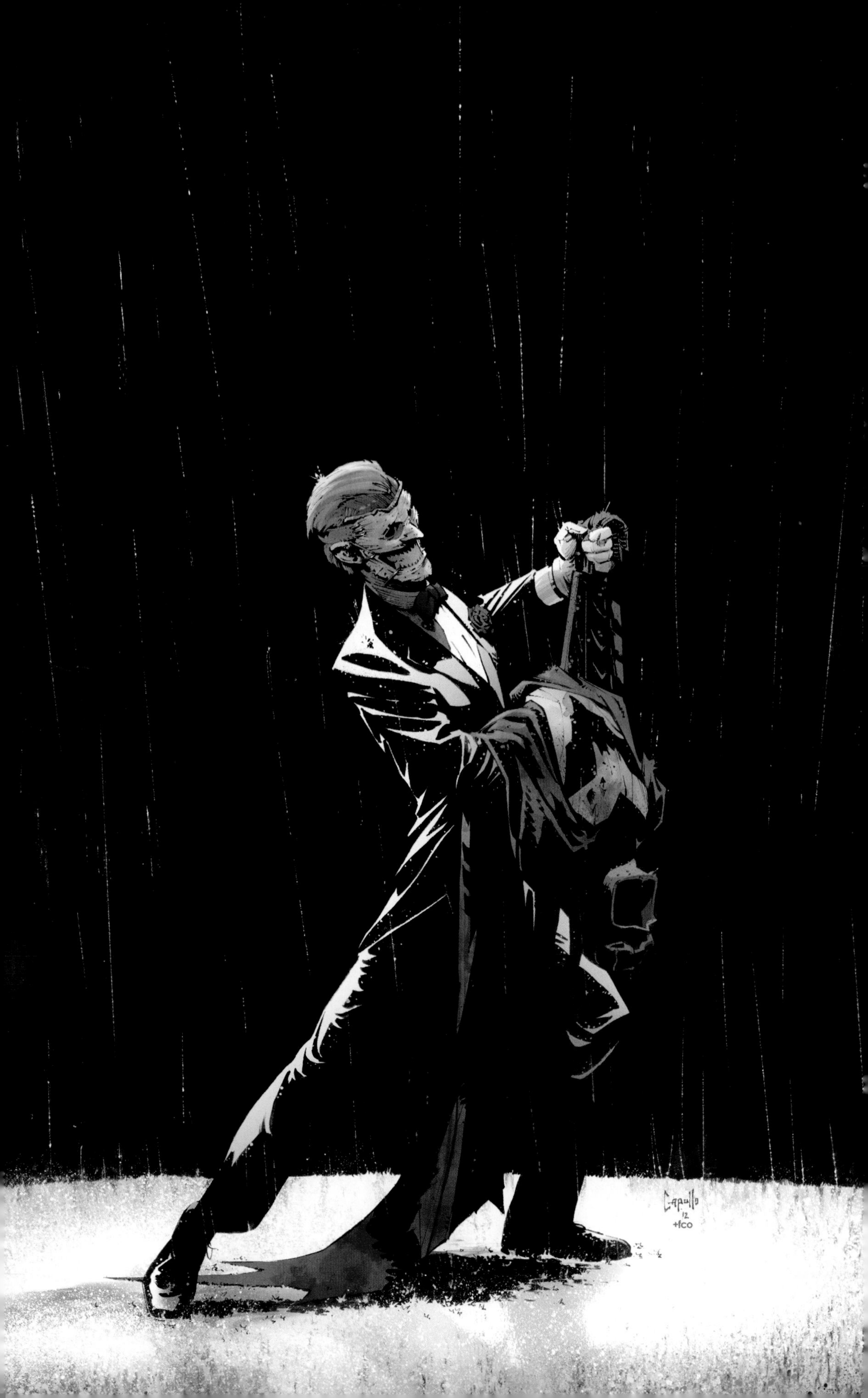

THE PUNCHLINE

SCOTT SNYDER writer GREG CAPULLO penciller JONATHAN GLAPION inker
cover by GREG CAPULLO & FCO PLASCENCIA

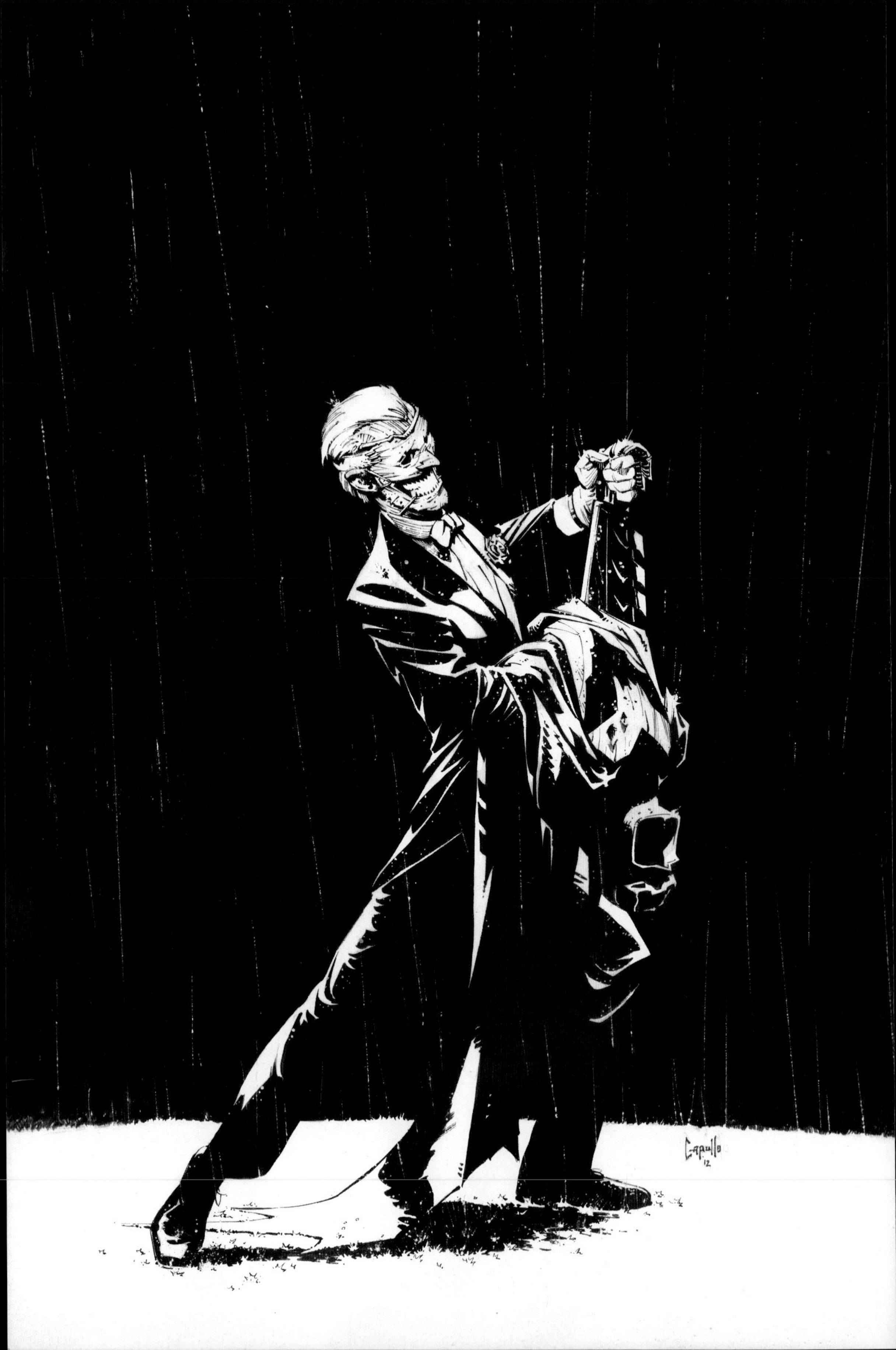

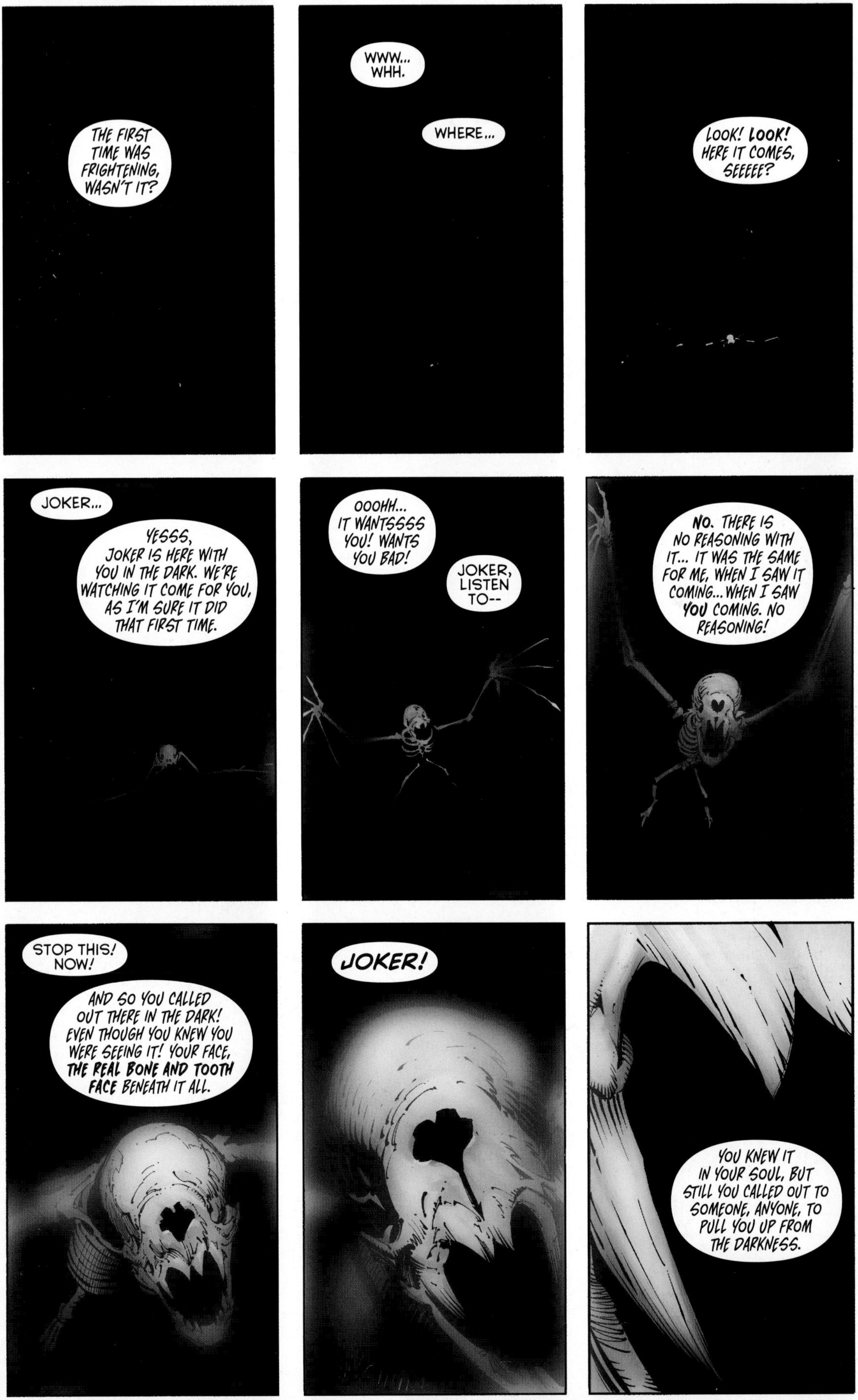
THE FIRST TIME WAS FRIGHTENING, WASN'T IT?
WWW... WHH.
WHERE...
LOOK! LOOK! HERE IT COMES, SEEEEE?
JOKER...
YESSS, JOKER IS HERE WITH YOU IN THE DARK. WE'RE WATCHING IT COME FOR YOU, AS I'M SURE IT DID THAT FIRST TIME.
OOOHH... IT WANTSSSS YOU! WANTS YOU BAD!
JOKER, LISTEN TO--
NO. THERE IS NO REASONING WITH IT... IT WAS THE SAME FOR ME, WHEN I SAW IT COMING... WHEN I SAW YOU COMING. NO REASONING!
STOP THIS! NOW!
AND SO YOU CALLED OUT THERE IN THE DARK! EVEN THOUGH YOU KNEW YOU WERE SEEING IT! YOUR FACE, THE REAL BONE AND TOOTH FACE BENEATH IT ALL.
JOKER!
YOU KNEW IT IN YOUR SOUL, BUT STILL YOU CALLED OUT TO SOMEONE, ANYONE, TO PULL YOU UP FROM THE DARKNESS.

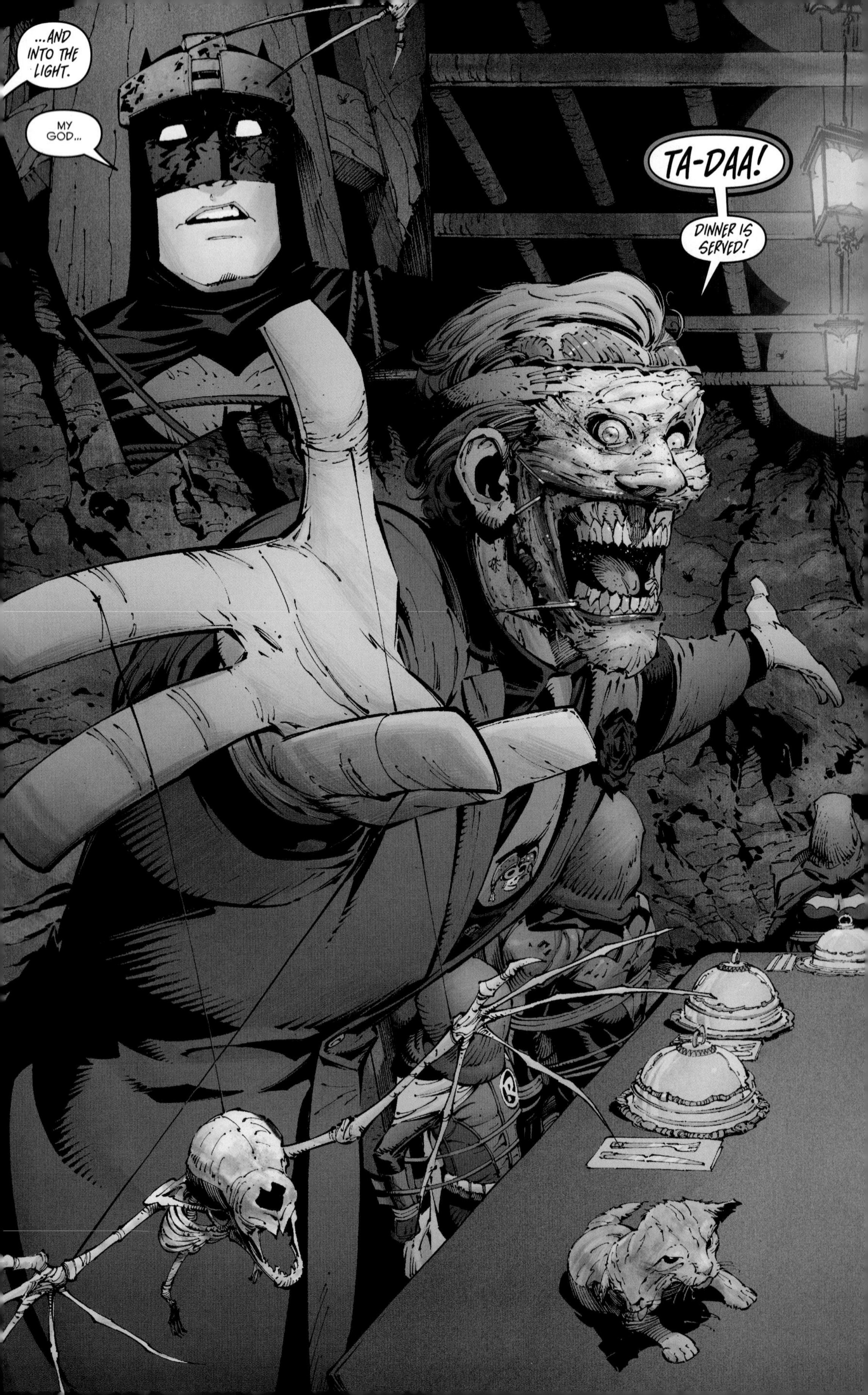
...AND INTO THE LIGHT.
MY GOD...
TA-DAA!
DINNER IS SERVED!

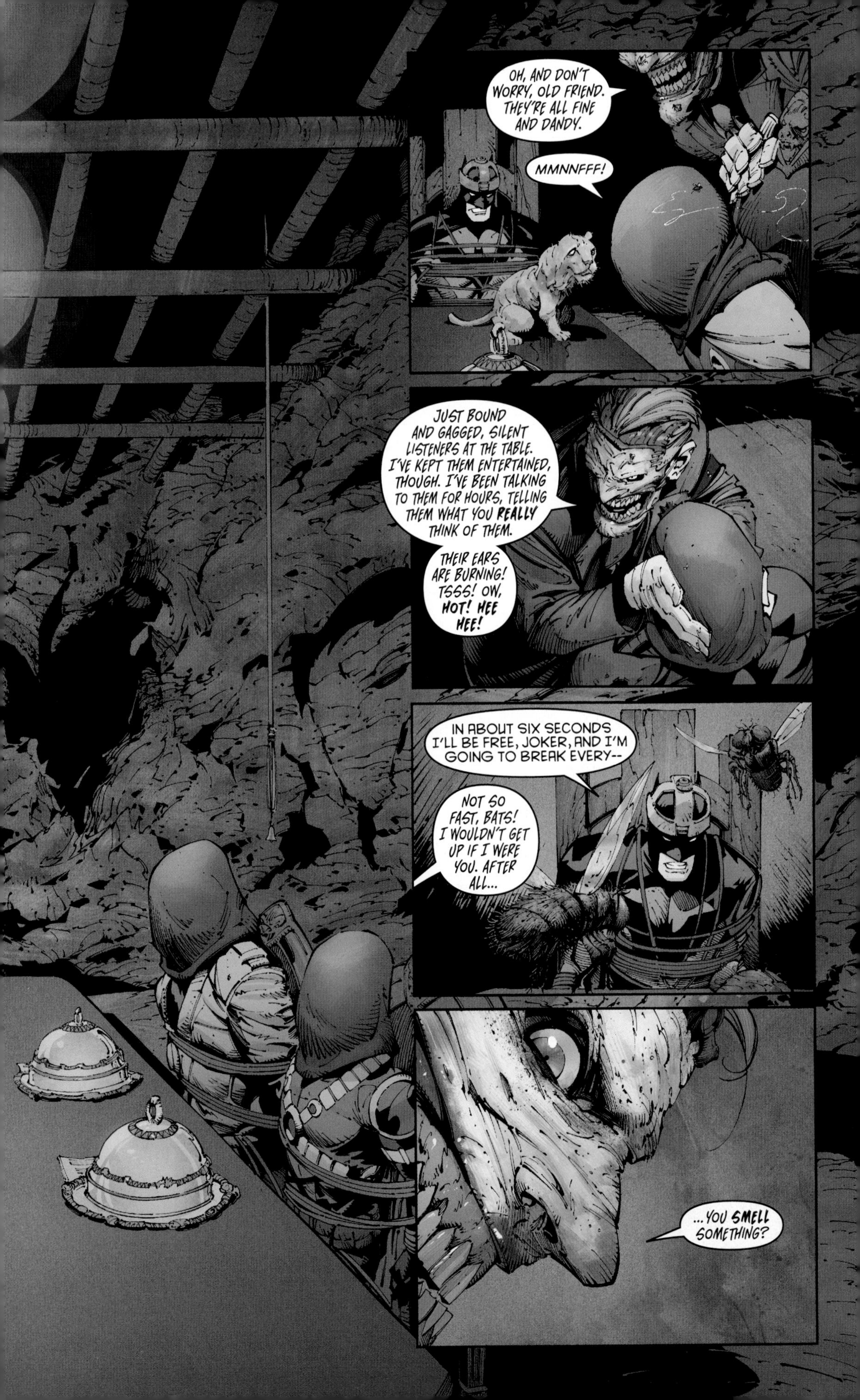
OH, AND DON'T WORRY, OLD FRIEND. THEY'RE ALL FINE AND DANDY.
MMNNFFF!
JUST BOUND AND GAGGED, SILENT LISTENERS AT THE TABLE. I'VE KEPT THEM ENTERTAINED, THOUGH. I'VE BEEN TALKING TO THEM FOR HOURS, TELLING THEM WHAT YOU **REALLY** THINK OF THEM.
THEIR EARS ARE BURNING! TSSS! OW, HOT! **HEE HEE!**
IN ABOUT SIX SECONDS I'LL BE FREE, JOKER, AND I'M GOING TO BREAK EVERY--
NOT SO FAST, BATS! I WOULDN'T GET UP IF I WERE YOU. AFTER ALL...
...YOU **SMELL** SOMETHING?

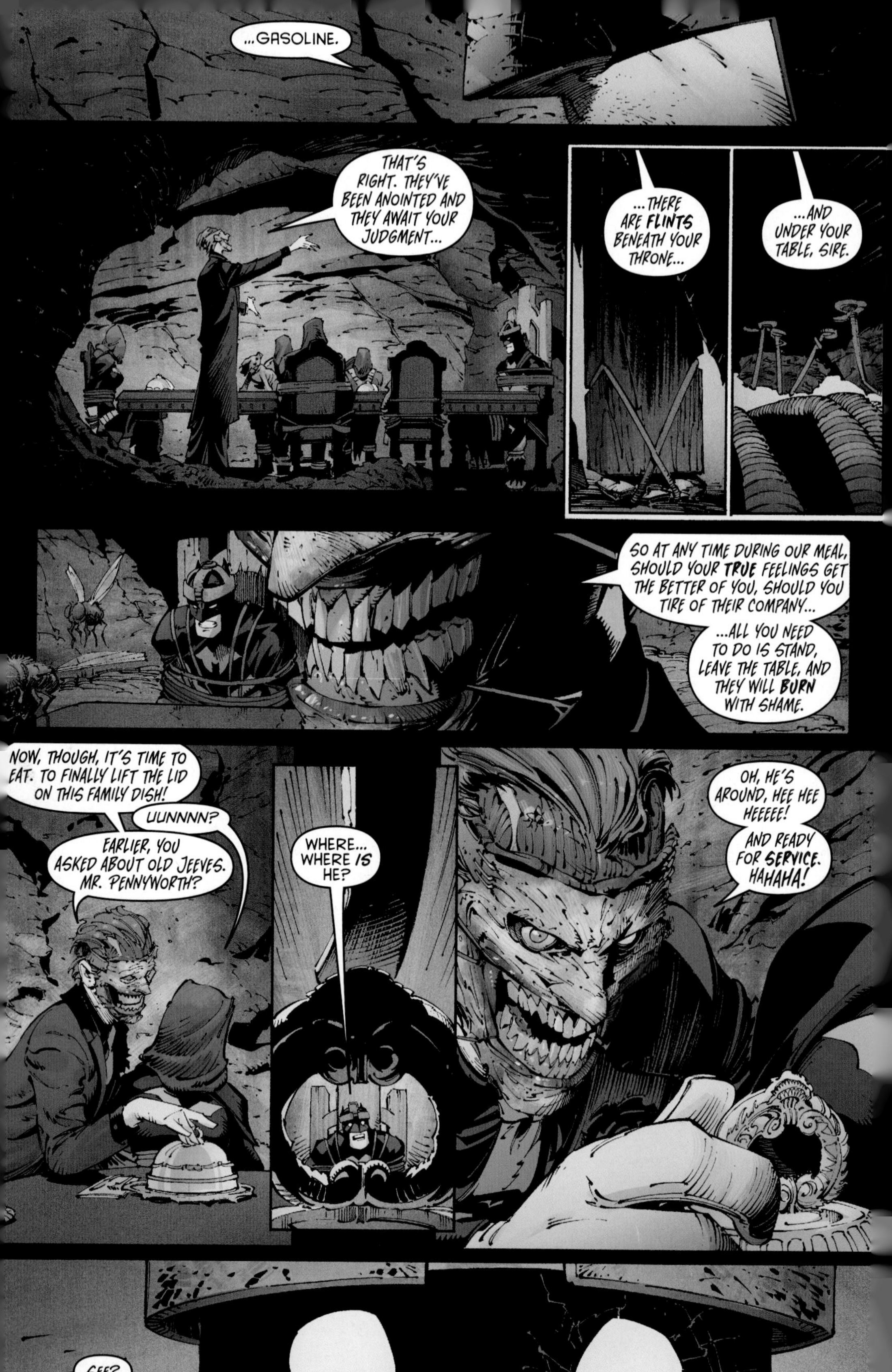
...GASOLINE.
THAT'S RIGHT. THEY'VE BEEN ANOINTED AND THEY AWAIT YOUR JUDGMENT...
...THERE ARE FLINTS BENEATH YOUR THRONE...
...AND UNDER YOUR TABLE, SIRE.
SO AT ANY TIME DURING OUR MEAL, SHOULD YOUR TRUE FEELINGS GET THE BETTER OF YOU, SHOULD YOU TIRE OF THEIR COMPANY...
...ALL YOU NEED TO DO IS STAND, LEAVE THE TABLE, AND THEY WILL BURN WITH SHAME.
NOW, THOUGH, IT'S TIME TO EAT. TO FINALLY LIFT THE LID ON THIS FAMILY DISH!
UUNNNN?
EARLIER, YOU ASKED ABOUT OLD JEEVES. MR. PENNYWORTH?
WHERE... WHERE IS HE?
OH, HE'S AROUND, HEE HEE HEEEEE!
AND READY FOR SERVICE. HAHAHA!
SEE?

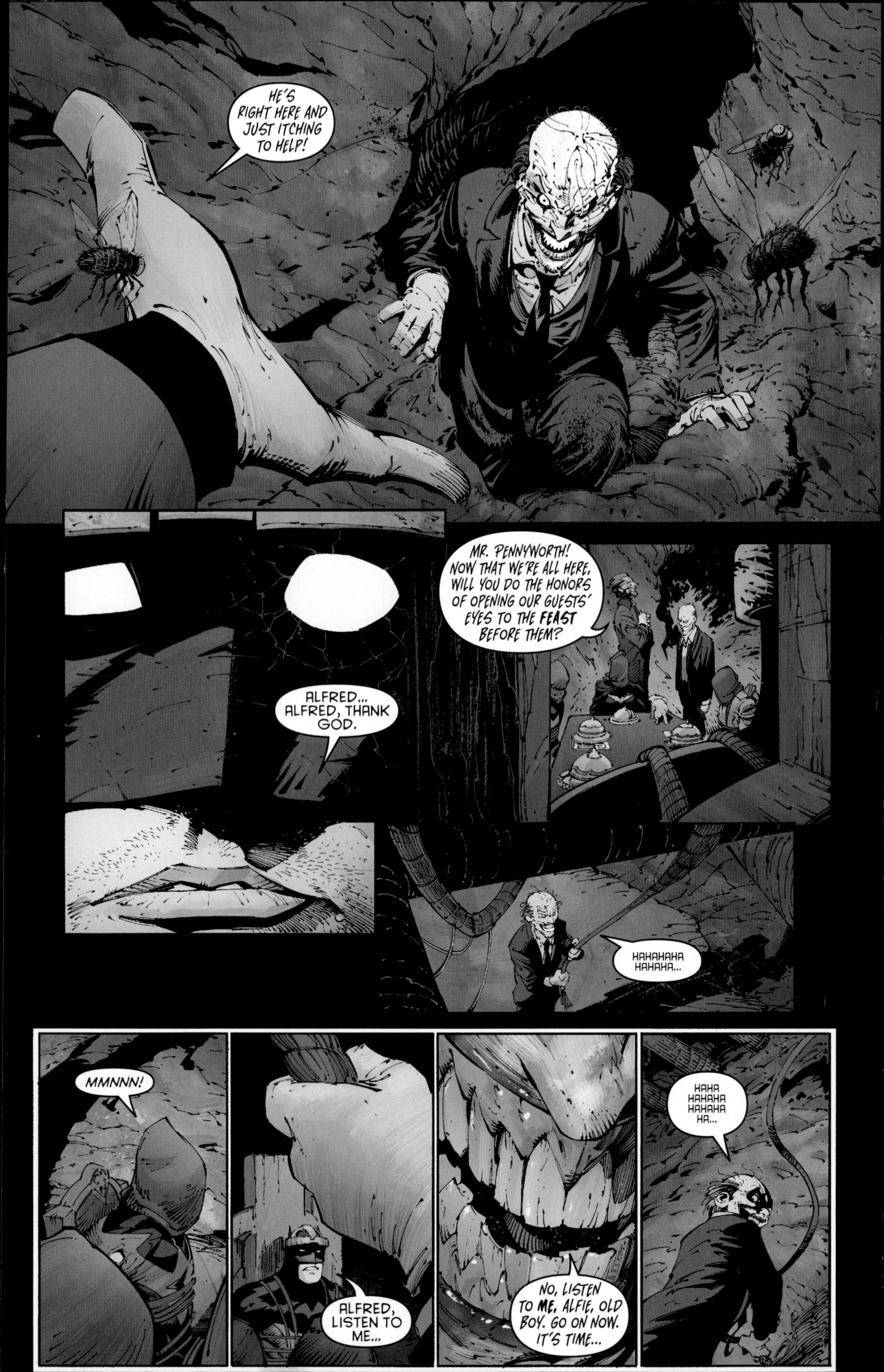
HE'S RIGHT HERE AND JUST ITCHING TO HELP!
MR. PENNYWORTH! NOW THAT WE'RE ALL HERE, WILL YOU DO THE HONORS OF OPENING OUR GUESTS' EYES TO THE FEAST BEFORE THEM?
ALFRED... ALFRED, THANK GOD.
HAHAHAHA HAHAHA...
MMNNN!
ALFRED, LISTEN TO ME...
NO, LISTEN TO ME, ALFIE, OLD BOY. GO ON NOW. IT'S TIME...
HAHA HAHAHA HAHAHA HA...

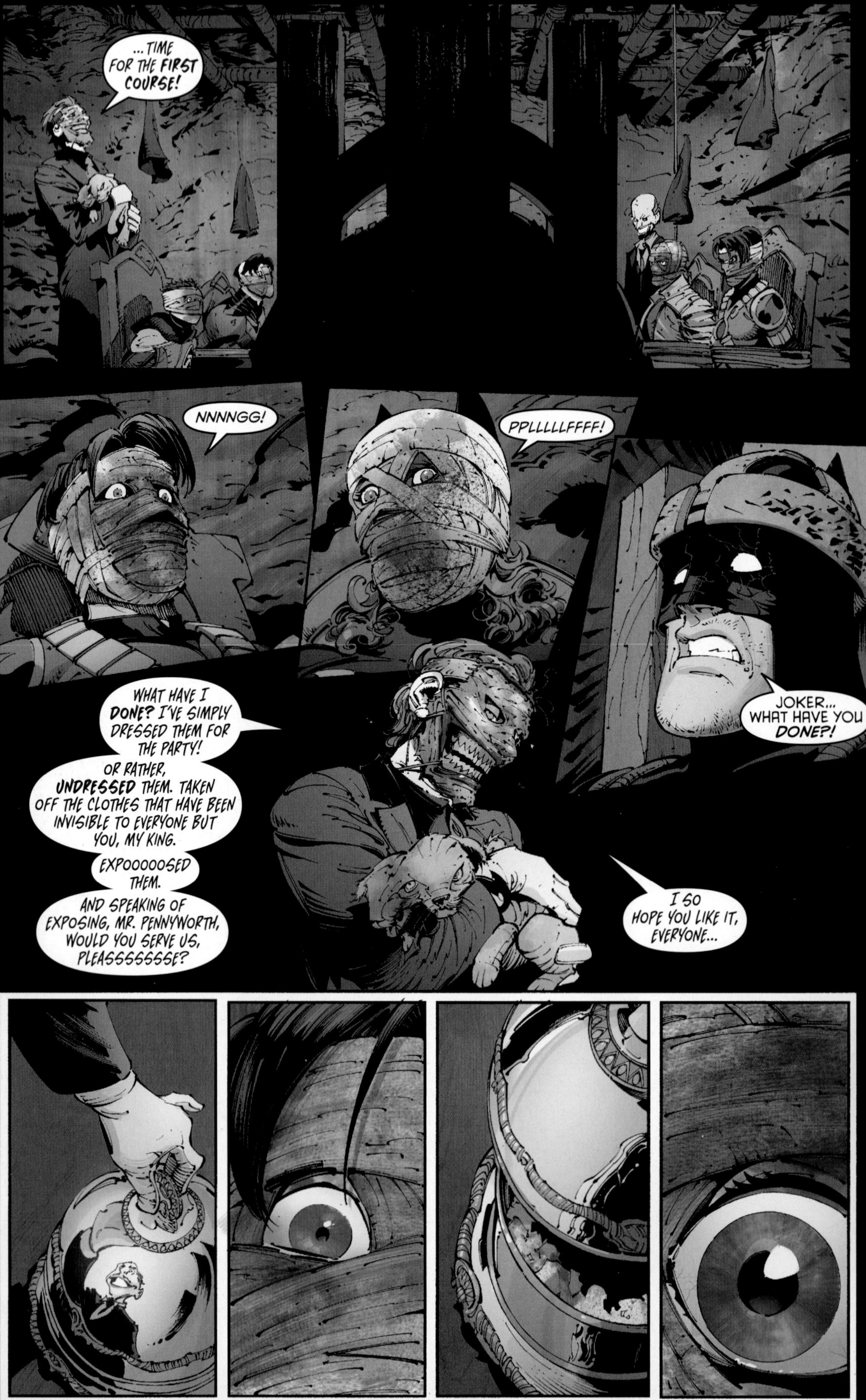
...TIME FOR THE FIRST COURSE!
NNNNGG!
PPLLLLLLFFFF!
JOKER... WHAT HAVE YOU DONE?!
WHAT HAVE I DONE? I'VE SIMPLY DRESSED THEM FOR THE PARTY!
OR RATHER, UNDRESSED THEM. TAKEN OFF THE CLOTHES THAT HAVE BEEN INVISIBLE TO EVERYONE BUT YOU, MY KING.
EXPOOOOOSED THEM.
AND SPEAKING OF EXPOSING, MR. PENNYWORTH, WOULD YOU SERVE US, PLEASSSSSSSE?
I SO HOPE YOU LIKE IT, EVERYONE...

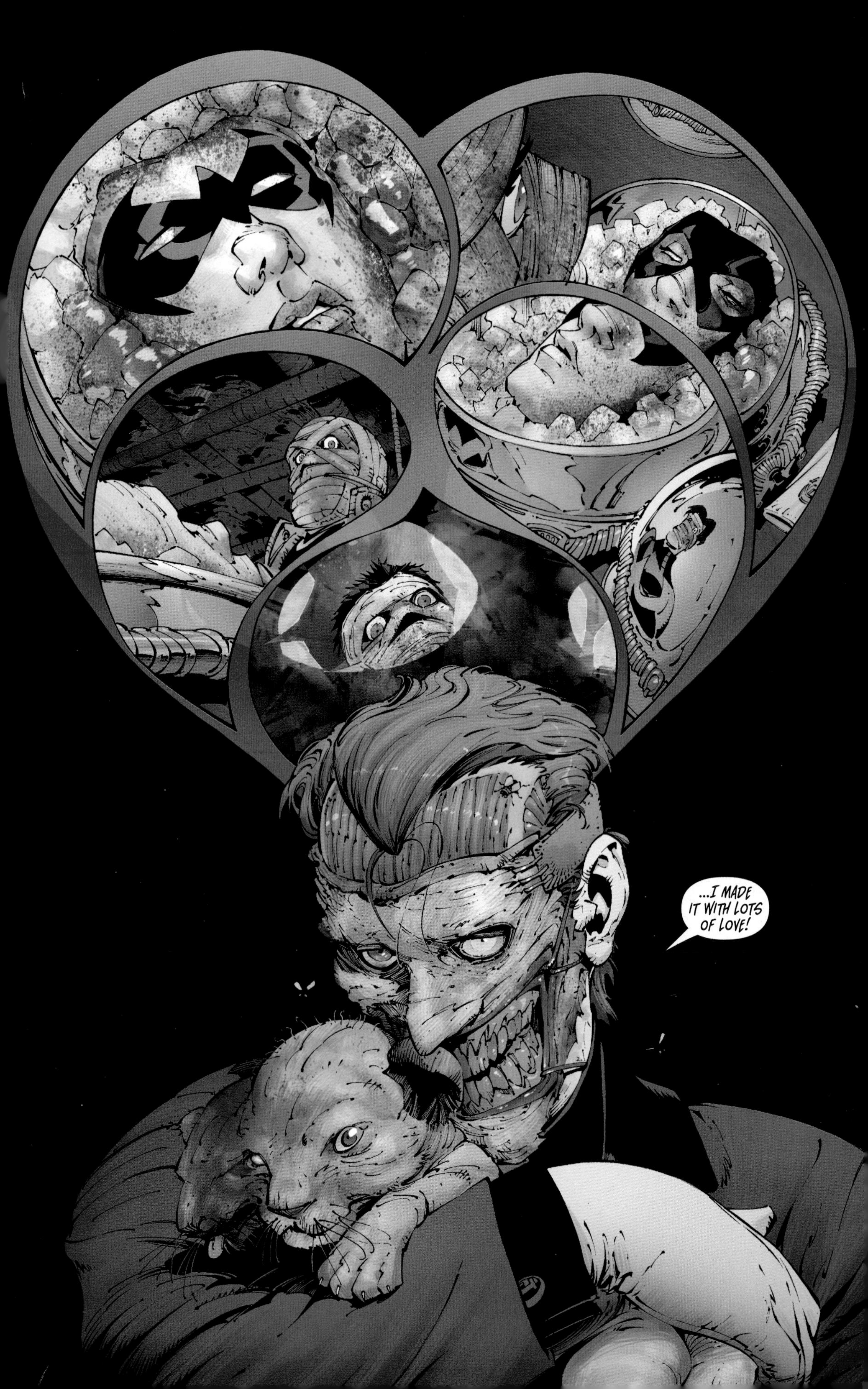
...I MADE IT WITH LOTS OF LOVE!

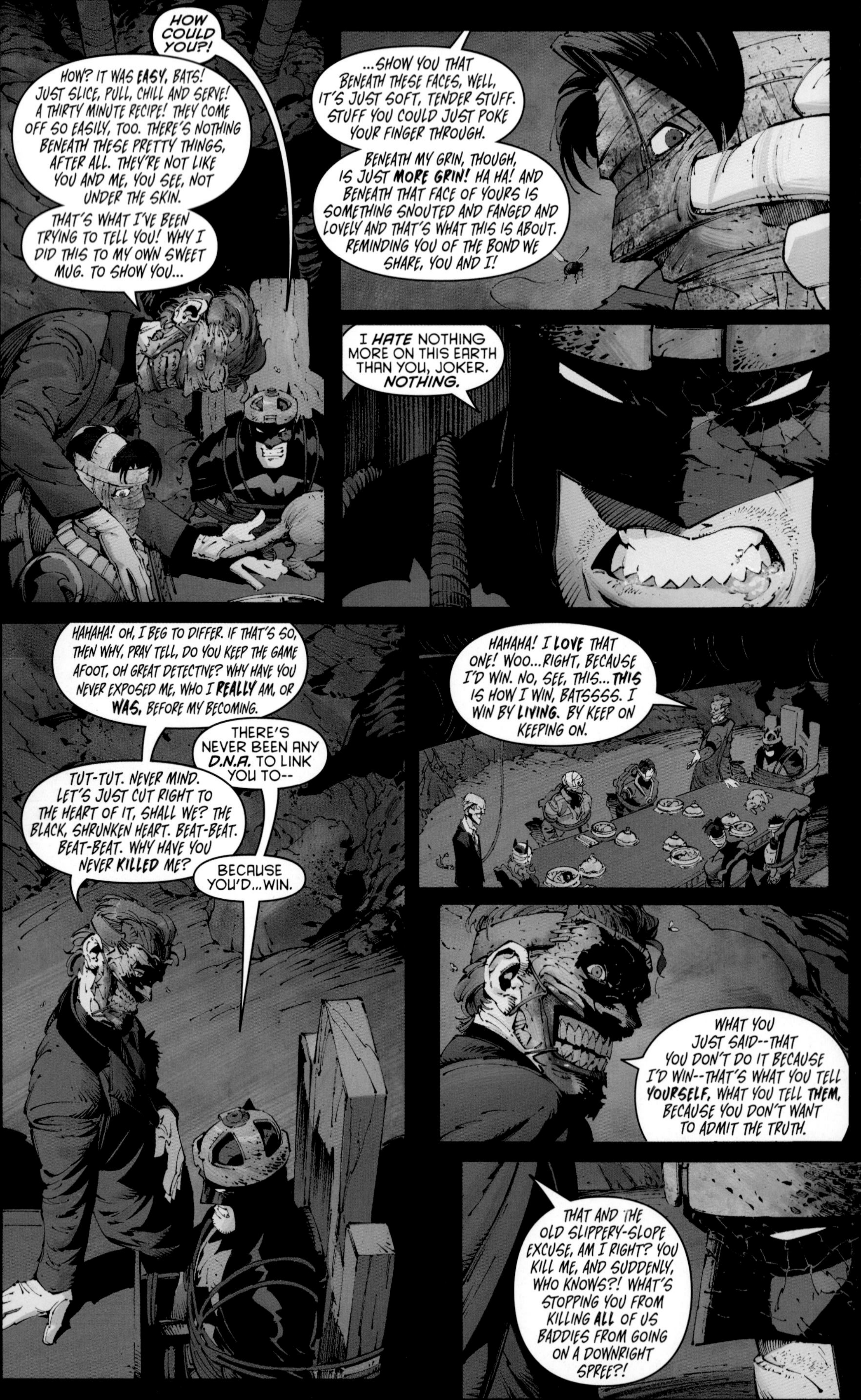

HOW COULD YOU?!
HOW? IT WAS EASY, BATS! JUST SLICE, PULL, CHILL AND SERVE! A THIRTY MINUTE RECIPE! THEY COME OFF SO EASILY, TOO. THERE'S NOTHING BENEATH THESE PRETTY THINGS, AFTER ALL. THEY'RE NOT LIKE YOU AND ME, YOU SEE, NOT UNDER THE SKIN.
THAT'S WHAT I'VE BEEN TRYING TO TELL YOU! WHY I DID THIS TO MY OWN SWEET MUG. TO SHOW YOU...
...SHOW YOU THAT BENEATH THESE FACES, WELL, IT'S JUST SOFT, TENDER STUFF. STUFF YOU COULD JUST POKE YOUR FINGER THROUGH.
BENEATH MY GRIN, THOUGH, IS JUST MORE GRIN! HA HA! AND BENEATH THAT FACE OF YOURS IS SOMETHING SNOUTED AND FANGED AND LOVELY AND THAT'S WHAT THIS IS ABOUT. REMINDING YOU OF THE BOND WE SHARE, YOU AND I!
I HATE NOTHING MORE ON THIS EARTH THAN YOU, JOKER. NOTHING.
HAHAHA! OH, I BEG TO DIFFER. IF THAT'S SO, THEN WHY, PRAY TELL, DO YOU KEEP THE GAME AFOOT, OH GREAT DETECTIVE? WHY HAVE YOU NEVER EXPOSED ME, WHO I REALLY AM, OR WAS, BEFORE MY BECOMING.
THERE'S NEVER BEEN ANY D.N.A. TO LINK YOU TO--
TUT-TUT. NEVER MIND. LET'S JUST CUT RIGHT TO THE HEART OF IT, SHALL WE? THE BLACK, SHRUNKEN HEART. BEAT-BEAT. BEAT-BEAT. WHY HAVE YOU NEVER KILLED ME?
BECAUSE YOU'D...WIN.
HAHAHA! I LOVE THAT ONE! WOO...RIGHT, BECAUSE I'D WIN. NO, SEE, THIS... THIS IS HOW I WIN, BATSSSS. I WIN BY LIVING. BY KEEP ON KEEPING ON.
WHAT YOU JUST SAID--THAT YOU DON'T DO IT BECAUSE I'D WIN--THAT'S WHAT YOU TELL YOURSELF, WHAT YOU TELL THEM, BECAUSE YOU DON'T WANT TO ADMIT THE TRUTH.
THAT AND THE OLD SLIPPERY-SLOPE EXCUSE, AM I RIGHT? YOU KILL ME, AND SUDDENLY, WHO KNOWS?! WHAT'S STOPPING YOU FROM KILLING ALL OF US BADDIES FROM GOING ON A DOWNRIGHT SPREE?!

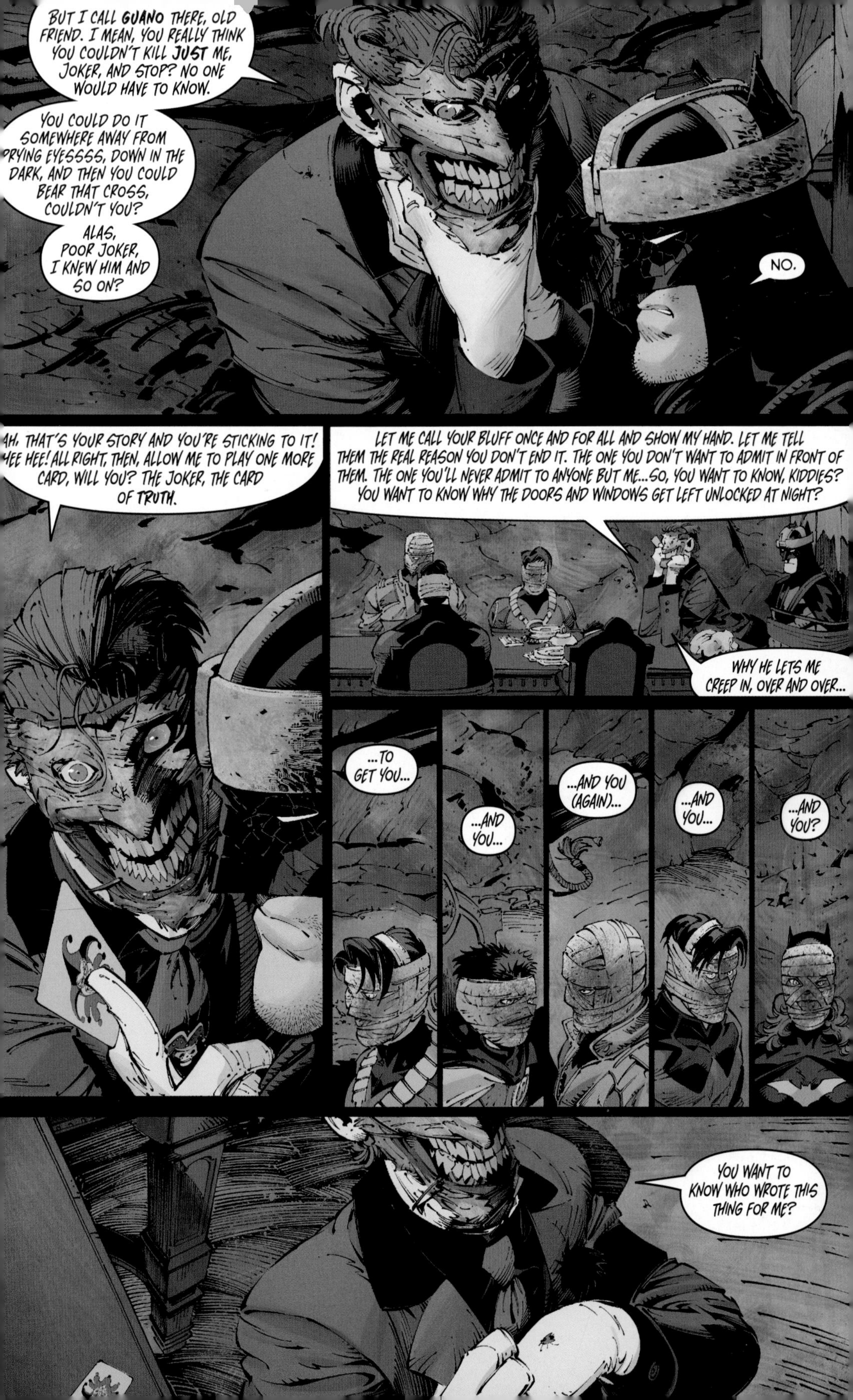
BUT I CALL GUANO THERE, OLD FRIEND. I MEAN, YOU REALLY THINK YOU COULDN'T KILL JUST ME, JOKER, AND STOP? NO ONE WOULD HAVE TO KNOW.
YOU COULD DO IT SOMEWHERE AWAY FROM PRYING EYESSSS, DOWN IN THE DARK, AND THEN YOU COULD BEAR THAT CROSS, COULDN'T YOU?
ALAS, POOR JOKER, I KNEW HIM AND SO ON?
NO.
AH, THAT'S YOUR STORY AND YOU'RE STICKING TO IT! HEE HEE! ALL RIGHT, THEN, ALLOW ME TO PLAY ONE MORE CARD, WILL YOU? THE JOKER, THE CARD OF TRUTH.
LET ME CALL YOUR BLUFF ONCE AND FOR ALL AND SHOW MY HAND. LET ME TELL THEM THE REAL REASON YOU DON'T END IT. THE ONE YOU DON'T WANT TO ADMIT IN FRONT OF THEM. THE ONE YOU'LL NEVER ADMIT TO ANYONE BUT ME...SO, YOU WANT TO KNOW, KIDDIES? YOU WANT TO KNOW WHY THE DOORS AND WINDOWS GET LEFT UNLOCKED AT NIGHT?
WHY HE LETS ME CREEP IN, OVER AND OVER...
...TO GET YOU...
...AND YOU...
...AND YOU (AGAIN)...
...AND YOU...
...AND YOU?
YOU WANT TO KNOW WHO WROTE THIS THING FOR ME?

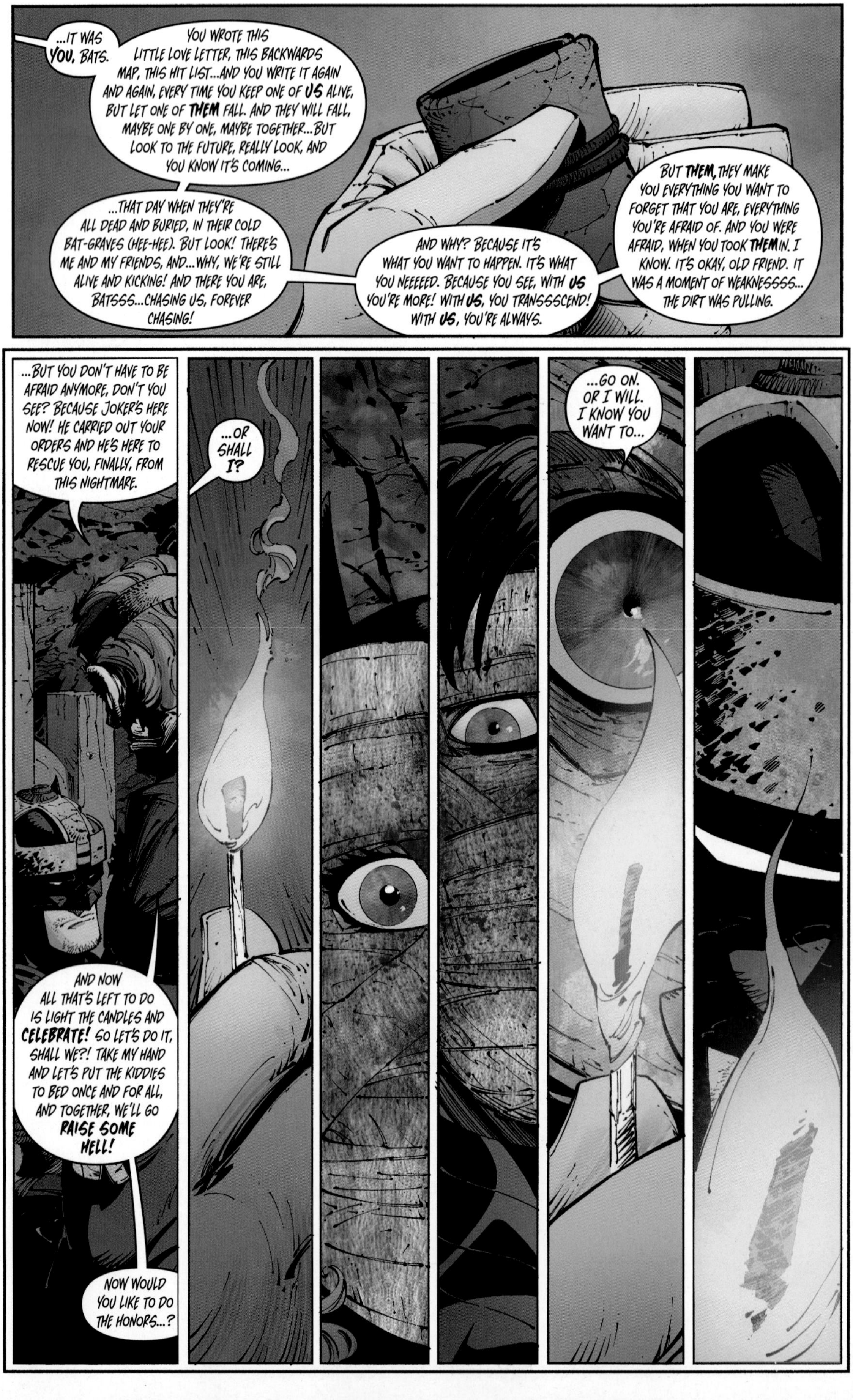
...IT WAS YOU, BATS.
YOU WROTE THIS LITTLE LOVE LETTER, THIS BACKWARDS MAP, THIS HIT LIST...AND YOU WRITE IT AGAIN AND AGAIN, EVERY TIME YOU KEEP ONE OF US ALIVE, BUT LET ONE OF THEM FALL. AND THEY WILL FALL, MAYBE ONE BY ONE, MAYBE TOGETHER...BUT LOOK TO THE FUTURE, REALLY LOOK, AND YOU KNOW IT'S COMING...
...THAT DAY WHEN THEY'RE ALL DEAD AND BURIED, IN THEIR COLD BAT-GRAVES (HEE-HEE). BUT LOOK! THERE'S ME AND MY FRIENDS, AND...WHY, WE'RE STILL ALIVE AND KICKING! AND THERE YOU ARE, BATSSS...CHASING US, FOREVER CHASING!
AND WHY? BECAUSE IT'S WHAT YOU WANT TO HAPPEN. IT'S WHAT YOU NEEEEED. BECAUSE YOU SEE, WITH US YOU'RE MORE! WITH US, YOU TRANSSSCEND! WITH US, YOU'RE ALWAYS.
BUT THEM, THEY MAKE YOU EVERYTHING YOU WANT TO FORGET THAT YOU ARE, EVERYTHING YOU'RE AFRAID OF. AND YOU WERE AFRAID, WHEN YOU TOOK THEM IN. I KNOW. IT'S OKAY, OLD FRIEND. IT WAS A MOMENT OF WEAKNESSSS... THE DIRT WAS PULLING.
...BUT YOU DON'T HAVE TO BE AFRAID ANYMORE, DON'T YOU SEE? BECAUSE JOKER'S HERE NOW! HE CARRIED OUT YOUR ORDERS AND HE'S HERE TO RESCUE YOU, FINALLY, FROM THIS NIGHTMARE.
AND NOW ALL THAT'S LEFT TO DO IS LIGHT THE CANDLES AND CELEBRATE! SO LET'S DO IT, SHALL WE?! TAKE MY HAND AND LET'S PUT THE KIDDIES TO BED ONCE AND FOR ALL, AND TOGETHER, WE'LL GO RAISE SOME HELL!
NOW WOULD YOU LIKE TO DO THE HONORS...?
...OR SHALL I?
...GO ON. OR I WILL. I KNOW YOU WANT TO...

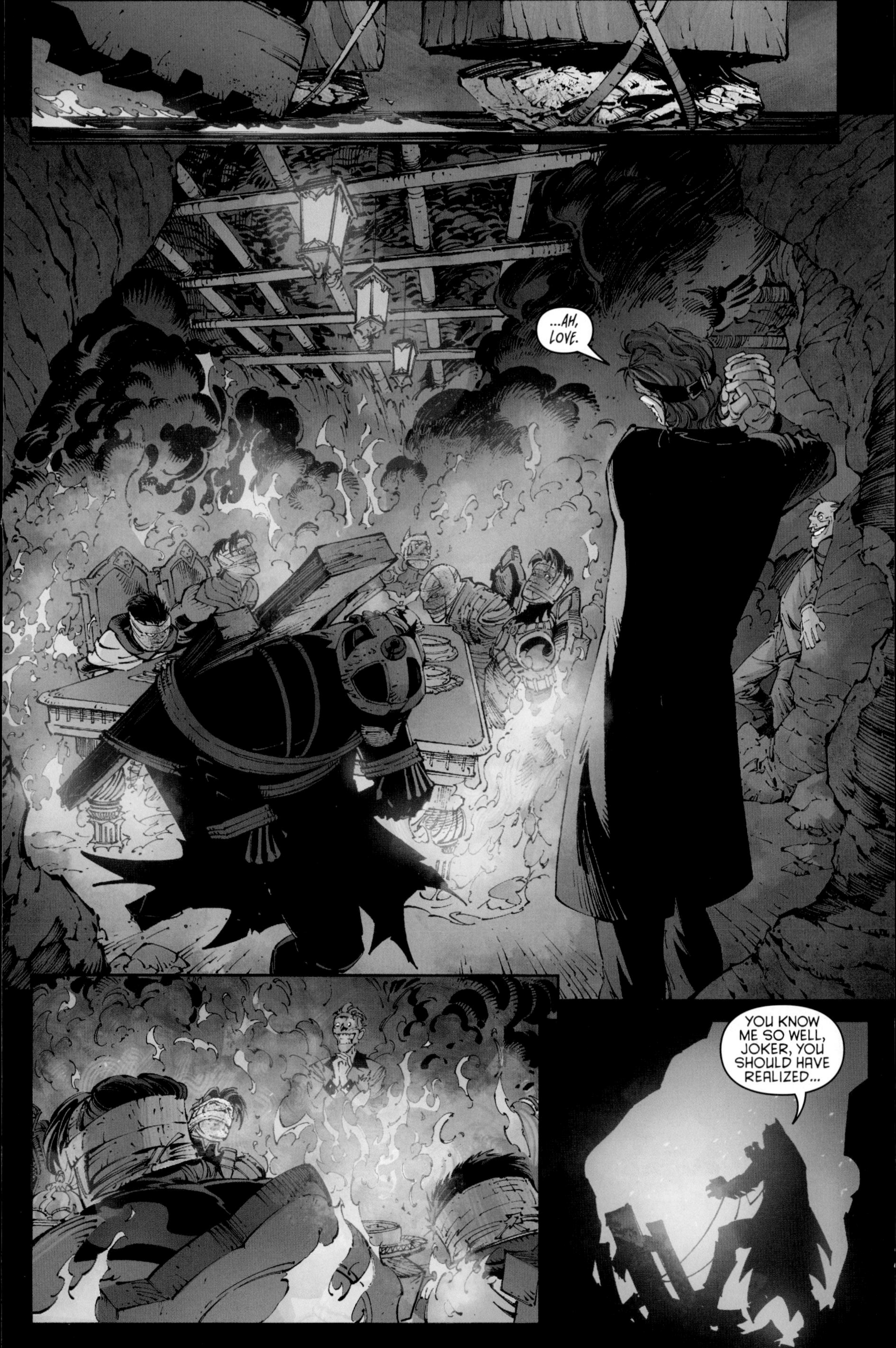
...AH, LOVE.
YOU KNOW ME SO WELL, JOKER, YOU SHOULD HAVE REALIZED...

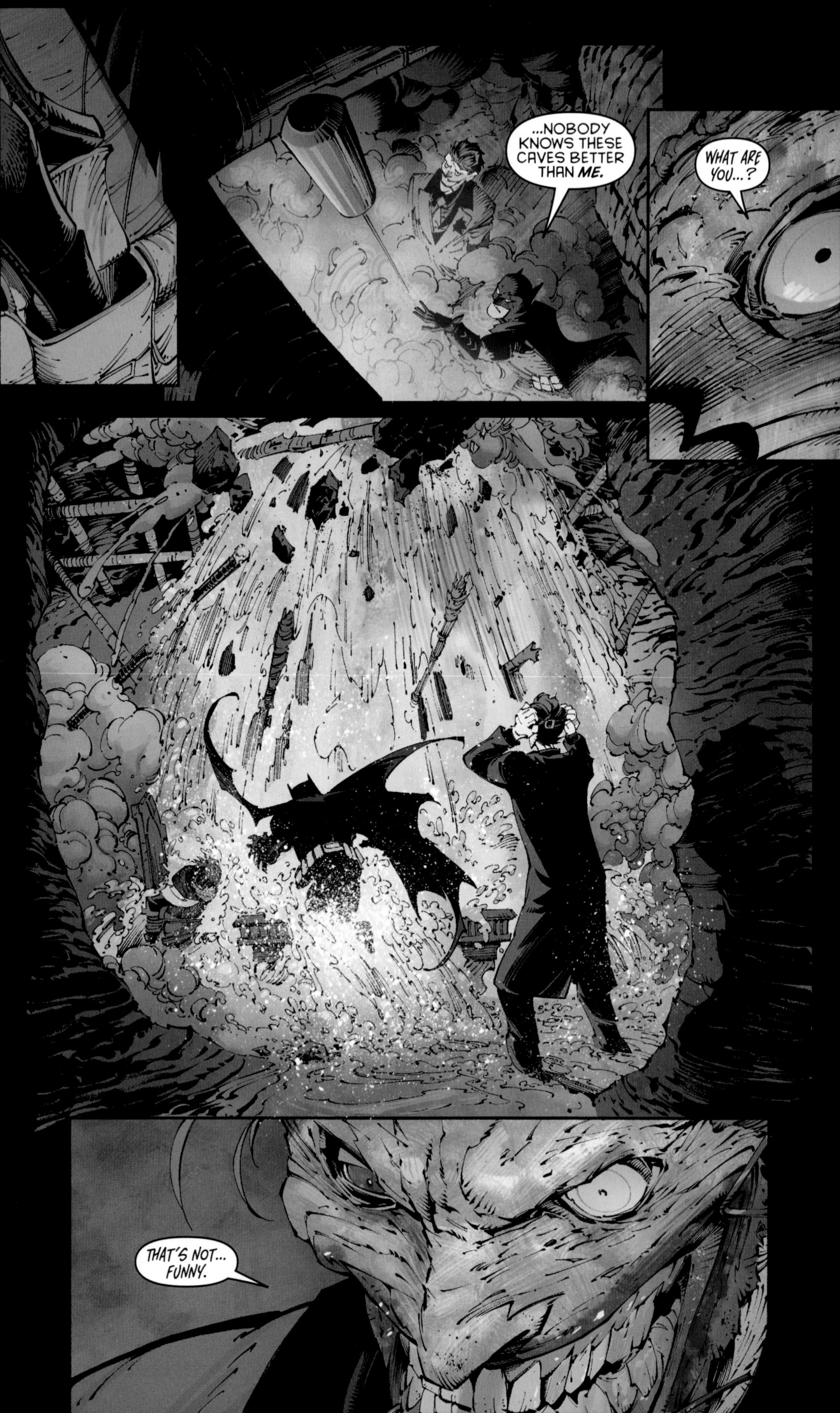
...NOBODY KNOWS THESE CAVES BETTER THAN *ME.*
WHAT ARE YOU...?
THAT'S NOT... FUNNY.

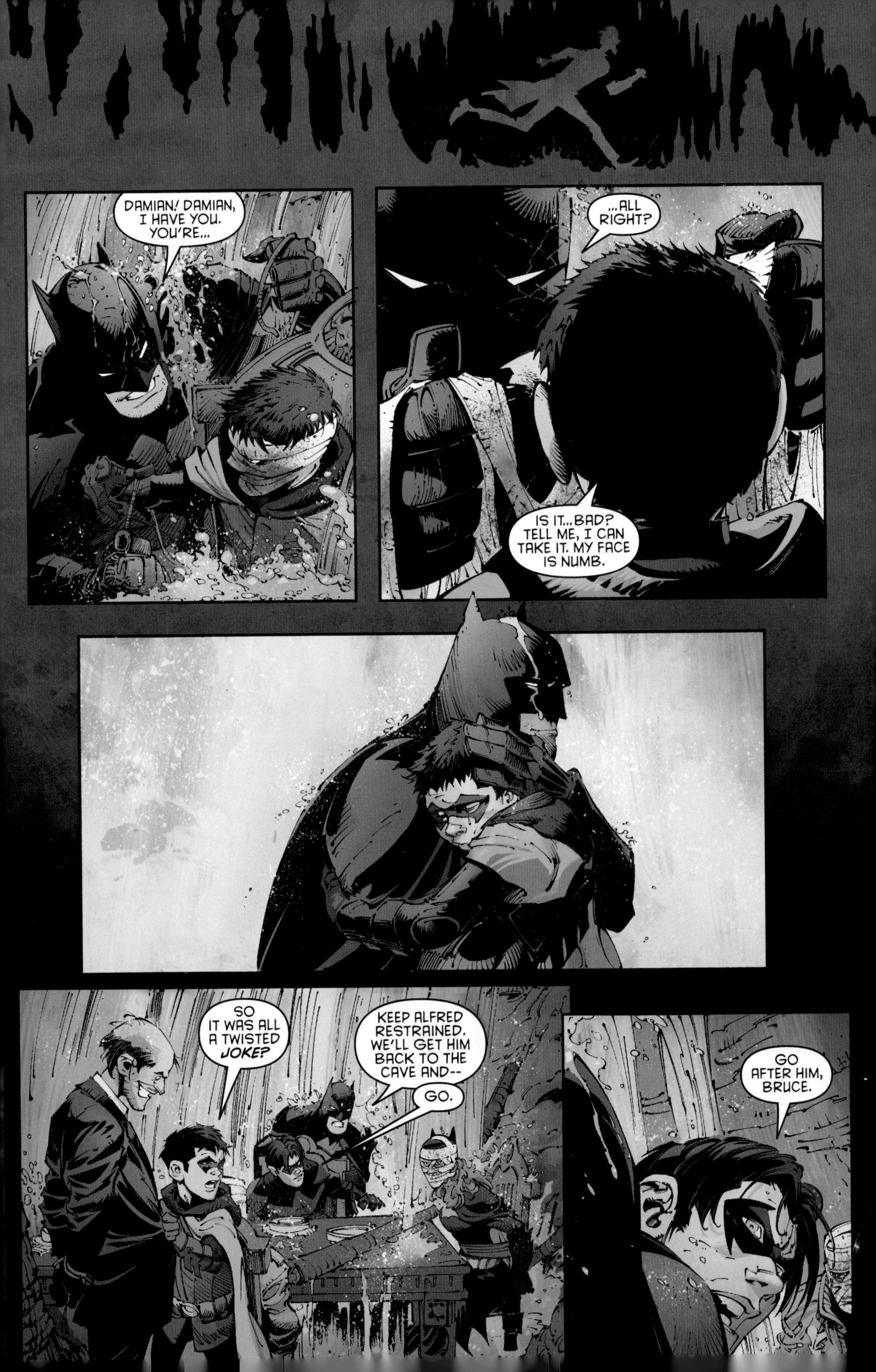
DAMIAN! DAMIAN, I HAVE YOU. YOU'RE...
...ALL RIGHT?
IS IT...BAD? TELL ME, I CAN TAKE IT. MY FACE IS NUMB.
SO IT WAS ALL A TWISTED JOKE?
KEEP ALFRED RESTRAINED. WE'LL GET HIM BACK TO THE CAVE AND--
GO.
GO AFTER HIM, BRUCE.

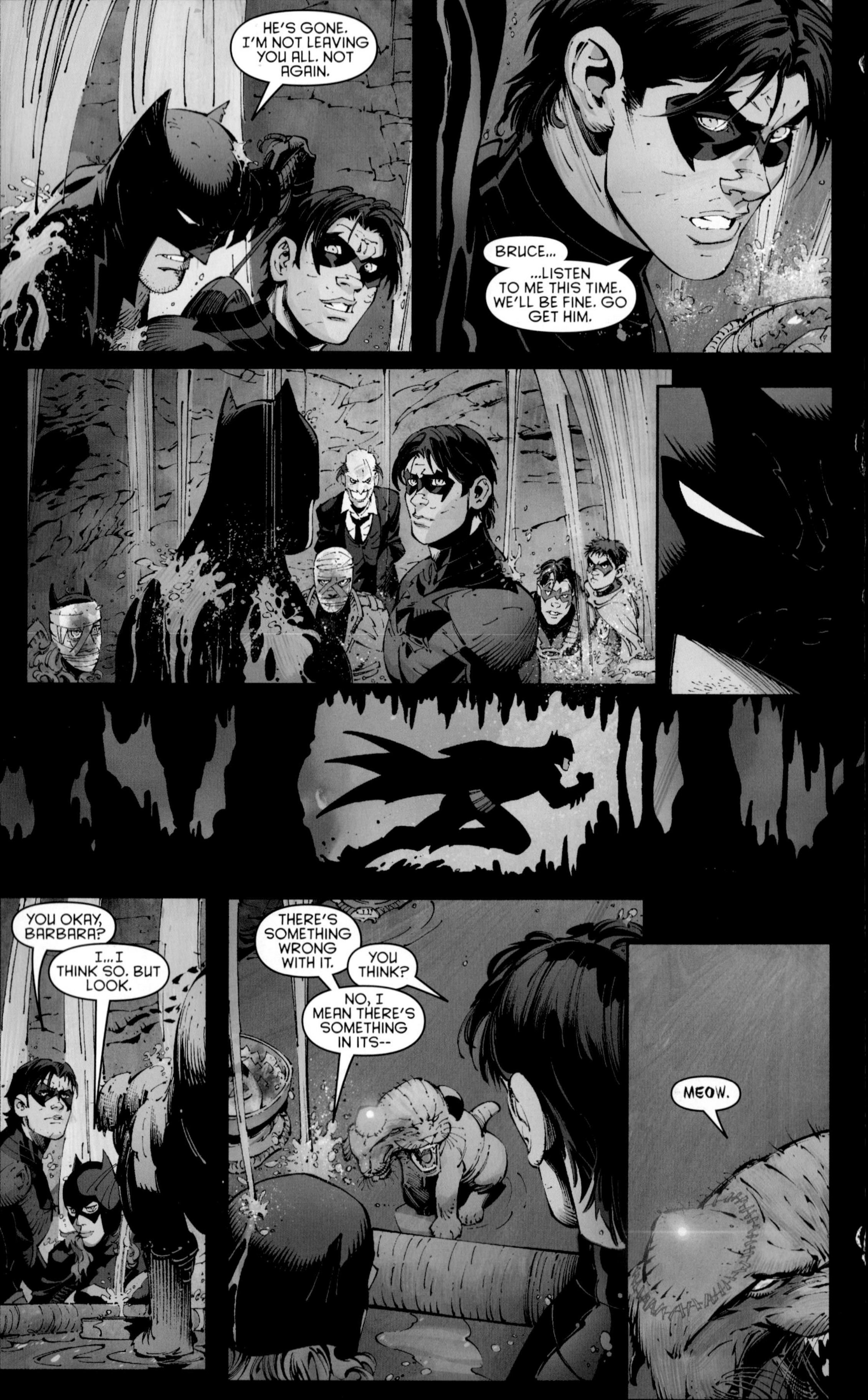
HE'S GONE. I'M NOT LEAVING YOU ALL. NOT AGAIN.
BRUCE...
...LISTEN TO ME THIS TIME. WE'LL BE FINE. GO GET HIM.
YOU OKAY, BARBARA?
I...I THINK SO. BUT LOOK.
THERE'S SOMETHING WRONG WITH IT.
YOU THINK?
NO, I MEAN THERE'S SOMETHING IN ITS--
MEOW.

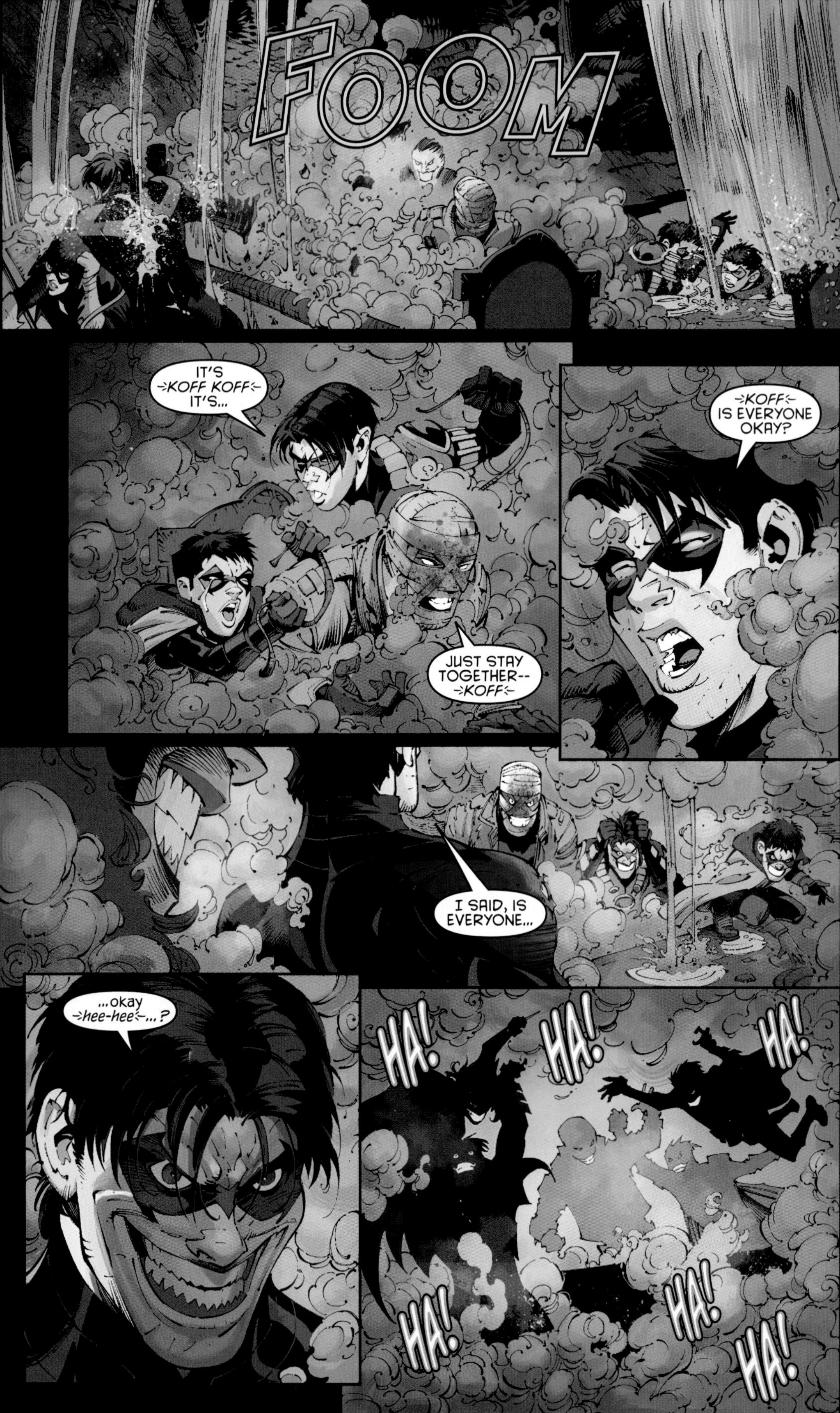
FOOM
IT'S -KOFF KOFF- IT'S...
JUST STAY TOGETHER-- -KOFF-
-KOFF- IS EVERYONE OKAY?
I SAID, IS EVERYONE...
...okay -hee-hee-...?
HA! HA! HA!
HA! HA! HA!

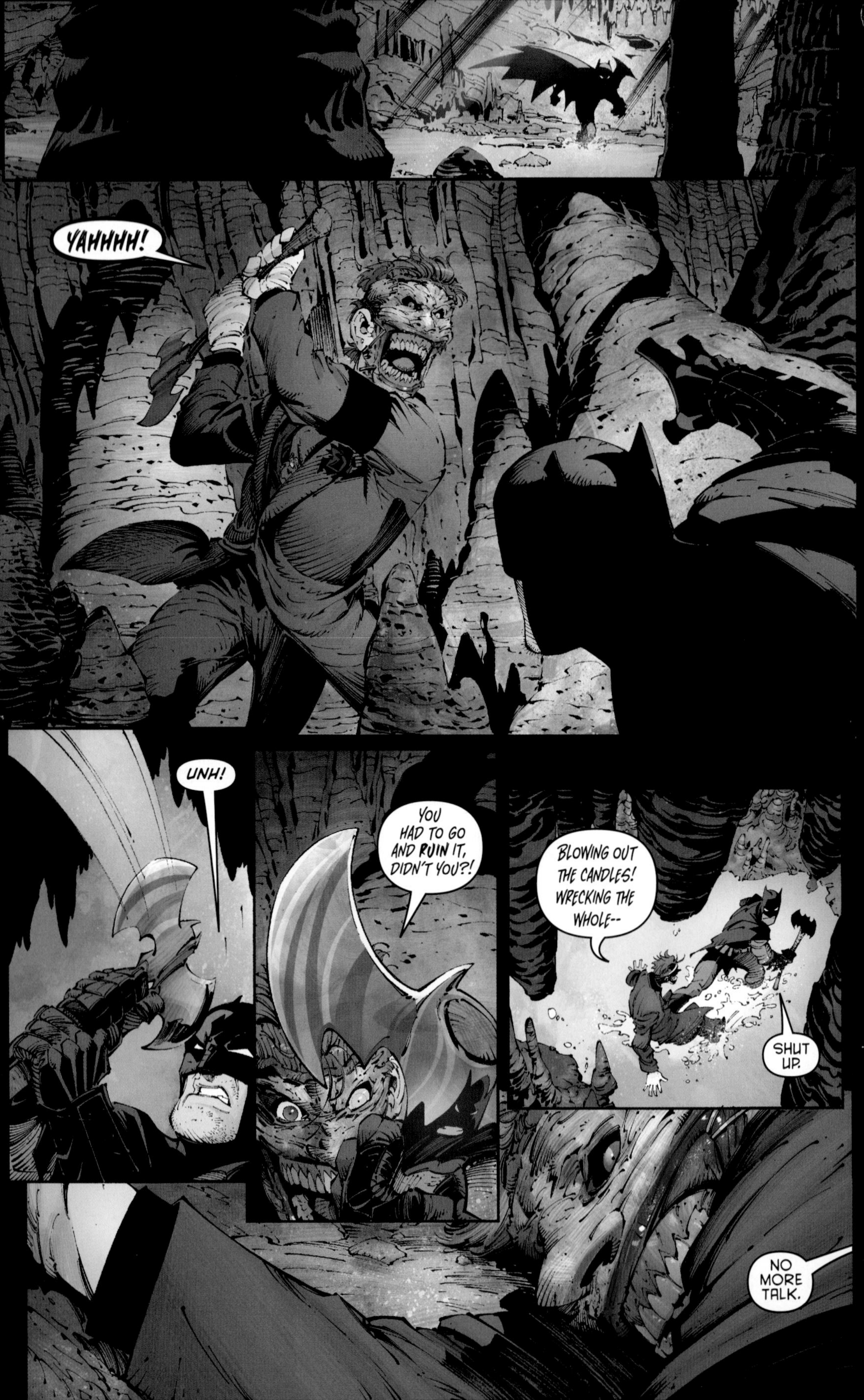
YAHHHH!
UNH!
YOU HAD TO GO AND RUIN IT, DIDN'T YOU?!
BLOWING OUT THE CANDLES! WRECKING THE WHOLE--
SHUT UP.
NO MORE TALK.

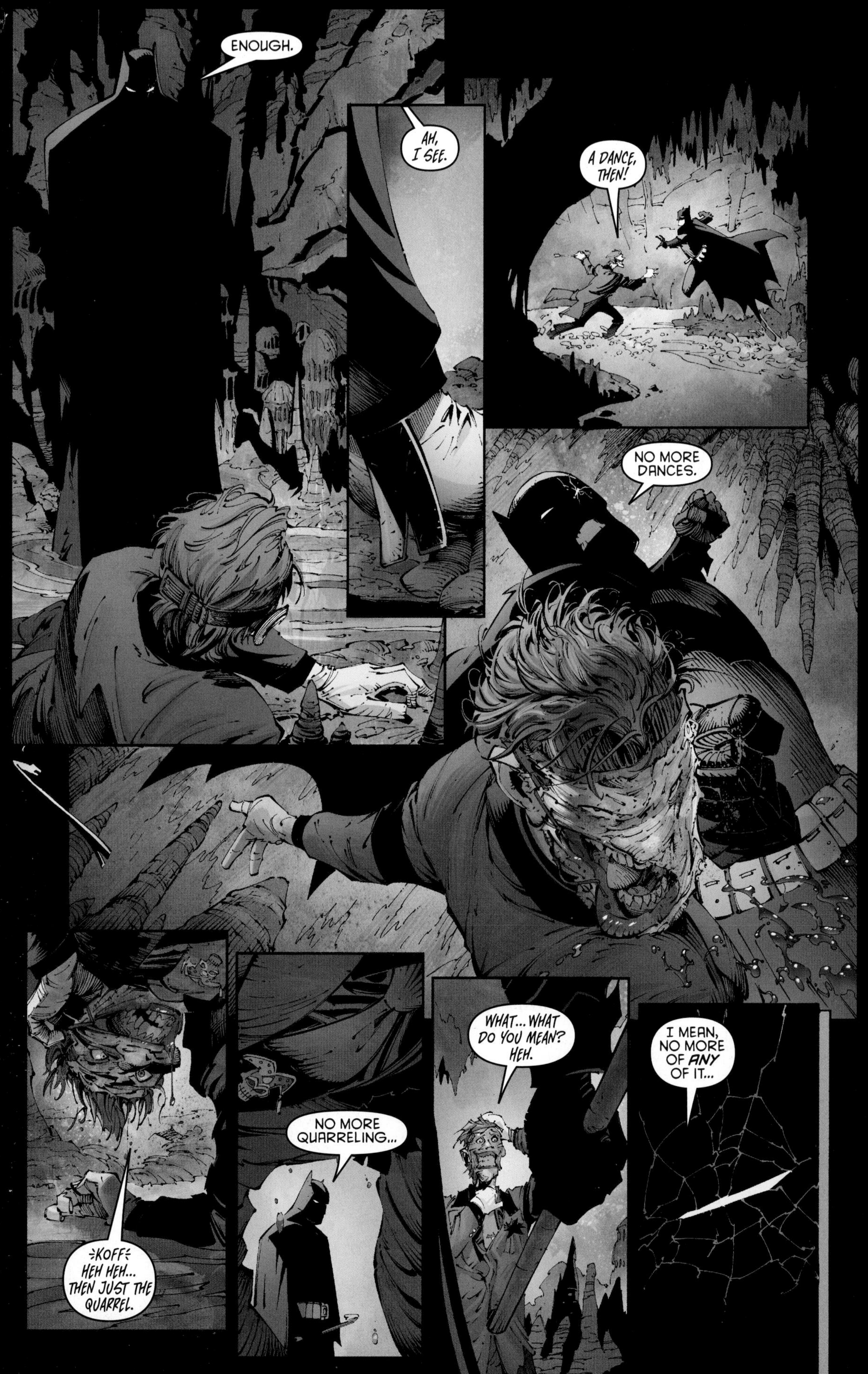
ENOUGH.
AH, I SEE.
A DANCE, THEN!
NO MORE DANCES.
≶KOFF≶ HEH HEH... THEN JUST THE QUARREL.
NO MORE QUARRELING...
WHAT... WHAT DO YOU MEAN? HEH.
I MEAN, NO MORE OF *ANY* OF IT...

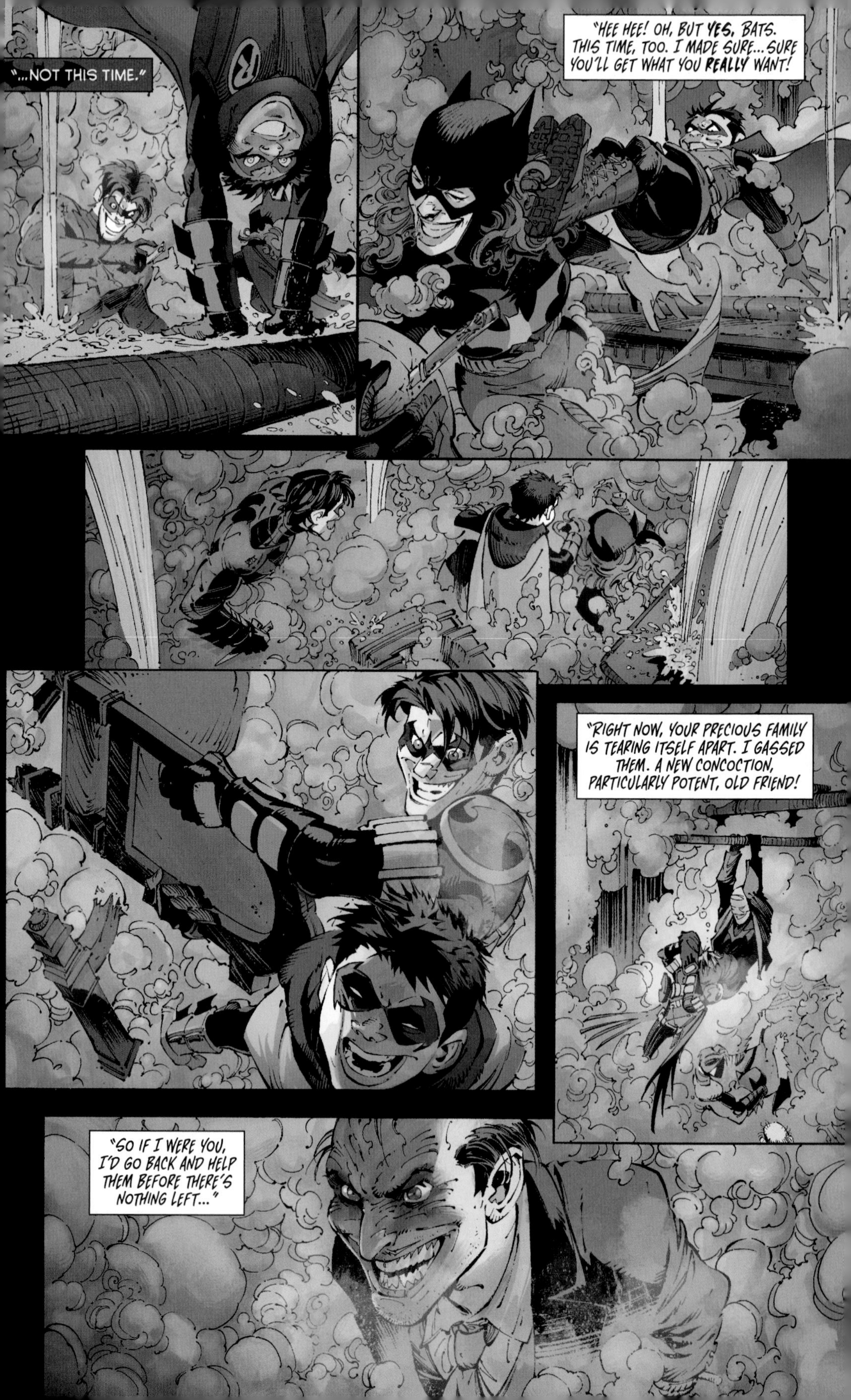
"...NOT THIS TIME."
"HEE HEE! OH, BUT YES, BATS. THIS TIME, TOO. I MADE SURE... SURE YOU'LL GET WHAT YOU REALLY WANT!
"RIGHT NOW, YOUR PRECIOUS FAMILY IS TEARING ITSELF APART. I GASSED THEM. A NEW CONCOCTION, PARTICULARLY POTENT, OLD FRIEND!
"SO IF I WERE YOU, I'D GO BACK AND HELP THEM BEFORE THERE'S NOTHING LEFT..."

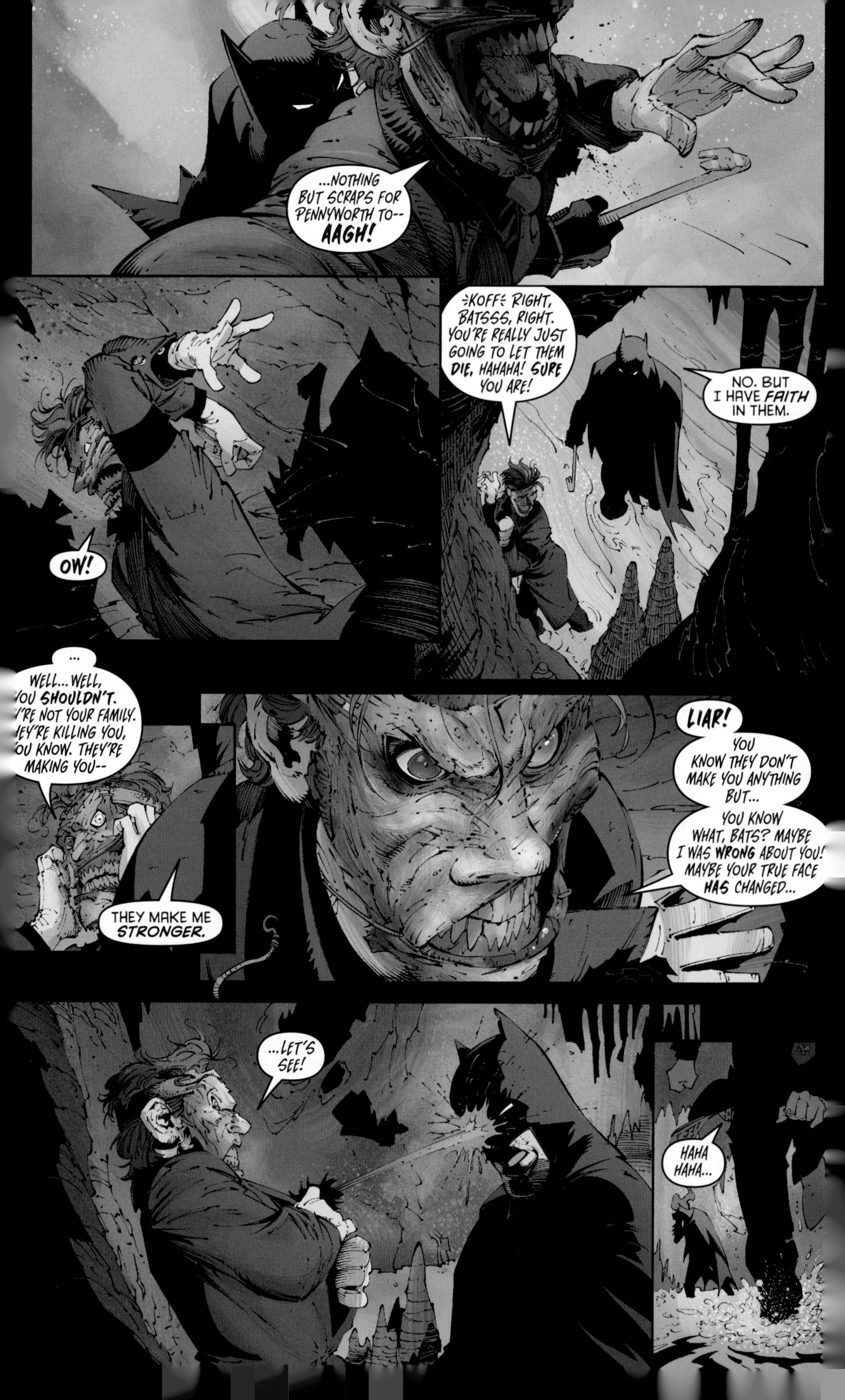
...NOTHING BUT SCRAPS FOR PENNYWORTH TO-- AAGH!
OW!
KOFF RIGHT, BATSSS, RIGHT. YOU'RE REALLY JUST GOING TO LET THEM DIE, HAHAHA! SURE YOU ARE!
NO. BUT I HAVE FAITH IN THEM.
...
WELL... WELL, YOU SHOULDN'T. Y'RE NOT YOUR FAMILY. HEY'RE KILLING YOU, YOU KNOW. THEY'RE MAKING YOU--
THEY MAKE ME STRONGER.
LIAR!
YOU KNOW THEY DON'T MAKE YOU ANYTHING BUT...
YOU KNOW WHAT, BATS? MAYBE I WAS WRONG ABOUT YOU! MAYBE YOUR TRUE FACE HAS CHANGED...
...LET'S SEE!
HAHA HAHA...

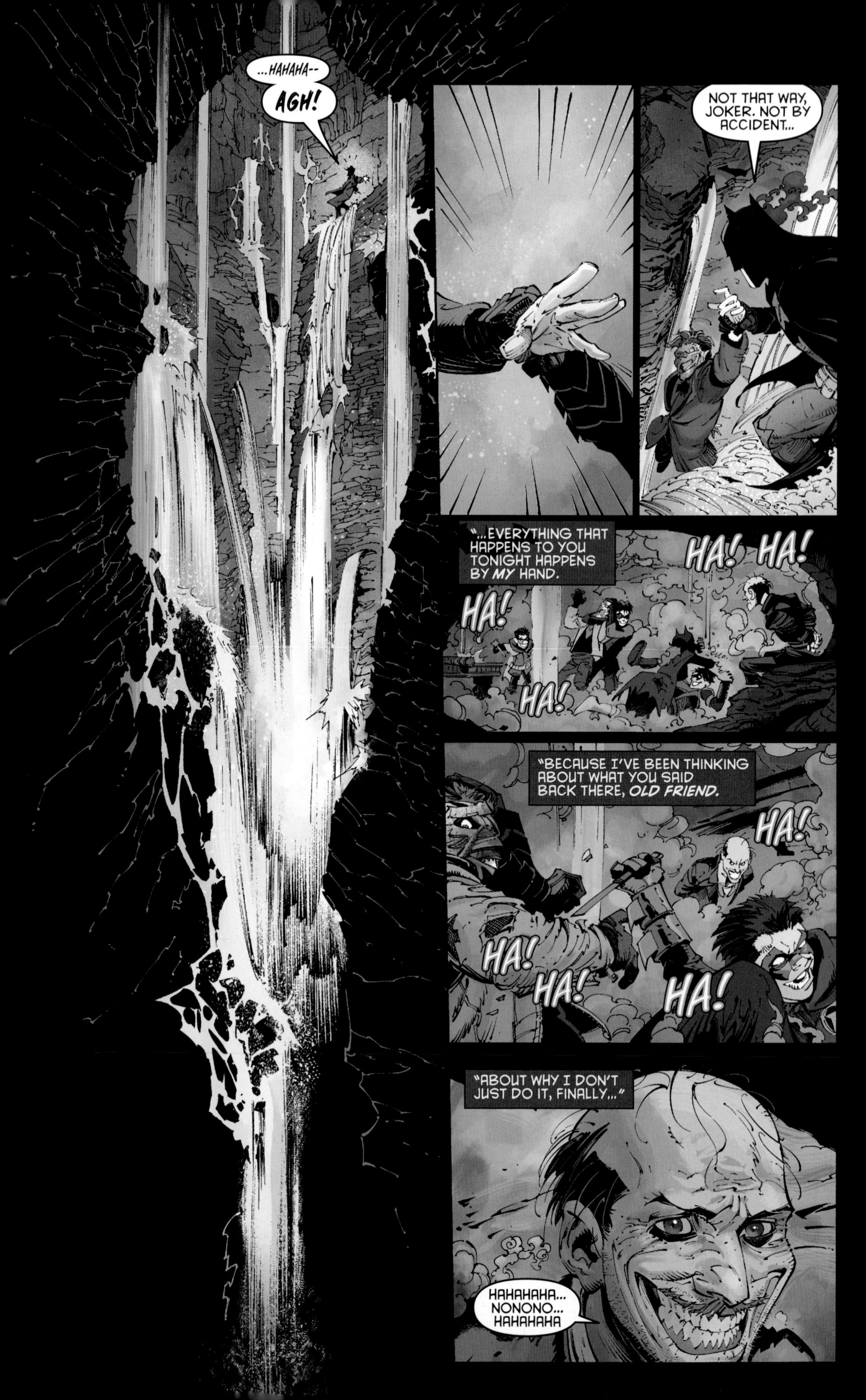
...HAHAHA--
AGH!
NOT THAT WAY, JOKER. NOT BY ACCIDENT...
"...EVERYTHING THAT HAPPENS TO YOU TONIGHT HAPPENS BY *MY* HAND.
HA! HA!
HA!
HA!
"BECAUSE I'VE BEEN THINKING ABOUT WHAT YOU SAID BACK THERE, *OLD FRIEND*.
HA!
HA!
HA!
HA!
"ABOUT WHY I DON'T JUST DO IT, FINALLY..."
HAHAHAHA... NONONO... HAHAHAHA

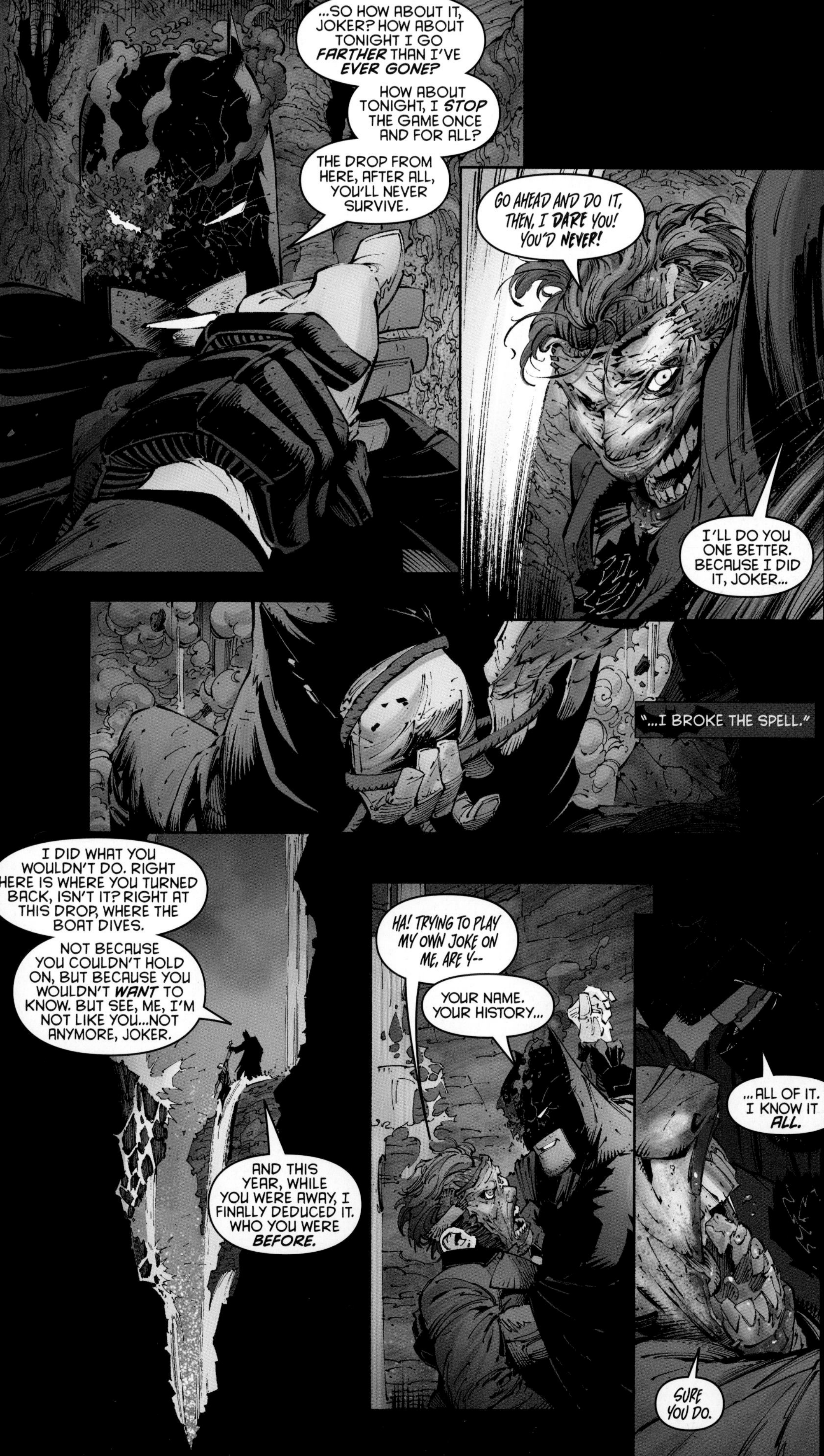
...SO HOW ABOUT IT, JOKER? HOW ABOUT TONIGHT I GO *FARTHER* THAN I'VE *EVER GONE?*
HOW ABOUT TONIGHT, I *STOP* THE GAME ONCE AND FOR ALL?
THE DROP FROM HERE, AFTER ALL, YOU'LL NEVER SURVIVE.
GO AHEAD AND DO IT, THEN, I *DARE* YOU! YOU'D *NEVER!*
I'LL DO YOU ONE BETTER. BECAUSE I DID IT, JOKER...
"...I BROKE THE SPELL."
I DID WHAT YOU WOULDN'T DO. RIGHT HERE IS WHERE YOU TURNED BACK, ISN'T IT? RIGHT AT THIS DROP, WHERE THE BOAT DIVES.
NOT BECAUSE YOU COULDN'T HOLD ON, BUT BECAUSE YOU WOULDN'T *WANT* TO KNOW. BUT SEE, ME, I'M NOT LIKE YOU...NOT ANYMORE, JOKER.
AND THIS YEAR, WHILE YOU WERE AWAY, I FINALLY DEDUCED IT. WHO YOU WERE *BEFORE.*
HA! TRYING TO PLAY MY OWN JOKE ON ME, ARE Y--
YOUR NAME. YOUR HISTORY...
...ALL OF IT. I KNOW IT *ALL.*
SURE YOU DO.

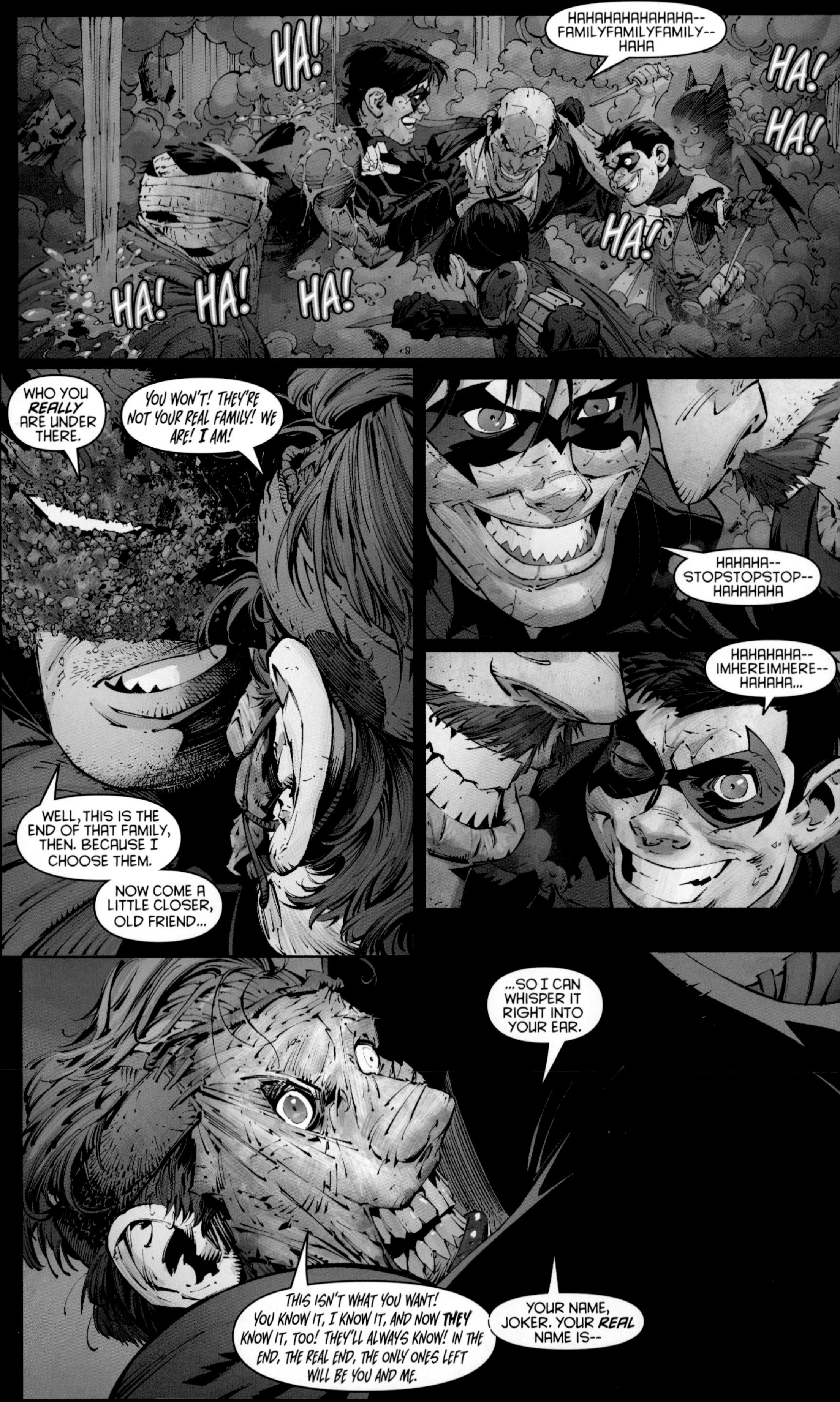

HA!
HAHAHAHAHAHAHA-- FAMILYFAMILYFAMILY-- HAHA
HA! HA!
HA!
HA! HA! HA!
WHO YOU REALLY ARE UNDER THERE.
YOU WON'T! THEY'RE NOT YOUR REAL FAMILY! WE ARE! I AM!
HAHAHA-- STOPSTOPSTOP-- HAHAHAHA
HAHAHAHA-- IMHEREIMHERE-- HAHAHA...
WELL, THIS IS THE END OF THAT FAMILY, THEN. BECAUSE I CHOOSE THEM.
NOW COME A LITTLE CLOSER, OLD FRIEND...
...SO I CAN WHISPER IT RIGHT INTO YOUR EAR.
THIS ISN'T WHAT YOU WANT! YOU KNOW IT, I KNOW IT, AND NOW THEY KNOW IT, TOO! THEY'LL ALWAYS KNOW! IN THE END, THE REAL END, THE ONLY ONES LEFT WILL BE YOU AND ME.
YOUR NAME, JOKER. YOUR REAL NAME IS--

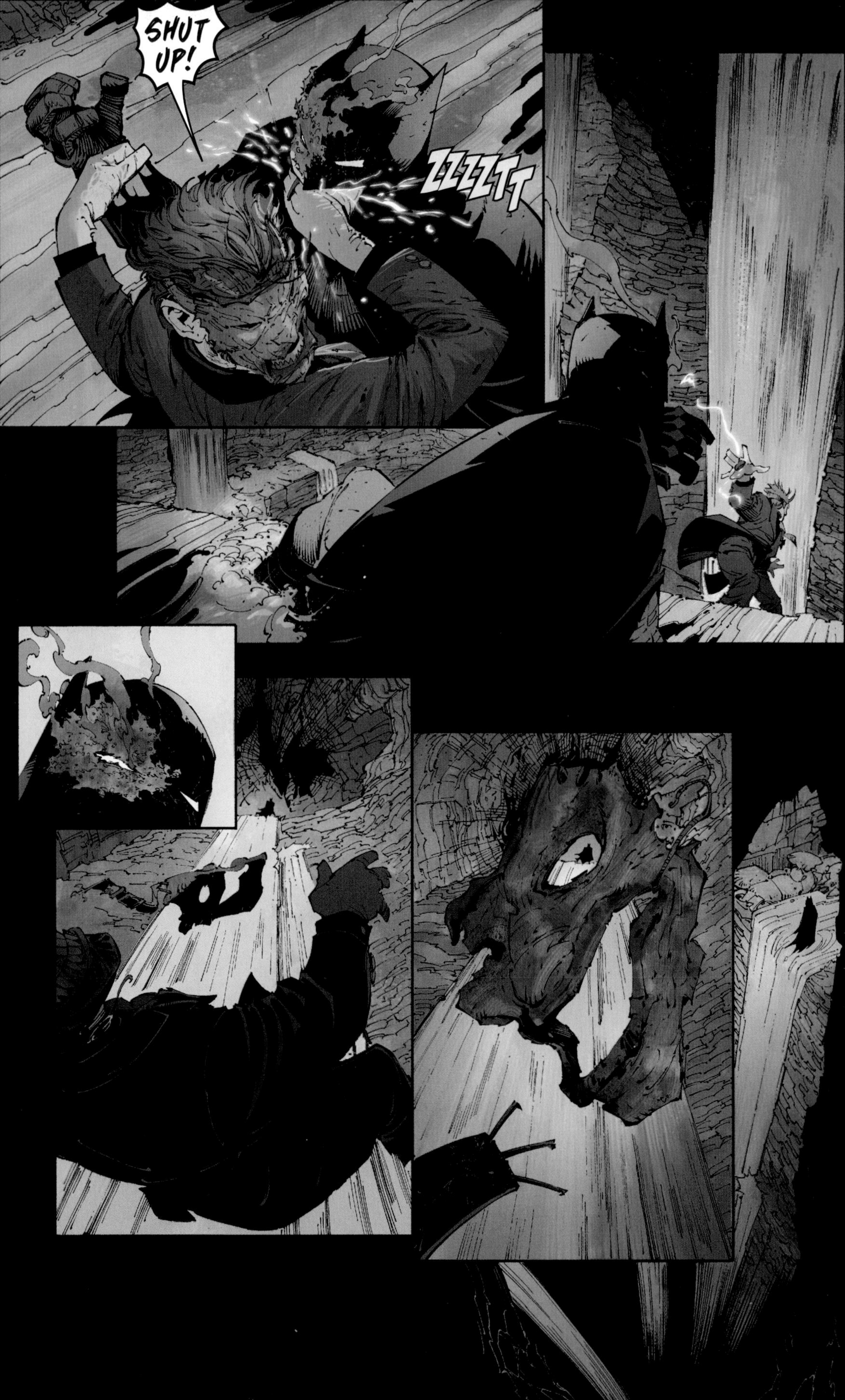
SHUT UP!
ZZZZTT

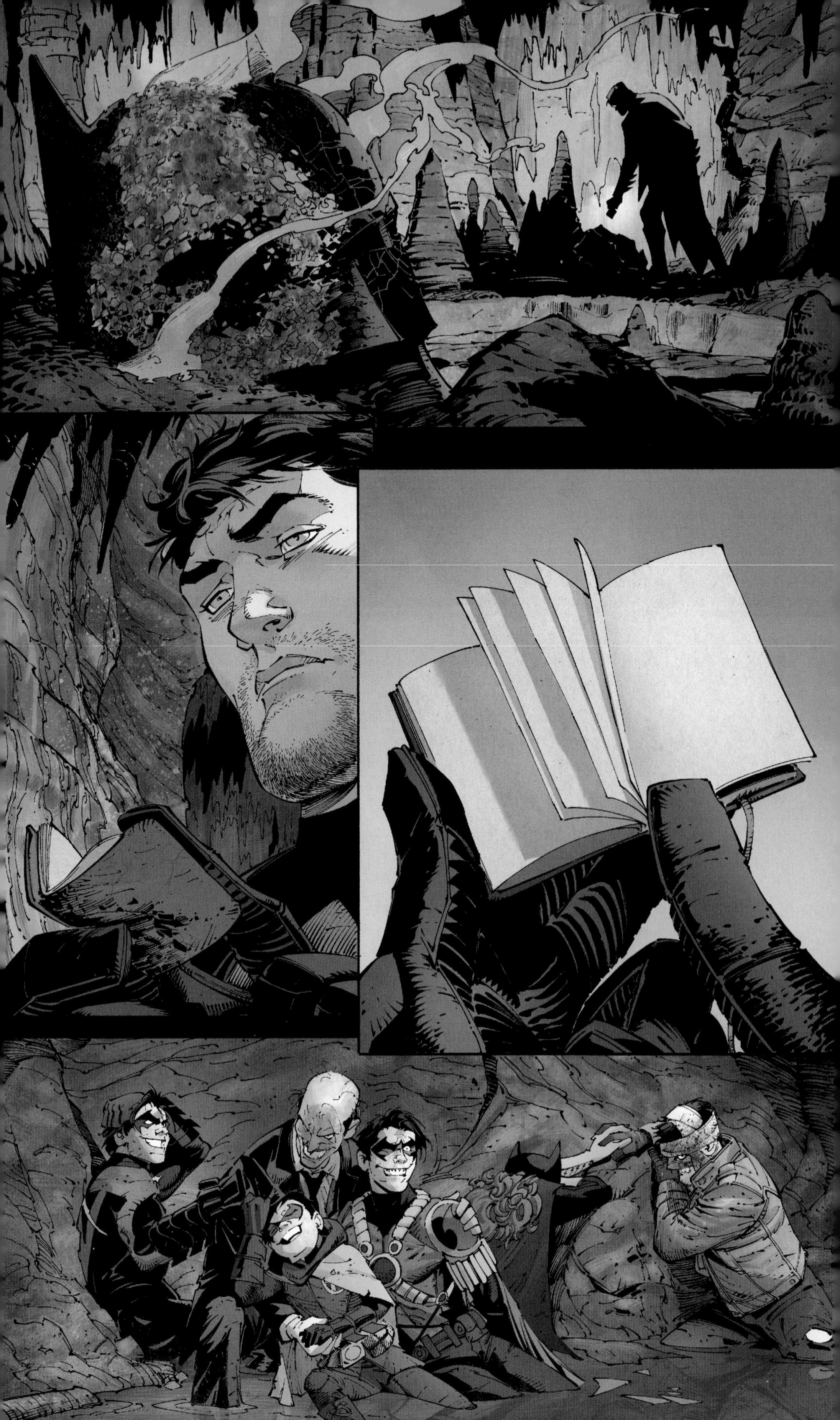

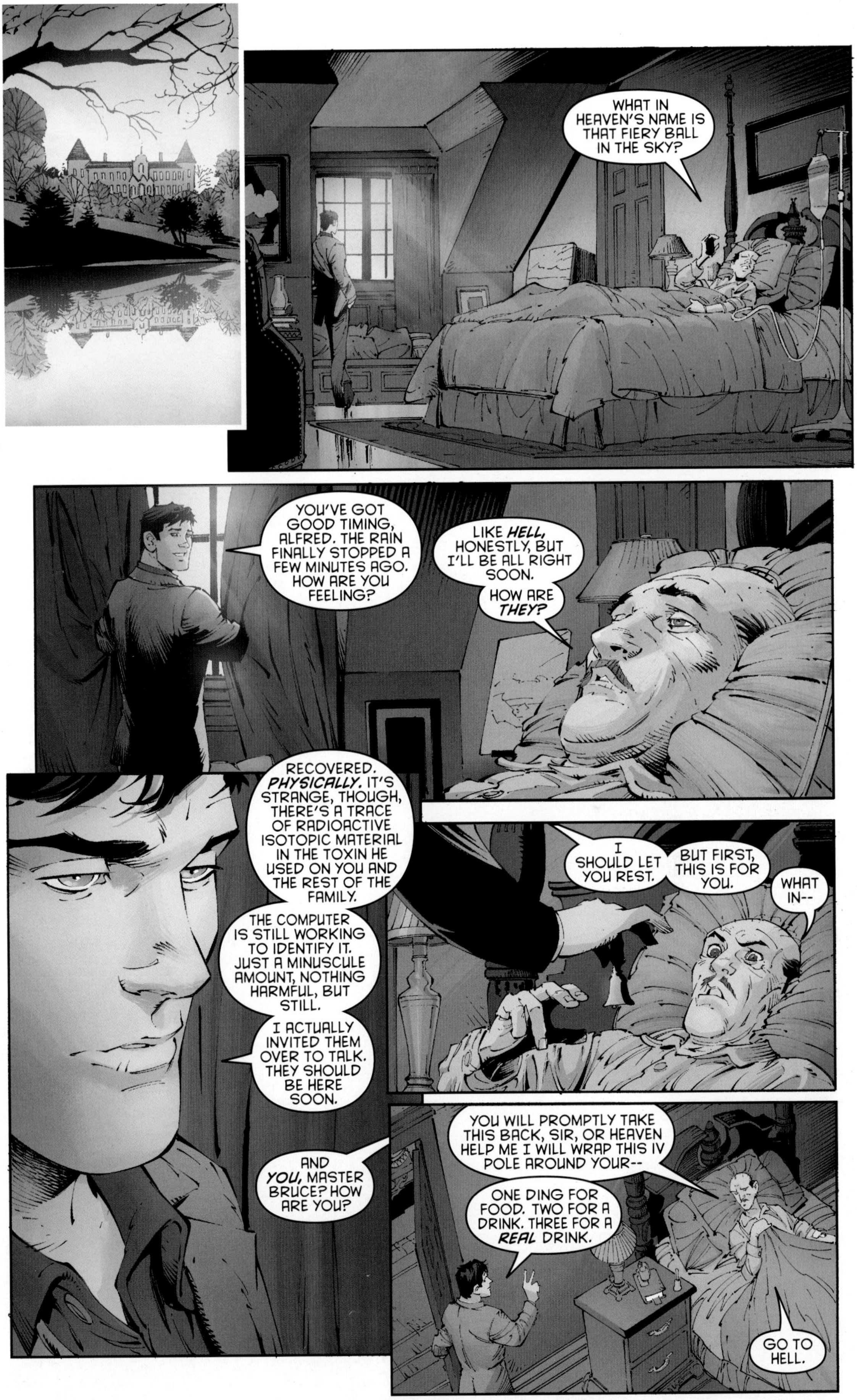
WHAT IN HEAVEN'S NAME IS THAT FIERY BALL IN THE SKY?
YOU'VE GOT GOOD TIMING, ALFRED. THE RAIN FINALLY STOPPED A FEW MINUTES AGO. HOW ARE YOU FEELING?
LIKE *HELL,* HONESTLY, BUT I'LL BE ALL RIGHT SOON.
HOW ARE *THEY?*
RECOVERED. *PHYSICALLY.* IT'S STRANGE, THOUGH, THERE'S A TRACE OF RADIOACTIVE ISOTOPIC MATERIAL IN THE TOXIN HE USED ON YOU AND THE REST OF THE FAMILY.
THE COMPUTER IS STILL WORKING TO IDENTIFY IT. JUST A MINUSCULE AMOUNT, NOTHING HARMFUL, BUT STILL.
I ACTUALLY INVITED THEM OVER TO TALK. THEY SHOULD BE HERE SOON.
AND *YOU,* MASTER BRUCE? HOW ARE YOU?
I SHOULD LET YOU REST.
BUT FIRST, THIS IS FOR YOU.
WHAT IN--
YOU WILL PROMPTLY TAKE THIS BACK, SIR, OR HEAVEN HELP ME I WILL WRAP THIS IV POLE AROUND YOUR--
ONE DING FOR FOOD. TWO FOR A DRINK. THREE FOR A *REAL* DRINK.
GO TO HELL.

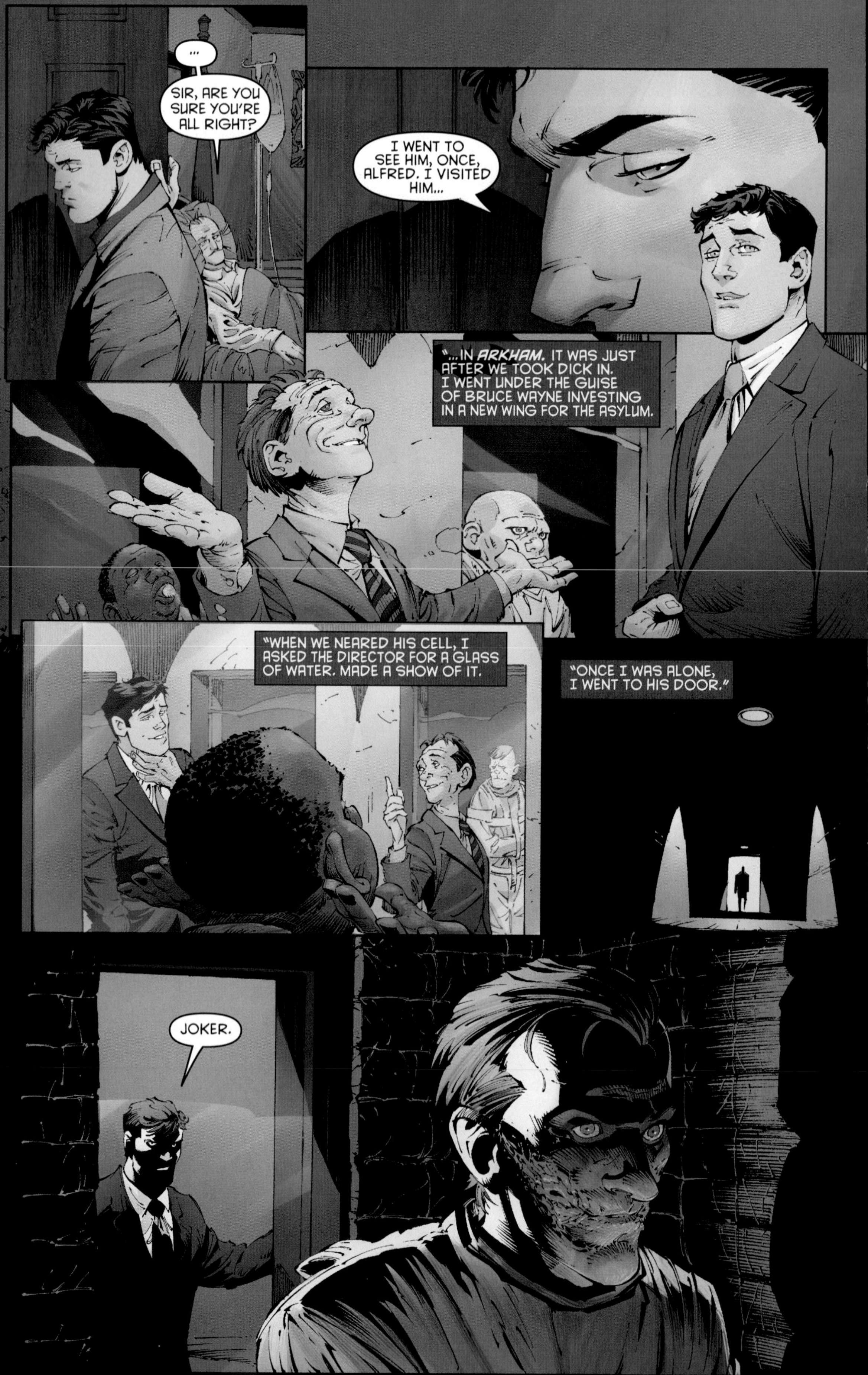
...
SIR, ARE YOU SURE YOU'RE ALL RIGHT?
I WENT TO SEE HIM, ONCE, ALFRED. I VISITED HIM...
"...IN ARKHAM. IT WAS JUST AFTER WE TOOK DICK IN. I WENT UNDER THE GUISE OF BRUCE WAYNE INVESTING IN A NEW WING FOR THE ASYLUM.
"WHEN WE NEARED HIS CELL, I ASKED THE DIRECTOR FOR A GLASS OF WATER. MADE A SHOW OF IT.
"ONCE I WAS ALONE, I WENT TO HIS DOOR."
JOKER.

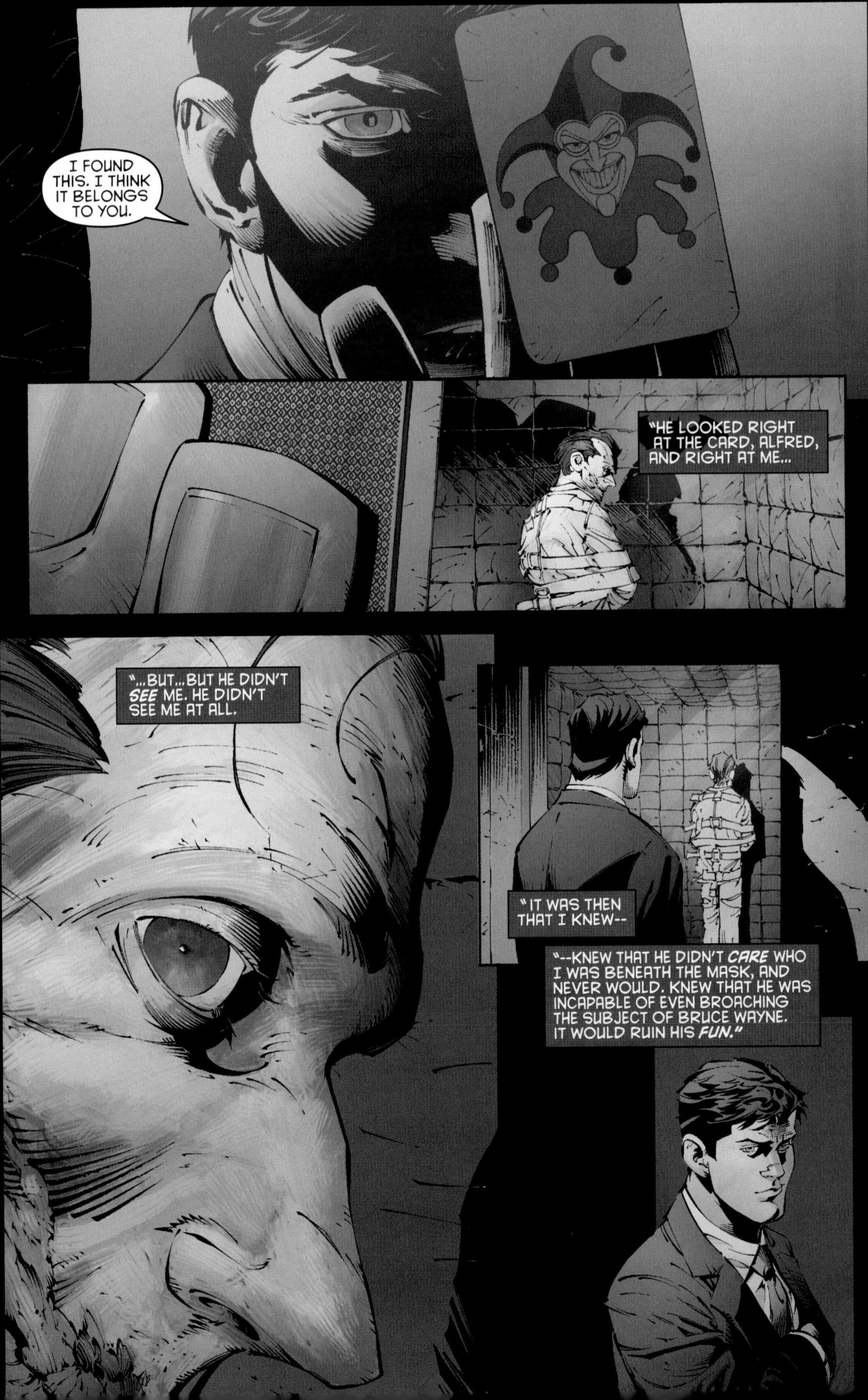
I FOUND THIS. I THINK IT BELONGS TO YOU.
"HE LOOKED RIGHT AT THE CARD, ALFRED, AND RIGHT AT ME...
"...BUT...BUT HE DIDN'T *SEE* ME. HE DIDN'T SEE ME AT ALL.
"IT WAS THEN THAT I KNEW--
"--KNEW THAT HE DIDN'T *CARE* WHO I WAS BENEATH THE MASK, AND NEVER WOULD. KNEW THAT HE WAS INCAPABLE OF EVEN BROACHING THE SUBJECT OF BRUCE WAYNE. IT WOULD RUIN HIS *FUN*."

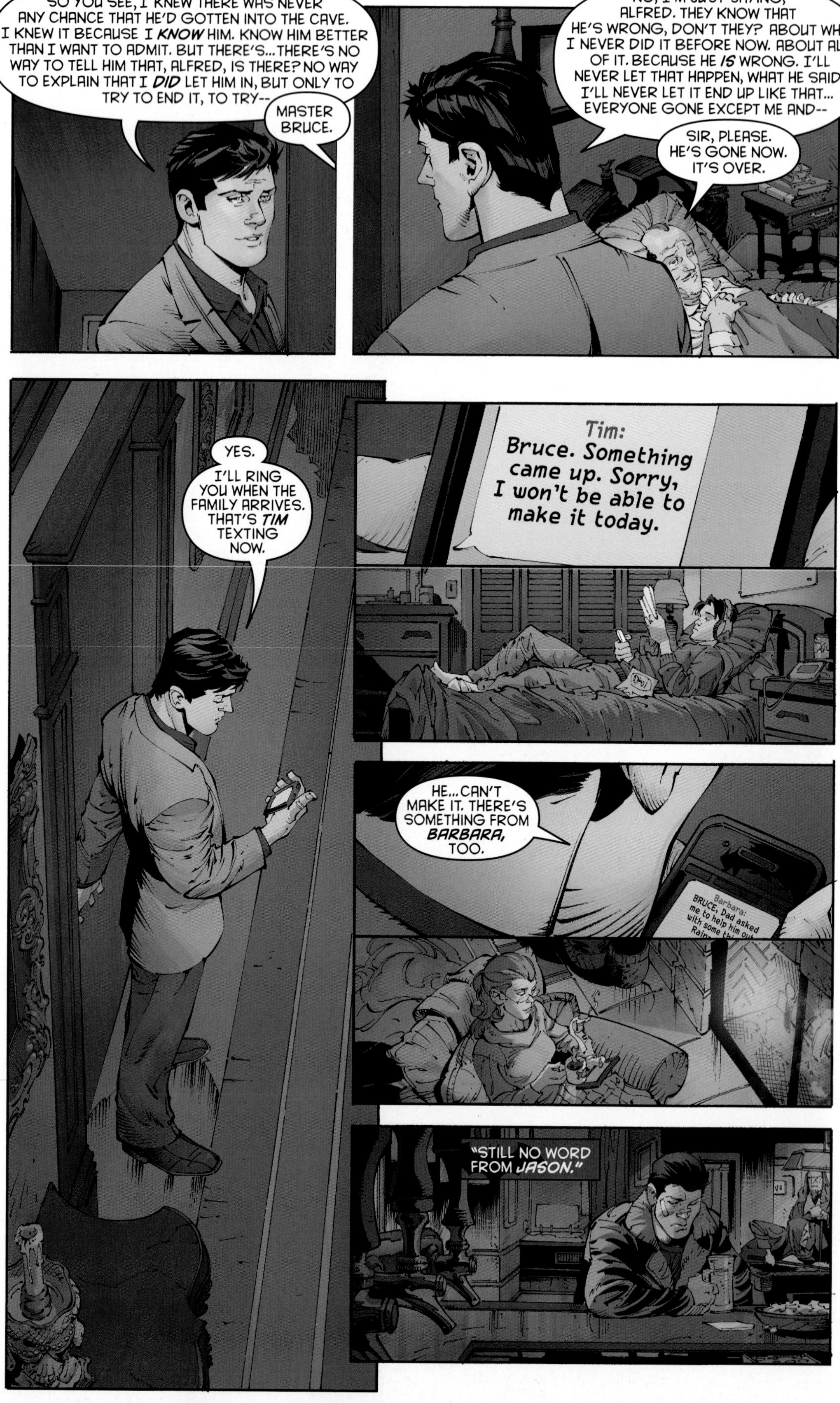
SO YOU SEE, I KNEW THERE WAS NEVER ANY CHANCE THAT HE'D GOTTEN INTO THE CAVE. I KNEW IT BECAUSE I **KNOW** HIM. KNOW HIM BETTER THAN I WANT TO ADMIT. BUT THERE'S...THERE'S NO WAY TO TELL HIM THAT, ALFRED, IS THERE? NO WAY TO EXPLAIN THAT I **DID** LET HIM IN, BUT ONLY TO TRY TO END IT, TO TRY--
MASTER BRUCE.
NO, I'M JUST SAYING, ALFRED. THEY KNOW THAT HE'S WRONG, DON'T THEY? ABOUT WHY I NEVER DID IT BEFORE NOW. ABOUT ALL OF IT. BECAUSE HE ***IS*** WRONG. I'LL NEVER LET THAT HAPPEN, WHAT HE SAID. I'LL NEVER LET IT END UP LIKE THAT... EVERYONE GONE EXCEPT ME AND--
SIR, PLEASE. HE'S GONE NOW. IT'S OVER.
YES.
I'LL RING YOU WHEN THE FAMILY ARRIVES. THAT'S *TIM* TEXTING NOW.
Tim:
Bruce. Something came up. Sorry, I won't be able to make it today.
HE...CAN'T MAKE IT. THERE'S SOMETHING FROM ***BARBARA,*** TOO.
Barbara:
BRUCE, Dad asked me to help him out with some
"STILL NO WORD FROM ***JASON.***"

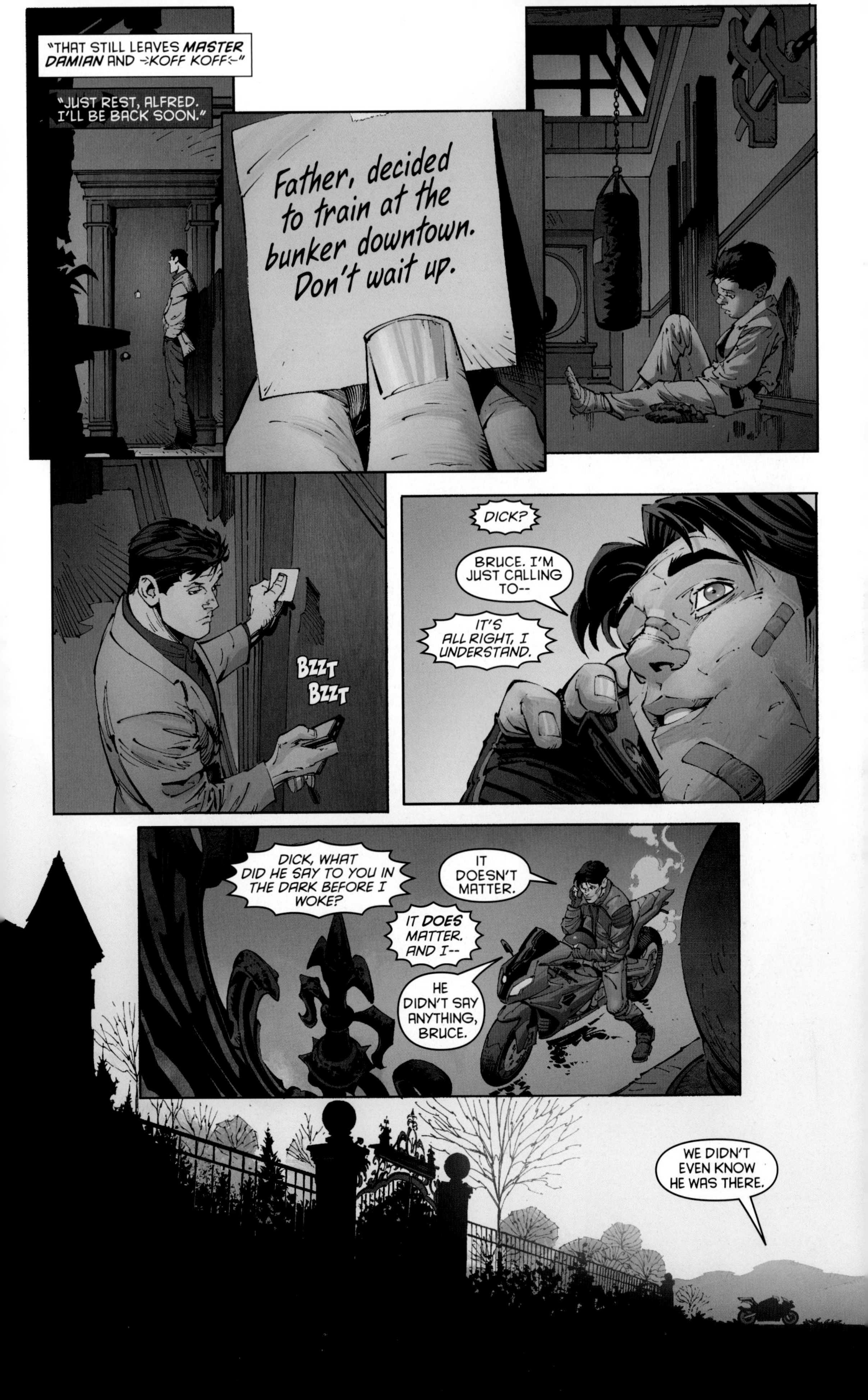
"THAT STILL LEAVES MASTER DAMIAN AND ~KOFF KOFF~"
"JUST REST, ALFRED. I'LL BE BACK SOON."
Father, decided to train at the bunker downtown. Don't wait up.
BZZT
BZZT
DICK?
BRUCE. I'M JUST CALLING TO--
IT'S ALL RIGHT, I UNDERSTAND.
DICK, WHAT DID HE SAY TO YOU IN THE DARK BEFORE I WOKE?
IT DOESN'T MATTER.
IT DOES MATTER. AND I--
HE DIDN'T SAY ANYTHING, BRUCE.
WE DIDN'T EVEN KNOW HE WAS THERE.

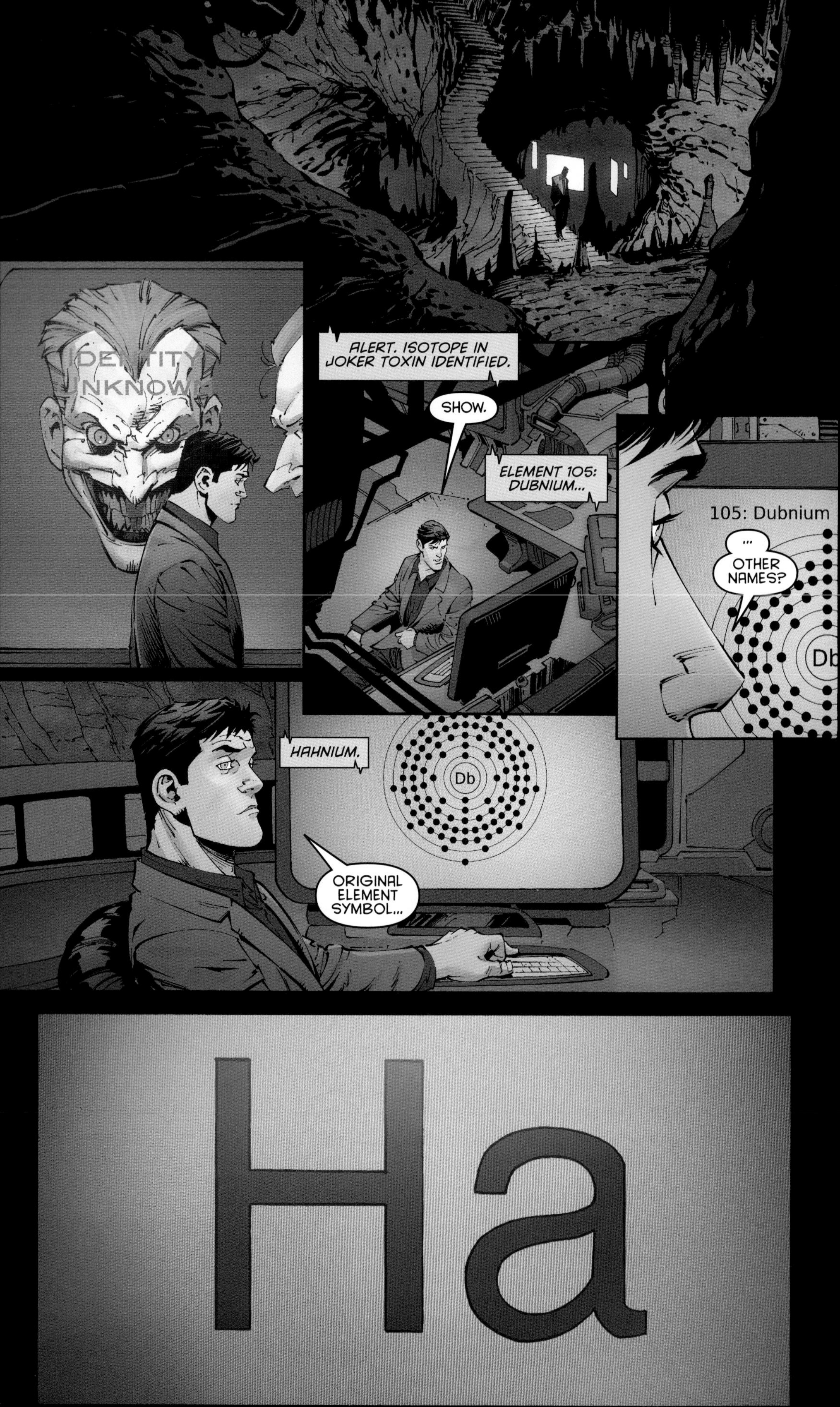
IDENTITY
UNKNOWN
ALERT. ISOTOPE IN JOKER TOXIN IDENTIFIED.
SHOW.
ELEMENT 105: DUBNIUM...
105: Dubnium
...
OTHER NAMES?
HAHNIUM.
Db
ORIGINAL ELEMENT SYMBOL...
Ha

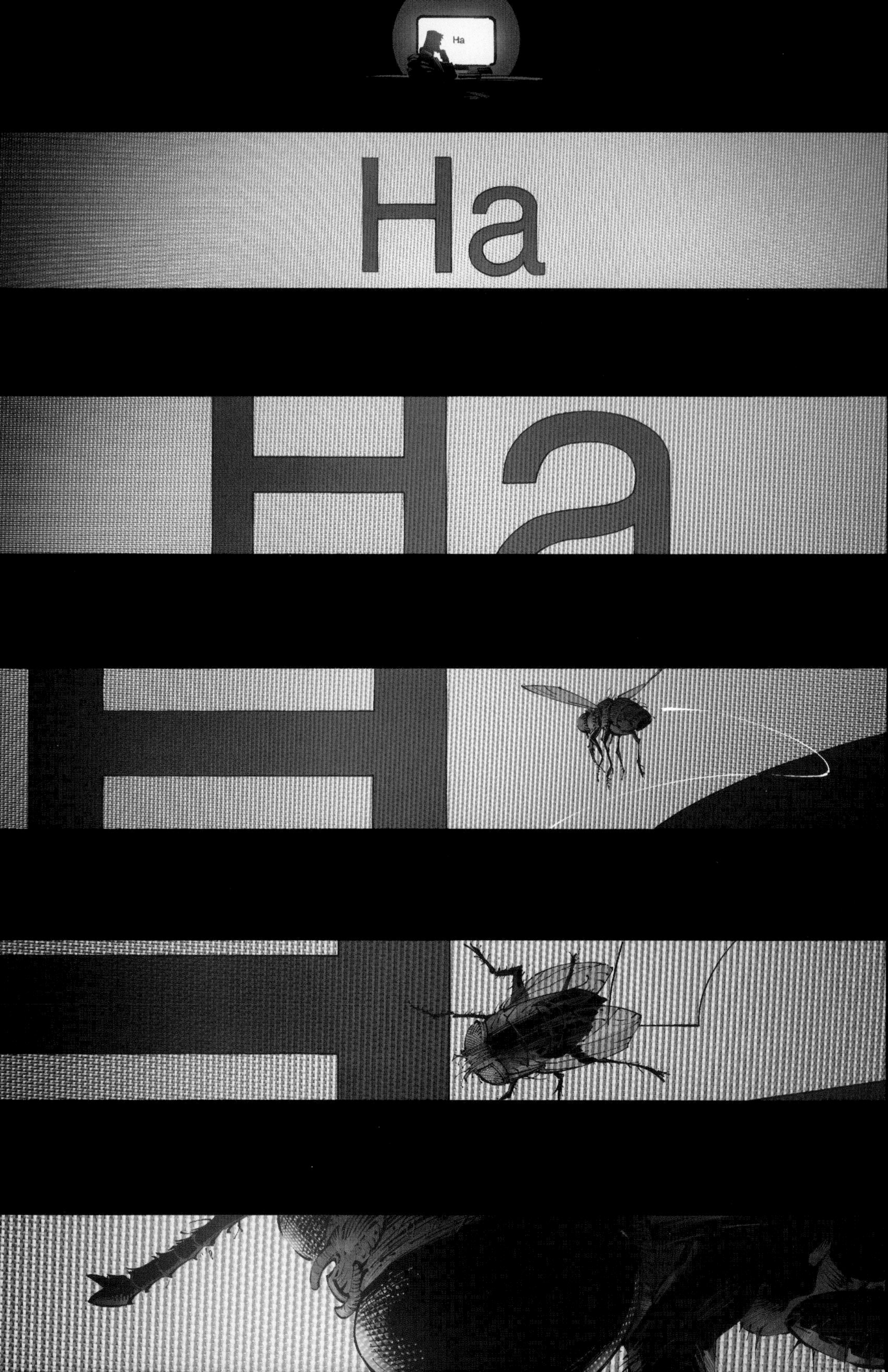
Ha
Ha

DREAMER

RAY FAWKES
writer

JULIUS GOPEZ
artist

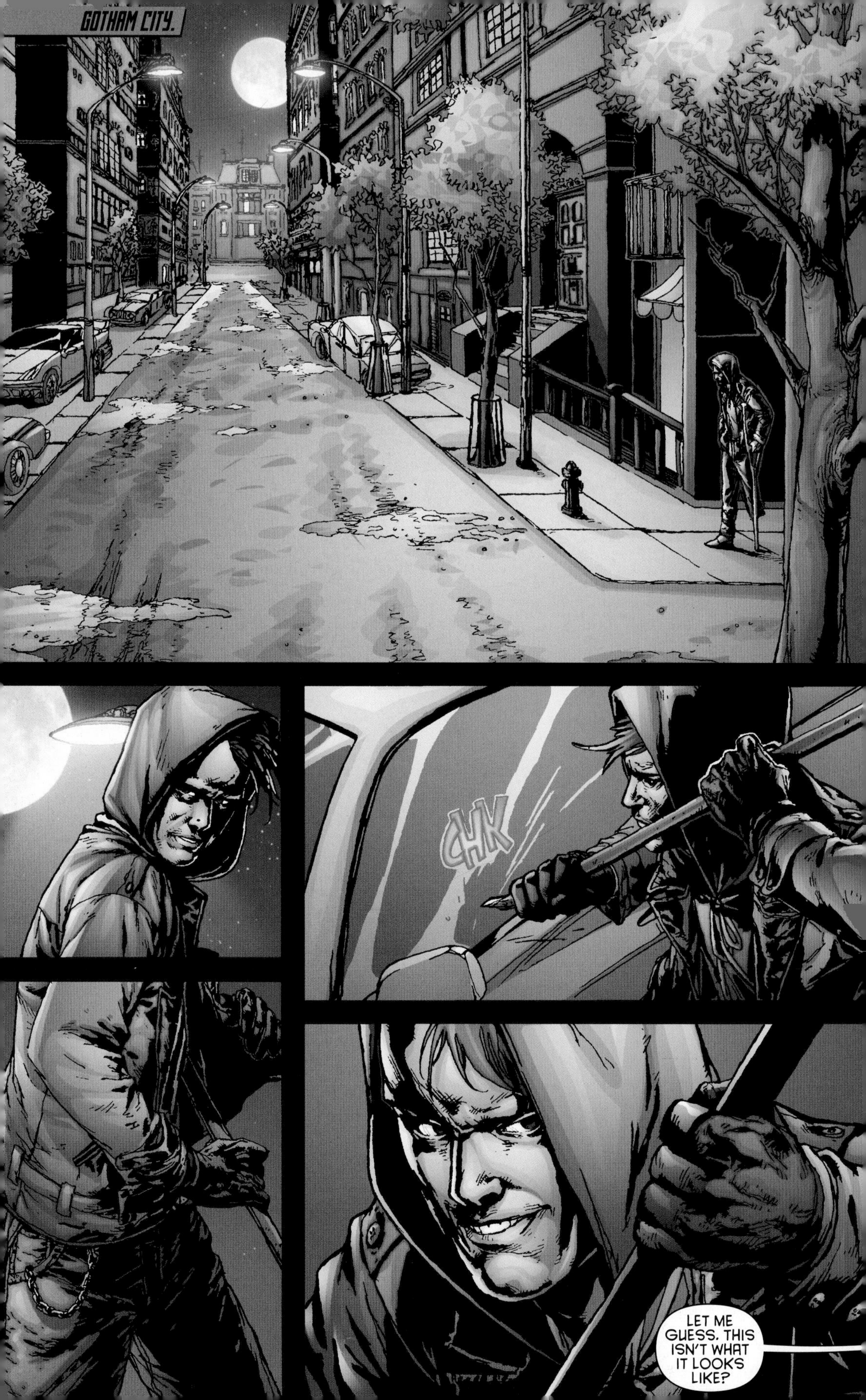
GOTHAM CITY.
CHK
LET ME GUESS. THIS ISN'T WHAT IT LOOKS LIKE?

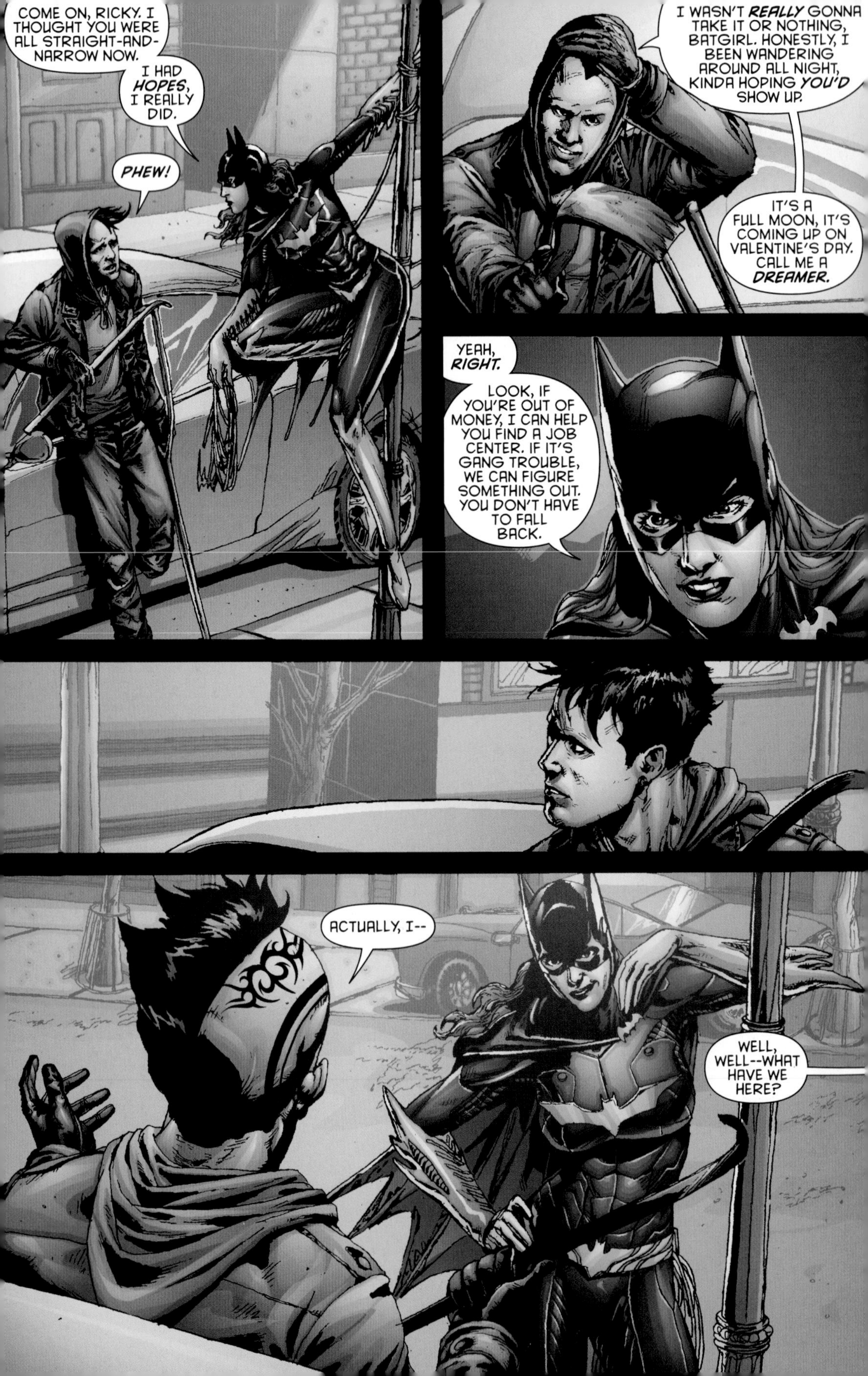
COME ON, RICKY. I THOUGHT YOU WERE ALL STRAIGHT-AND-NARROW NOW.
I HAD *HOPES*, I REALLY DID.
PHEW!
I WASN'T *REALLY* GONNA TAKE IT OR NOTHING, BATGIRL. HONESTLY, I BEEN WANDERING AROUND ALL NIGHT, KINDA HOPING *YOU'D* SHOW UP.
IT'S A FULL MOON, IT'S COMING UP ON VALENTINE'S DAY. CALL ME A *DREAMER*.
YEAH, *RIGHT*.
LOOK, IF YOU'RE OUT OF MONEY, I CAN HELP YOU FIND A JOB CENTER. IF IT'S GANG TROUBLE, WE CAN FIGURE SOMETHING OUT. YOU DON'T HAVE TO FALL BACK.
ACTUALLY, I--
WELL, WELL--WHAT HAVE WE HERE?

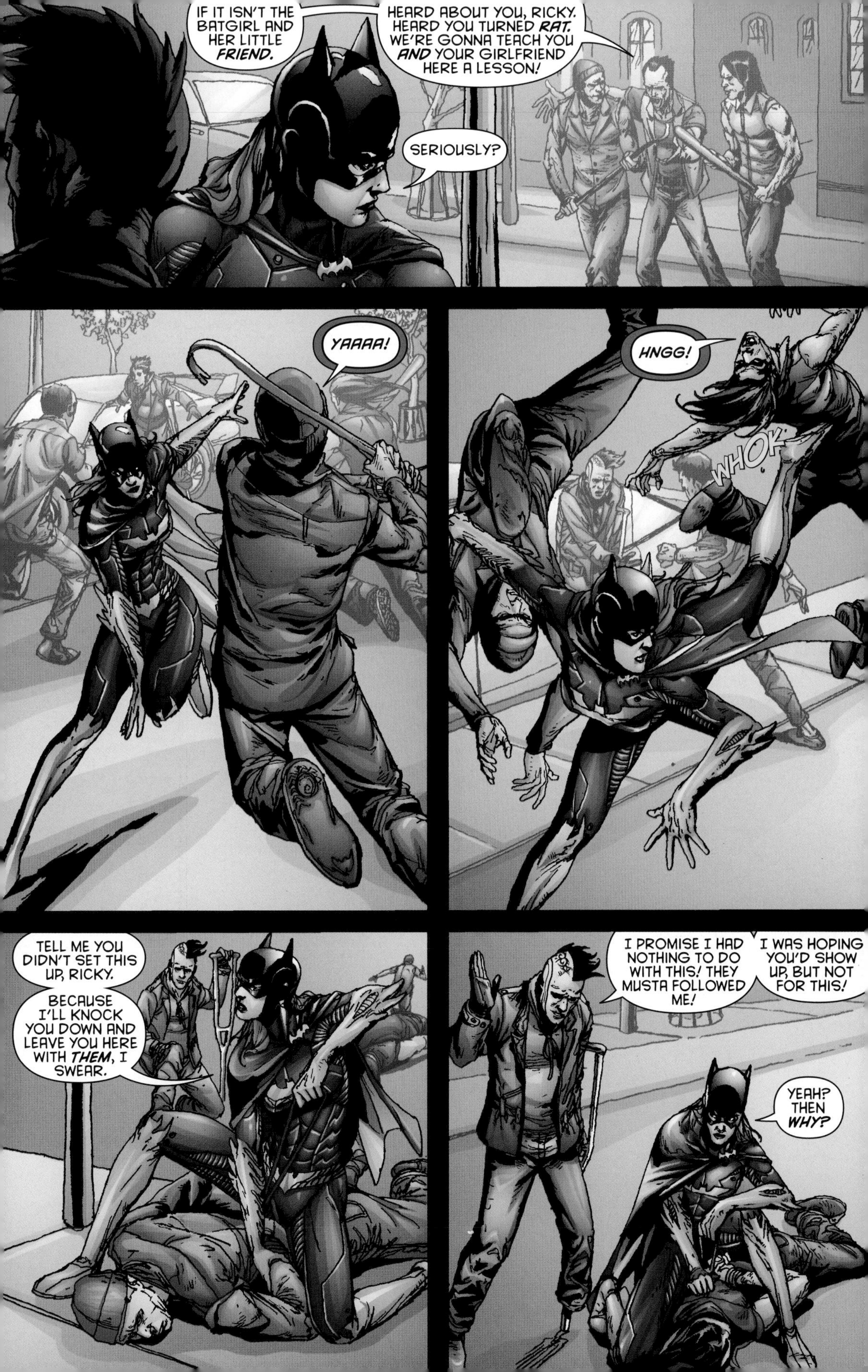
IF IT ISN'T THE BATGIRL AND HER LITTLE FRIEND.
HEARD ABOUT YOU, RICKY. HEARD YOU TURNED RAT. WE'RE GONNA TEACH YOU AND YOUR GIRLFRIEND HERE A LESSON!
SERIOUSLY?
YAAAA!
HNGG!
WHOK
TELL ME YOU DIDN'T SET THIS UP, RICKY.
BECAUSE I'LL KNOCK YOU DOWN AND LEAVE YOU HERE WITH THEM, I SWEAR.
I PROMISE I HAD NOTHING TO DO WITH THIS! THEY MUSTA FOLLOWED ME!
I WAS HOPING YOU'D SHOW UP, BUT NOT FOR THIS!
YEAH? THEN WHY?

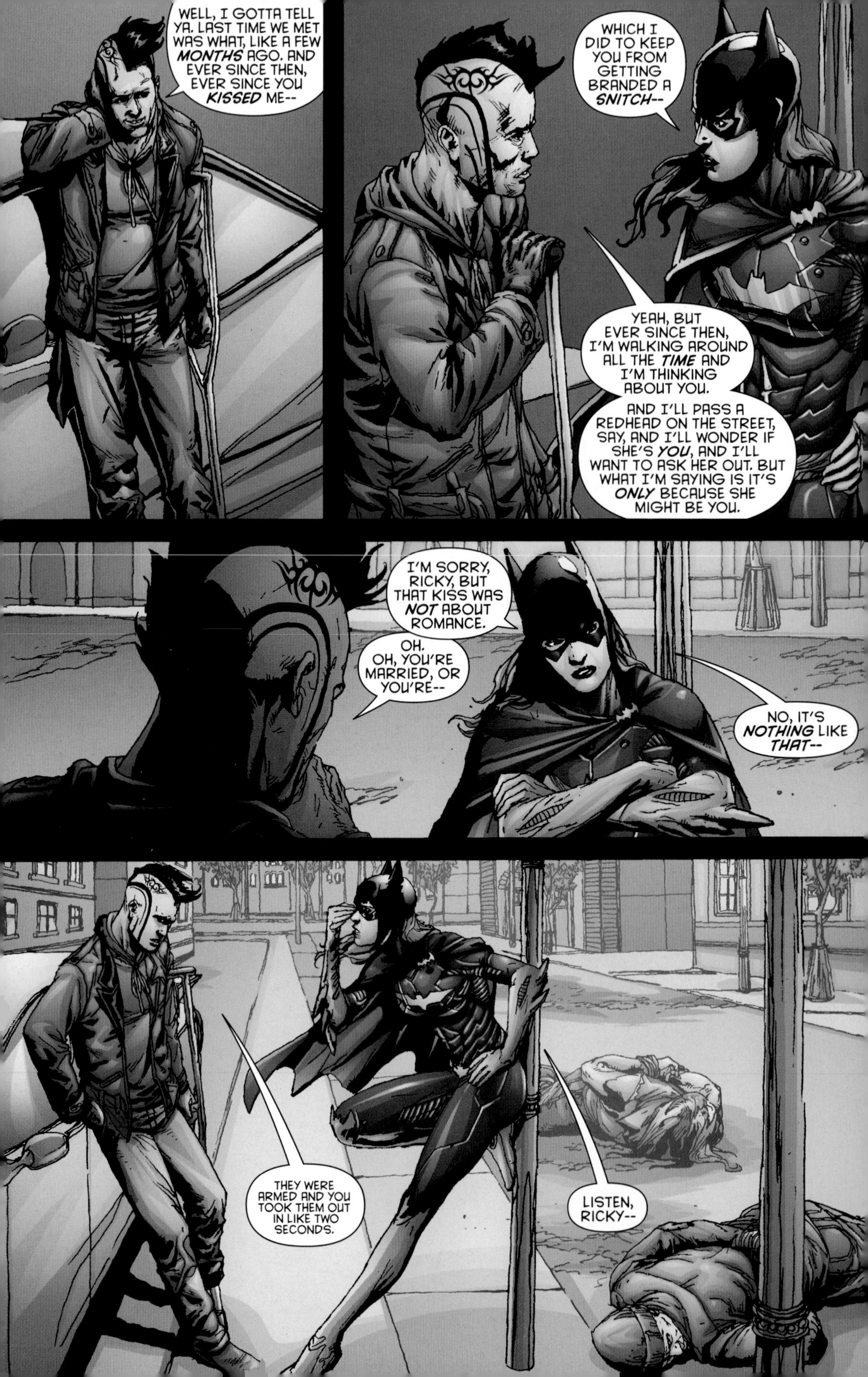
WELL, I GOTTA TELL YA. LAST TIME WE MET WAS WHAT, LIKE A FEW *MONTHS* AGO. AND EVER SINCE THEN, EVER SINCE YOU *KISSED* ME--
WHICH I DID TO KEEP YOU FROM GETTING BRANDED A *SNITCH*--
YEAH, BUT EVER SINCE THEN, I'M WALKING AROUND ALL THE *TIME* AND I'M THINKING ABOUT YOU.
AND I'LL PASS A REDHEAD ON THE STREET, SAY, AND I'LL WONDER IF SHE'S *YOU*, AND I'LL WANT TO ASK HER OUT. BUT WHAT I'M SAYING IS IT'S *ONLY* BECAUSE SHE MIGHT BE YOU.
I'M SORRY, RICKY, BUT THAT KISS WAS *NOT* ABOUT ROMANCE.
OH. OH, YOU'RE MARRIED, OR YOU'RE--
NO, IT'S *NOTHING* LIKE *THAT*--
THEY WERE ARMED AND YOU TOOK THEM OUT IN LIKE TWO SECONDS.
LISTEN, RICKY--

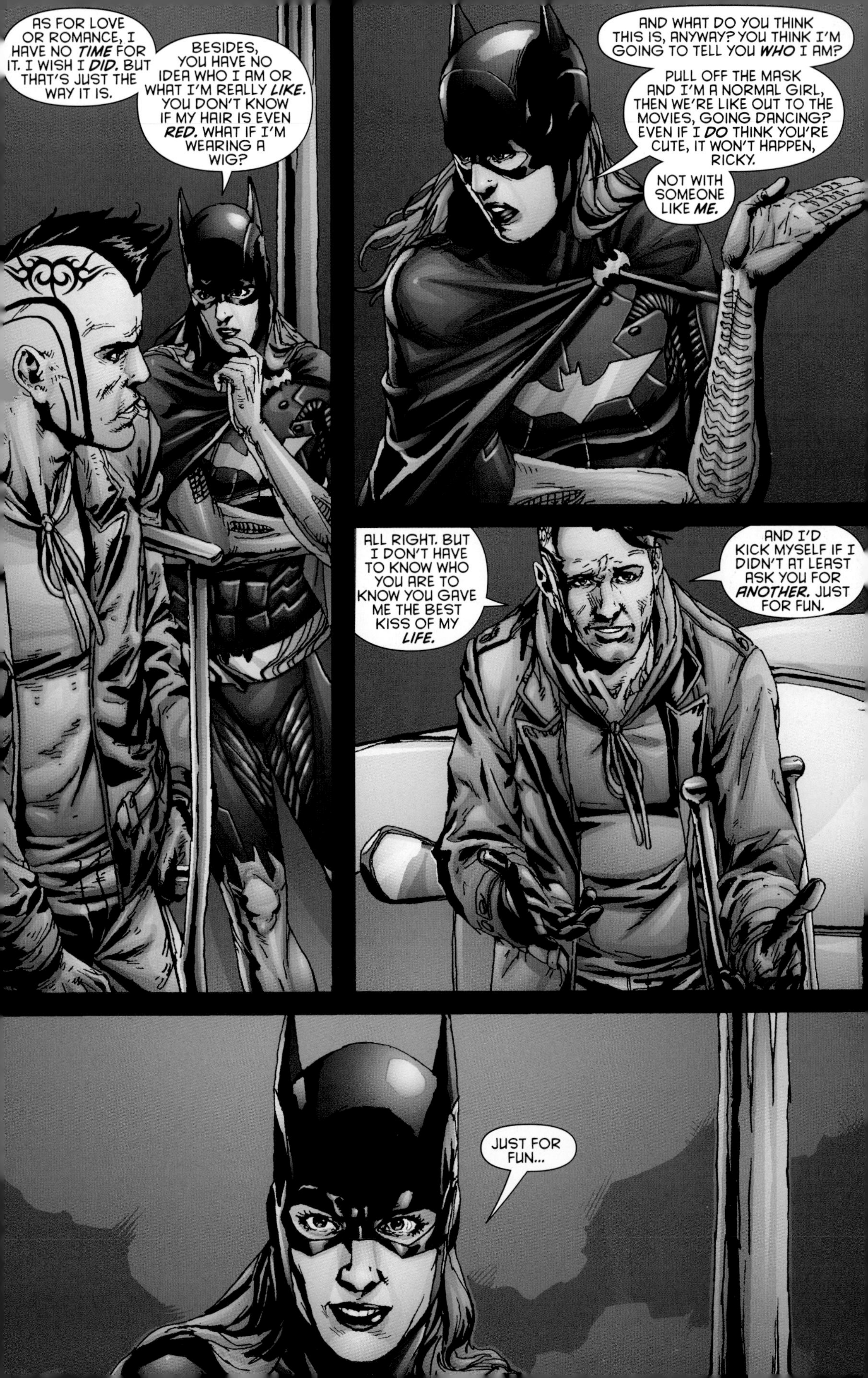
AS FOR LOVE OR ROMANCE, I HAVE NO TIME FOR IT. I WISH I DID. BUT THAT'S JUST THE WAY IT IS.
BESIDES, YOU HAVE NO IDEA WHO I AM OR WHAT I'M REALLY LIKE. YOU DON'T KNOW IF MY HAIR IS EVEN RED. WHAT IF I'M WEARING A WIG?
AND WHAT DO YOU THINK THIS IS, ANYWAY? YOU THINK I'M GOING TO TELL YOU WHO I AM?
PULL OFF THE MASK AND I'M A NORMAL GIRL, THEN WE'RE LIKE OUT TO THE MOVIES, GOING DANCING? EVEN IF I DO THINK YOU'RE CUTE, IT WON'T HAPPEN, RICKY.
NOT WITH SOMEONE LIKE ME.
ALL RIGHT. BUT I DON'T HAVE TO KNOW WHO YOU ARE TO KNOW YOU GAVE ME THE BEST KISS OF MY LIFE.
AND I'D KICK MYSELF IF I DIDN'T AT LEAST ASK YOU FOR ANOTHER. JUST FOR FUN.
JUST FOR FUN...

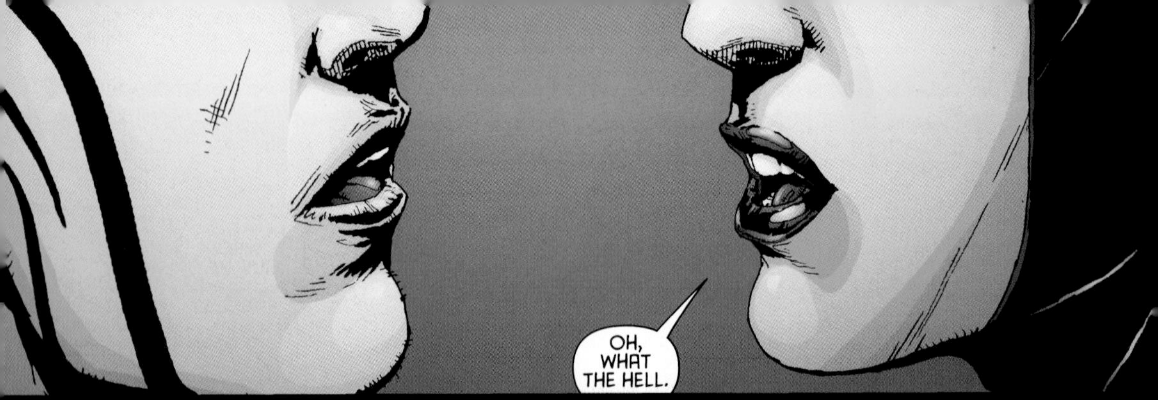
OH, WHAT THE HELL.

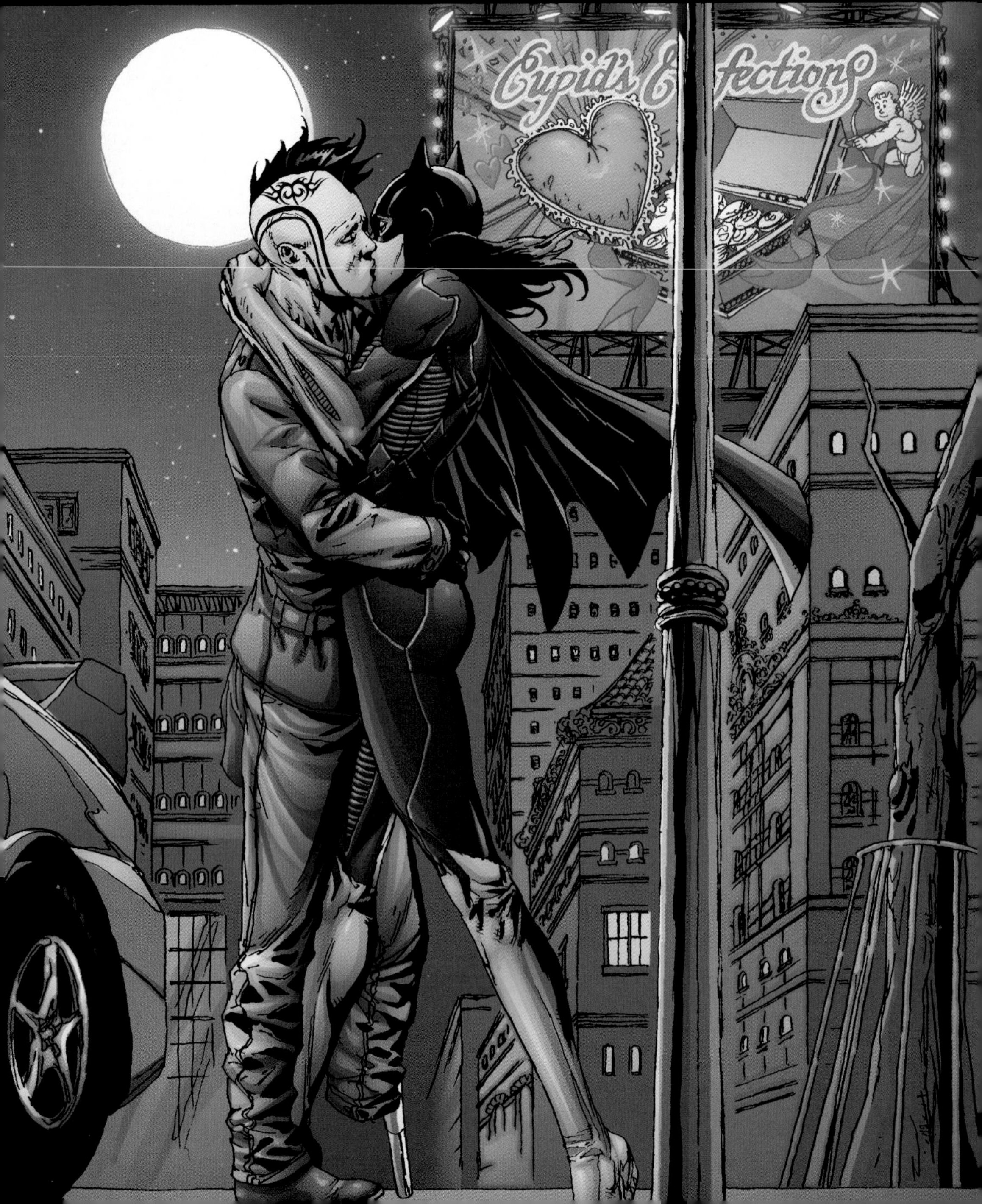
Cupid's

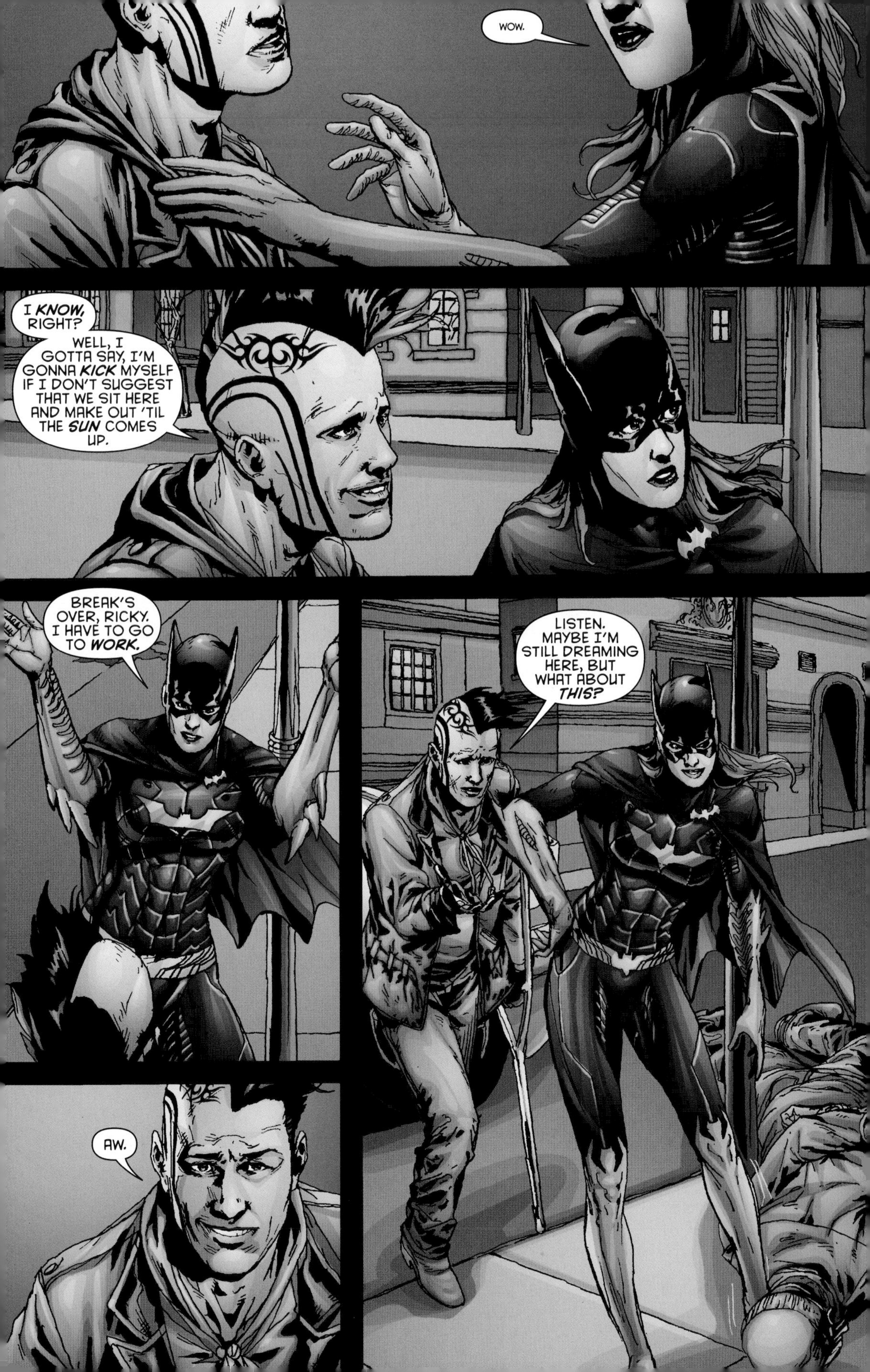
WOW.
I KNOW, RIGHT?
WELL, I GOTTA SAY, I'M GONNA KICK MYSELF IF I DON'T SUGGEST THAT WE SIT HERE AND MAKE OUT 'TIL THE SUN COMES UP.
BREAK'S OVER, RICKY. I HAVE TO GO TO WORK.
LISTEN. MAYBE I'M STILL DREAMING HERE, BUT WHAT ABOUT THIS?
AW.

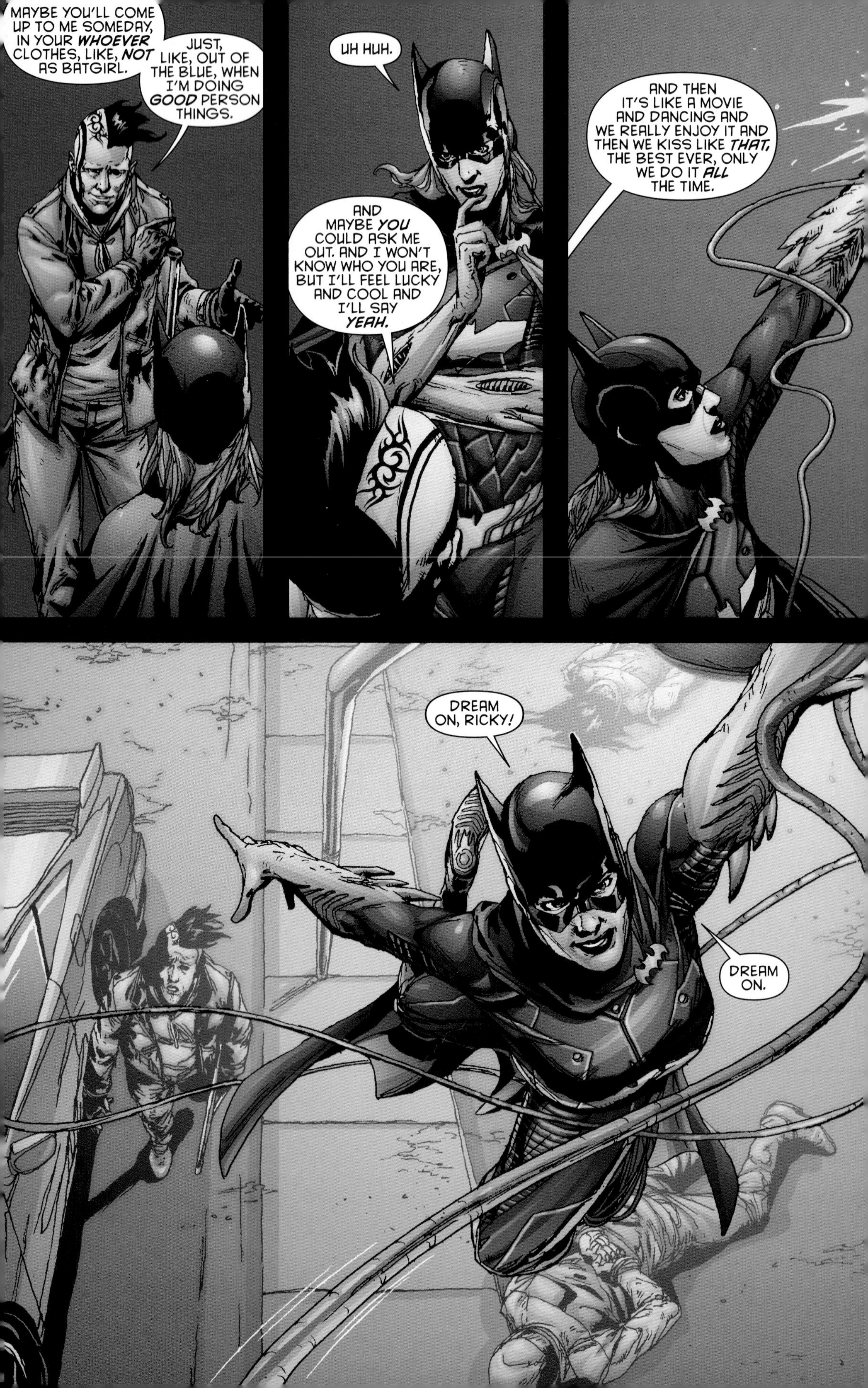
MAYBE YOU'LL COME UP TO ME SOMEDAY, IN YOUR *WHOEVER* CLOTHES, LIKE, *NOT* AS BATGIRL.
JUST, LIKE, OUT OF THE BLUE, WHEN I'M DOING *GOOD* PERSON THINGS.
UH HUH.
AND MAYBE *YOU* COULD ASK ME OUT. AND I WON'T KNOW WHO YOU ARE, BUT I'LL FEEL LUCKY AND COOL AND I'LL SAY *YEAH.*
AND THEN IT'S LIKE A MOVIE AND DANCING AND WE REALLY ENJOY IT AND THEN WE KISS LIKE *THAT,* THE BEST EVER, ONLY WE DO IT *ALL* THE TIME.
DREAM ON, RICKY!
DREAM ON.

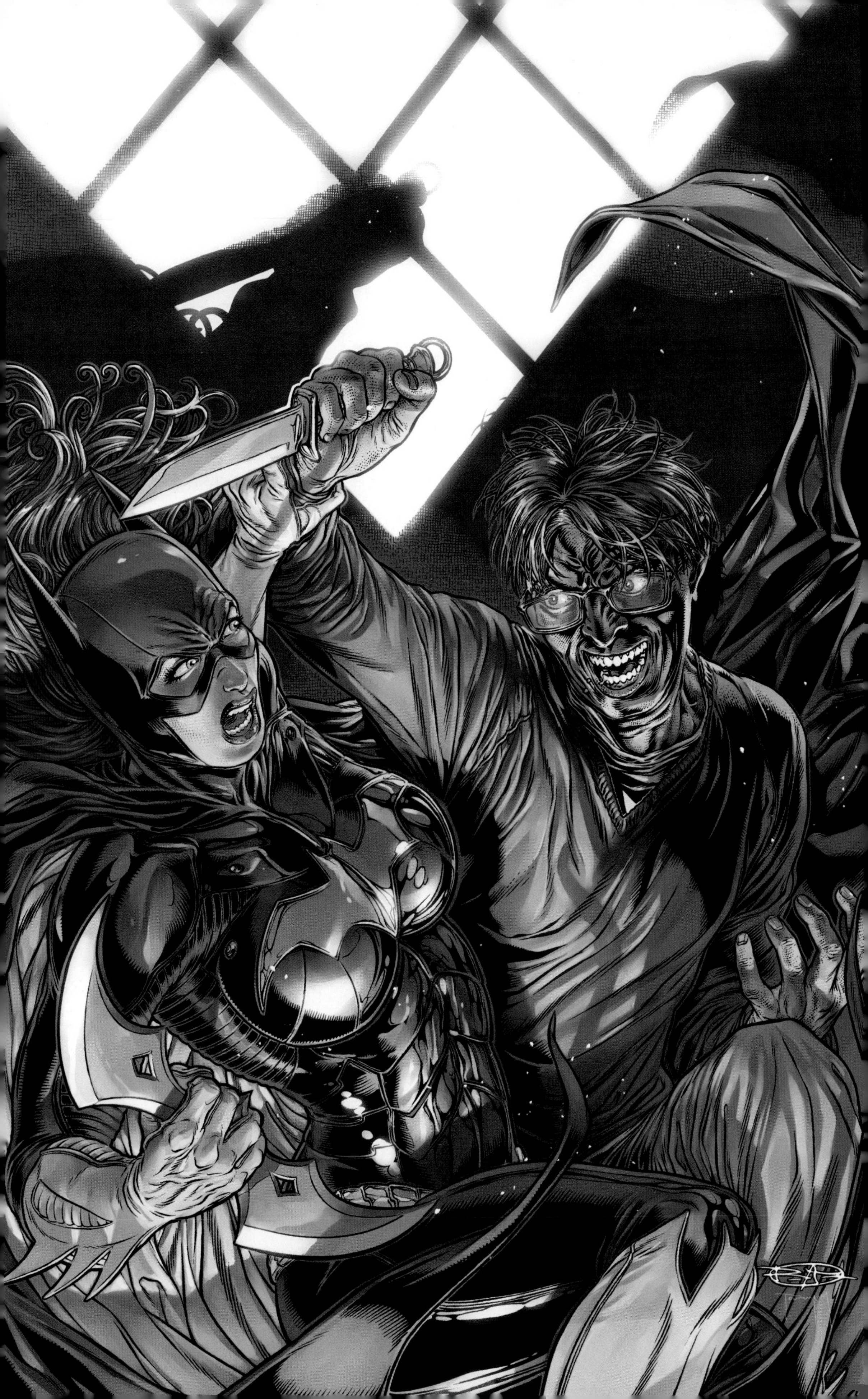

ENDURE THE FLAME

RAY FAWKES writer DANIEL SAMPERE penciller VICENTE CIFUENTES inker
cover by JUAN JOSE RYP & TOMEU MOREY

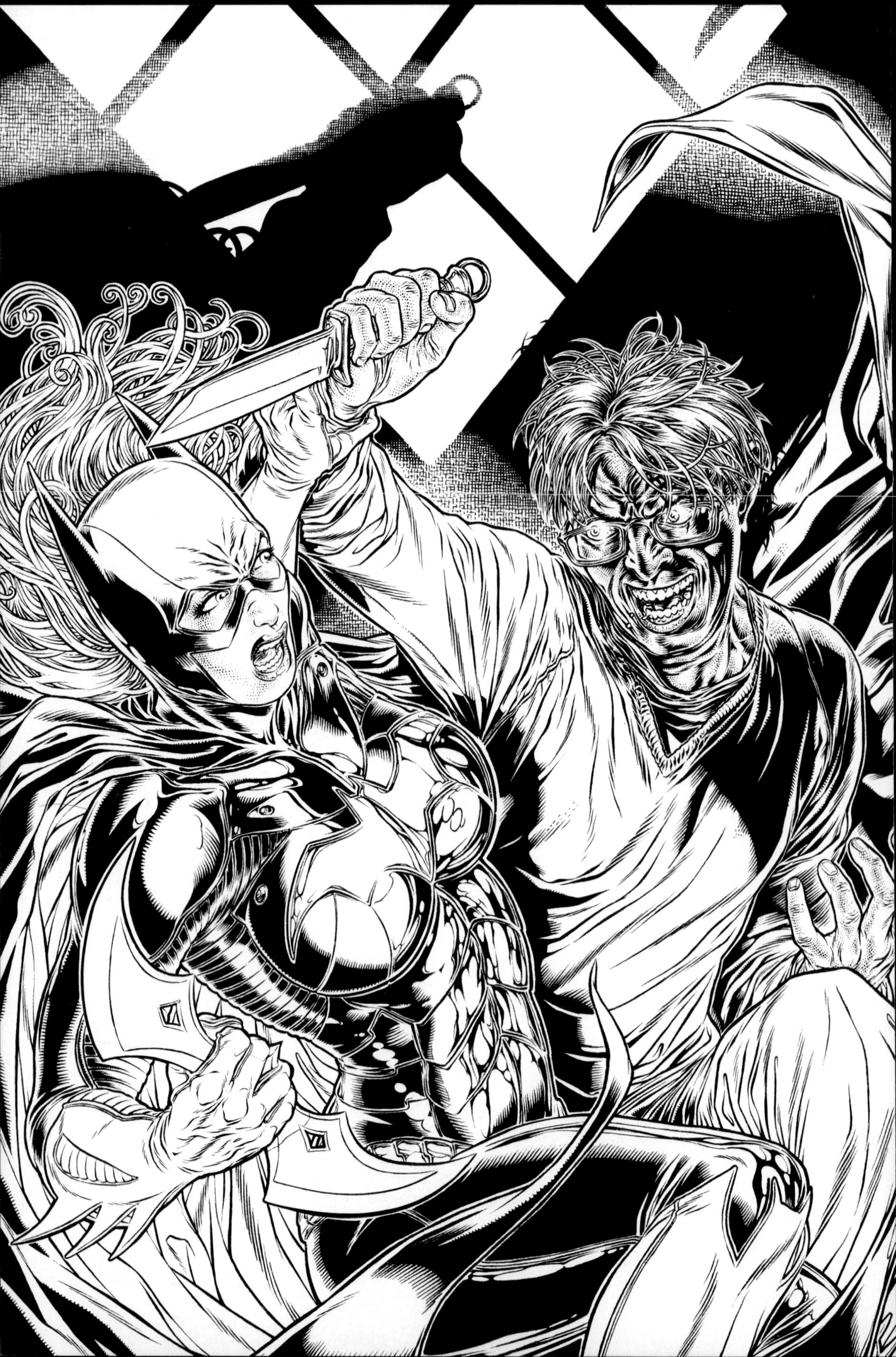

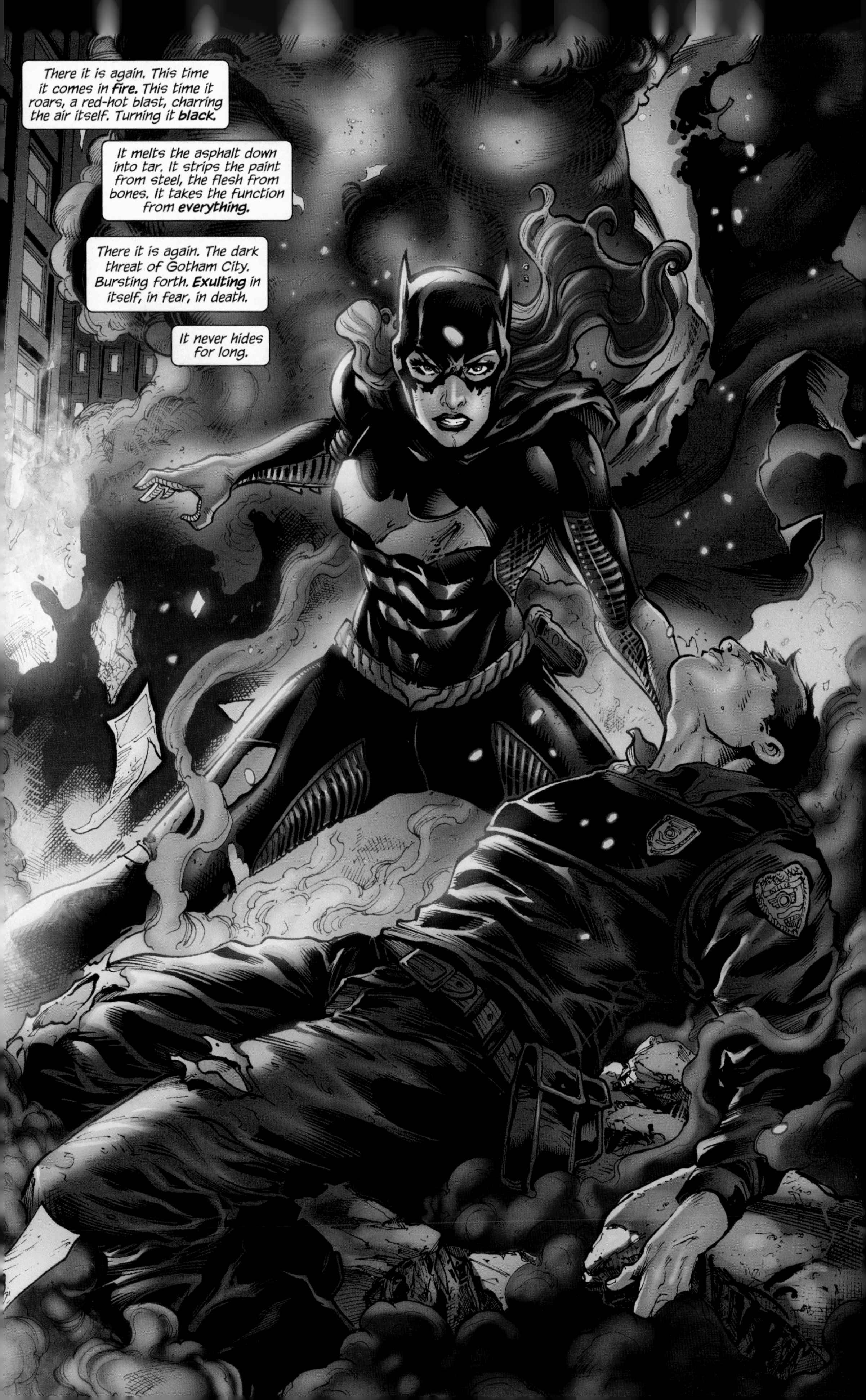
There it is again. This time it comes in fire. This time it roars, a red-hot blast, charring the air itself. Turning it black.
It melts the asphalt down into tar. It strips the paint from steel, the flesh from bones. It takes the function from everything.
There it is again. The dark threat of Gotham City. Bursting forth. Exulting in itself, in fear, in death.
It never hides for long.

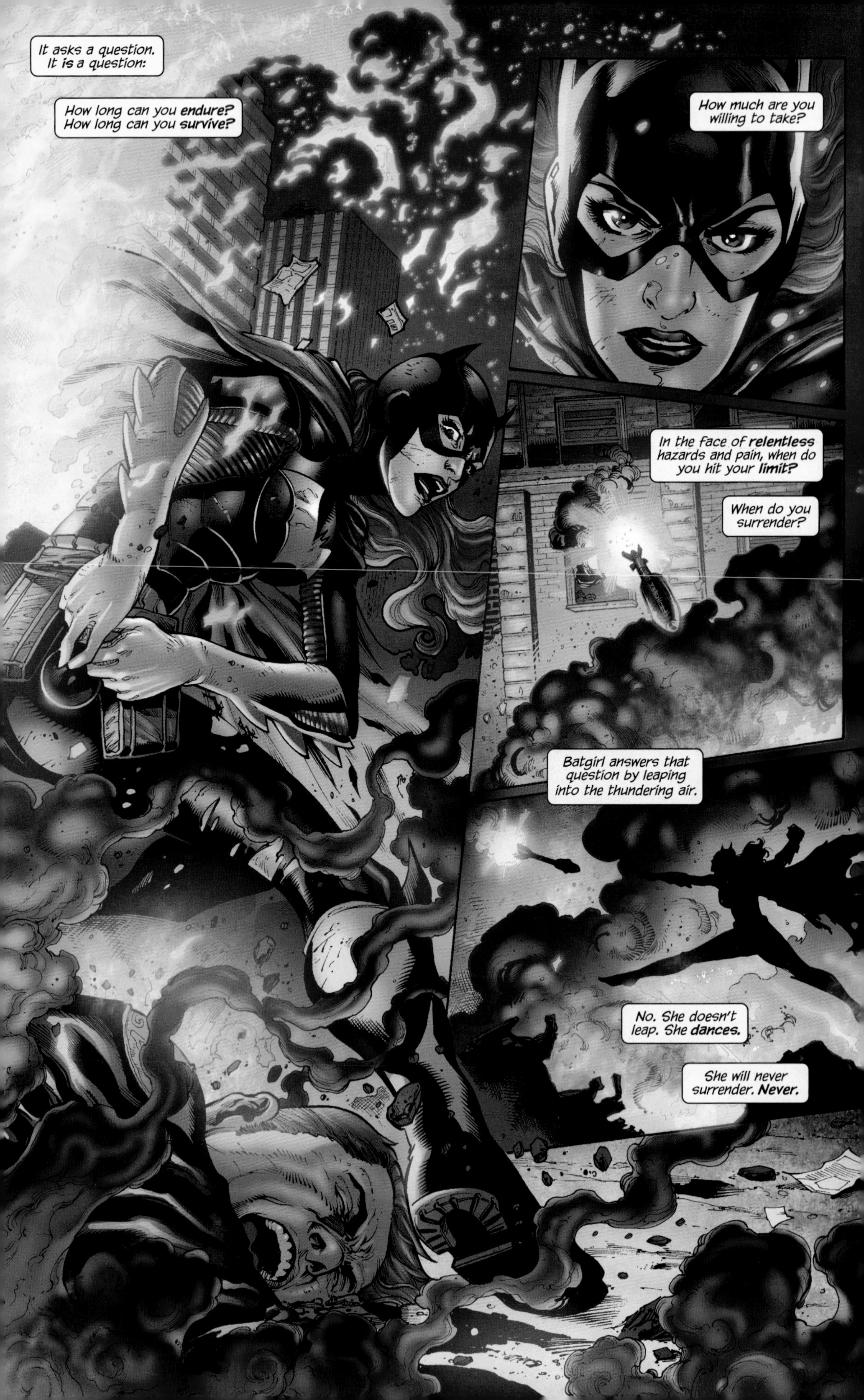
It asks a question.
It **is** a question:
How long can you **endure?**
How long can you **survive?**
How much are you
willing to take?
In the face of **relentless**
hazards and pain, when do
you hit your **limit?**
When do you
surrender?
Batgirl answers that
question by leaping
into the thundering air.
No. She doesn't
leap. She **dances.**
She will never
surrender. **Never.**

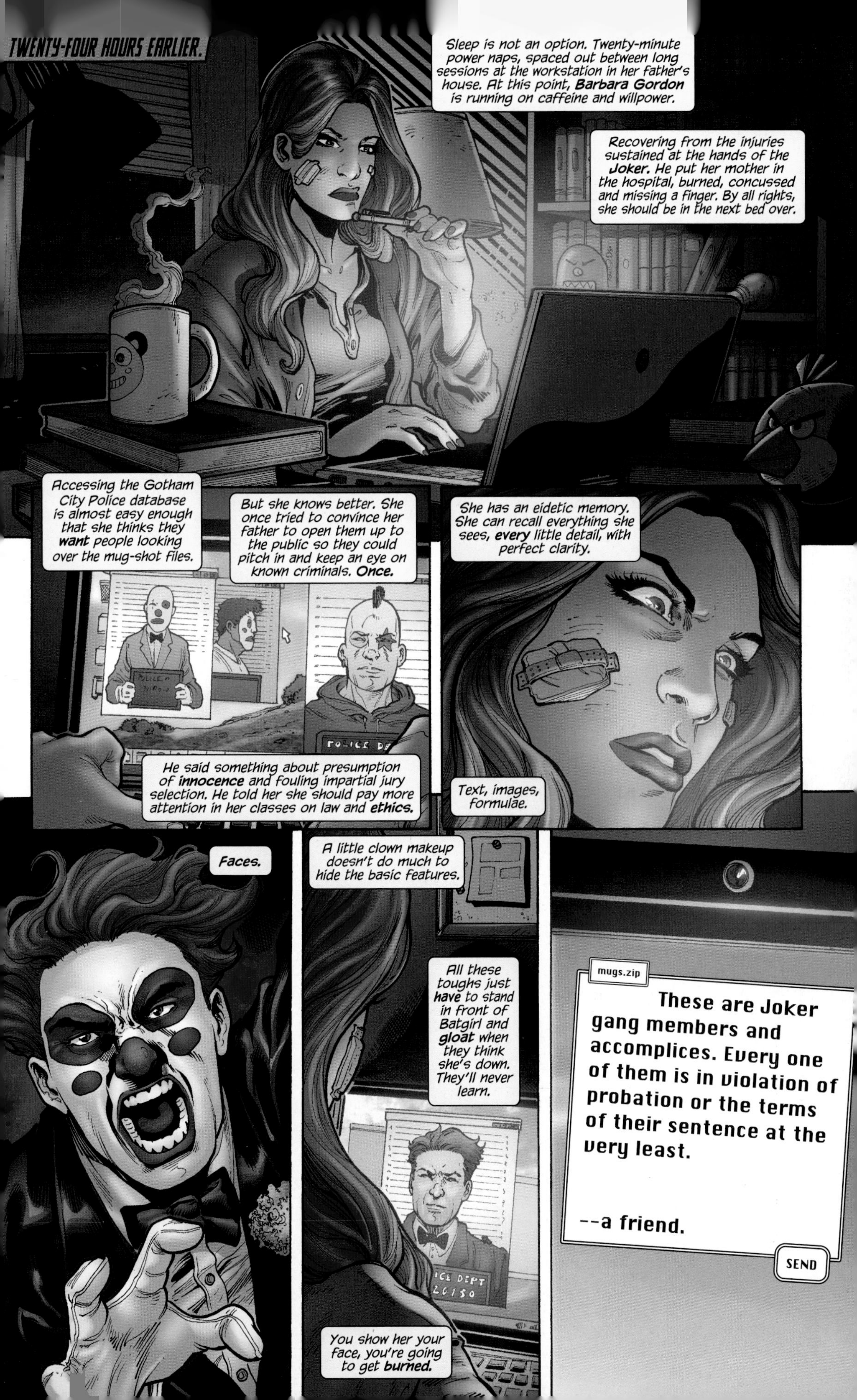
TWENTY-FOUR HOURS EARLIER.
Sleep is not an option. Twenty-minute power naps, spaced out between long sessions at the workstation in her father's house. At this point, Barbara Gordon is running on caffeine and willpower.
Recovering from the injuries sustained at the hands of the Joker. He put her mother in the hospital, burned, concussed and missing a finger. By all rights, she should be in the next bed over.
Accessing the Gotham City Police database is almost easy enough that she thinks they want people looking over the mug-shot files.
But she knows better. She once tried to convince her father to open them up to the public so they could pitch in and keep an eye on known criminals. Once.
He said something about presumption of innocence and fouling impartial jury selection. He told her she should pay more attention in her classes on law and ethics.
She has an eidetic memory. She can recall everything she sees, every little detail, with perfect clarity.
Text, images, formulae.
Faces.
A little clown makeup doesn't do much to hide the basic features.
All these toughs just have to stand in front of Batgirl and gloat when they think she's down. They'll never learn.
You show her your face, you're going to get burned.
mugs.zip
These are Joker gang members and accomplices. Every one of them is in violation of probation or the terms of their sentence at the very least.
--a friend.
SEND

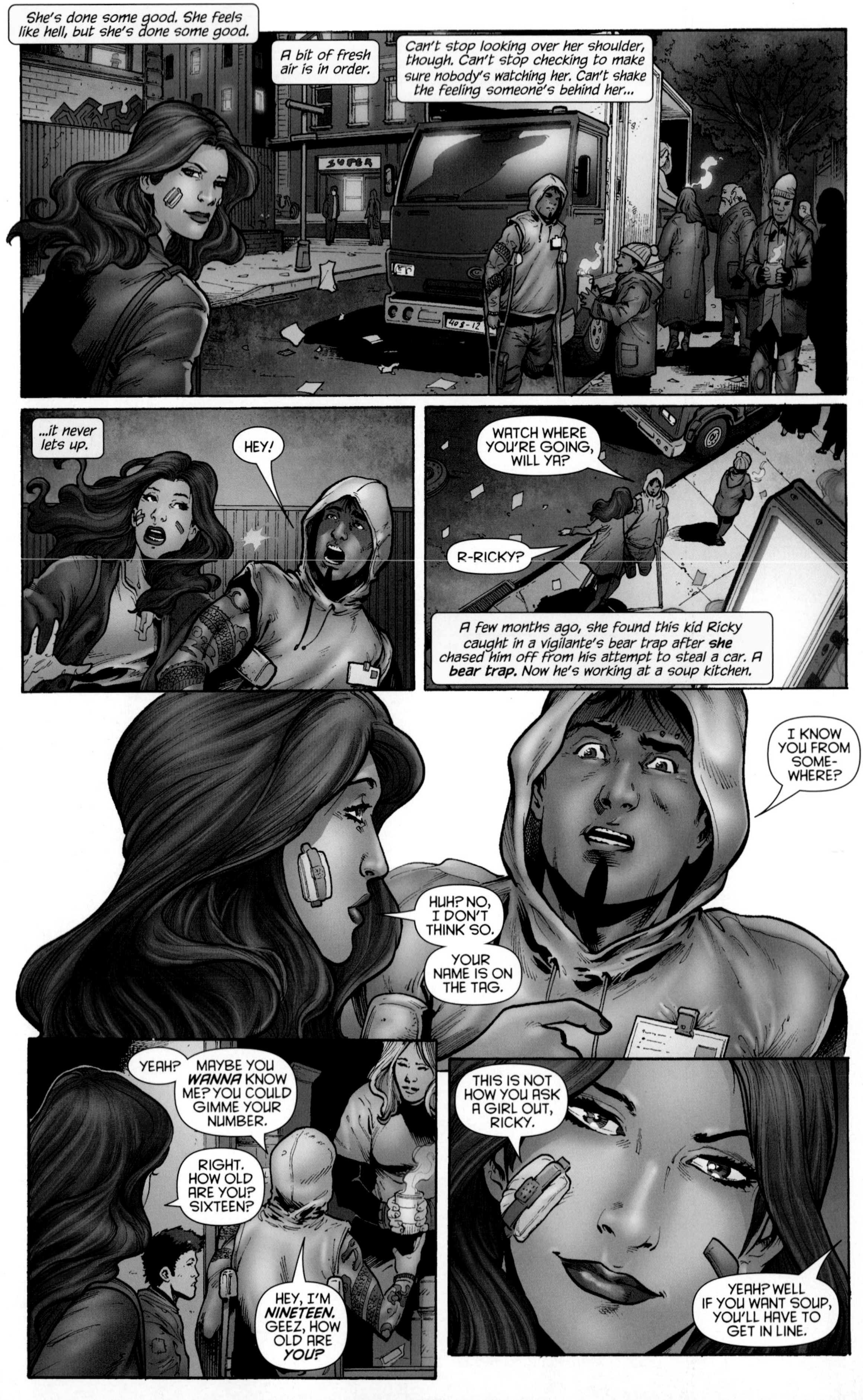
She's done some good. She feels like hell, but she's done some good.
A bit of fresh air is in order.
Can't stop looking over her shoulder, though. Can't stop checking to make sure nobody's watching her. Can't shake the feeling someone's behind her...
SUPER
...it never lets up.
HEY!
WATCH WHERE YOU'RE GOING, WILL YA?
R-RICKY?
A few months ago, she found this kid Ricky caught in a vigilante's bear trap after **she** chased him off from his attempt to steal a car. A **bear trap.** Now he's working at a soup kitchen.
I KNOW YOU FROM SOME-WHERE?
HUH? NO, I DON'T THINK SO.
YOUR NAME IS ON THE TAG.
YEAH?
MAYBE YOU ***WANNA*** KNOW ME? YOU COULD GIMME YOUR NUMBER.
RIGHT. HOW OLD ARE YOU? SIXTEEN?
HEY, I'M ***NINETEEN.*** GEEZ, HOW OLD ARE ***YOU?***
THIS IS NOT HOW YOU ASK A GIRL OUT, RICKY.
YEAH? WELL IF YOU WANT SOUP, YOU'LL HAVE TO GET IN LINE.

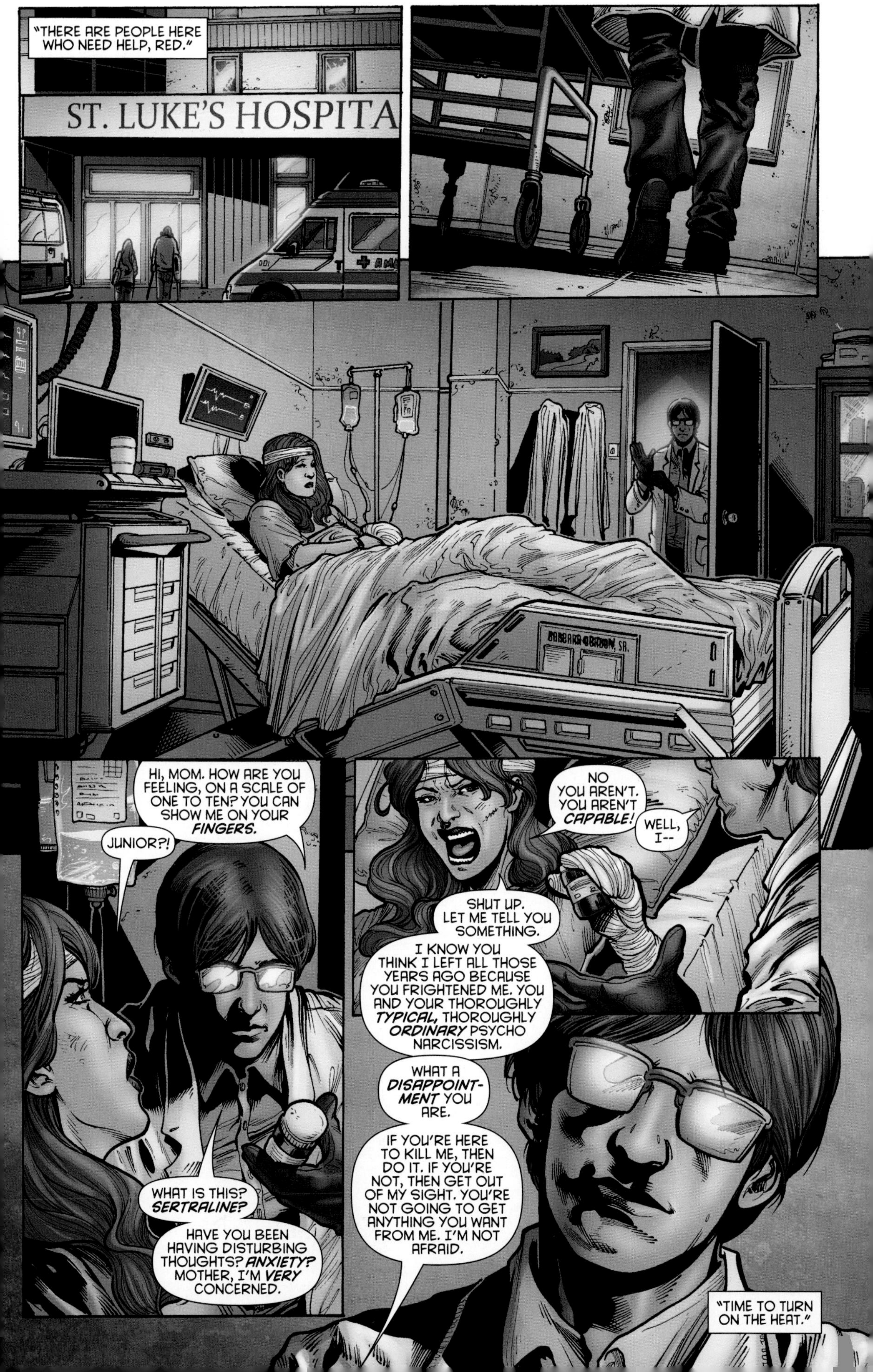
"THERE ARE PEOPLE HERE WHO NEED HELP, RED."
ST. LUKE'S HOSPITA
HI, MOM. HOW ARE YOU FEELING, ON A SCALE OF ONE TO TEN? YOU CAN SHOW ME ON YOUR *FINGERS.*
JUNIOR?!
WHAT IS THIS? *SERTRALINE?*
HAVE YOU BEEN HAVING DISTURBING THOUGHTS? *ANXIETY?* MOTHER, I'M *VERY* CONCERNED.
NO YOU AREN'T. YOU AREN'T *CAPABLE!*
WELL, I--
SHUT UP. LET ME TELL YOU SOMETHING.
I KNOW YOU THINK I LEFT ALL THOSE YEARS AGO BECAUSE YOU FRIGHTENED ME. YOU AND YOUR THOROUGHLY *TYPICAL,* THOROUGHLY *ORDINARY* PSYCHO NARCISSISM.
WHAT A *DISAPPOINTMENT* YOU ARE.
IF YOU'RE HERE TO KILL ME, THEN DO IT. IF YOU'RE NOT, THEN GET OUT OF MY SIGHT. YOU'RE NOT GOING TO GET ANYTHING YOU WANT FROM ME. I'M NOT AFRAID.
"TIME TO TURN ON THE HEAT."

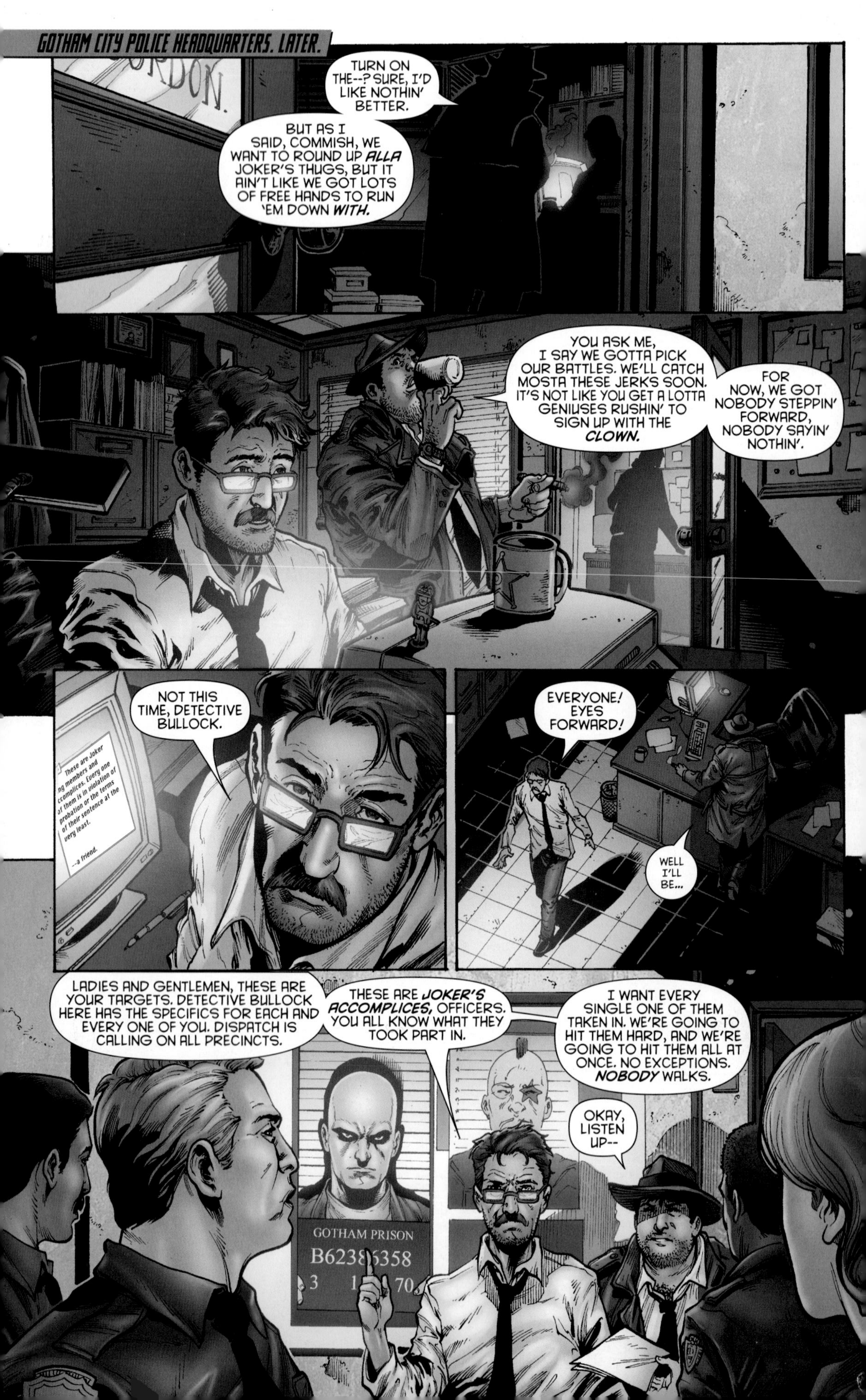
GOTHAM CITY POLICE HEADQUARTERS. LATER.
TURN ON THE--? SURE, I'D LIKE NOTHIN' BETTER.
BUT AS I SAID, COMMISH, WE WANT TO ROUND UP ALLA JOKER'S THUGS, BUT IT AIN'T LIKE WE GOT LOTS OF FREE HANDS TO RUN 'EM DOWN WITH.
YOU ASK ME, I SAY WE GOTTA PICK OUR BATTLES. WE'LL CATCH MOSTA THESE JERKS SOON. IT'S NOT LIKE YOU GET A LOTTA GENIUSES RUSHIN' TO SIGN UP WITH THE CLOWN.
FOR NOW, WE GOT NOBODY STEPPIN' FORWARD, NOBODY SAYIN' NOTHIN'.
NOT THIS TIME, DETECTIVE BULLOCK.
These are Joker
ng members and
ccomplices. Every one
of them is in violation of
probation or the terms
of their sentence at the
very least.
--a friend.
EVERYONE! EYES FORWARD!
WELL I'LL BE...
LADIES AND GENTLEMEN, THESE ARE YOUR TARGETS. DETECTIVE BULLOCK HERE HAS THE SPECIFICS FOR EACH AND EVERY ONE OF YOU. DISPATCH IS CALLING ON ALL PRECINCTS.
THESE ARE JOKER'S ACCOMPLICES, OFFICERS. YOU ALL KNOW WHAT THEY TOOK PART IN.
I WANT EVERY SINGLE ONE OF THEM TAKEN IN. WE'RE GOING TO HIT THEM HARD, AND WE'RE GOING TO HIT THEM ALL AT ONCE. NO EXCEPTIONS. NOBODY WALKS.
OKAY, LISTEN UP--
GOTHAM PRISON

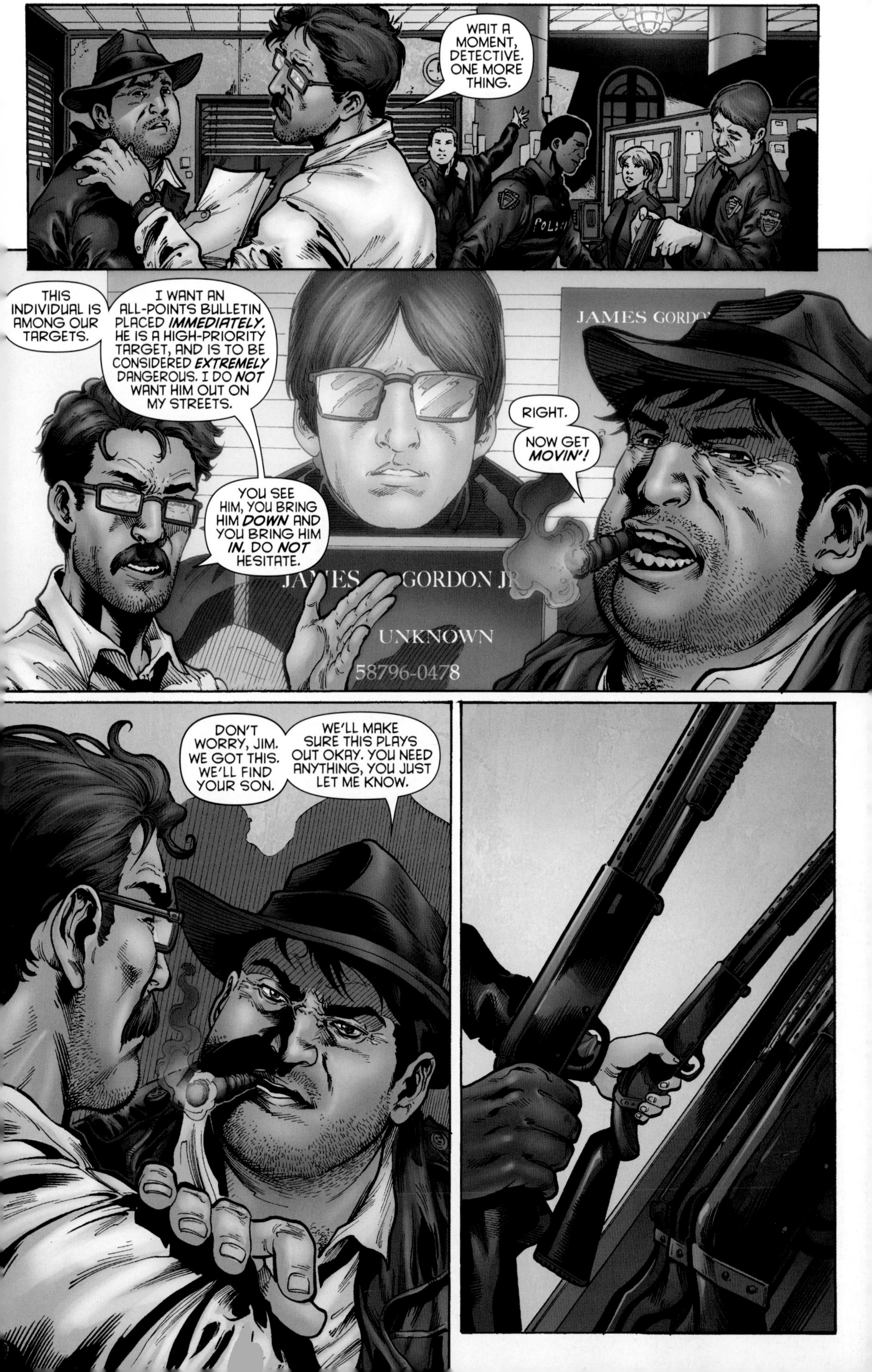
WAIT A MOMENT, DETECTIVE. ONE MORE THING.
THIS INDIVIDUAL IS AMONG OUR TARGETS.
I WANT AN ALL-POINTS BULLETIN PLACED IMMEDIATELY. HE IS A HIGH-PRIORITY TARGET, AND IS TO BE CONSIDERED EXTREMELY DANGEROUS. I DO NOT WANT HIM OUT ON MY STREETS.
YOU SEE HIM, YOU BRING HIM DOWN AND YOU BRING HIM IN. DO NOT HESITATE.
RIGHT.
NOW GET MOVIN'!
JAMES GORDON JR
UNKNOWN
58796-0478
DON'T WORRY, JIM. WE GOT THIS. WE'LL FIND YOUR SON.
WE'LL MAKE SURE THIS PLAYS OUT OKAY. YOU NEED ANYTHING, YOU JUST LET ME KNOW.

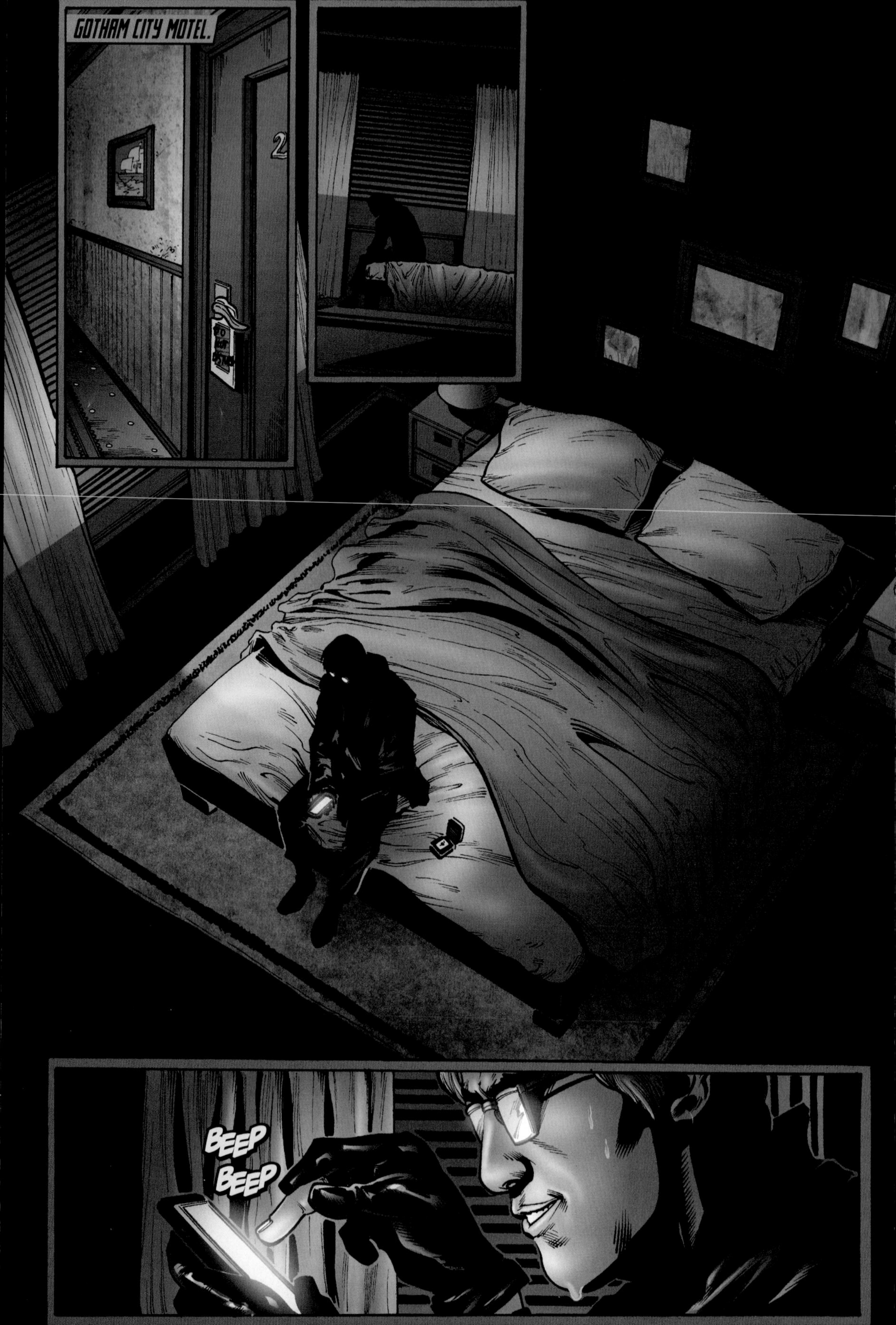
GOTHAM CITY MOTEL.
BEEP
BEEP

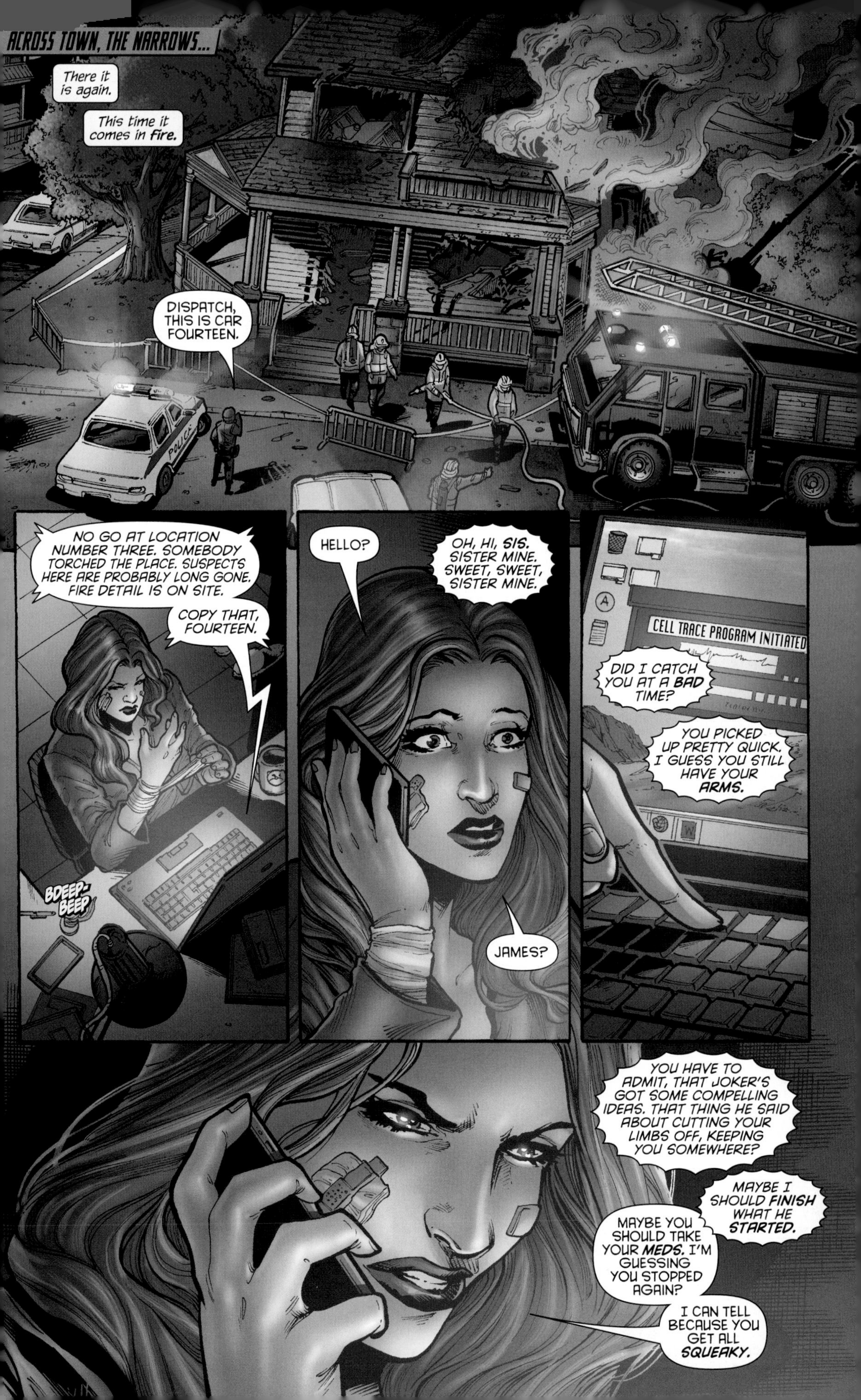
ACROSS TOWN, THE NARROWS...
There it is again.
This time it comes in fire.
DISPATCH, THIS IS CAR FOURTEEN.
NO GO AT LOCATION NUMBER THREE. SOMEBODY TORCHED THE PLACE. SUSPECTS HERE ARE PROBABLY LONG GONE. FIRE DETAIL IS ON SITE.
COPY THAT, FOURTEEN.
BDEEP-BEEP
HELLO?
OH, HI, SIS. SISTER MINE. SWEET, SWEET, SISTER MINE.
JAMES?
CELL TRACE PROGRAM INITIATED
DID I CATCH YOU AT A BAD TIME?
YOU PICKED UP PRETTY QUICK. I GUESS YOU STILL HAVE YOUR ARMS.
YOU HAVE TO ADMIT, THAT JOKER'S GOT SOME COMPELLING IDEAS. THAT THING HE SAID ABOUT CUTTING YOUR LIMBS OFF, KEEPING YOU SOMEWHERE?
MAYBE I SHOULD FINISH WHAT HE STARTED.
MAYBE YOU SHOULD TAKE YOUR MEDS. I'M GUESSING YOU STOPPED AGAIN?
I CAN TELL BECAUSE YOU GET ALL SQUEAKY.

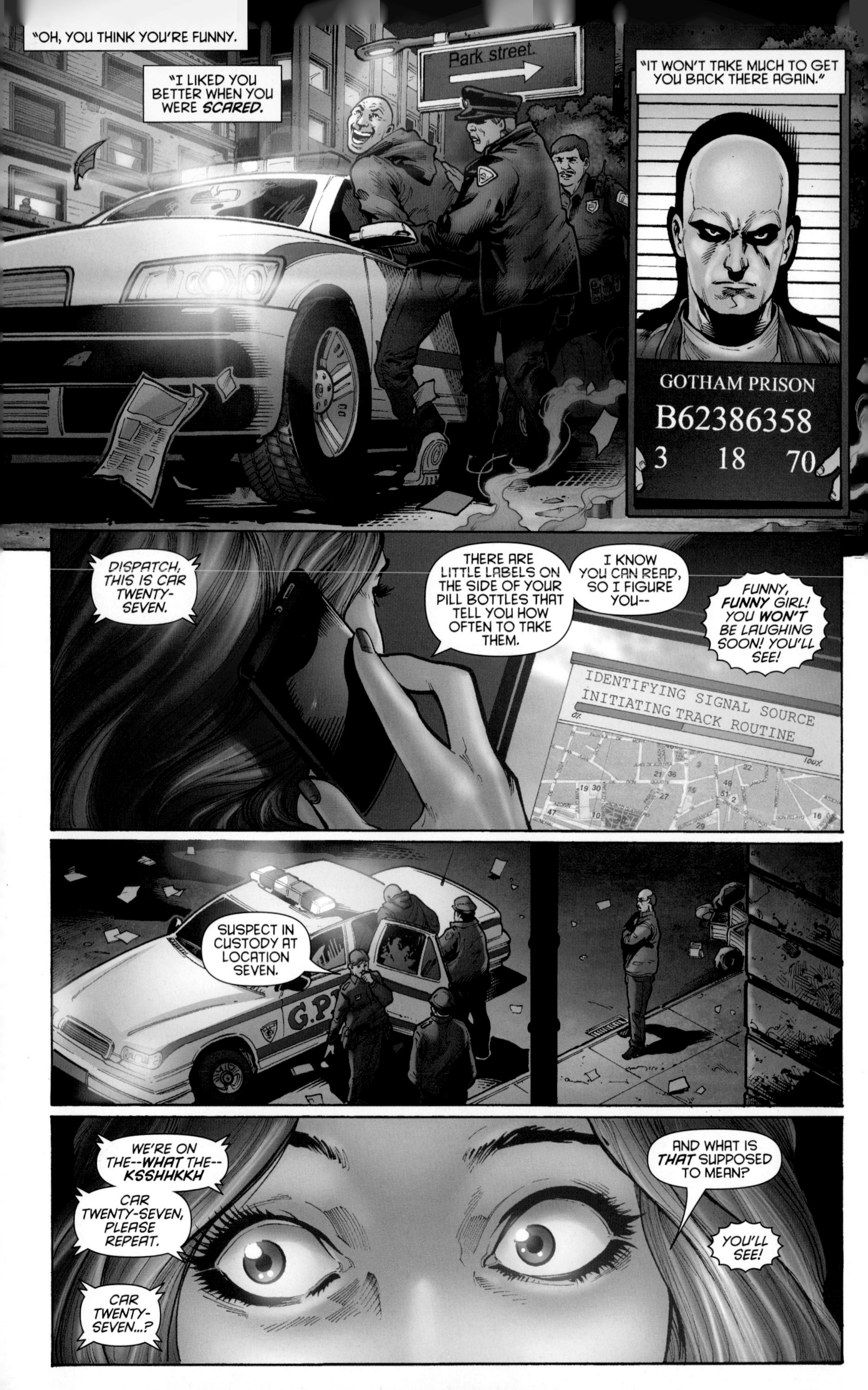
"OH, YOU THINK YOU'RE FUNNY.
"I LIKED YOU BETTER WHEN YOU WERE SCARED.
Park street.
"IT WON'T TAKE MUCH TO GET YOU BACK THERE AGAIN."
GOTHAM PRISON
B62386358
3 18 70
DISPATCH, THIS IS CAR TWENTY-SEVEN.
THERE ARE LITTLE LABELS ON THE SIDE OF YOUR PILL BOTTLES THAT TELL YOU HOW OFTEN TO TAKE THEM.
I KNOW YOU CAN READ, SO I FIGURE YOU--
FUNNY, FUNNY GIRL! YOU WON'T BE LAUGHING SOON! YOU'LL SEE!
IDENTIFYING SIGNAL SOURCE
INITIATING TRACK ROUTINE
SUSPECT IN CUSTODY AT LOCATION SEVEN.
WE'RE ON THE--WHAT THE--
KSSHHKKH
CAR TWENTY-SEVEN, PLEASE REPEAT.
CAR TWENTY-SEVEN...?
AND WHAT IS THAT SUPPOSED TO MEAN?
YOU'LL SEE!

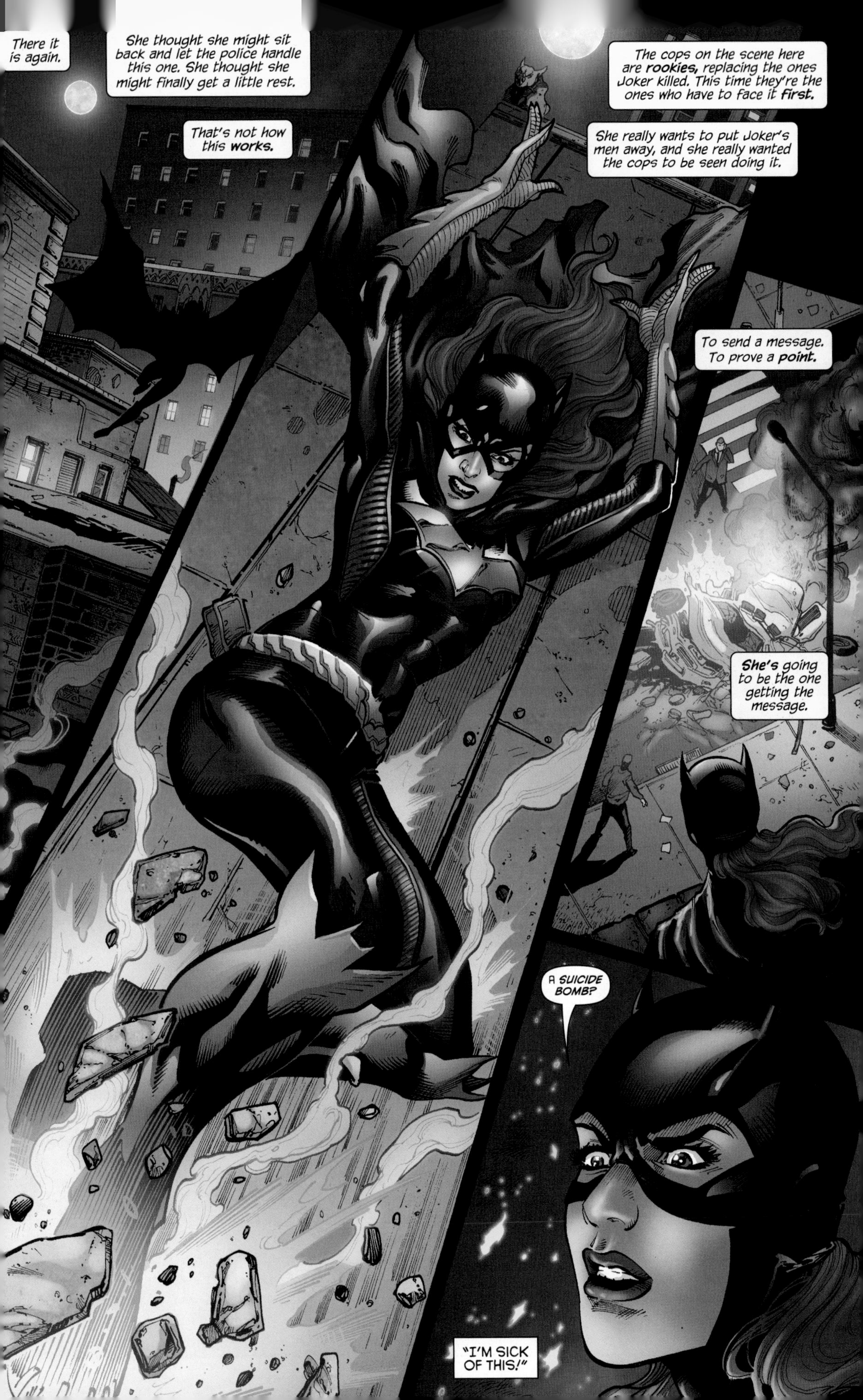
There it is again.
She thought she might sit back and let the police handle this one. She thought she might finally get a little rest.
That's not how this works.
The cops on the scene here are rookies, replacing the ones Joker killed. This time they're the ones who have to face it first.
She really wants to put Joker's men away, and she really wanted the cops to be seen doing it.
To send a message. To prove a point.
She's going to be the one getting the message.
A SUICIDE BOMB?
"I'M SICK OF THIS!"

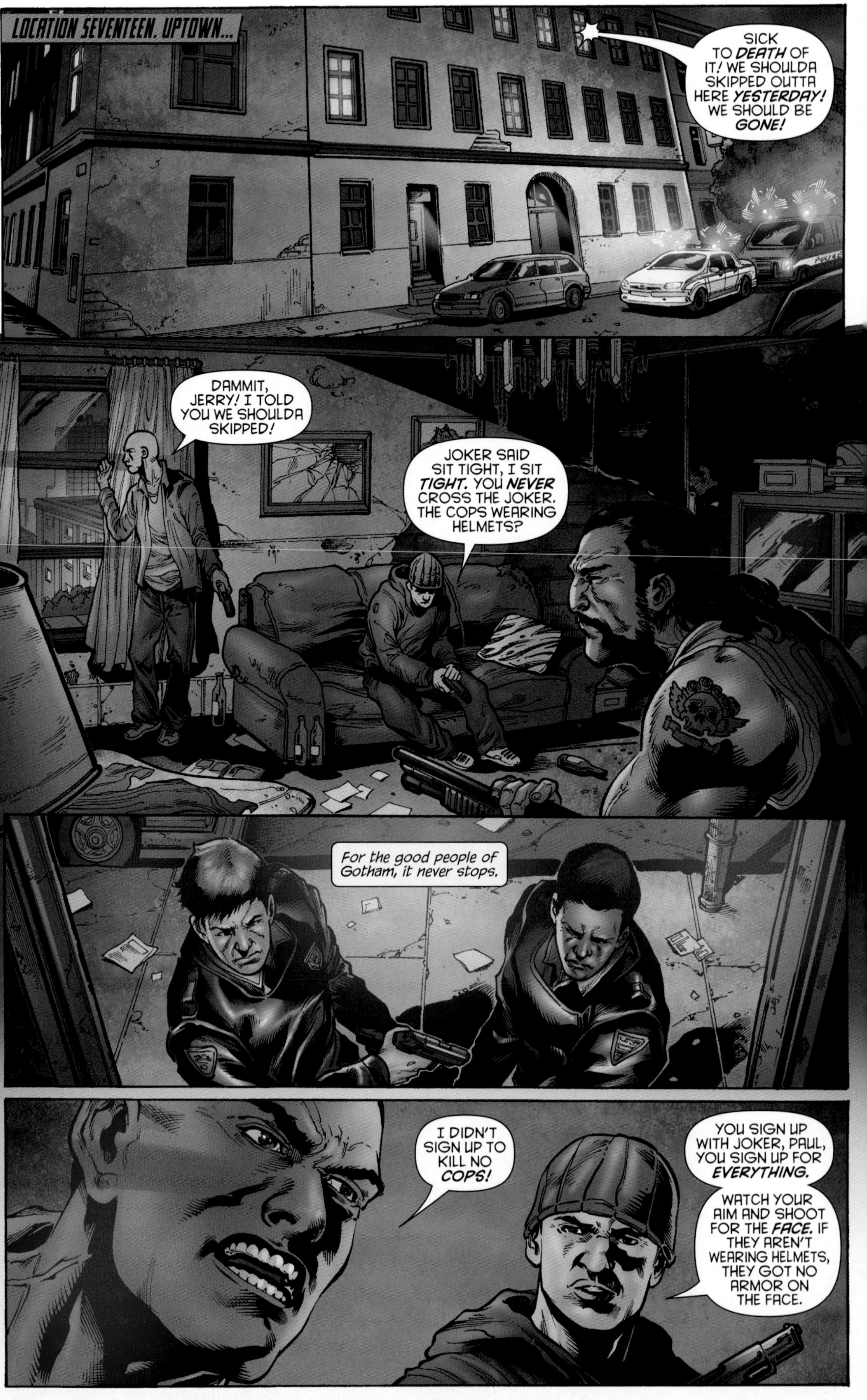
LOCATION SEVENTEEN. UPTOWN...
SICK TO DEATH OF IT! WE SHOULDA SKIPPED OUTTA HERE YESTERDAY! WE SHOULD BE GONE!
DAMMIT, JERRY! I TOLD YOU WE SHOULDA SKIPPED!
JOKER SAID SIT TIGHT, I SIT TIGHT. YOU NEVER CROSS THE JOKER. THE COPS WEARING HELMETS?
For the good people of Gotham, it never stops.
I DIDN'T SIGN UP TO KILL NO COPS!
YOU SIGN UP WITH JOKER, PAUL, YOU SIGN UP FOR EVERYTHING.
WATCH YOUR AIM AND SHOOT FOR THE FACE. IF THEY AREN'T WEARING HELMETS, THEY GOT NO ARMOR ON THE FACE.

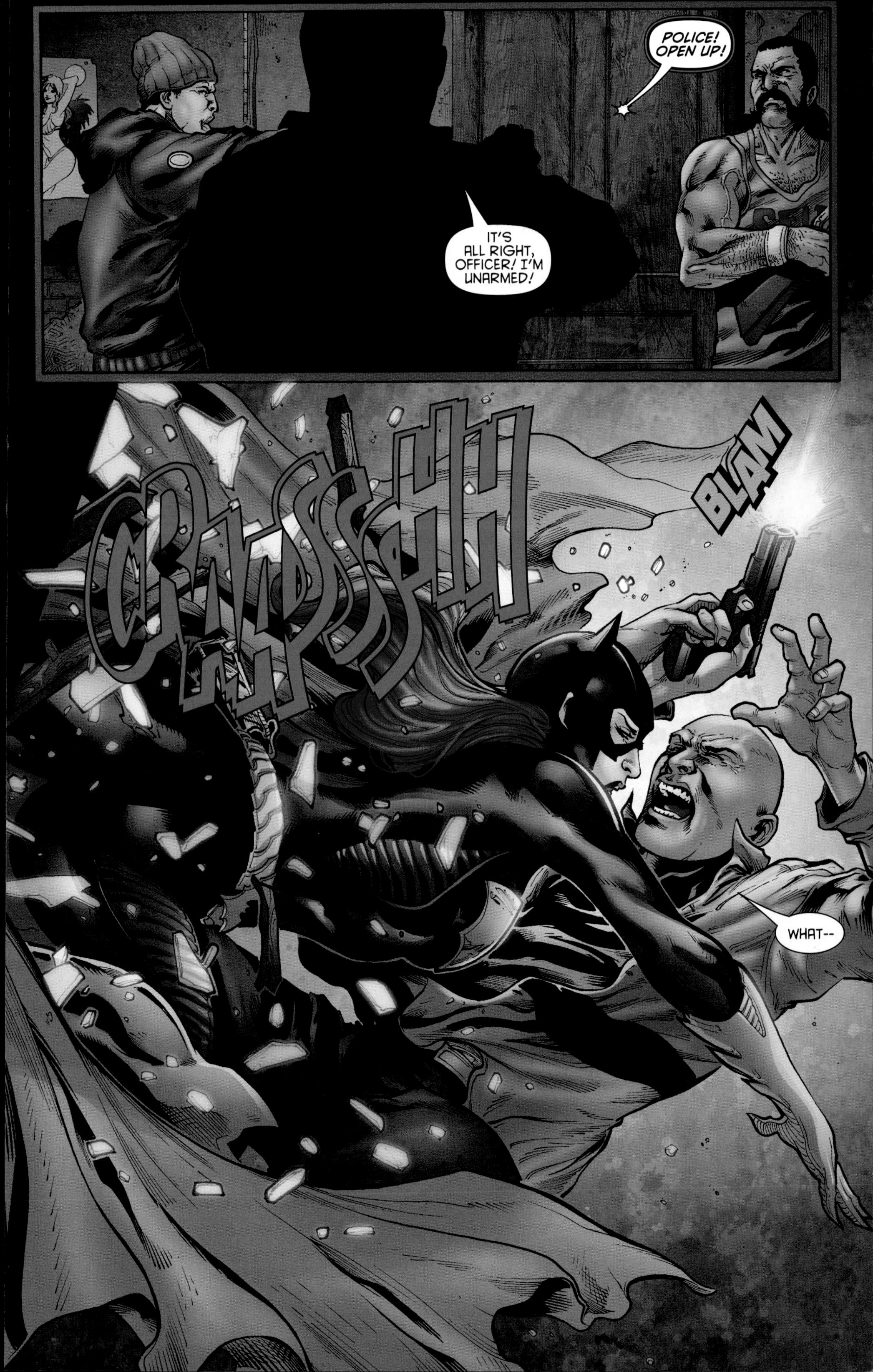
POLICE! OPEN UP!
IT'S ALL RIGHT, OFFICER! I'M UNARMED!
BLAM
WHAT--

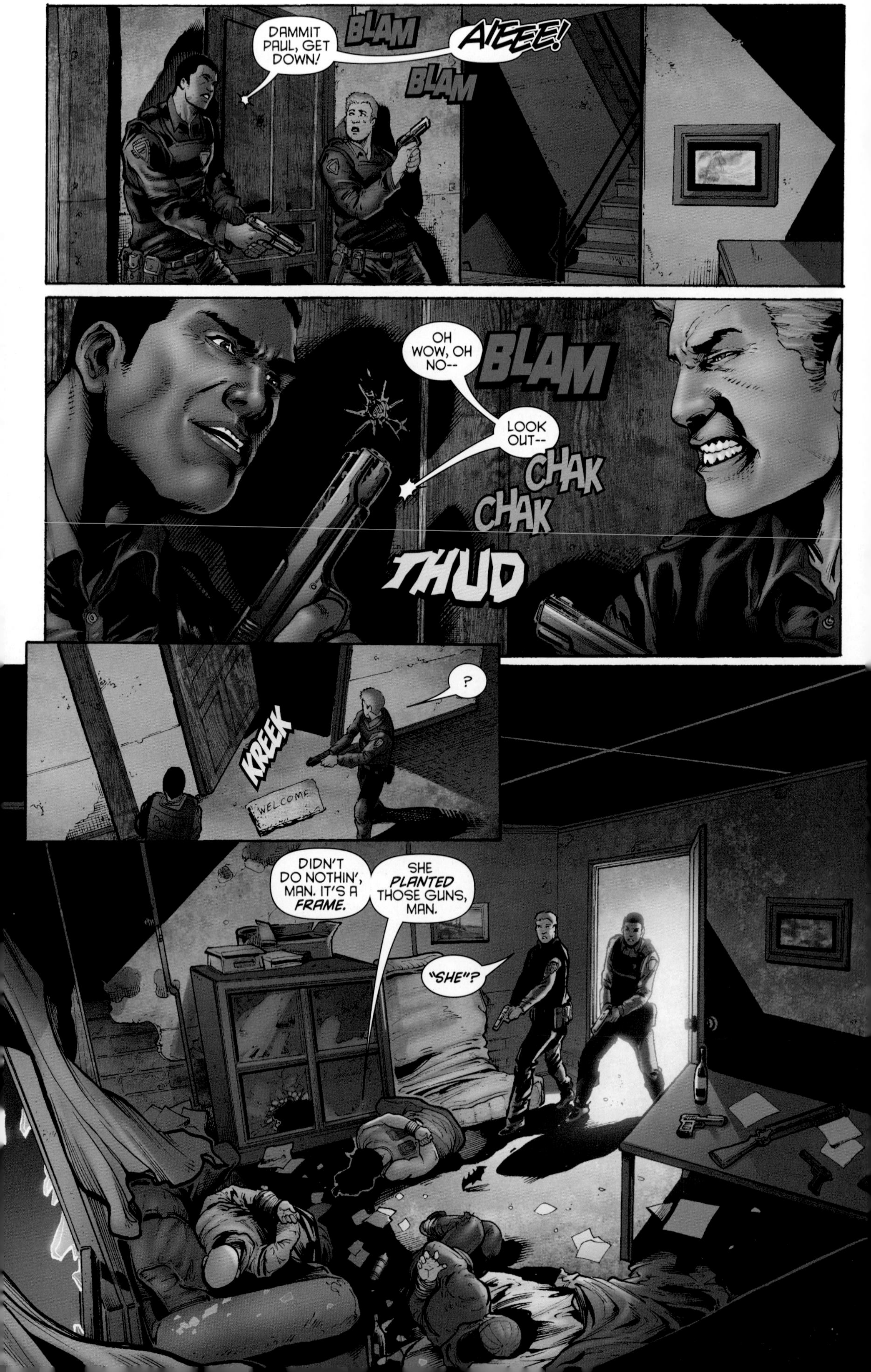
DAMMIT PAUL, GET DOWN!
BLAM
AIEEE!
BLAM
OH WOW, OH NO--
BLAM
LOOK OUT--
CHAK
CHAK
THUD
KREEK
?
WELCOME
DIDN'T DO NOTHIN', MAN. IT'S A *FRAME.*
SHE *PLANTED* THOSE GUNS, MAN.
"SHE"?

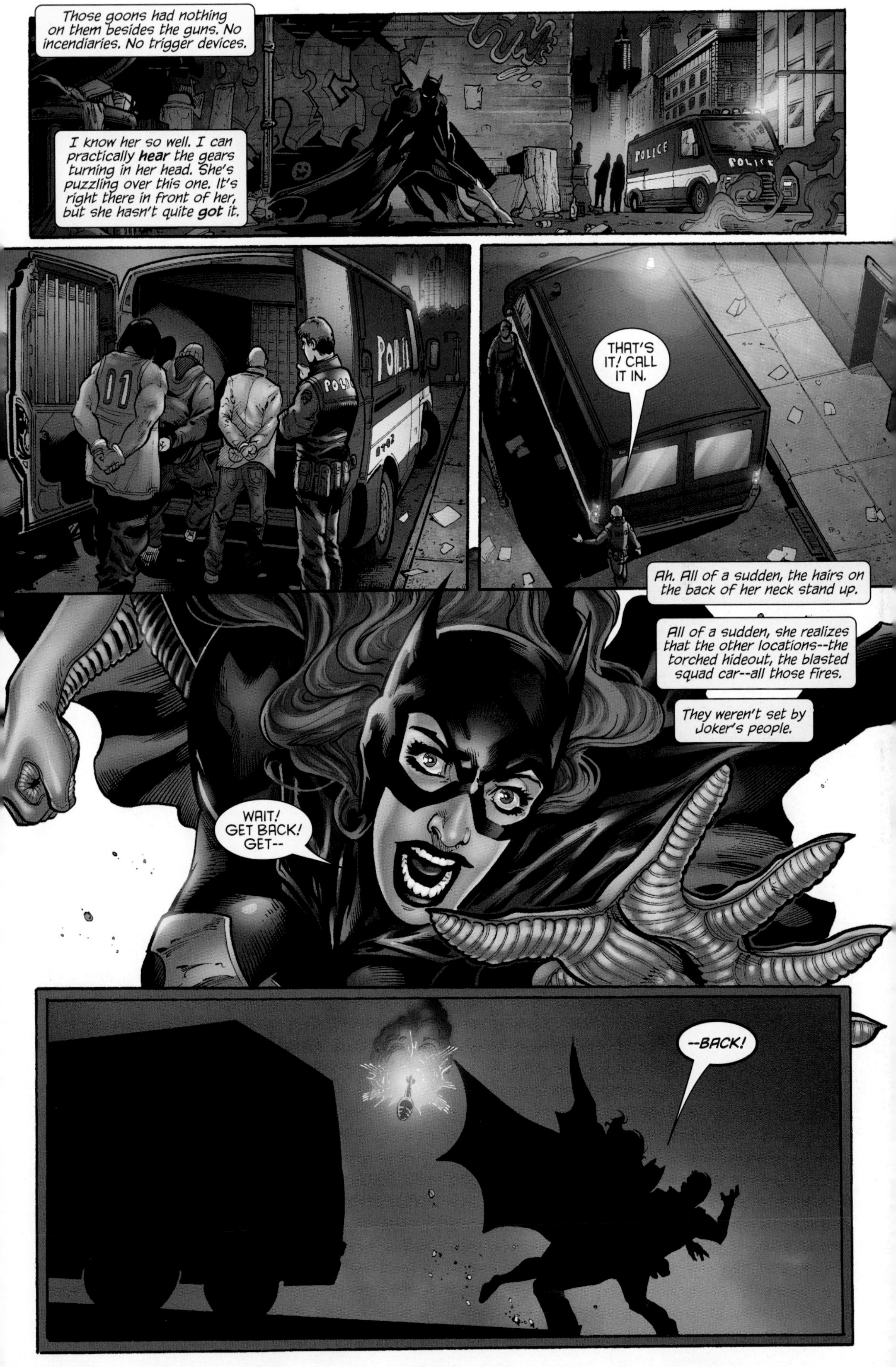
Those goons had nothing on them besides the guns. No incendiaries. No trigger devices.
I know her so well. I can practically hear the gears turning in her head. She's puzzling over this one. It's right there in front of her, but she hasn't quite got it.
POLICE
POLICE
THAT'S IT! CALL IT IN.
Ah. All of a sudden, the hairs on the back of her neck stand up.
All of a sudden, she realizes that the other locations--the torched hideout, the blasted squad car--all those fires.
They weren't set by Joker's people.
WAIT! GET BACK! GET--
--BACK!

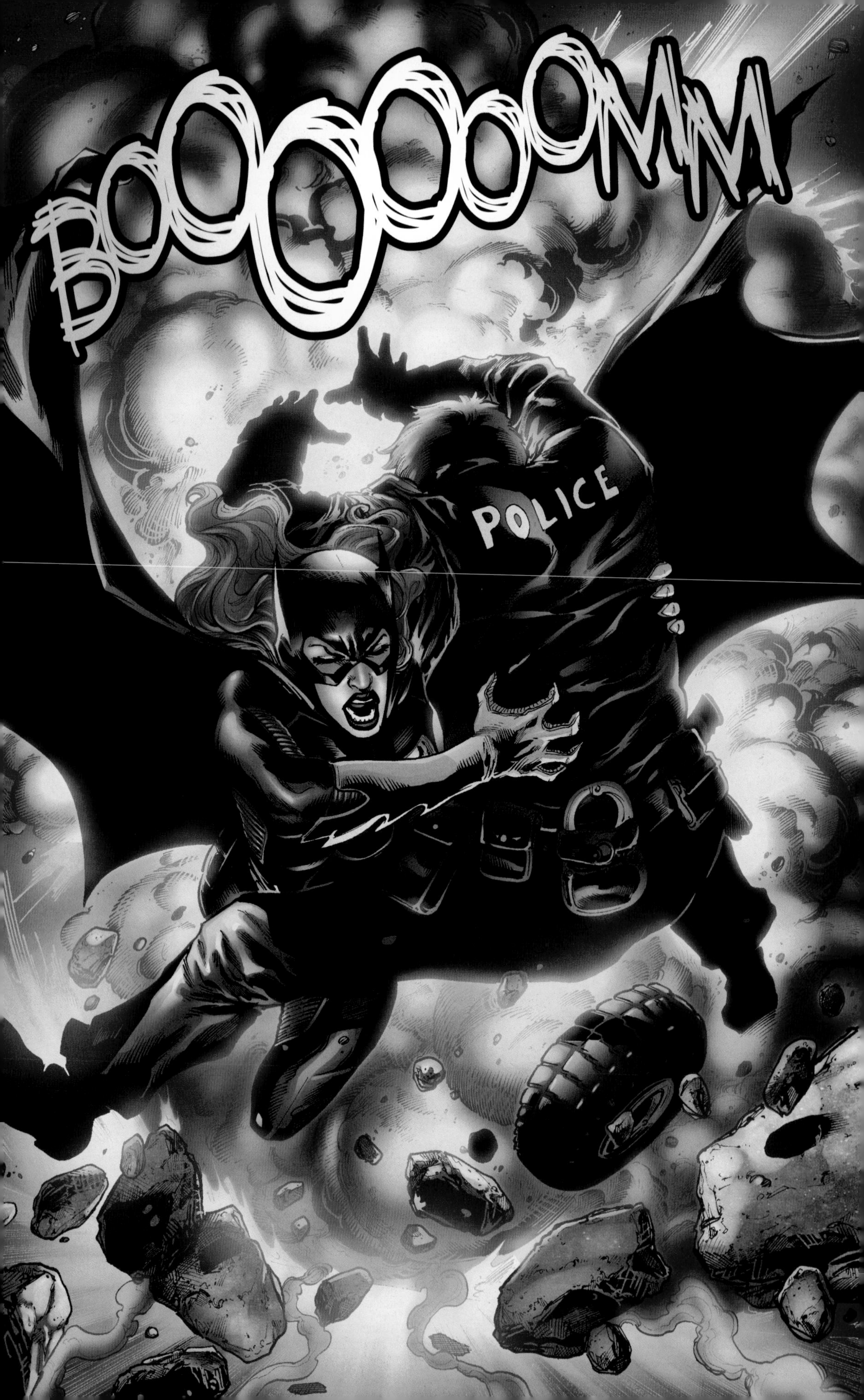
BOOOOOOOMM
POLICE

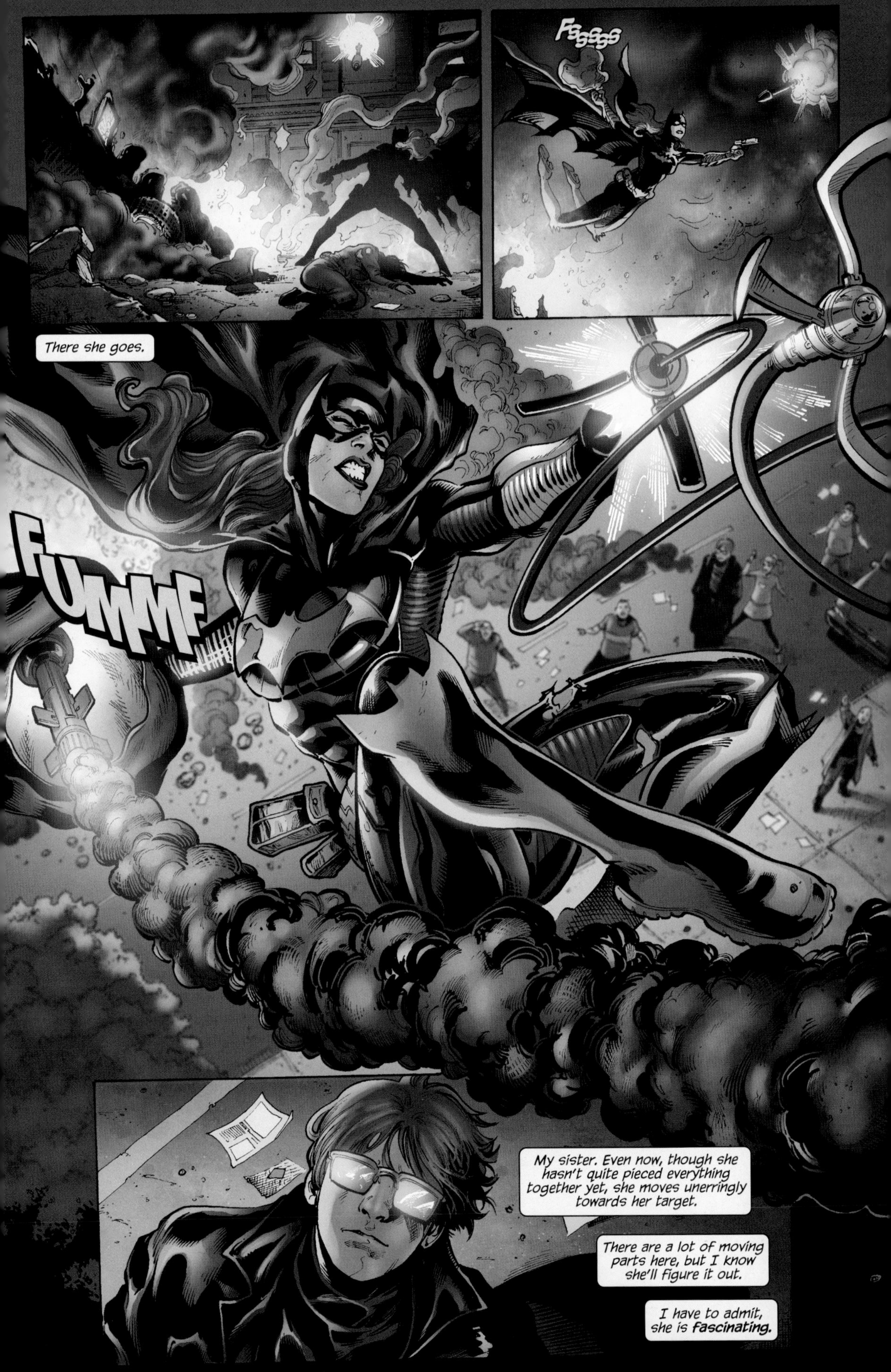
FSSSSS
There she goes.
FUMMF
My sister. Even now, though she hasn't quite pieced everything together yet, she moves unerringly towards her target.
There are a lot of moving parts here, but I know she'll figure it out.
I have to admit, she is **fascinating.**

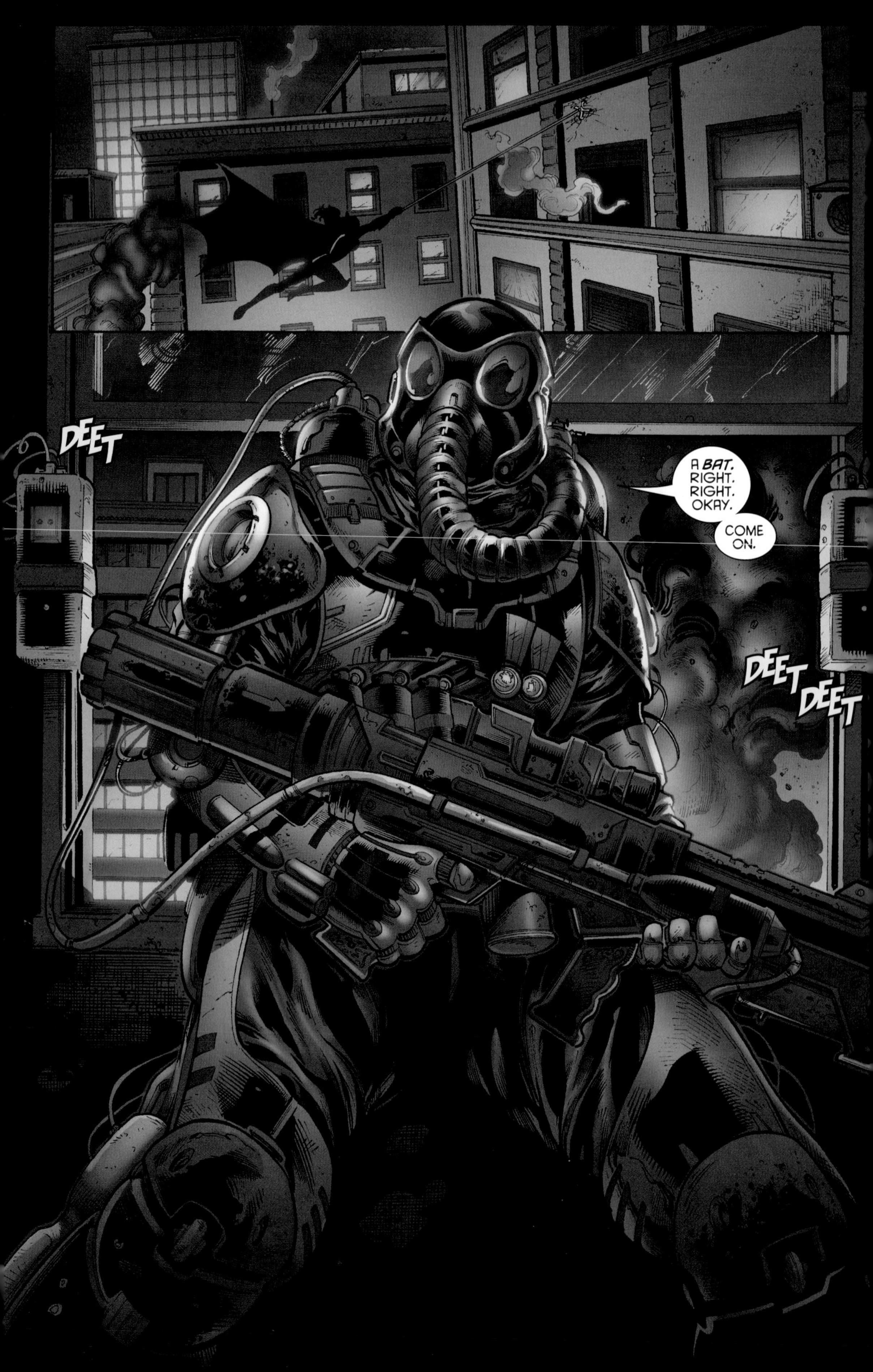
DEET
A BAT. RIGHT. RIGHT. OKAY.
COME ON.
DEET DEET

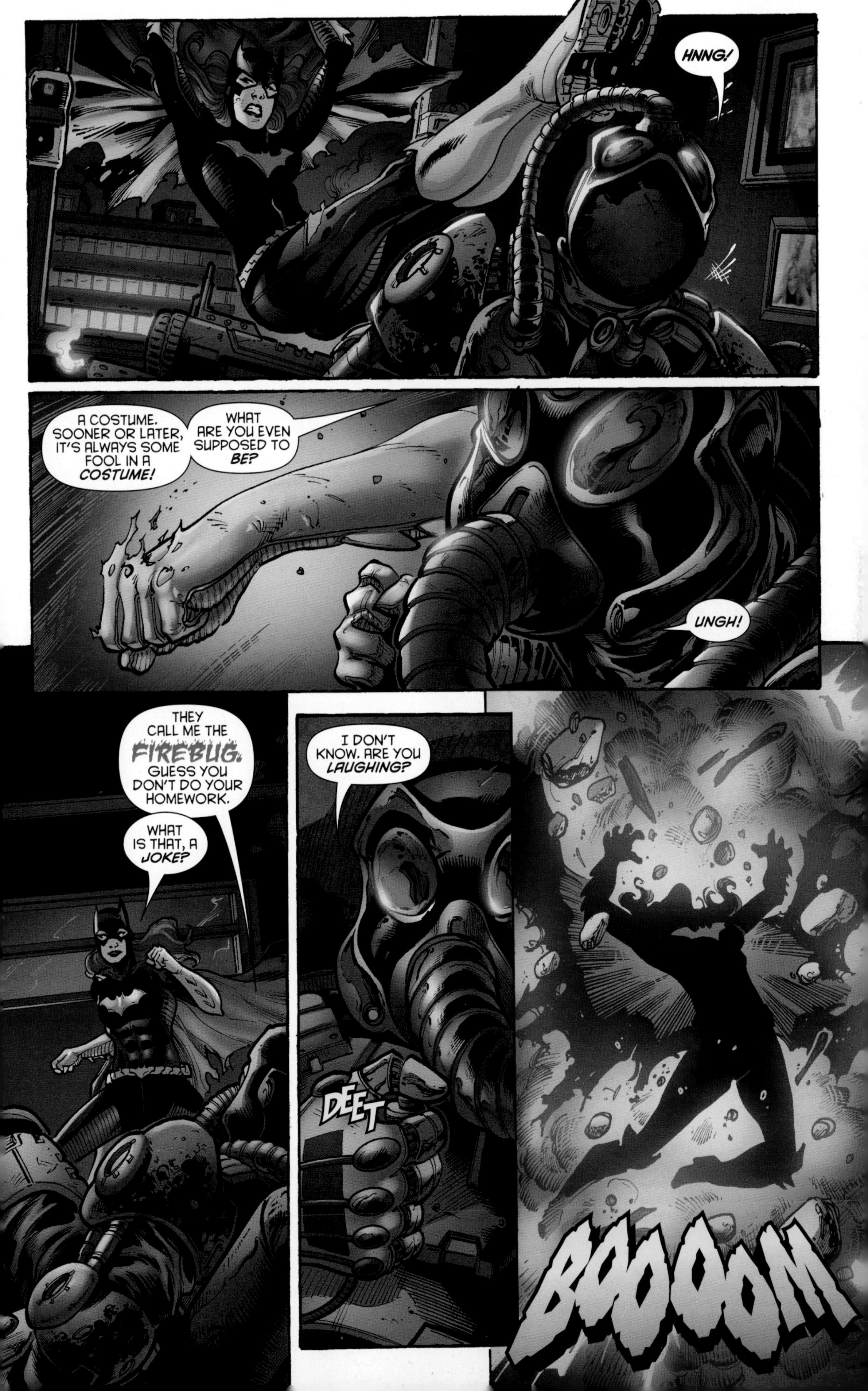
HNNG!
A COSTUME. SOONER OR LATER, IT'S ALWAYS SOME FOOL IN A COSTUME!
WHAT ARE YOU EVEN SUPPOSED TO BE?
UNGH!
THEY CALL ME THE FIREBUG. GUESS YOU DON'T DO YOUR HOMEWORK.
WHAT IS THAT, A JOKE?
I DON'T KNOW. ARE YOU LAUGHING?
DEET
BOOOOM

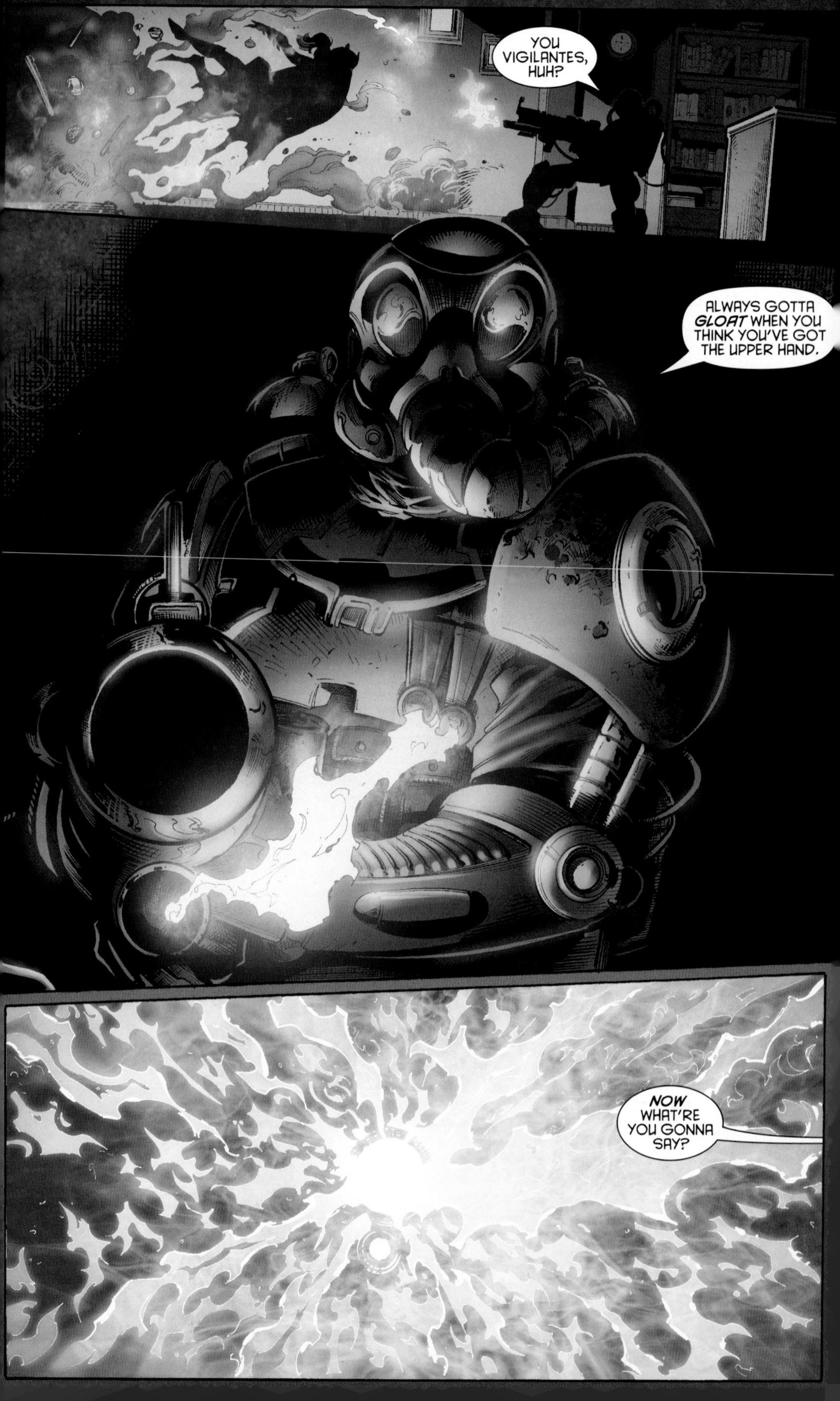
YOU VIGILANTES, HUH?
ALWAYS GOTTA GLOAT WHEN YOU THINK YOU'VE GOT THE UPPER HAND.
NOW WHAT'RE YOU GONNA SAY?

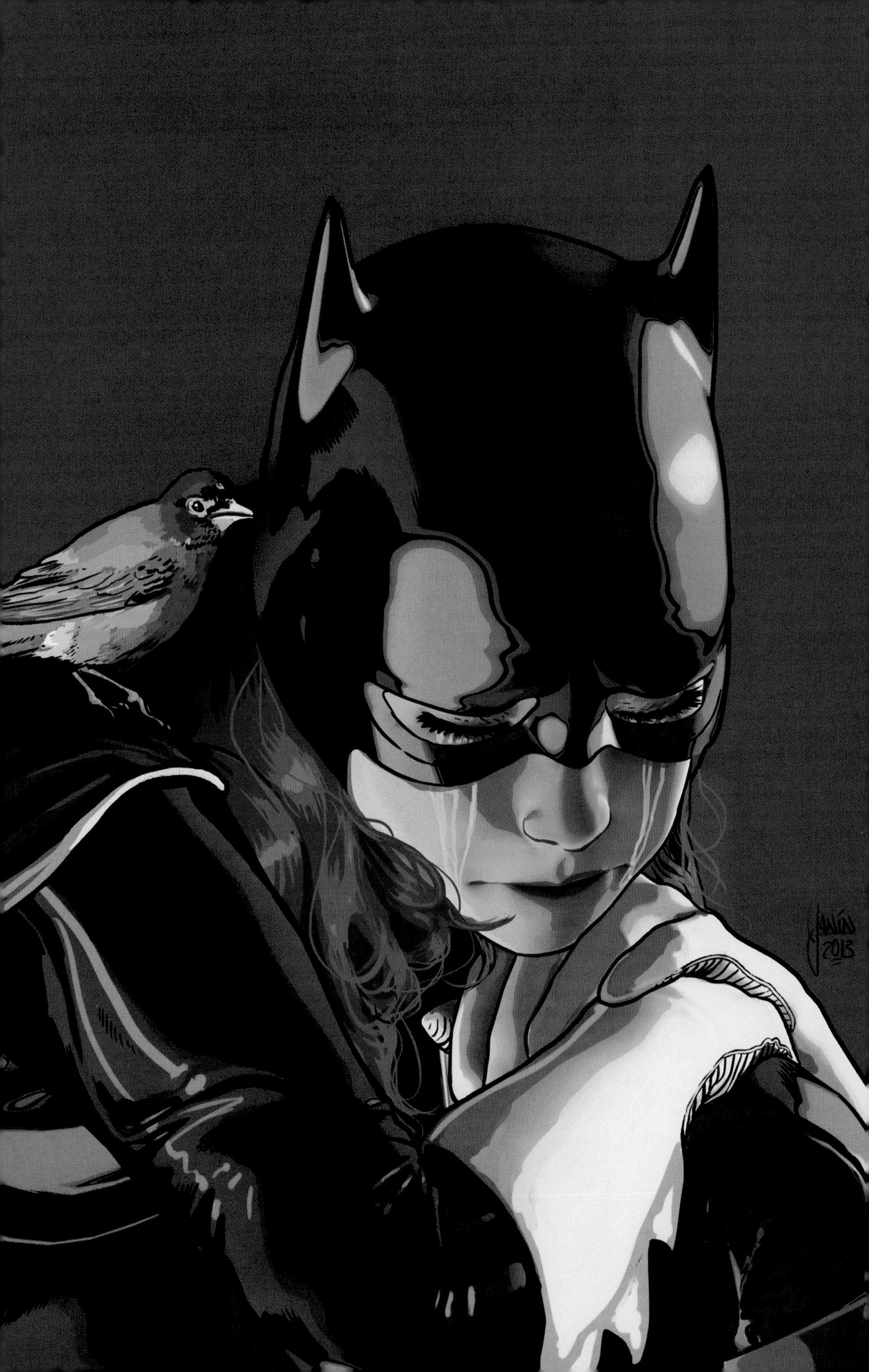

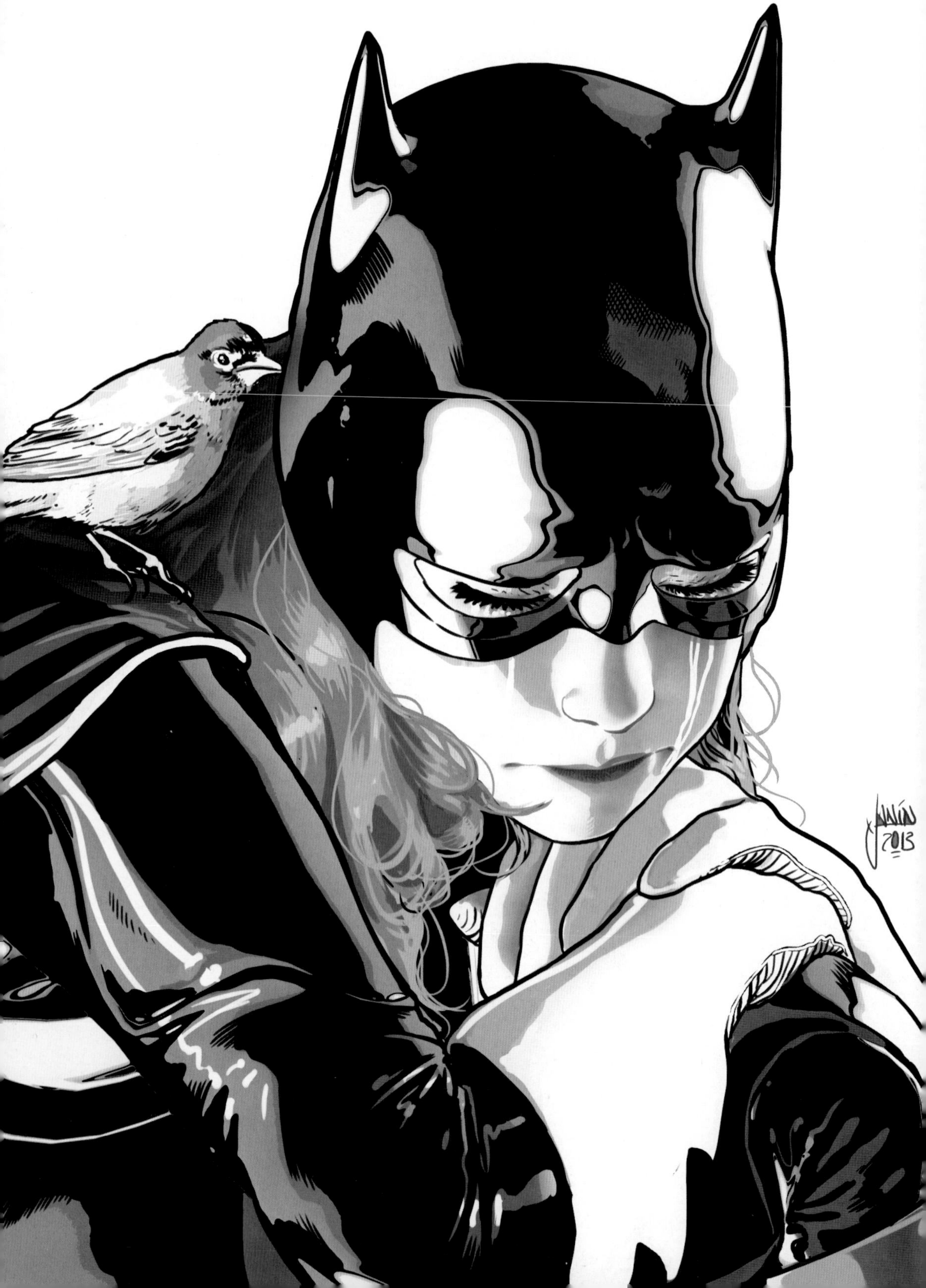

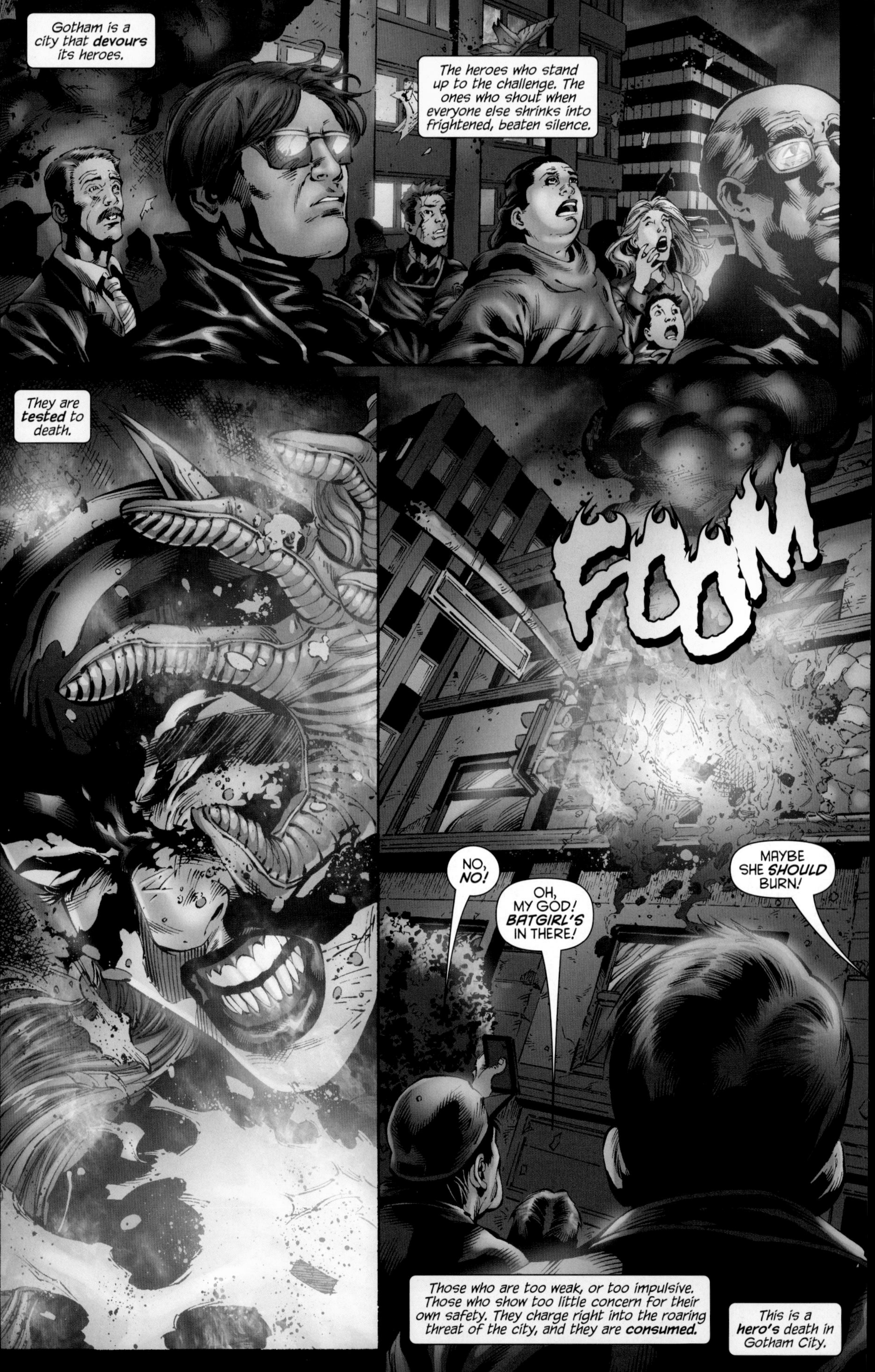
Gotham is a city that **devours** its heroes.
The heroes who stand up to the challenge. The ones who shout when everyone else shrinks into frightened, beaten silence.
They are **tested** to death.
FOOM
NO, ***NO!***
OH, MY GOD! ***BATGIRL'S*** IN THERE!
MAYBE SHE ***SHOULD*** BURN!
Those who are too weak, or too impulsive. Those who show too little concern for their own safety. They charge right into the roaring threat of the city, and they are **consumed.**
This is a **hero's** death in Gotham City.

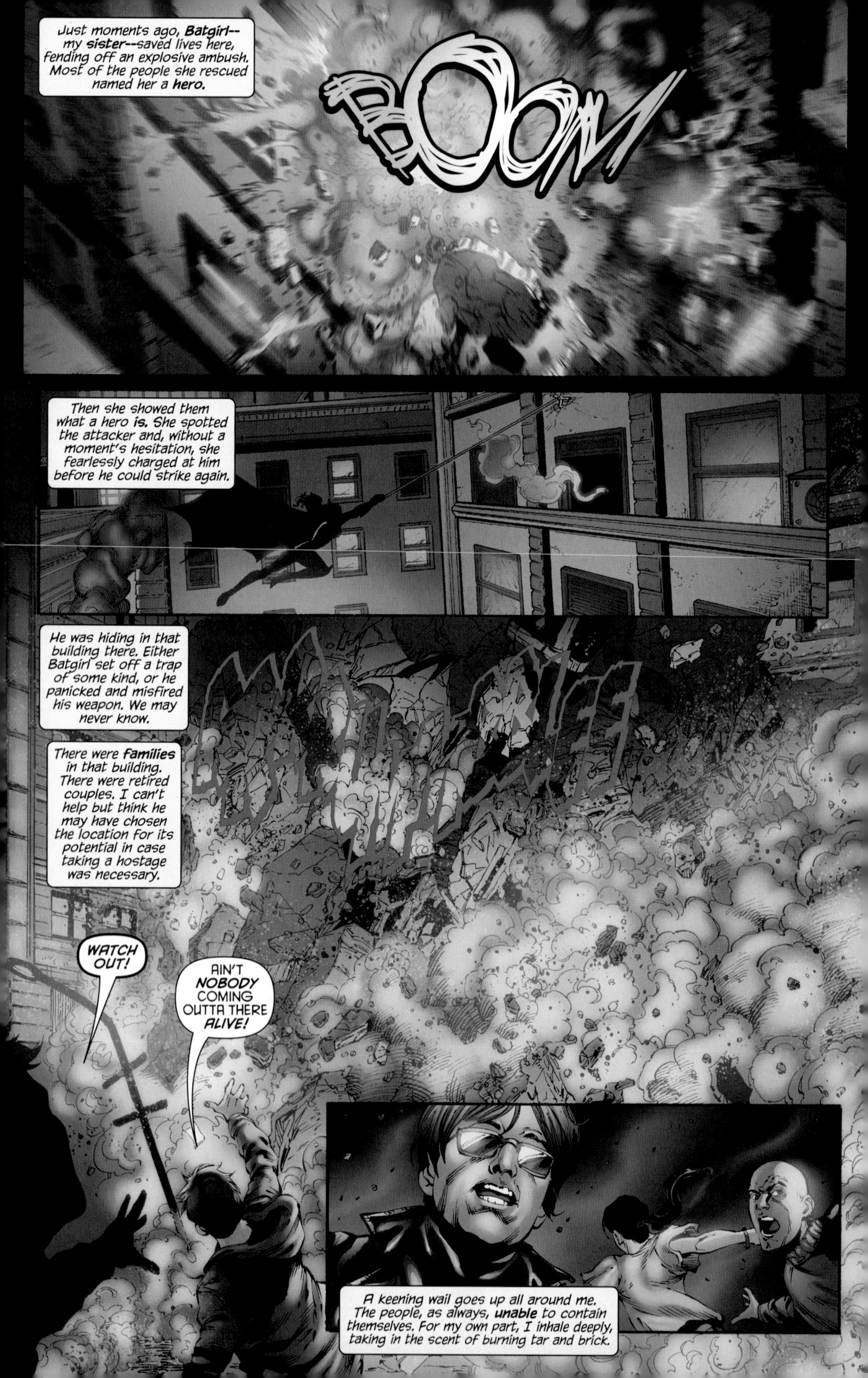
Just moments ago, Batgirl--my sister--saved lives here, fending off an explosive ambush. Most of the people she rescued named her a hero.
BOOM
Then she showed them what a hero is. She spotted the attacker and, without a moment's hesitation, she fearlessly charged at him before he could strike again.
He was hiding in that building there. Either Batgirl set off a trap of some kind, or he panicked and misfired his weapon. We may never know.
There were families in that building. There were retired couples. I can't help but think he may have chosen the location for its potential in case taking a hostage was necessary.
WATCH OUT!
AIN'T NOBODY COMING OUTTA THERE ALIVE!
A keening wail goes up all around me. The people, as always, unable to contain themselves. For my own part, I inhale deeply, taking in the scent of burning tar and brick.

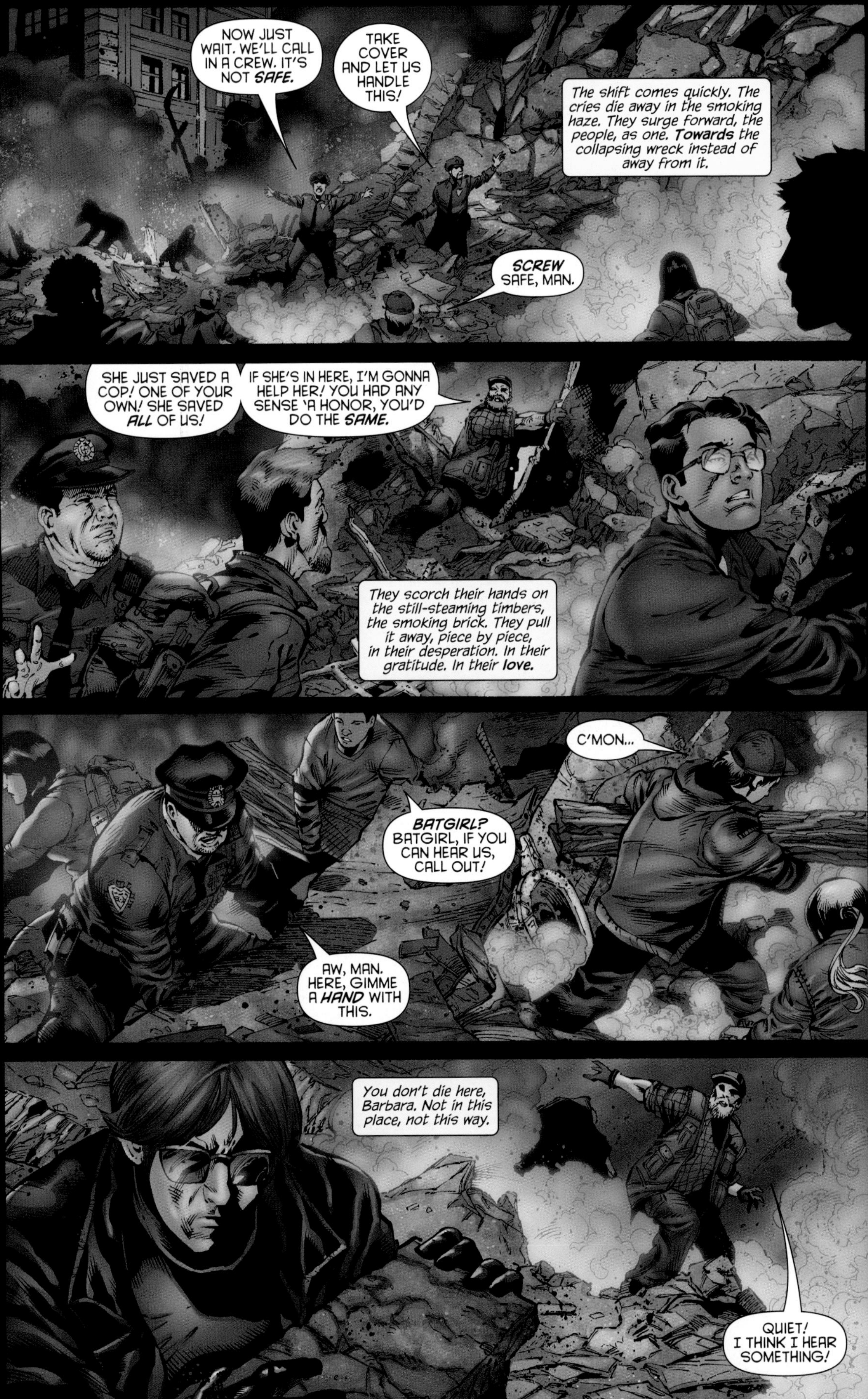
NOW JUST WAIT. WE'LL CALL IN A CREW. IT'S NOT *SAFE.*
TAKE COVER AND LET US HANDLE THIS!
The shift comes quickly. The cries die away in the smoking haze. They surge forward, the people, as one. ***Towards*** *the collapsing wreck instead of away from it.*
SCREW SAFE, MAN.
SHE JUST SAVED A COP! ONE OF YOUR OWN! SHE SAVED ***ALL*** OF US!
IF SHE'S IN HERE, I'M GONNA HELP HER! YOU HAD ANY SENSE 'A HONOR, YOU'D DO THE ***SAME.***
They scorch their hands on the still-steaming timbers, the smoking brick. They pull it away, piece by piece, in their desperation. In their gratitude. In their ***love.***
C'MON...
BATGIRL? BATGIRL, IF YOU CAN HEAR US, CALL OUT!
AW, MAN. HERE, GIMME A ***HAND*** WITH THIS.
You don't die here, Barbara. Not in this place, not this way.
QUIET! I THINK I HEAR SOMETHING!

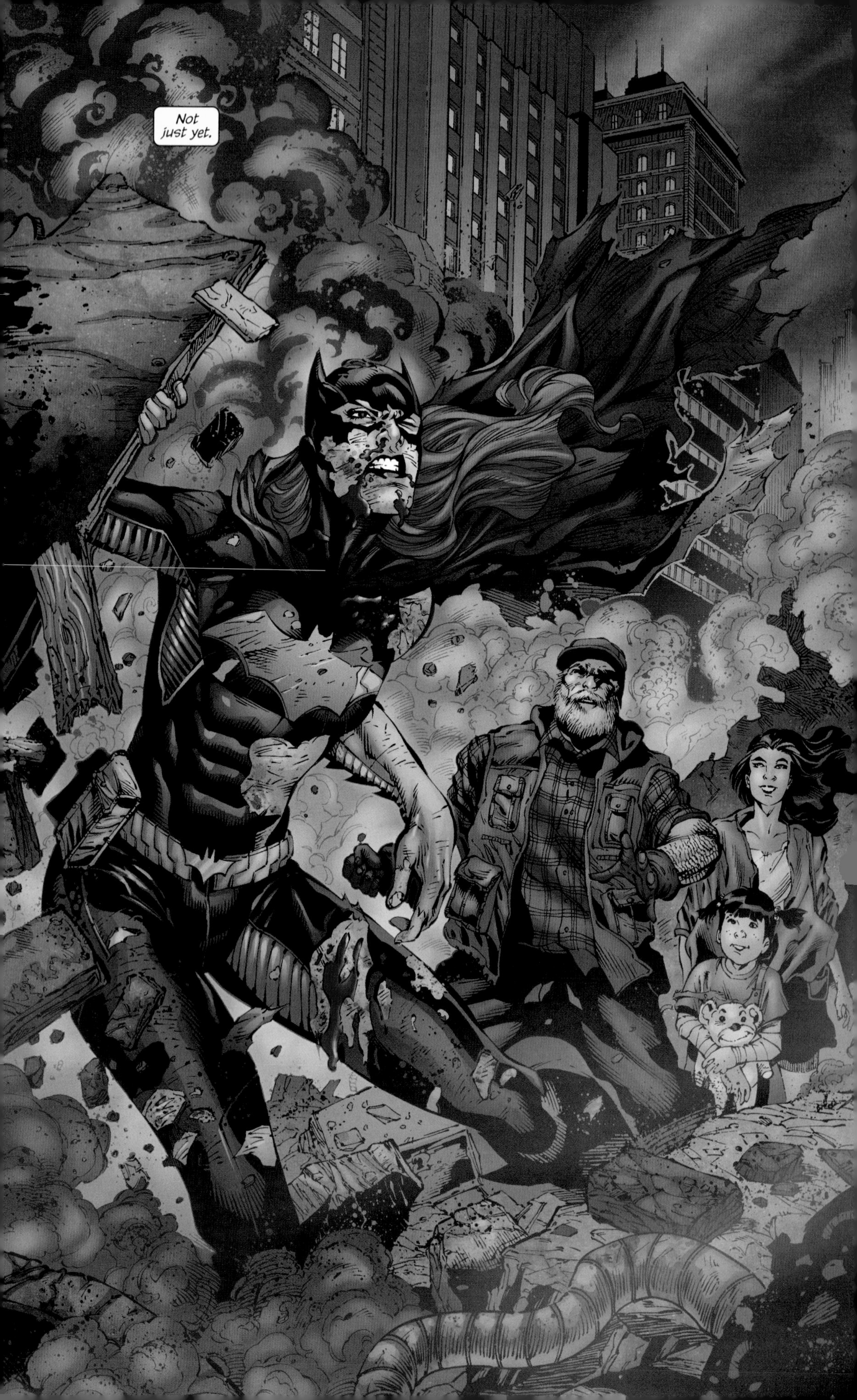
Not just yet.

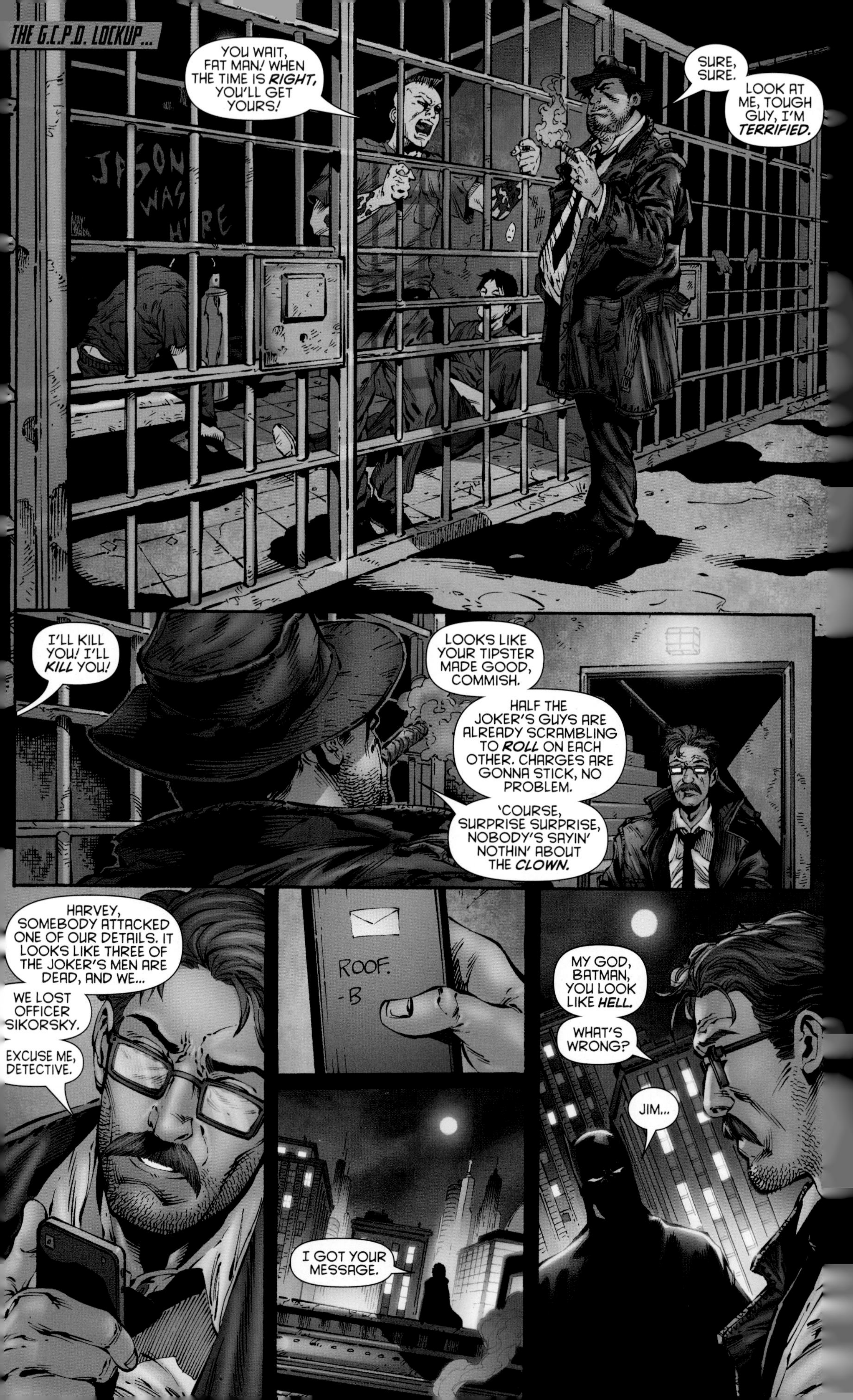
THE G.C.P.D. LOCKUP...
YOU WAIT, FAT MAN! WHEN THE TIME IS RIGHT, YOU'LL GET YOURS!
SURE, SURE.
LOOK AT ME, TOUGH GUY, I'M TERRIFIED.
JASON WAS HERE
I'LL KILL YOU! I'LL KILL YOU!
LOOKS LIKE YOUR TIPSTER MADE GOOD, COMMISH.
HALF THE JOKER'S GUYS ARE ALREADY SCRAMBLING TO ROLL ON EACH OTHER. CHARGES ARE GONNA STICK, NO PROBLEM.
'COURSE, SURPRISE SURPRISE, NOBODY'S SAYIN' NOTHIN' ABOUT THE CLOWN.
HARVEY, SOMEBODY ATTACKED ONE OF OUR DETAILS. IT LOOKS LIKE THREE OF THE JOKER'S MEN ARE DEAD, AND WE...
WE LOST OFFICER SIKORSKY.
EXCUSE ME, DETECTIVE.
ROOF. -B
I GOT YOUR MESSAGE.
MY GOD, BATMAN, YOU LOOK LIKE HELL.
WHAT'S WRONG?
JIM...

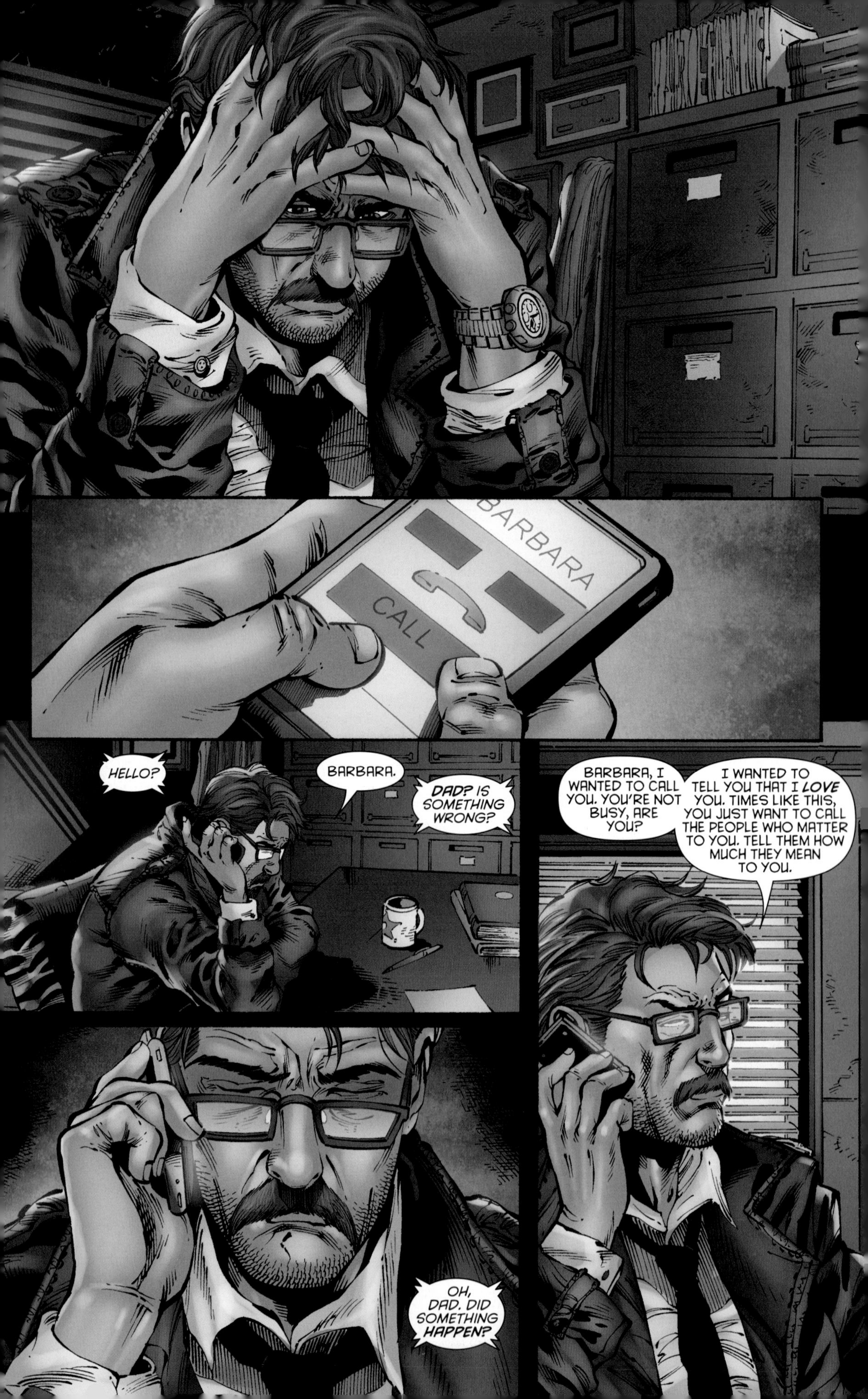

BARBARA
CALL
HELLO?
BARBARA.
DAD? IS SOMETHING WRONG?
BARBARA, I WANTED TO CALL YOU. YOU'RE NOT BUSY, ARE YOU?
I WANTED TO TELL YOU THAT I LOVE YOU. TIMES LIKE THIS, YOU JUST WANT TO CALL THE PEOPLE WHO MATTER TO YOU. TELL THEM HOW MUCH THEY MEAN TO YOU.
OH, DAD. DID SOMETHING HAPPEN?

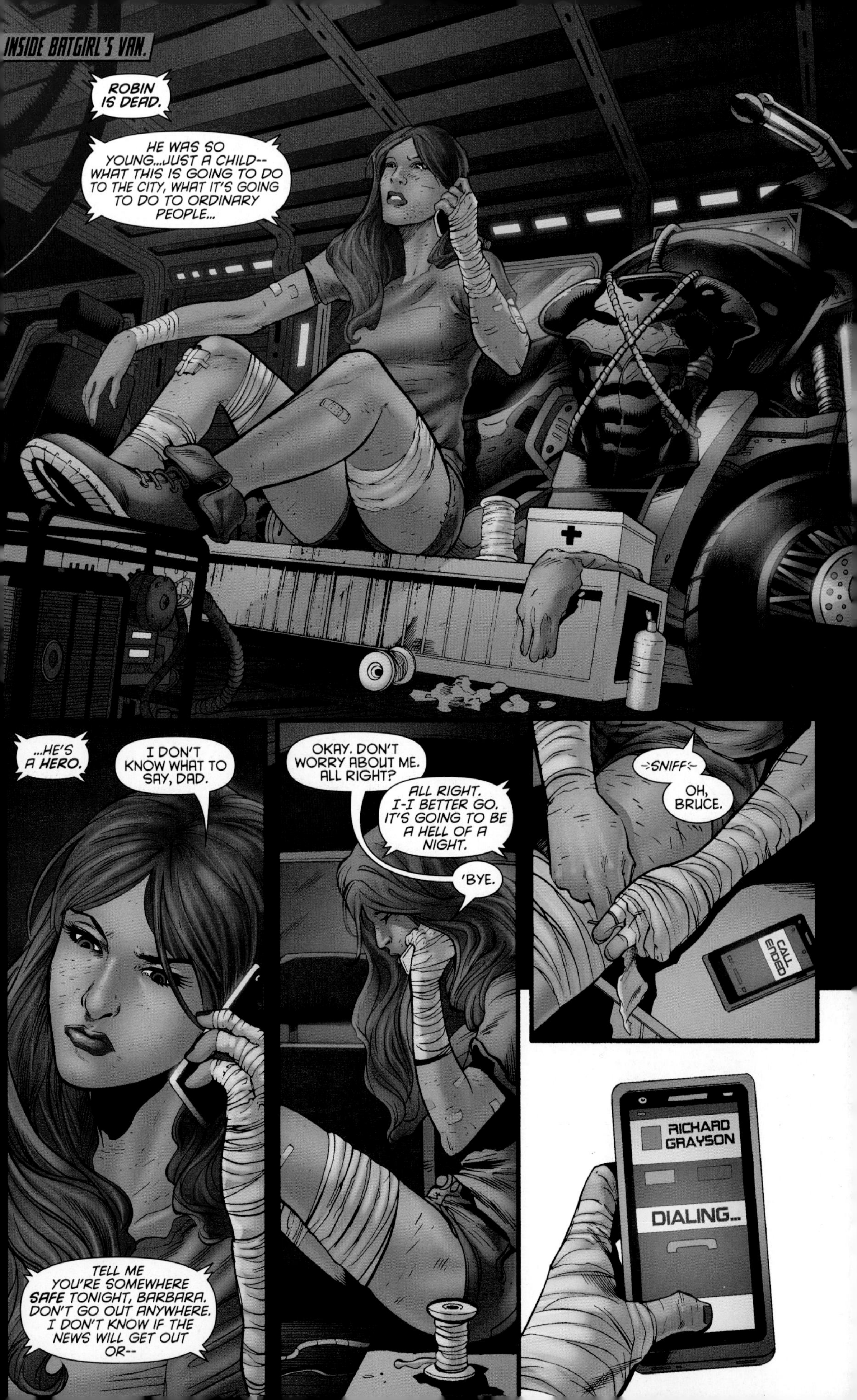
INSIDE BATGIRL'S VAN.
ROBIN IS DEAD.
HE WAS SO YOUNG...JUST A CHILD-- WHAT THIS IS GOING TO DO TO THE CITY, WHAT IT'S GOING TO DO TO ORDINARY PEOPLE...
...HE'S A HERO.
I DON'T KNOW WHAT TO SAY, DAD.
TELL ME YOU'RE SOMEWHERE SAFE TONIGHT, BARBARA. DON'T GO OUT ANYWHERE. I DON'T KNOW IF THE NEWS WILL GET OUT OR--
OKAY. DON'T WORRY ABOUT ME. ALL RIGHT?
ALL RIGHT. I-I BETTER GO. IT'S GOING TO BE A HELL OF A NIGHT.
'BYE.
-SNIFF-
OH, BRUCE.
CALL ENDED
RICHARD GRAYSON
DIALING...

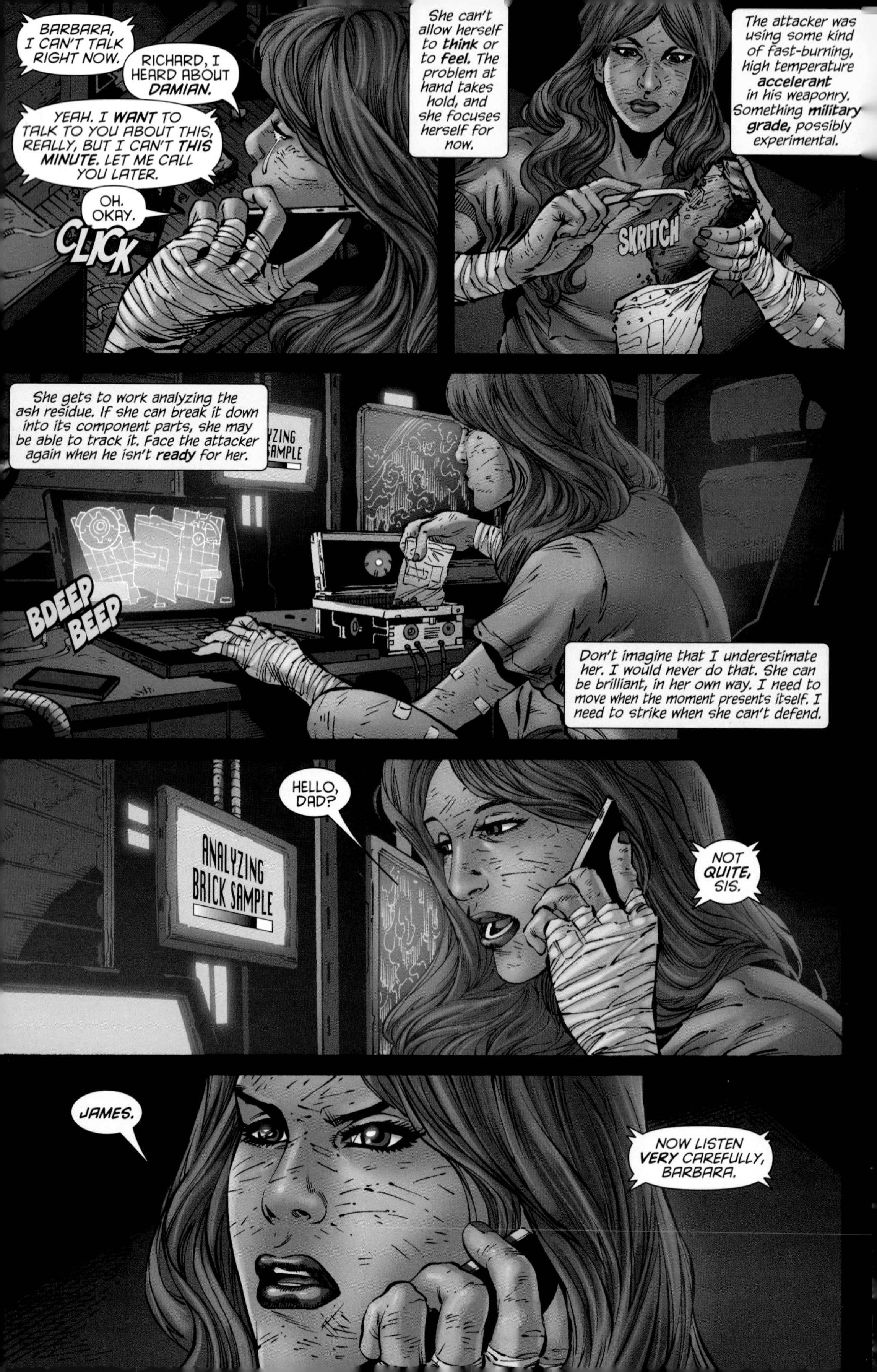
BARBARA, I CAN'T TALK RIGHT NOW.
RICHARD, I HEARD ABOUT DAMIAN.
YEAH. I WANT TO TALK TO YOU ABOUT THIS, REALLY, BUT I CAN'T THIS MINUTE. LET ME CALL YOU LATER.
OH. OKAY.
CLICK
She can't allow herself to think or to feel. The problem at hand takes hold, and she focuses herself for now.
The attacker was using some kind of fast-burning, high temperature accelerant in his weaponry. Something military grade, possibly experimental.
SKRITCH
She gets to work analyzing the ash residue. If she can break it down into its component parts, she may be able to track it. Face the attacker again when he isn't ready for her.
BDEEP BEEP
Don't imagine that I underestimate her. I would never do that. She can be brilliant, in her own way. I need to move when the moment presents itself. I need to strike when she can't defend.
ANALYZING BRICK SAMPLE
HELLO, DAD?
NOT QUITE, SIS.
JAMES.
NOW LISTEN VERY CAREFULLY, BARBARA.

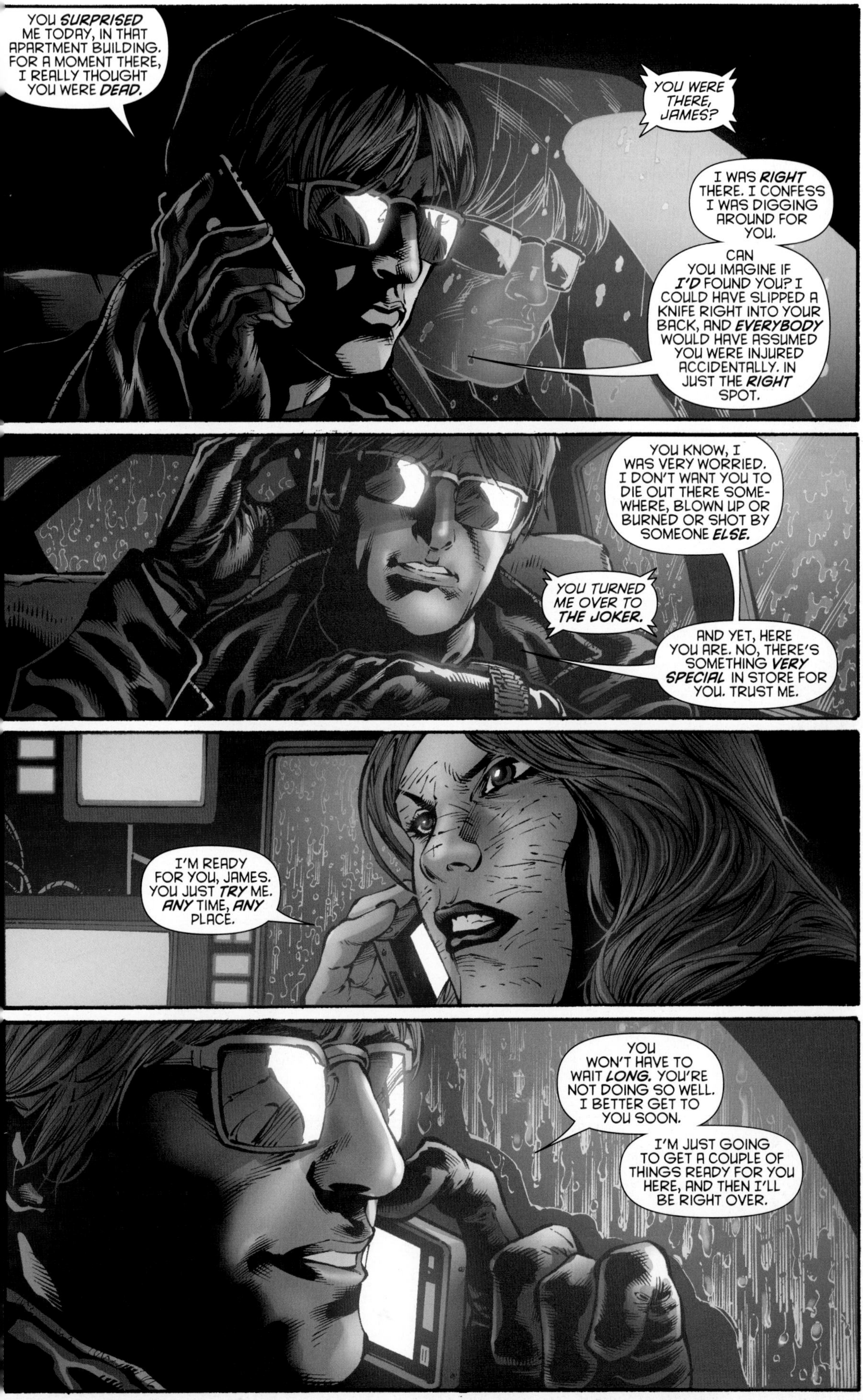
YOU SURPRISED ME TODAY, IN THAT APARTMENT BUILDING. FOR A MOMENT THERE, I REALLY THOUGHT YOU WERE DEAD.
YOU WERE THERE, JAMES?
I WAS RIGHT THERE. I CONFESS I WAS DIGGING AROUND FOR YOU.
CAN YOU IMAGINE IF I'D FOUND YOU? I COULD HAVE SLIPPED A KNIFE RIGHT INTO YOUR BACK, AND EVERYBODY WOULD HAVE ASSUMED YOU WERE INJURED ACCIDENTALLY. IN JUST THE RIGHT SPOT.
YOU KNOW, I WAS VERY WORRIED. I DON'T WANT YOU TO DIE OUT THERE SOME-WHERE, BLOWN UP OR BURNED OR SHOT BY SOMEONE ELSE.
YOU TURNED ME OVER TO THE JOKER.
AND YET, HERE YOU ARE. NO, THERE'S SOMETHING VERY SPECIAL IN STORE FOR YOU. TRUST ME.
I'M READY FOR YOU, JAMES. YOU JUST TRY ME. ANY TIME, ANY PLACE.
YOU WON'T HAVE TO WAIT LONG. YOU'RE NOT DOING SO WELL. I BETTER GET TO YOU SOON.
I'M JUST GOING TO GET A COUPLE OF THINGS READY FOR YOU HERE, AND THEN I'LL BE RIGHT OVER.

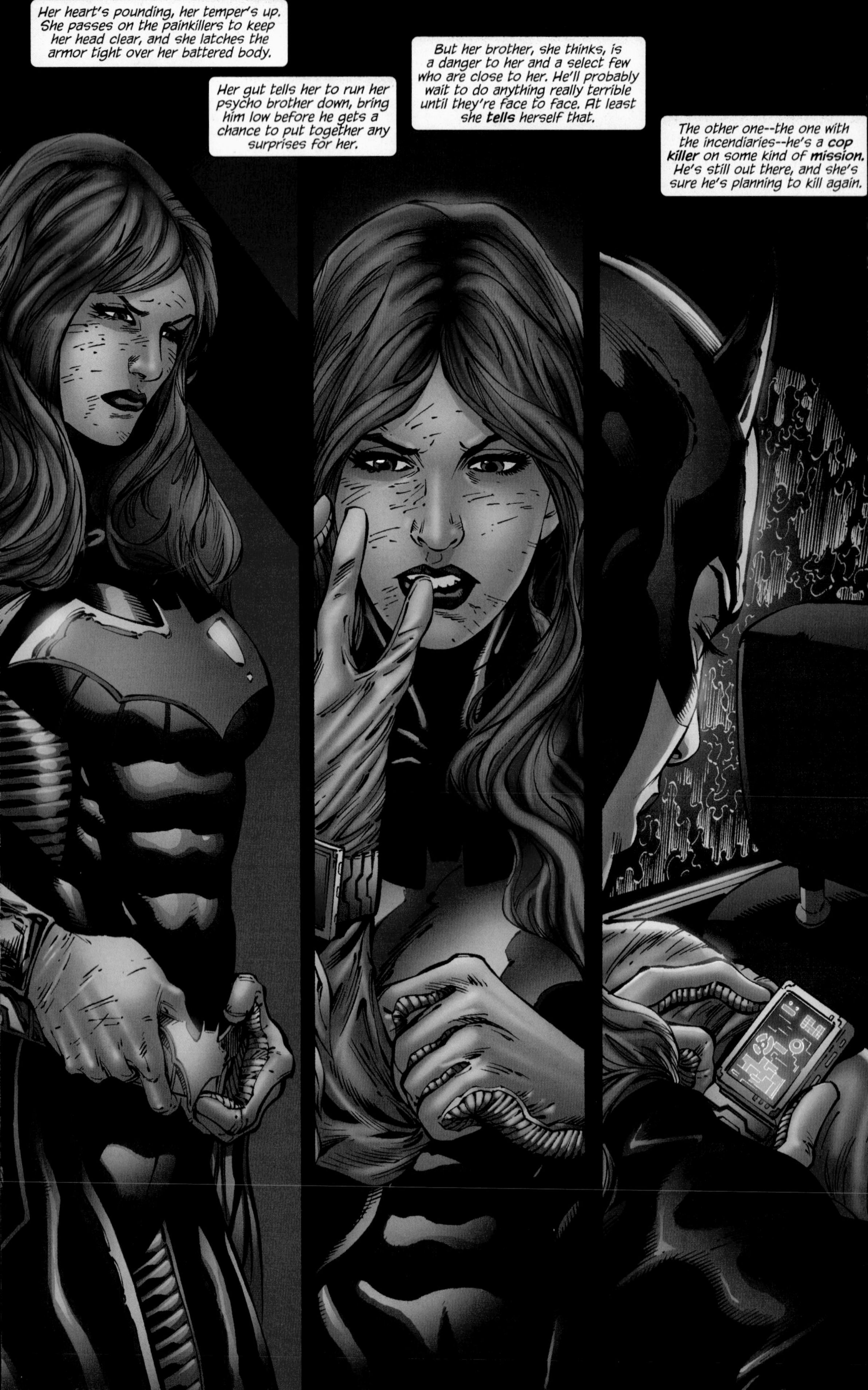
Her heart's pounding, her temper's up. She passes on the painkillers to keep her head clear, and she latches the armor tight over her battered body.
Her gut tells her to run her psycho brother down, bring him low before he gets a chance to put together any surprises for her.
But her brother, she thinks, is a danger to her and a select few who are close to her. He'll probably wait to do anything really terrible until they're face to face. At least she **tells** herself that.
The other one--the one with the incendiaries--he's a **cop killer** on some kind of **mission.** He's still out there, and she's sure he's planning to kill again.

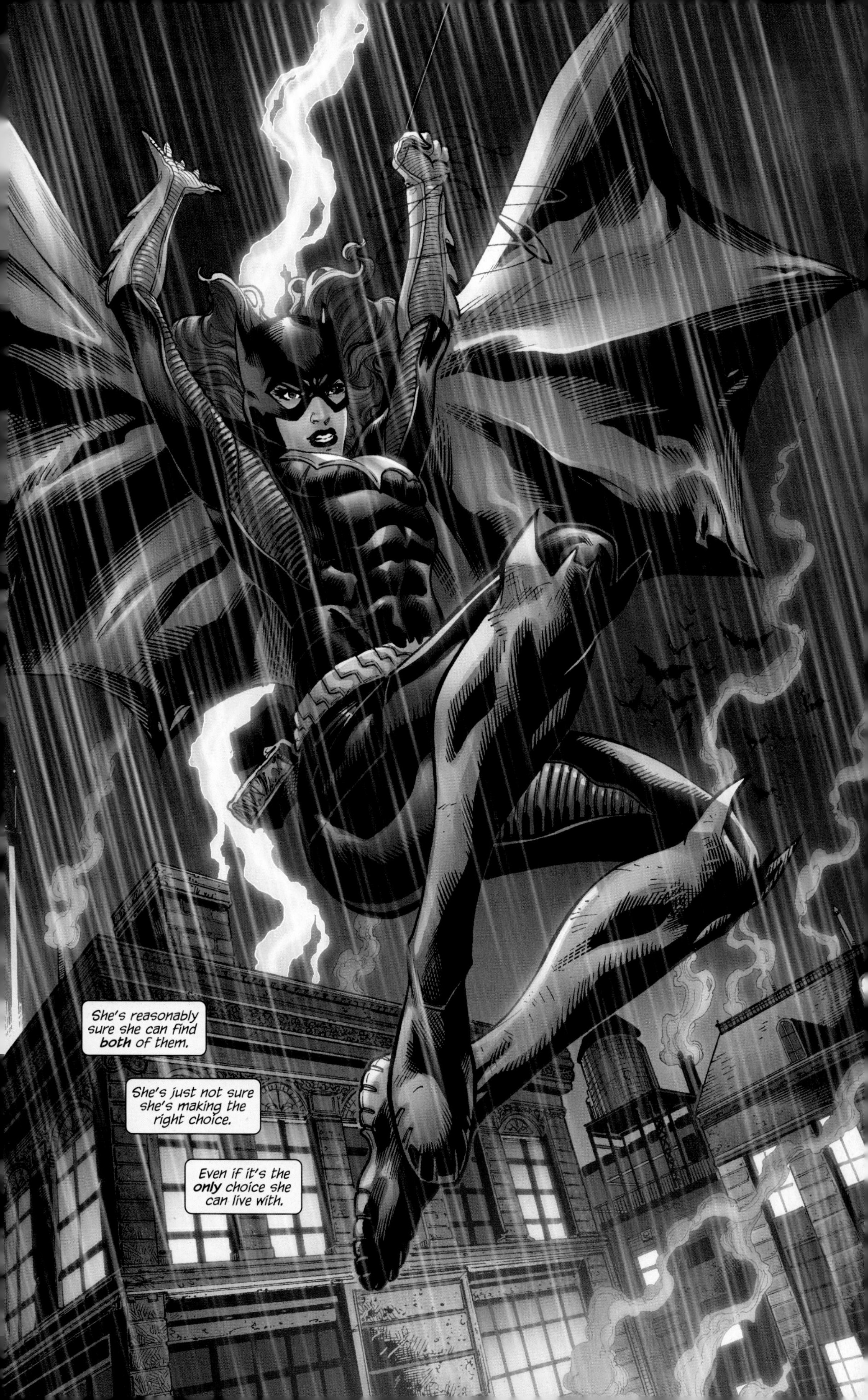
She's reasonably sure she can find **both** of them.
She's just not sure she's making the right choice.
Even if it's the **only** choice she can live with.

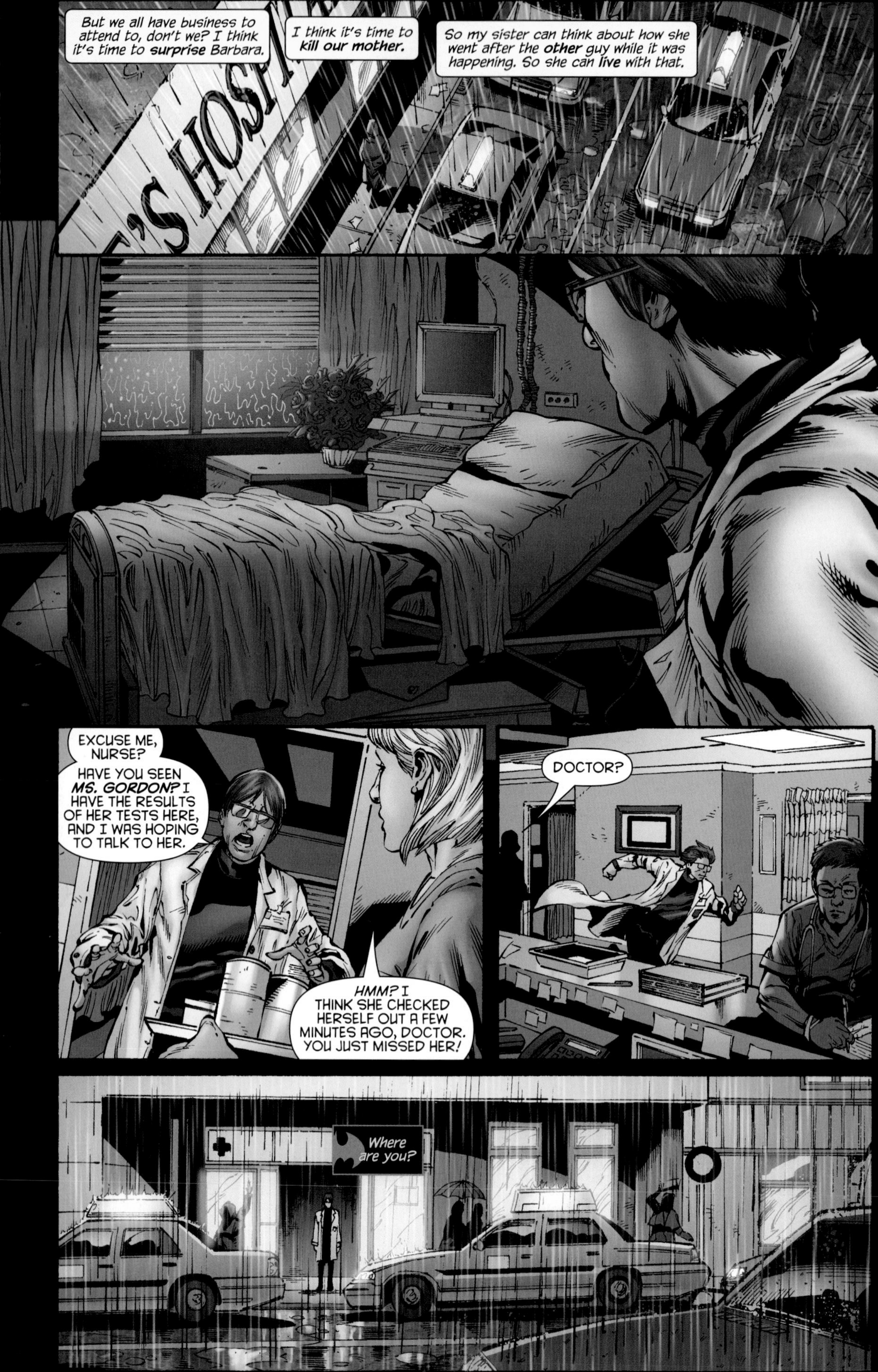
But we all have business to attend to, don't we? I think it's time to **surprise** Barbara.
I think it's time to **kill our mother.**
So my sister can think about how she went after the **other** guy while it was happening. So she can **live** with that.
'S HOSP
EXCUSE ME, NURSE?
HAVE YOU SEEN ***MS. GORDON?*** I HAVE THE RESULTS OF HER TESTS HERE, AND I WAS HOPING TO TALK TO HER.
HMM? I THINK SHE CHECKED HERSELF OUT A FEW MINUTES AGO, DOCTOR. YOU JUST MISSED HER!
DOCTOR?
Where are you?

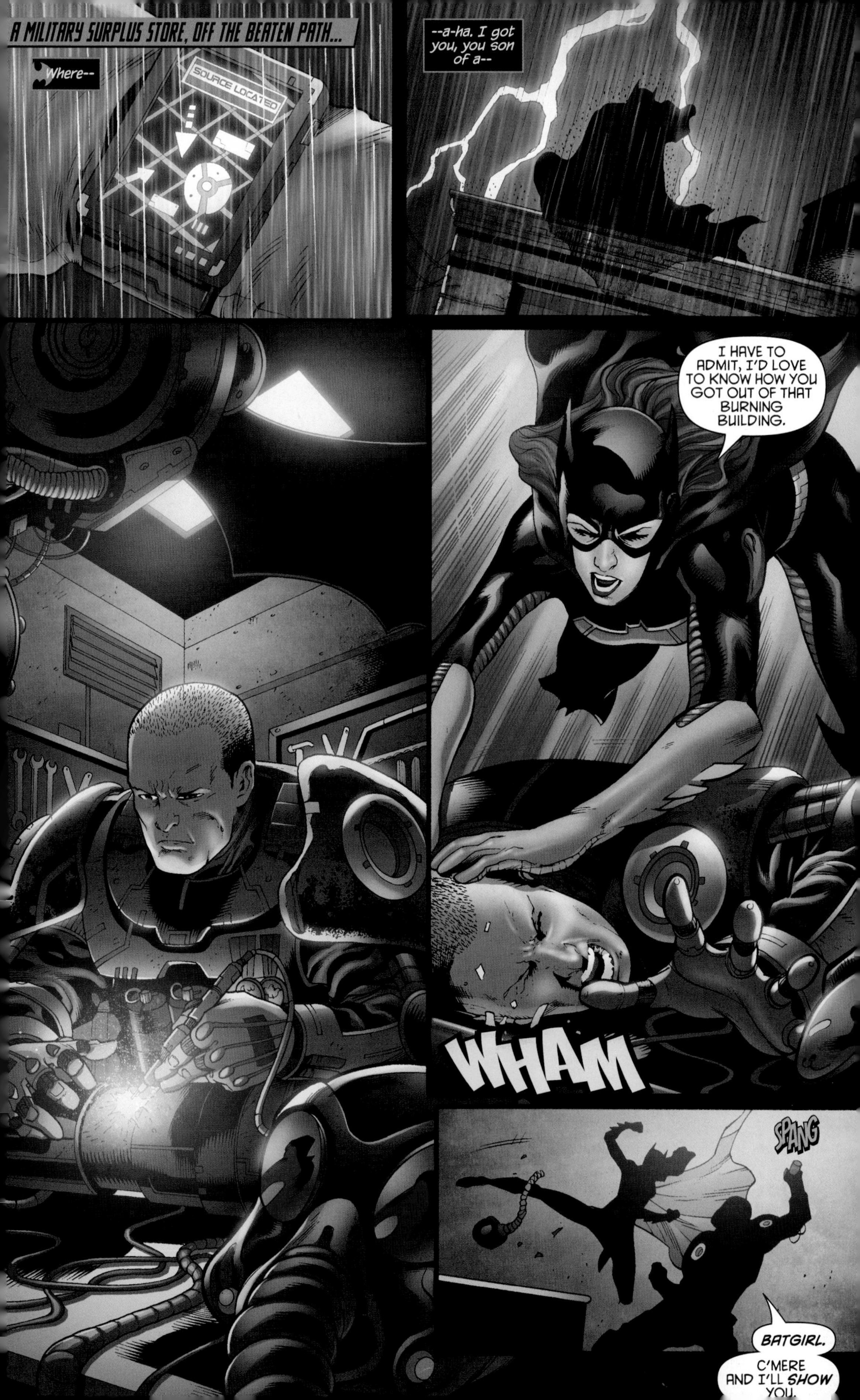

A MILITARY SURPLUS STORE, OFF THE BEATEN PATH...
Where--
SOURCE LOCATED
--a-ha. I got you, you son of a--
I HAVE TO ADMIT, I'D LOVE TO KNOW HOW YOU GOT OUT OF THAT BURNING BUILDING.
WHAM
SPANG
BATGIRL.
C'MERE AND I'LL SHOW YOU.

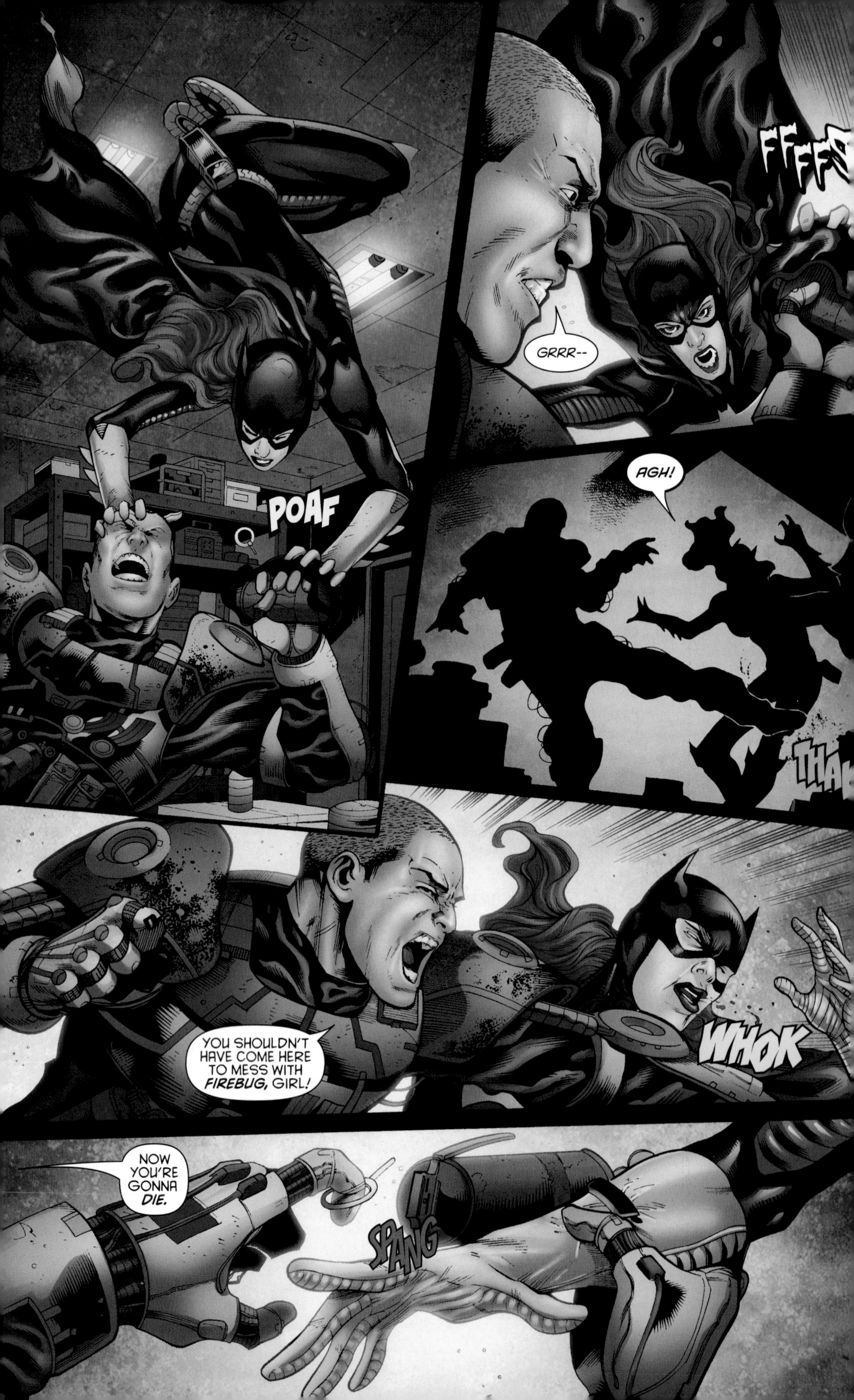
POAF
FFFF
GRRR--
AGH!
THA
YOU SHOULDN'T HAVE COME HERE TO MESS WITH *FIREBUG*, GIRL!
WHOK
NOW YOU'RE GONNA *DIE.*
SPANG

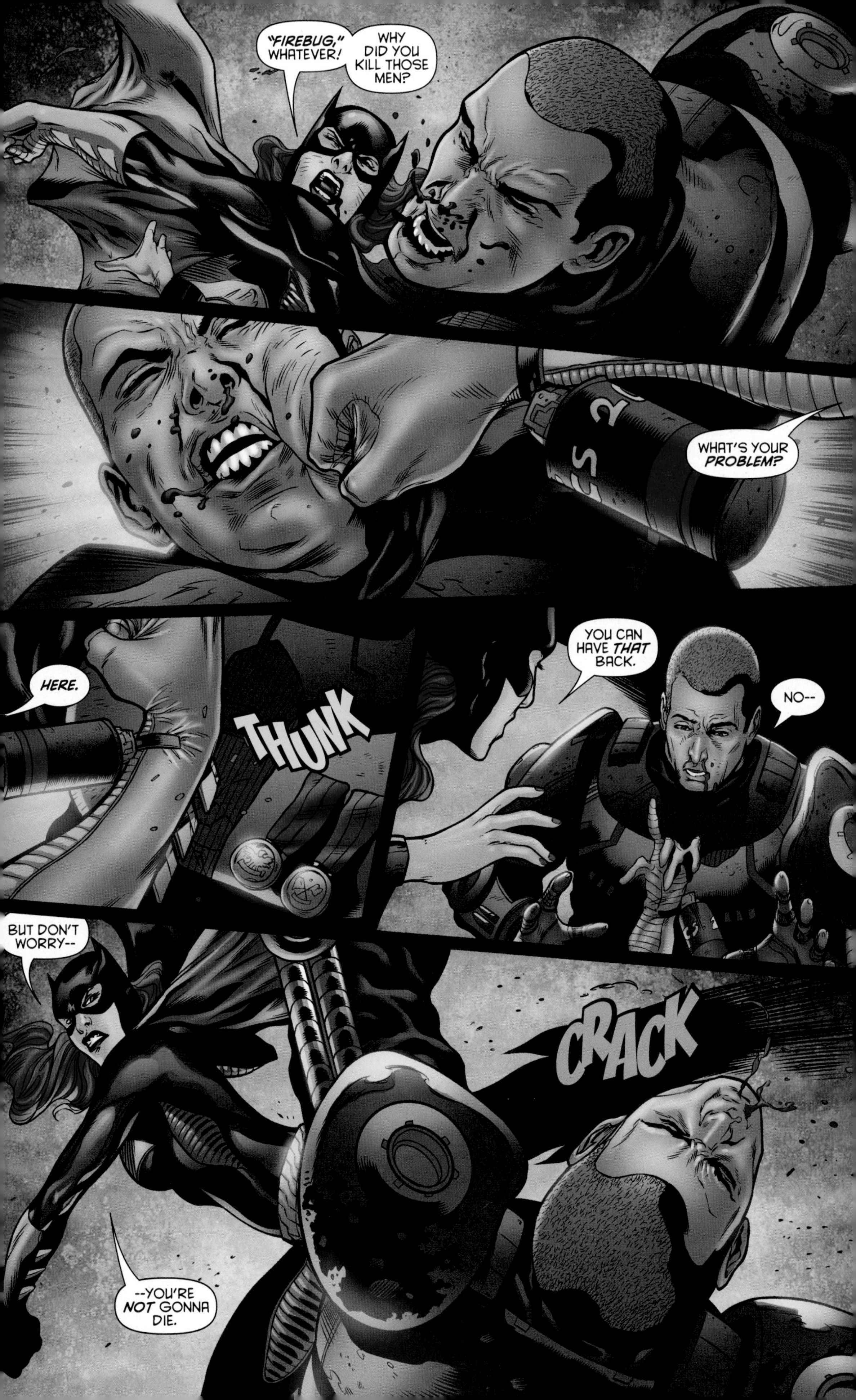
"FIREBUG," WHATEVER!
WHY DID YOU KILL THOSE MEN?
WHAT'S YOUR PROBLEM?
HERE.
THUNK
YOU CAN HAVE THAT BACK.
NO--
BUT DON'T WORRY--
CRACK
--YOU'RE NOT GONNA DIE.

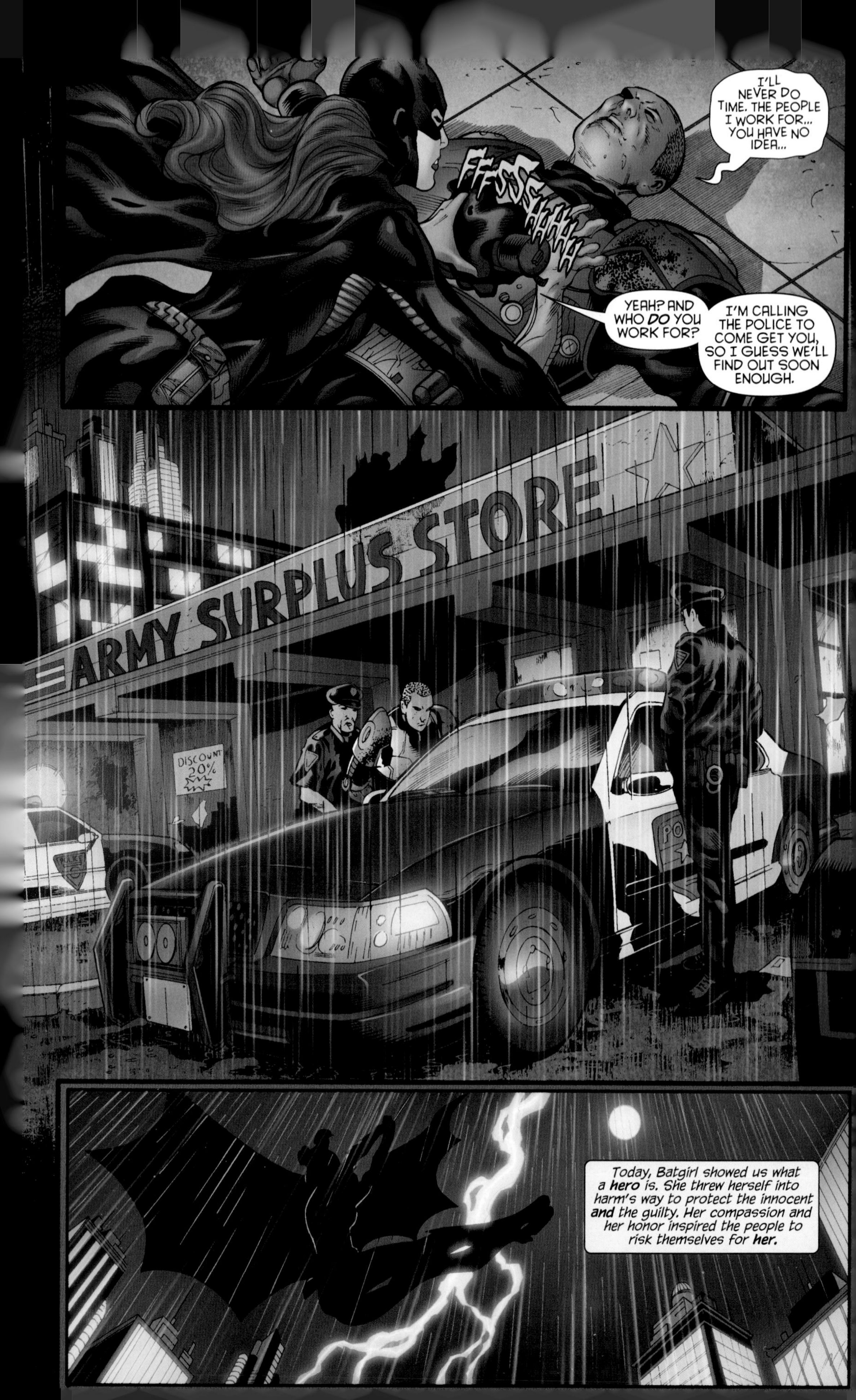
I'LL NEVER DO TIME. THE PEOPLE I WORK FOR... YOU HAVE NO IDEA...
FFFSSSHHHH
YEAH? AND WHO DO YOU WORK FOR?
I'M CALLING THE POLICE TO COME GET YOU, SO I GUESS WE'LL FIND OUT SOON ENOUGH.
ARMY SURPLUS STORE
DISCOUNT 20%
POLICE
Today, Batgirl showed us what a hero is. She threw herself into harm's way to protect the innocent and the guilty. Her compassion and her honor inspired the people to risk themselves for her.

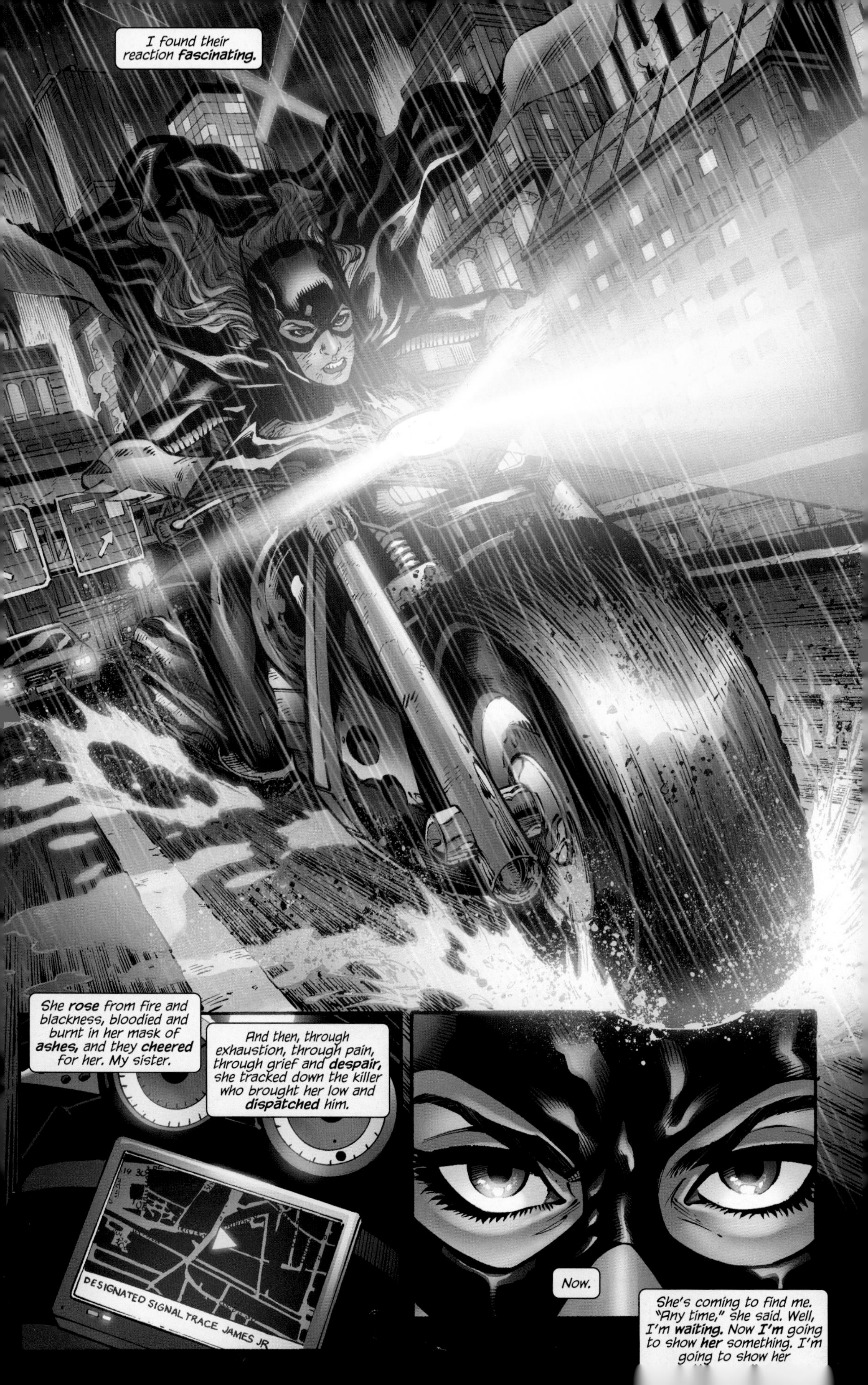
I found their reaction **fascinating.**
She **rose** from fire and blackness, bloodied and burnt in her mask of **ashes,** and they **cheered** for her. My sister.
And then, through exhaustion, through pain, through grief and **despair,** she tracked down the killer who brought her low and **dispatched** him.
DESIGNATED SIGNAL TRACE JAMES JR
Now.
She's coming to find me. "Any time," she said. Well, I'm **waiting.** Now **I'm** going to show **her** something. I'm going to show her

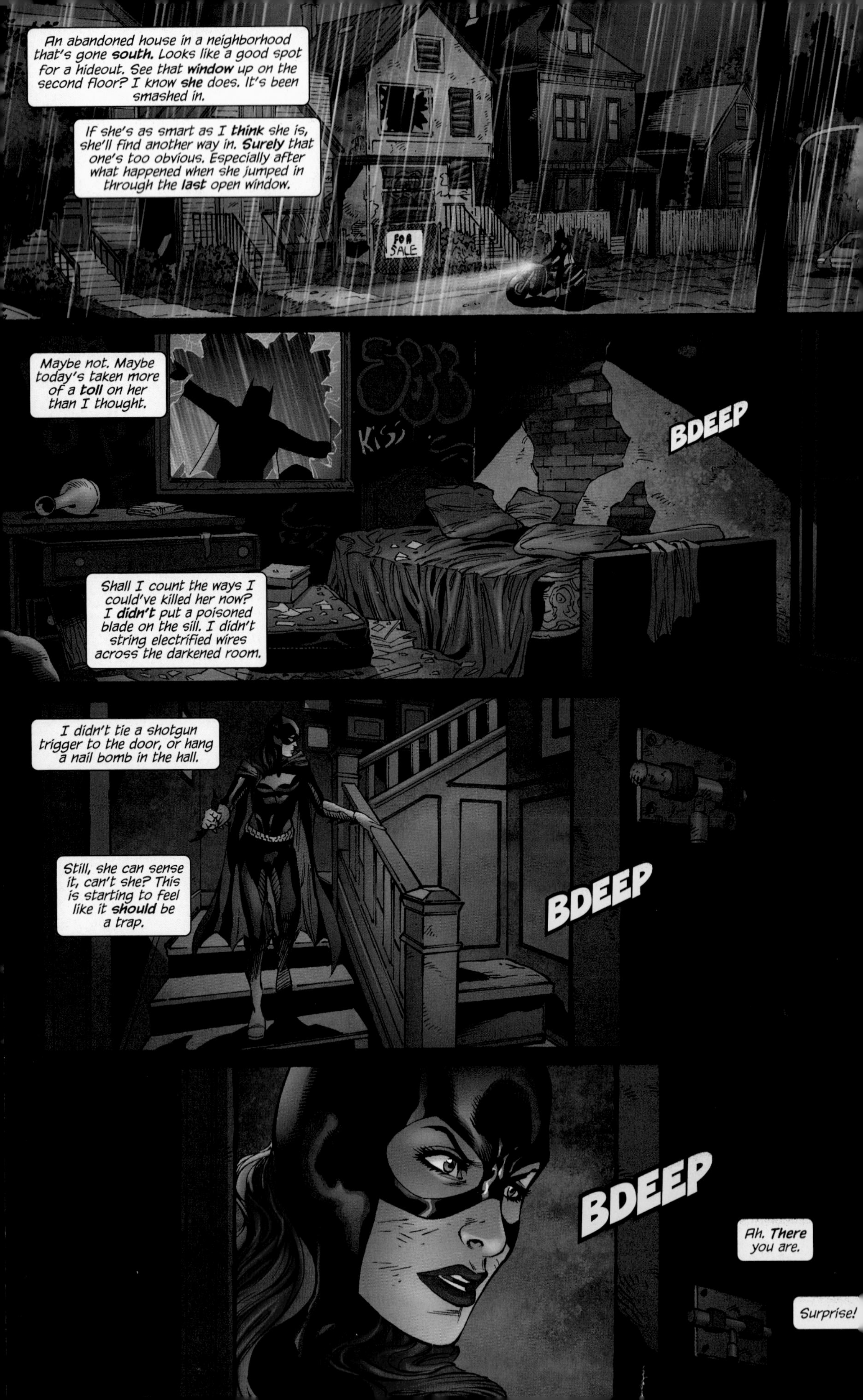

An abandoned house in a neighborhood that's gone **south.** Looks like a good spot for a hideout. See that **window** up on the second floor? I know **she** does. It's been smashed in.
If she's as smart as I **think** she is, she'll find another way in. **Surely** that one's too obvious. Especially after what happened when she jumped in through the **last** open window.
FOR SALE
Maybe not. Maybe today's taken more of a **toll** on her than I thought.
BDEEP
Shall I count the ways I could've killed her now? I **didn't** put a poisoned blade on the sill. I didn't string electrified wires across the darkened room.
I didn't tie a shotgun trigger to the door, or hang a nail bomb in the hall.
Still, she can sense it, can't she? This is starting to feel like it **should** be a trap.
BDEEP
BDEEP
Ah. **There** you are.
Surprise!

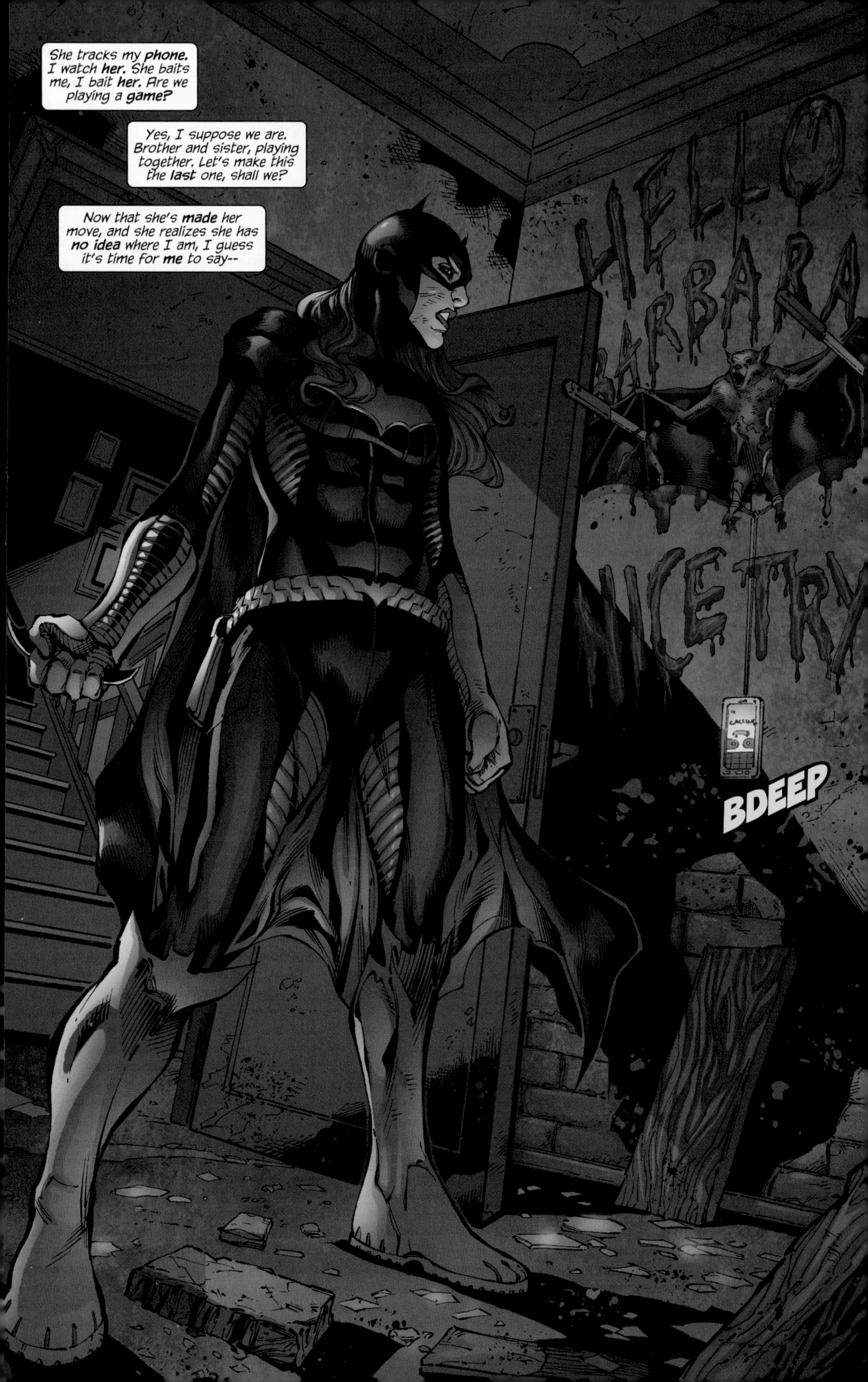
She tracks my **phone.** I watch **her.** She baits me, I bait **her.** Are we playing a **game?**
Yes, I suppose we are. Brother and sister, playing together. Let's make this the **last** one, shall we?
Now that she's **made** her move, and she realizes she has **no idea** where I am, I guess it's time for **me** to say--
HELLO BARBARA
NICE TRY
BDEEP

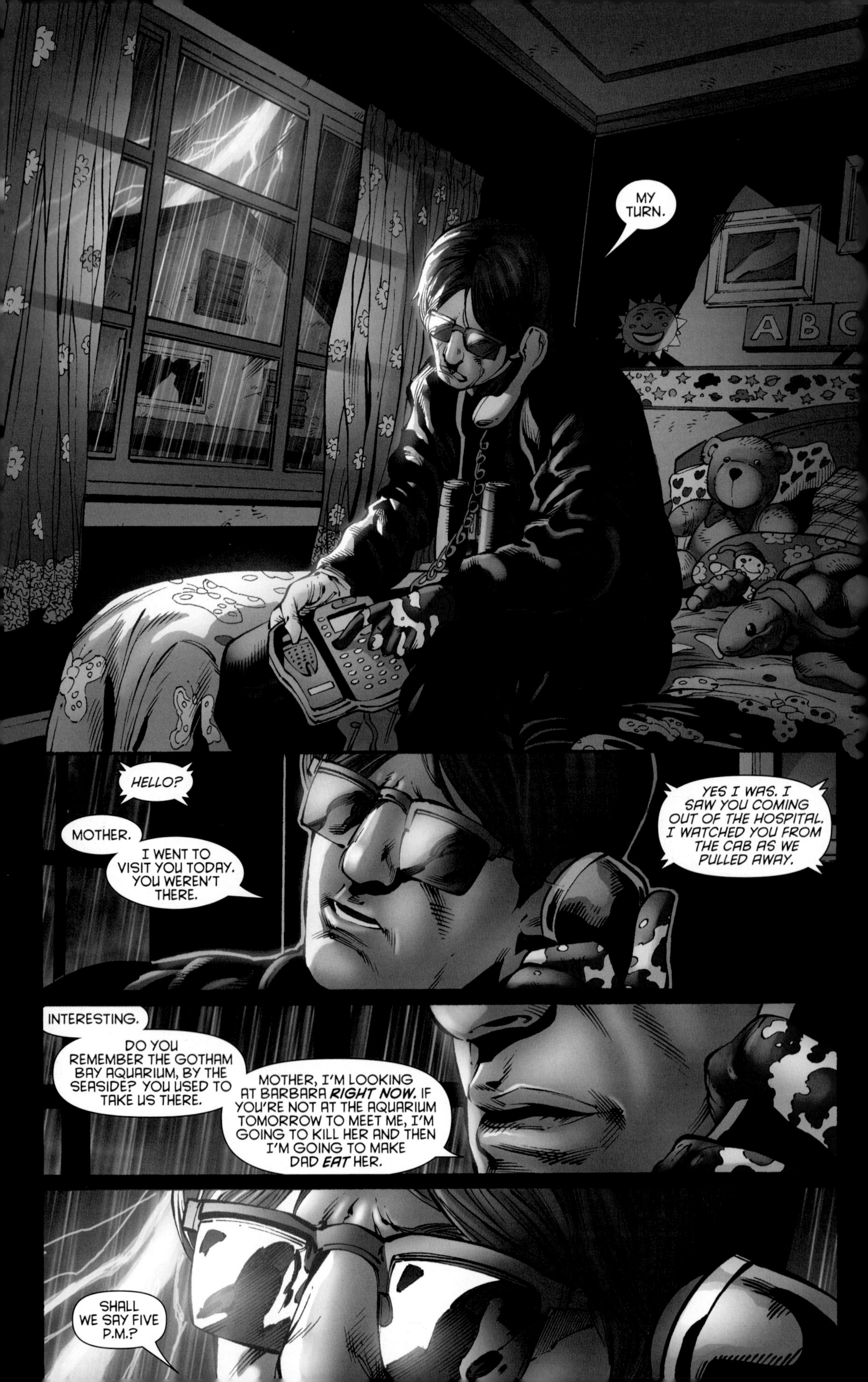
MY TURN.
HELLO?
MOTHER.
I WENT TO VISIT YOU TODAY. YOU WEREN'T THERE.
YES I WAS. I SAW YOU COMING OUT OF THE HOSPITAL. I WATCHED YOU FROM THE CAB AS WE PULLED AWAY.
INTERESTING.
DO YOU REMEMBER THE GOTHAM BAY AQUARIUM, BY THE SEASIDE? YOU USED TO TAKE US THERE.
MOTHER, I'M LOOKING AT BARBARA *RIGHT NOW.* IF YOU'RE NOT AT THE AQUARIUM TOMORROW TO MEET ME, I'M GOING TO KILL HER AND THEN I'M GOING TO MAKE DAD *EAT* HER.
SHALL WE SAY FIVE P.M.?

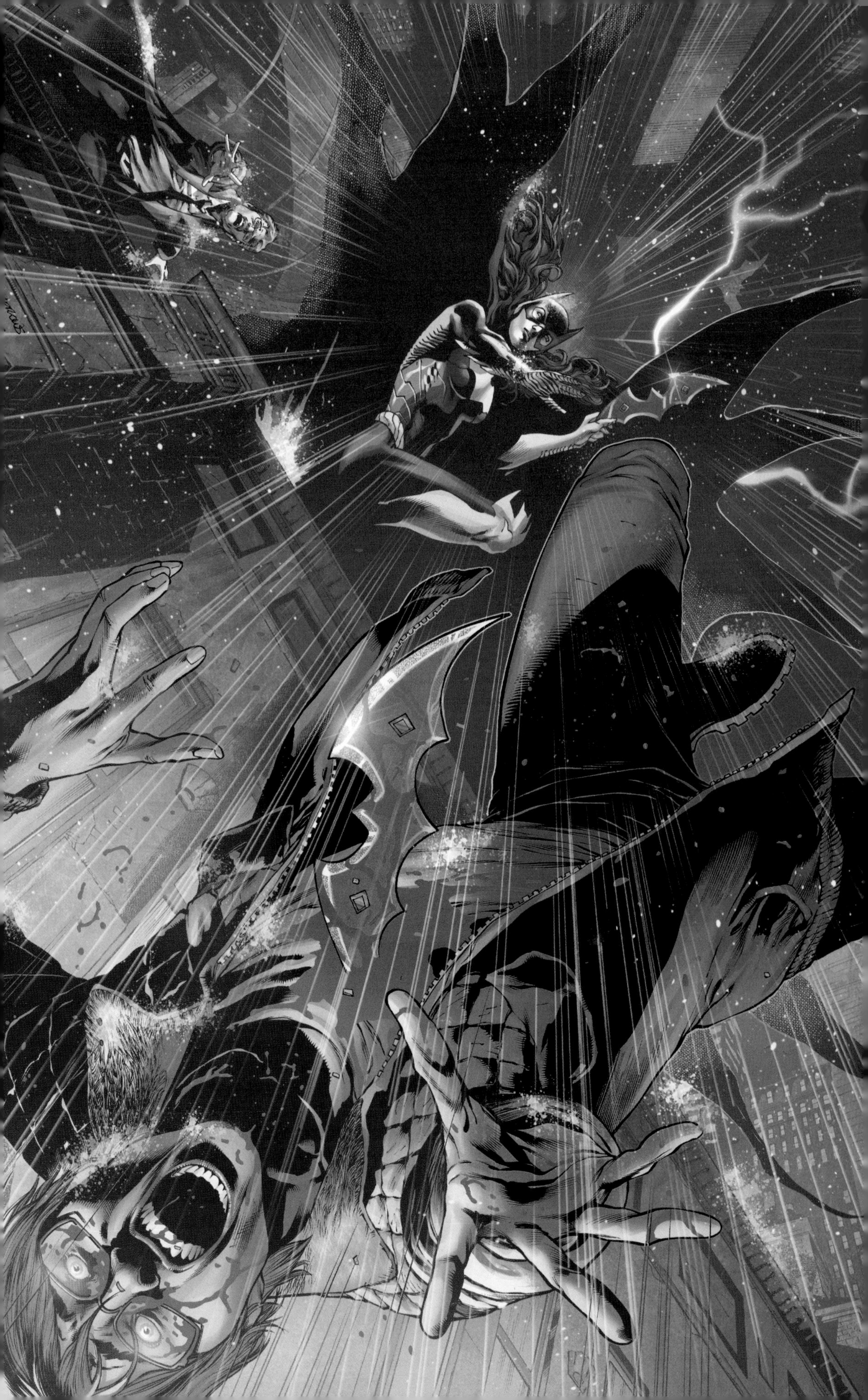

A BLADE FROM THE SHADOWS

GAIL SIMONE writer **DANIEL SAMPERE** penciller **JONATHAN GLAPION MARC DEERING** inkers
cover by **EDDY BARROWS, EBER FERREIRA & MARCELO MAIOLO**

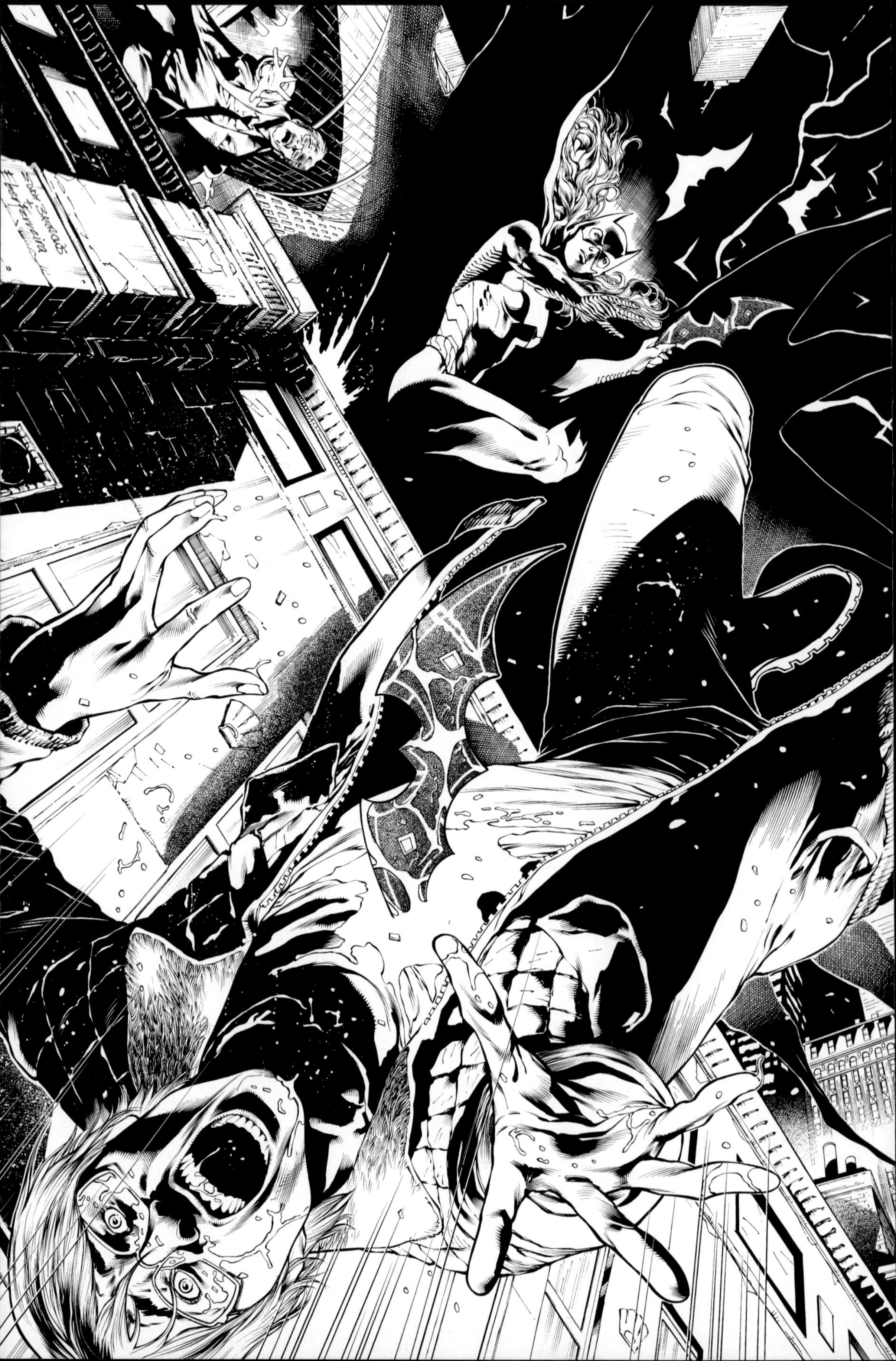

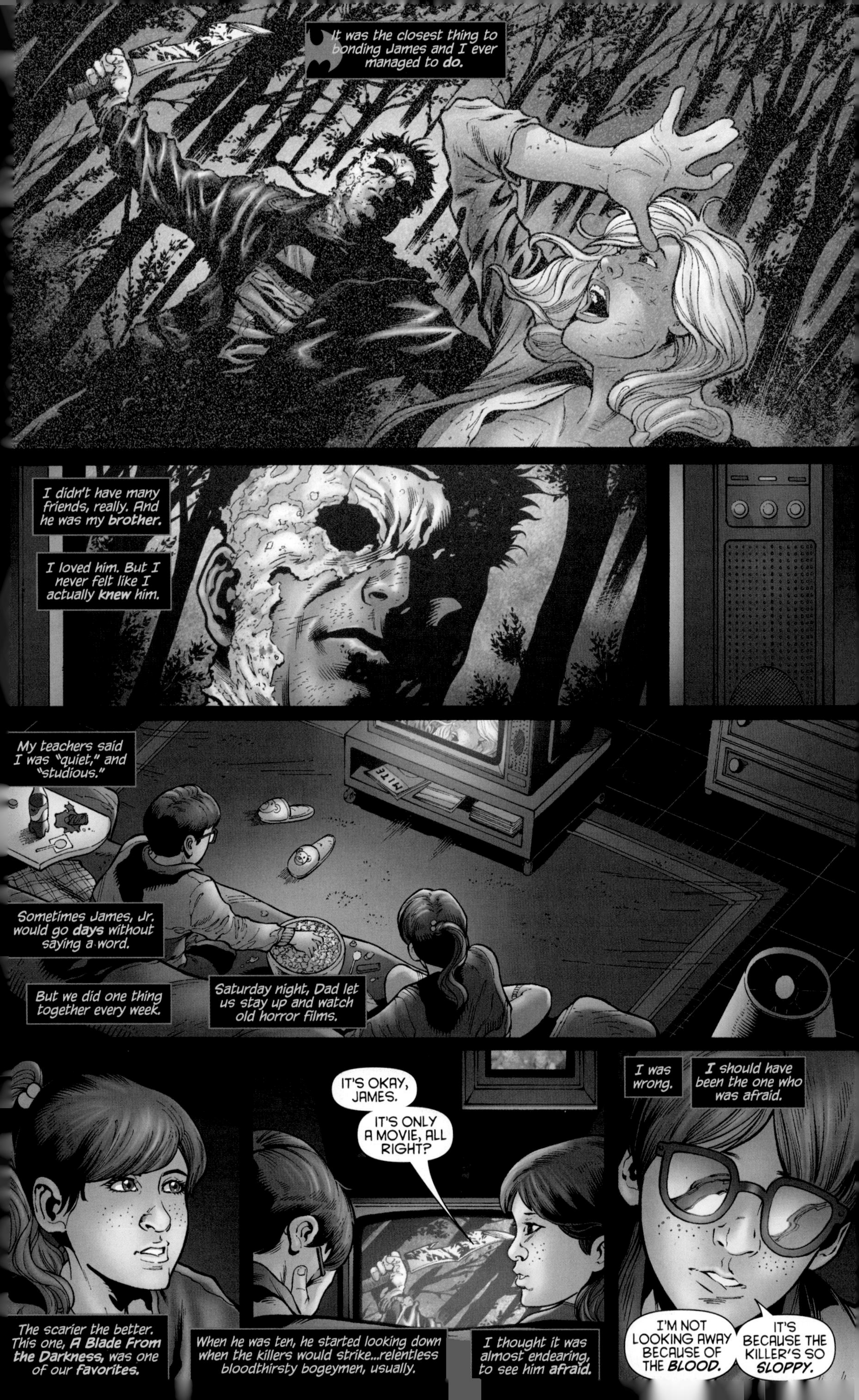
It was the closest thing to bonding James and I ever managed to do.
I didn't have many friends, really. And he was my brother.
I loved him. But I never felt like I actually knew him.
My teachers said I was "quiet," and "studious."
Sometimes James, Jr. would go days without saying a word.
But we did one thing together every week.
Saturday night, Dad let us stay up and watch old horror films.
The scarier the better. This one, A Blade From the Darkness, was one of our favorites.
IT'S OKAY, JAMES.
IT'S ONLY A MOVIE, ALL RIGHT?
When he was ten, he started looking down when the killers would strike...relentless bloodthirsty bogeymen, usually.
I thought it was almost endearing, to see him afraid.
I was wrong.
I should have been the one who was afraid.
I'M NOT LOOKING AWAY BECAUSE OF THE BLOOD.
IT'S BECAUSE THE KILLER'S SO SLOPPY.

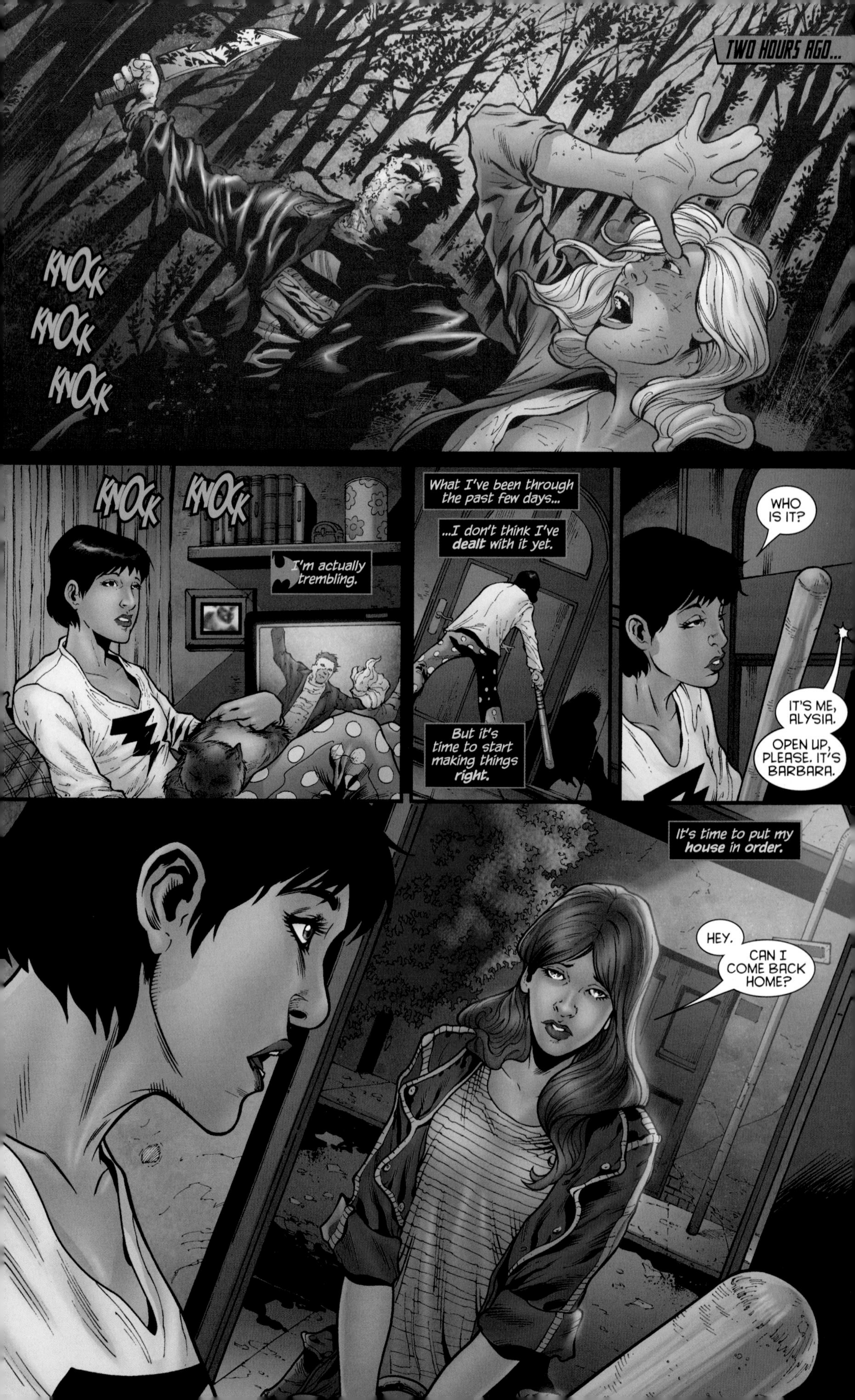
TWO HOURS AGO...
KNOCK
KNOCK
KNOCK
KNOCK
KNOCK
I'm actually trembling.
What I've been through the past few days...
...I don't think I've dealt with it yet.
But it's time to start making things right.
WHO IS IT?
IT'S ME, ALYSIA.
OPEN UP, PLEASE. IT'S BARBARA.
It's time to put my house in order.
HEY.
CAN I COME BACK HOME?

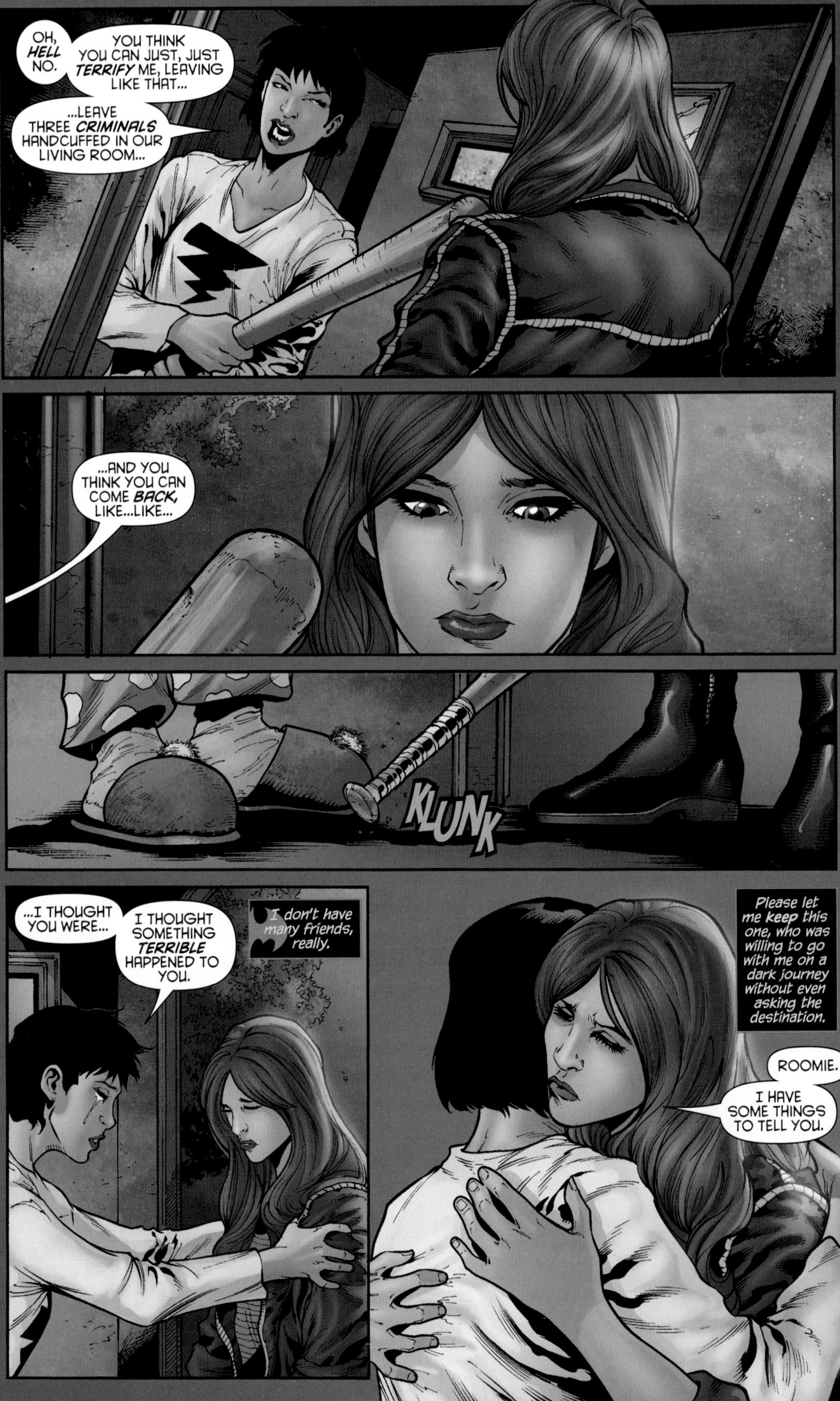
OH, HELL NO.
YOU THINK YOU CAN JUST, JUST TERRIFY ME, LEAVING LIKE THAT...
...LEAVE THREE CRIMINALS HANDCUFFED IN OUR LIVING ROOM...
...AND YOU THINK YOU CAN COME BACK, LIKE...LIKE...
KLUNK
...I THOUGHT YOU WERE...
I THOUGHT SOMETHING TERRIBLE HAPPENED TO YOU.
I don't have many friends, really.
Please let me keep this one, who was willing to go with me on a dark journey without even asking the destination.
ROOMIE.
I HAVE SOME THINGS TO TELL YOU.

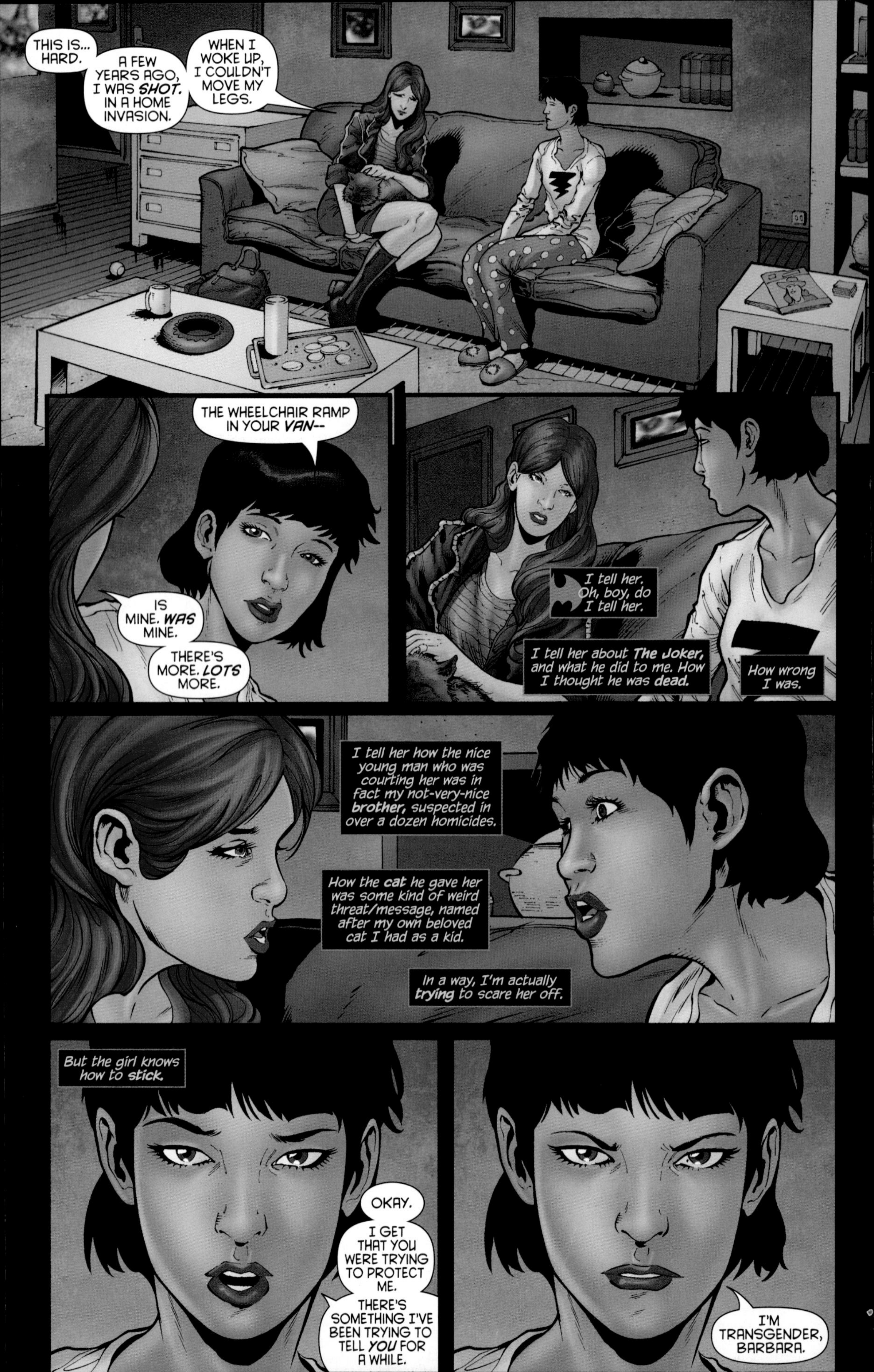
THIS IS... HARD.
A FEW YEARS AGO, I WAS SHOT. IN A HOME INVASION.
WHEN I WOKE UP, I COULDN'T MOVE MY LEGS.
THE WHEELCHAIR RAMP IN YOUR VAN--
IS MINE. WAS MINE.
THERE'S MORE. LOTS MORE.
I tell her. Oh, boy, do I tell her.
I tell her about The Joker, and what he did to me. How I thought he was dead.
How wrong I was.
I tell her how the nice young man who was courting her was in fact my not-very-nice brother, suspected in over a dozen homicides.
How the cat he gave her was some kind of weird threat/message, named after my own beloved cat I had as a kid.
In a way, I'm actually trying to scare her off.
But the girl knows how to stick.
OKAY.
I GET THAT YOU WERE TRYING TO PROTECT ME.
THERE'S SOMETHING I'VE BEEN TRYING TO TELL YOU FOR A WHILE.
I'M TRANSGENDER, BARBARA.

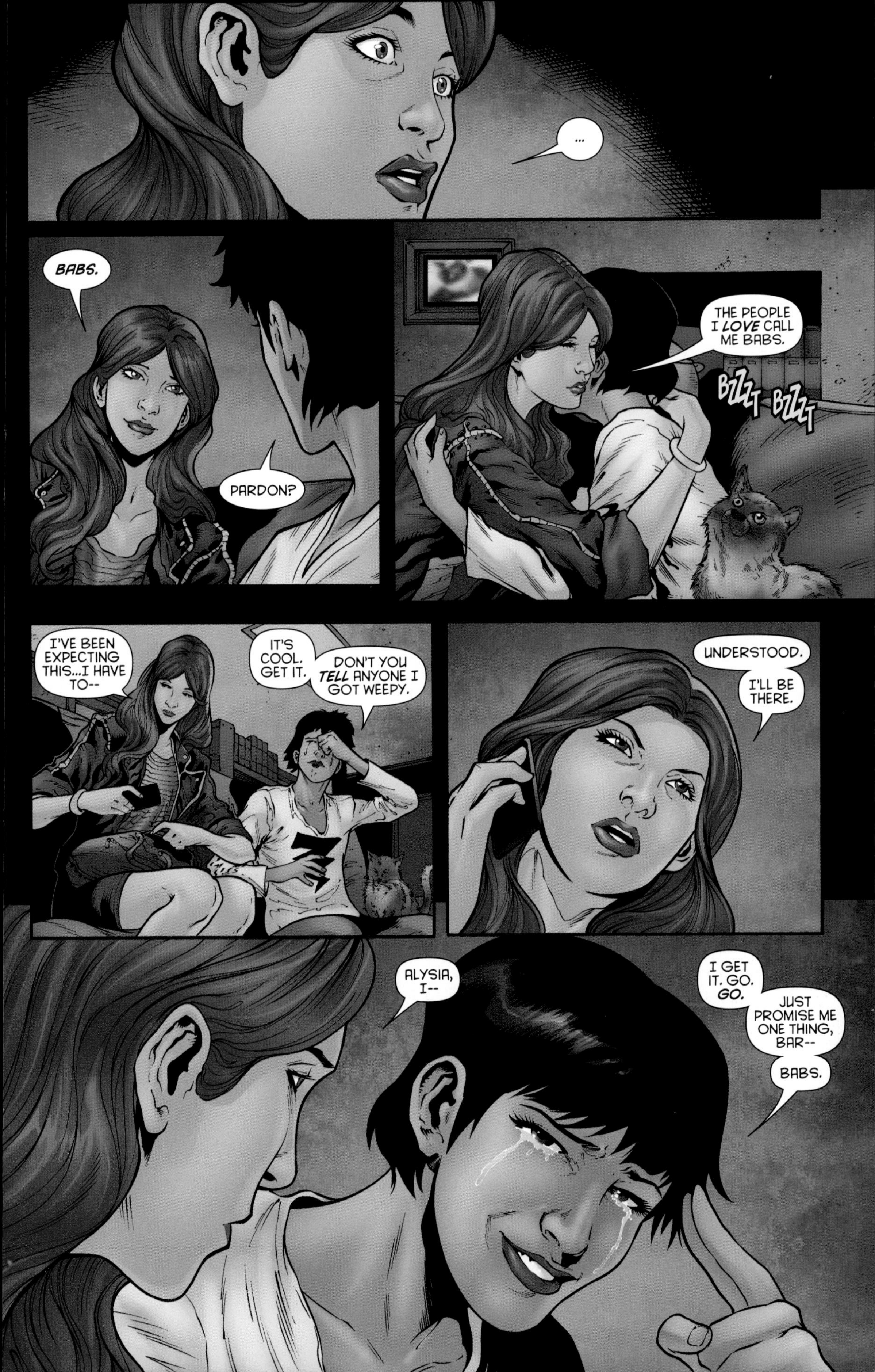
...
BABS.
PARDON?
THE PEOPLE I LOVE CALL ME BABS.
BZZZT BZZZT
I'VE BEEN EXPECTING THIS...I HAVE TO--
IT'S COOL. GET IT.
DON'T YOU TELL ANYONE I GOT WEEPY.
UNDERSTOOD.
I'LL BE THERE.
ALYSIA, I--
I GET IT. GO. GO.
JUST PROMISE ME ONE THING, BAR--
BABS.

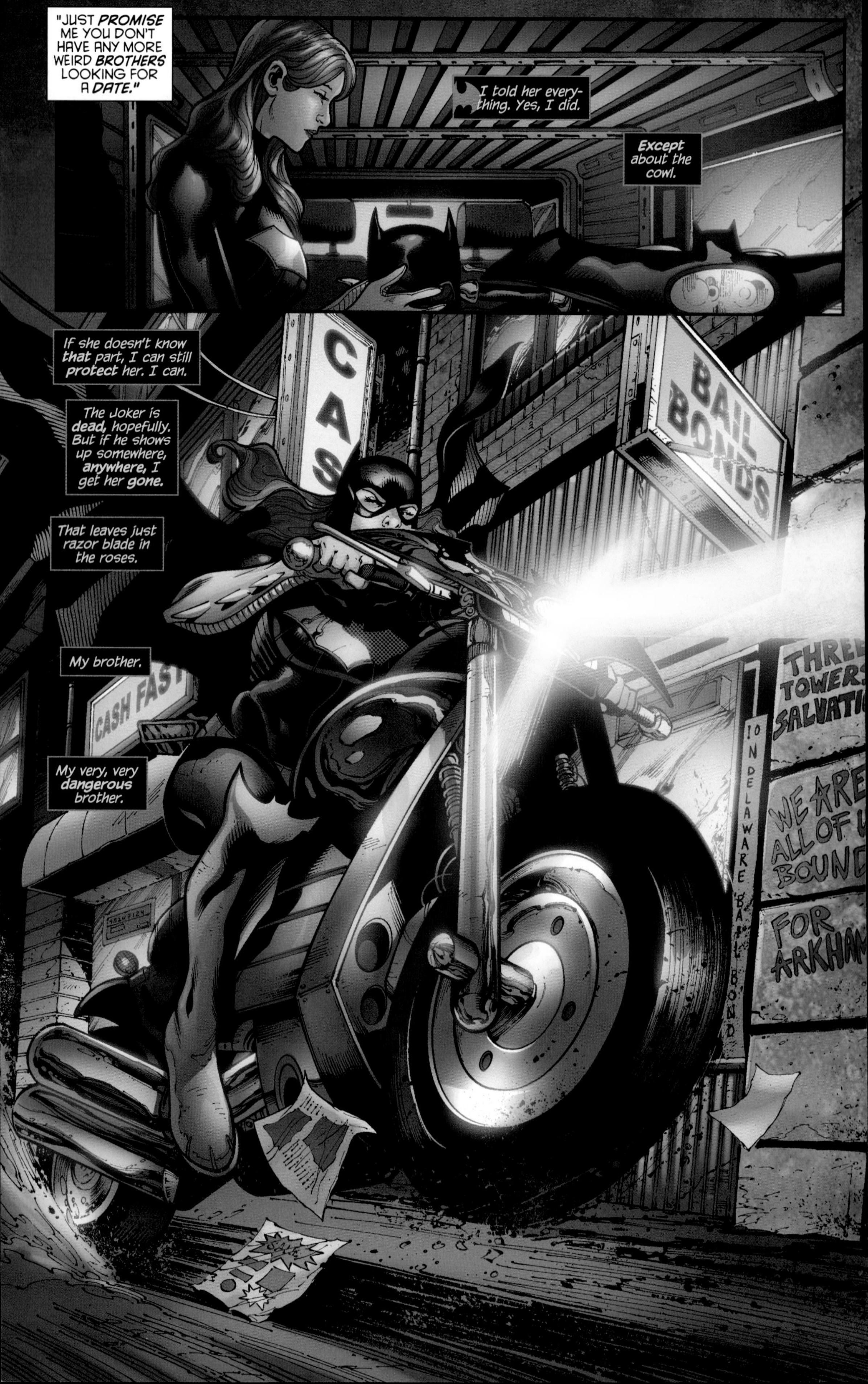
"JUST PROMISE ME YOU DON'T HAVE ANY MORE WEIRD BROTHERS LOOKING FOR A DATE."
I told her everything. Yes, I did.
Except about the cowl.
If she doesn't know that part, I can still protect her. I can.
The Joker is dead, hopefully. But if he shows up somewhere, anywhere, I get her gone.
That leaves just razor blade in the roses.
My brother.
My very, very dangerous brother.
BAIL BONDS
CASH FAST
DELAWARE BAIL BOND
FOR ARKHAM

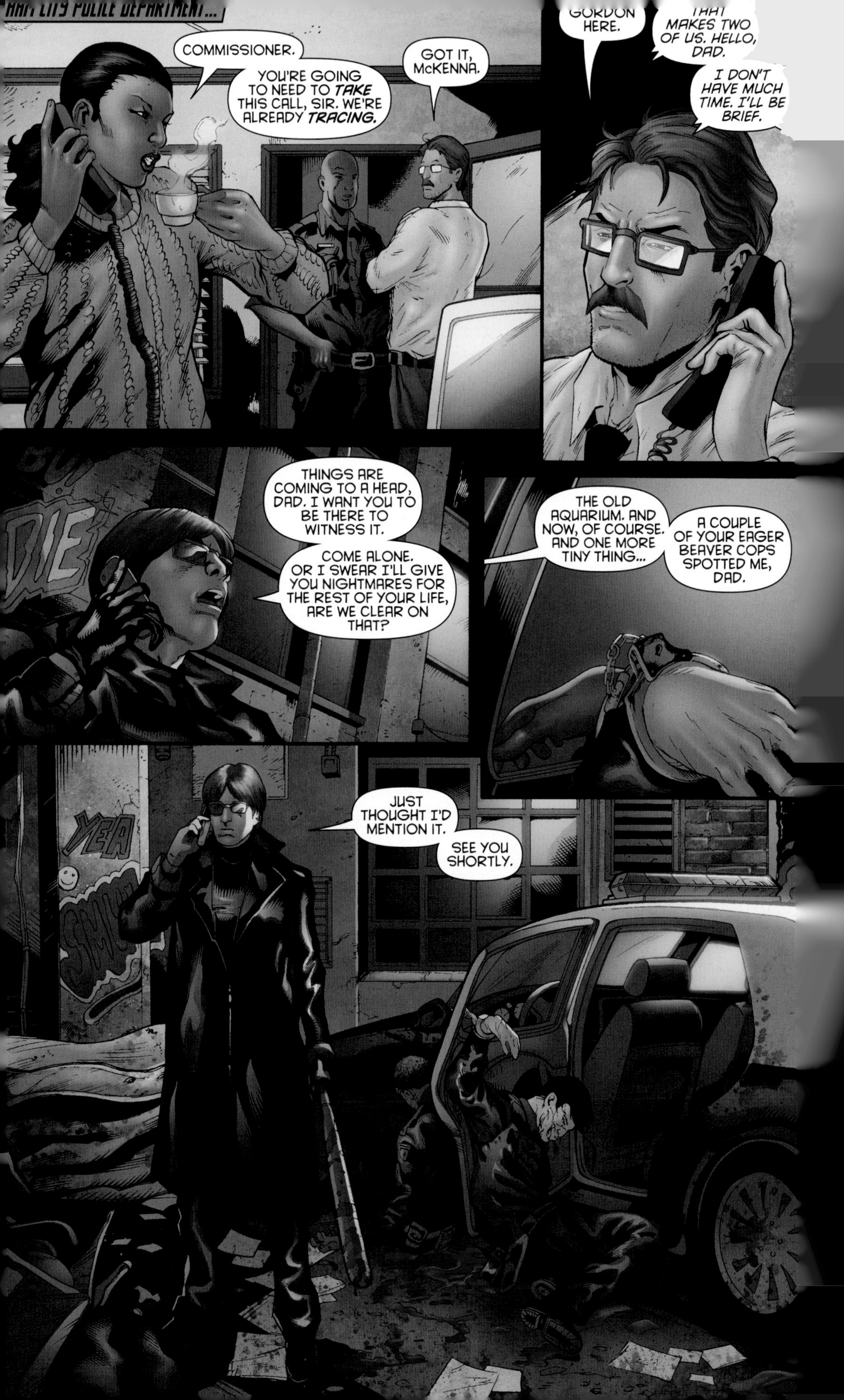
COMMISSIONER.
YOU'RE GOING TO NEED TO *TAKE* THIS CALL, SIR. WE'RE ALREADY *TRACING.*
GOT IT, McKENNA.
GORDON HERE.
THAT MAKES TWO OF US. HELLO, DAD.
I DON'T HAVE MUCH TIME. I'LL BE BRIEF.
THINGS ARE COMING TO A HEAD, DAD. I WANT YOU TO BE THERE TO WITNESS IT.
COME ALONE. OR I SWEAR I'LL GIVE YOU NIGHTMARES FOR THE REST OF YOUR LIFE, ARE WE CLEAR ON THAT?
THE OLD AQUARIUM. AND NOW, OF COURSE. AND ONE MORE TINY THING...
A COUPLE OF YOUR EAGER BEAVER COPS SPOTTED ME, DAD.
JUST THOUGHT I'D MENTION IT.
SEE YOU SHORTLY.

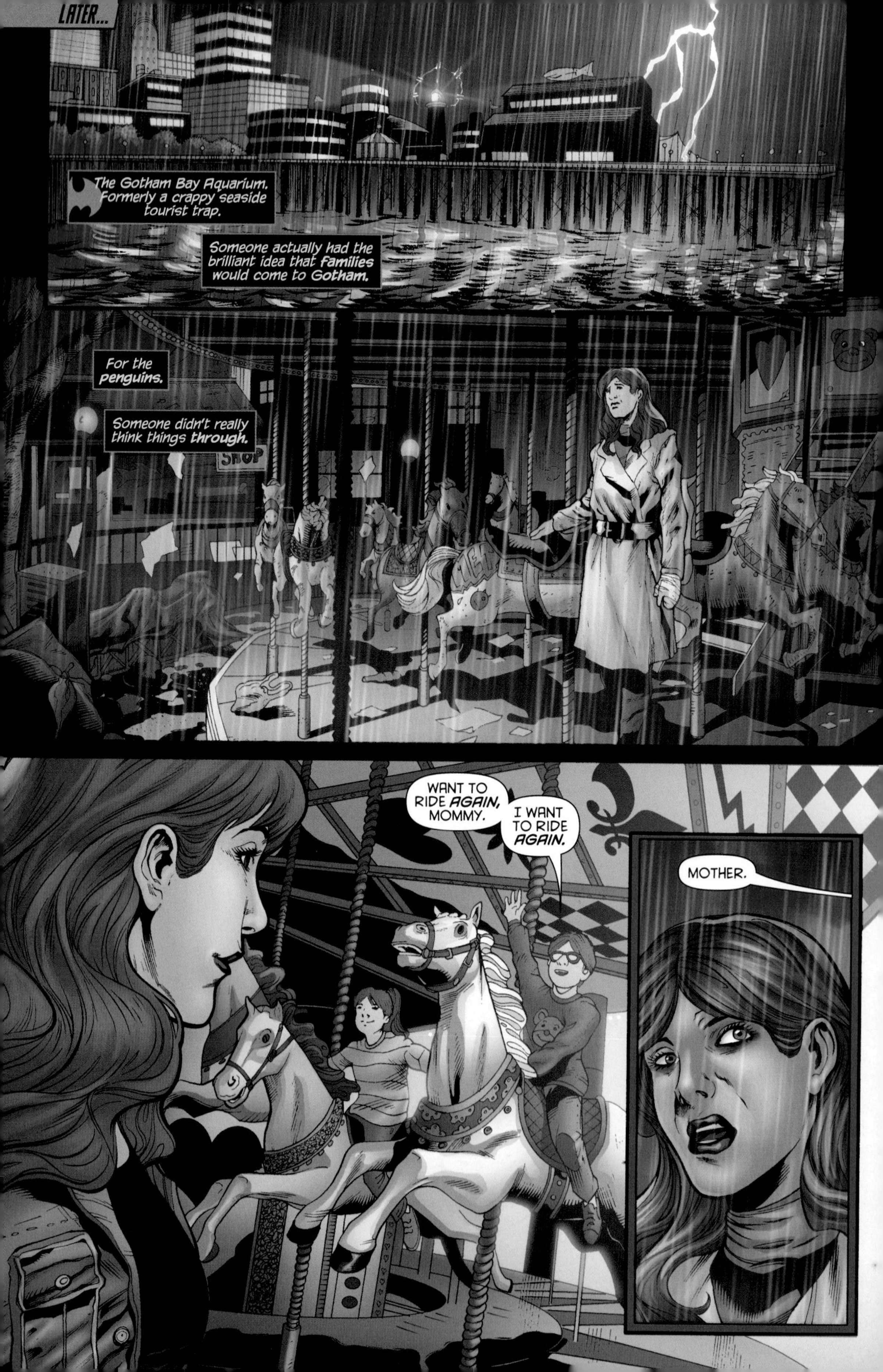
LATER...
The Gotham Bay Aquarium. Formerly a crappy seaside tourist trap.
Someone actually had the brilliant idea that families would come to Gotham.
For the penguins.
Someone didn't really think things through.
SHOP
WANT TO RIDE AGAIN, MOMMY.
I WANT TO RIDE AGAIN.
MOTHER.

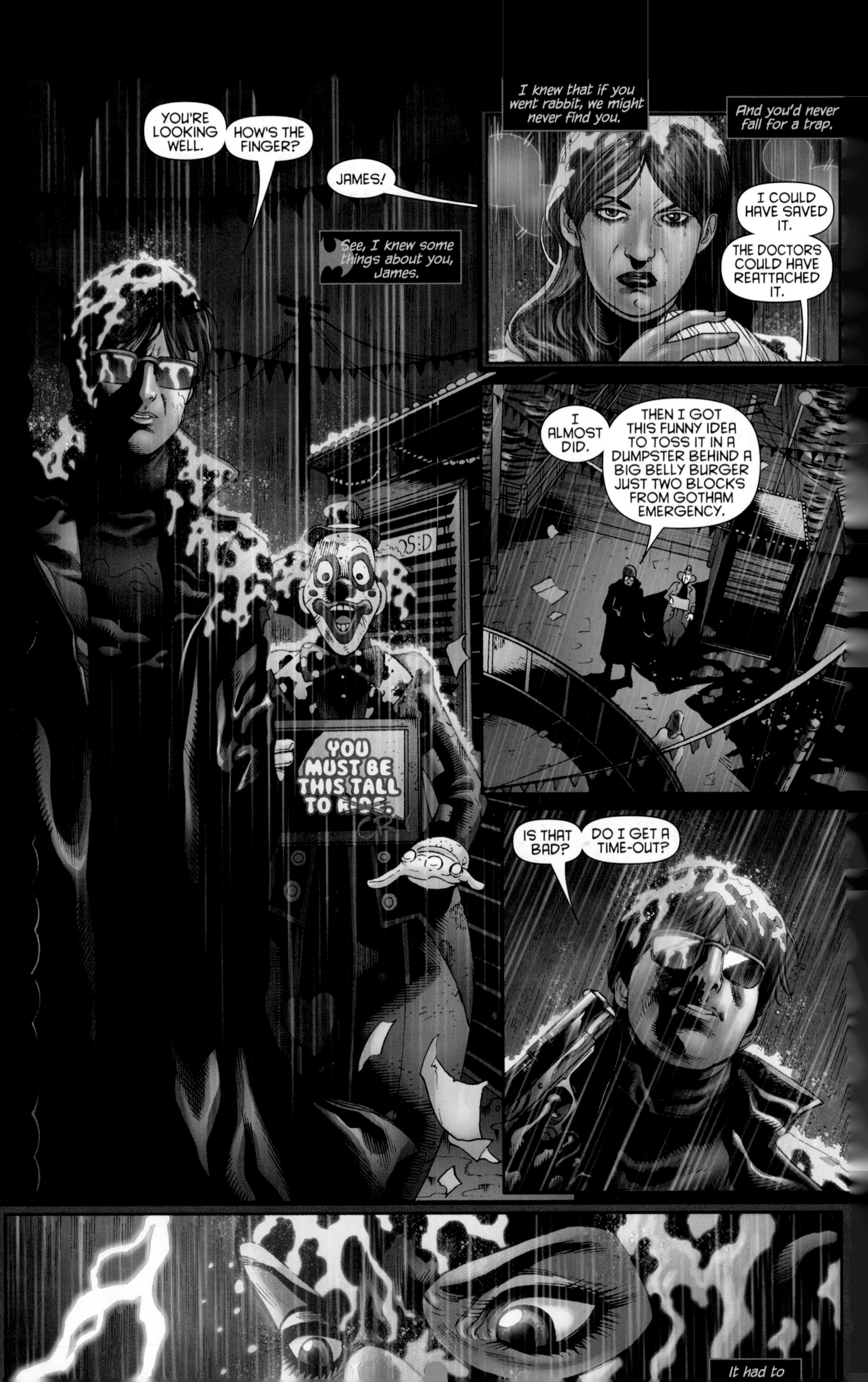
YOU'RE LOOKING WELL.
HOW'S THE FINGER?
JAMES!
See, I knew some things about you, James.
YOU MUST BE THIS TALL TO RIDE.
I knew that if you went rabbit, we might never find you.
And you'd never fall for a trap.
I COULD HAVE SAVED IT.
THE DOCTORS COULD HAVE REATTACHED IT.
I ALMOST DID.
THEN I GOT THIS FUNNY IDEA TO TOSS IT IN A DUMPSTER BEHIND A BIG BELLY BURGER JUST TWO BLOCKS FROM GOTHAM EMERGENCY.
IS THAT BAD?
DO I GET A TIME-OUT?
It had to

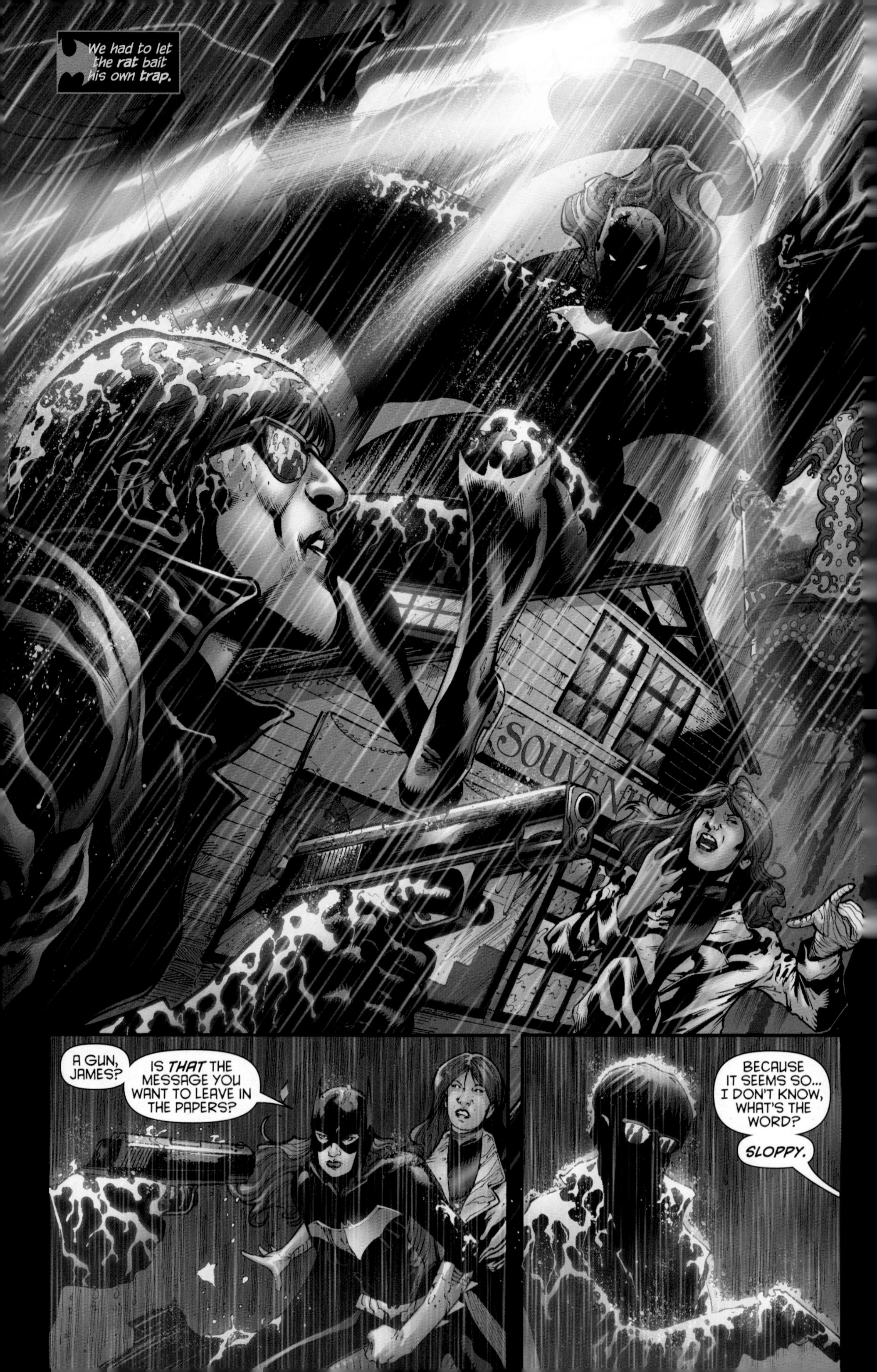
We had to let the rat bait his own trap.
SOUVEN
A GUN, JAMES?
IS THAT THE MESSAGE YOU WANT TO LEAVE IN THE PAPERS?
BECAUSE IT SEEMS SO... I DON'T KNOW, WHAT'S THE WORD?
SLOPPY.

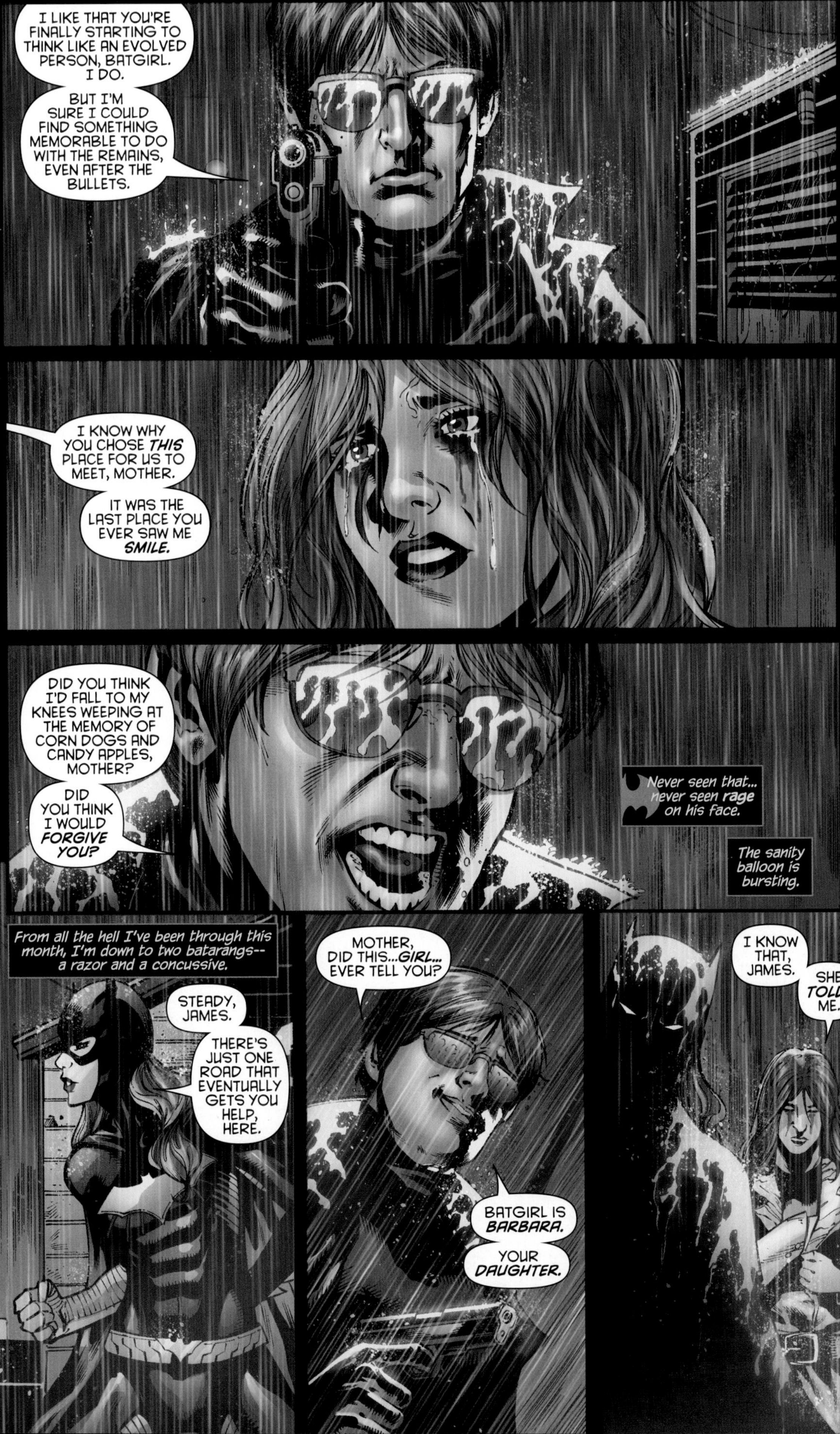
I LIKE THAT YOU'RE FINALLY STARTING TO THINK LIKE AN EVOLVED PERSON, BATGIRL. I DO.
BUT I'M SURE I COULD FIND SOMETHING MEMORABLE TO DO WITH THE REMAINS, EVEN AFTER THE BULLETS.
I KNOW WHY YOU CHOSE *THIS* PLACE FOR US TO MEET, MOTHER.
IT WAS THE LAST PLACE YOU EVER SAW ME *SMILE.*
DID YOU THINK I'D FALL TO MY KNEES WEEPING AT THE MEMORY OF CORN DOGS AND CANDY APPLES, MOTHER?
DID YOU THINK I WOULD *FORGIVE YOU?*
*Never seen that... never seen **rage** on his face.*
The sanity balloon is bursting.
From all the hell I've been through this month, I'm down to two batarangs-- a razor and a concussive.
STEADY, JAMES.
THERE'S JUST ONE ROAD THAT EVENTUALLY GETS YOU HELP, HERE.
MOTHER, DID THIS...*GIRL...* EVER TELL YOU?
BATGIRL IS *BARBARA.*
YOUR *DAUGHTER.*
I KNOW THAT, JAMES.
SHE *TOLD* ME.

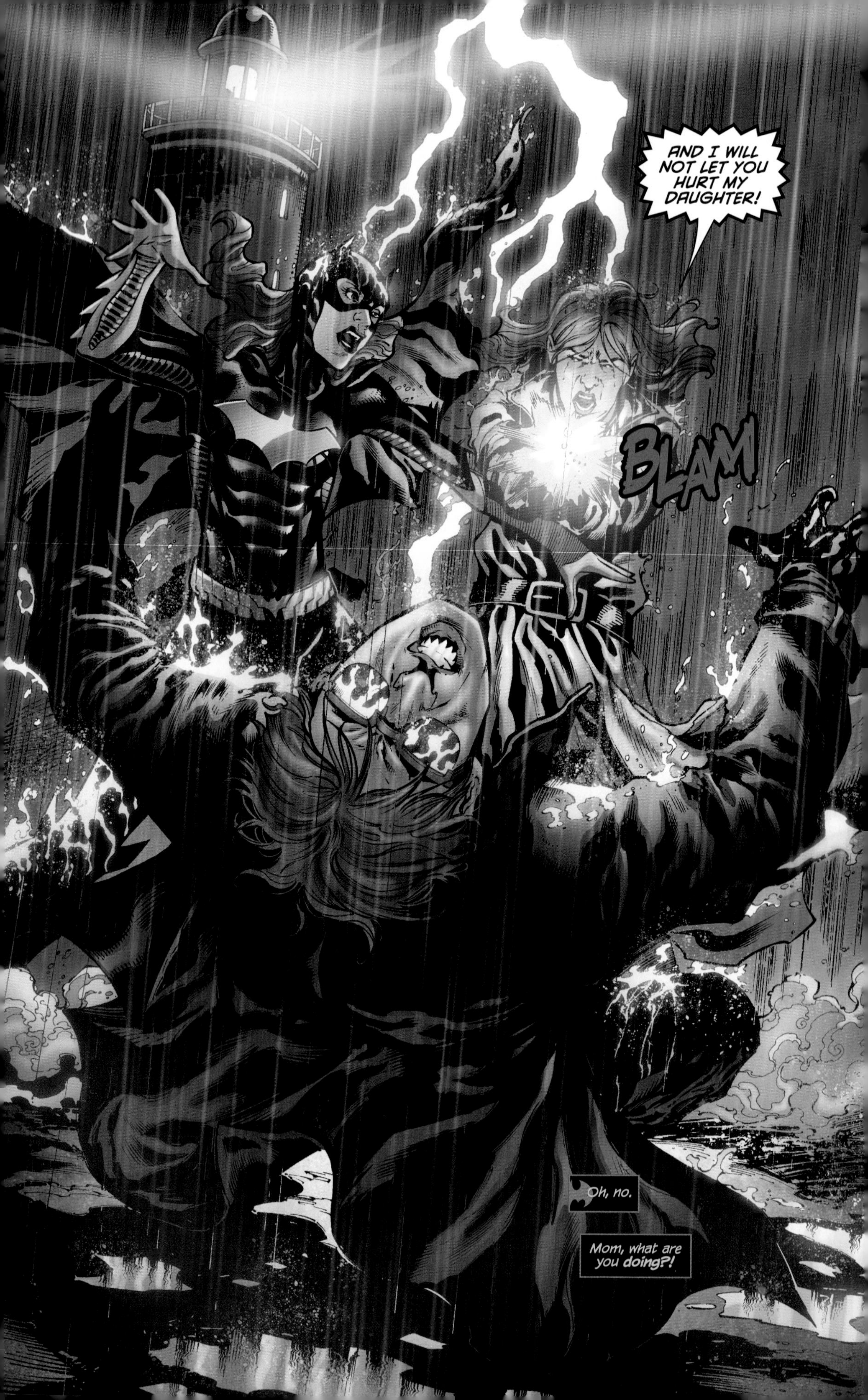
AND I WILL NOT LET YOU HURT MY DAUGHTER!
BLAM
Oh, no.
Mom, what are you doing?!

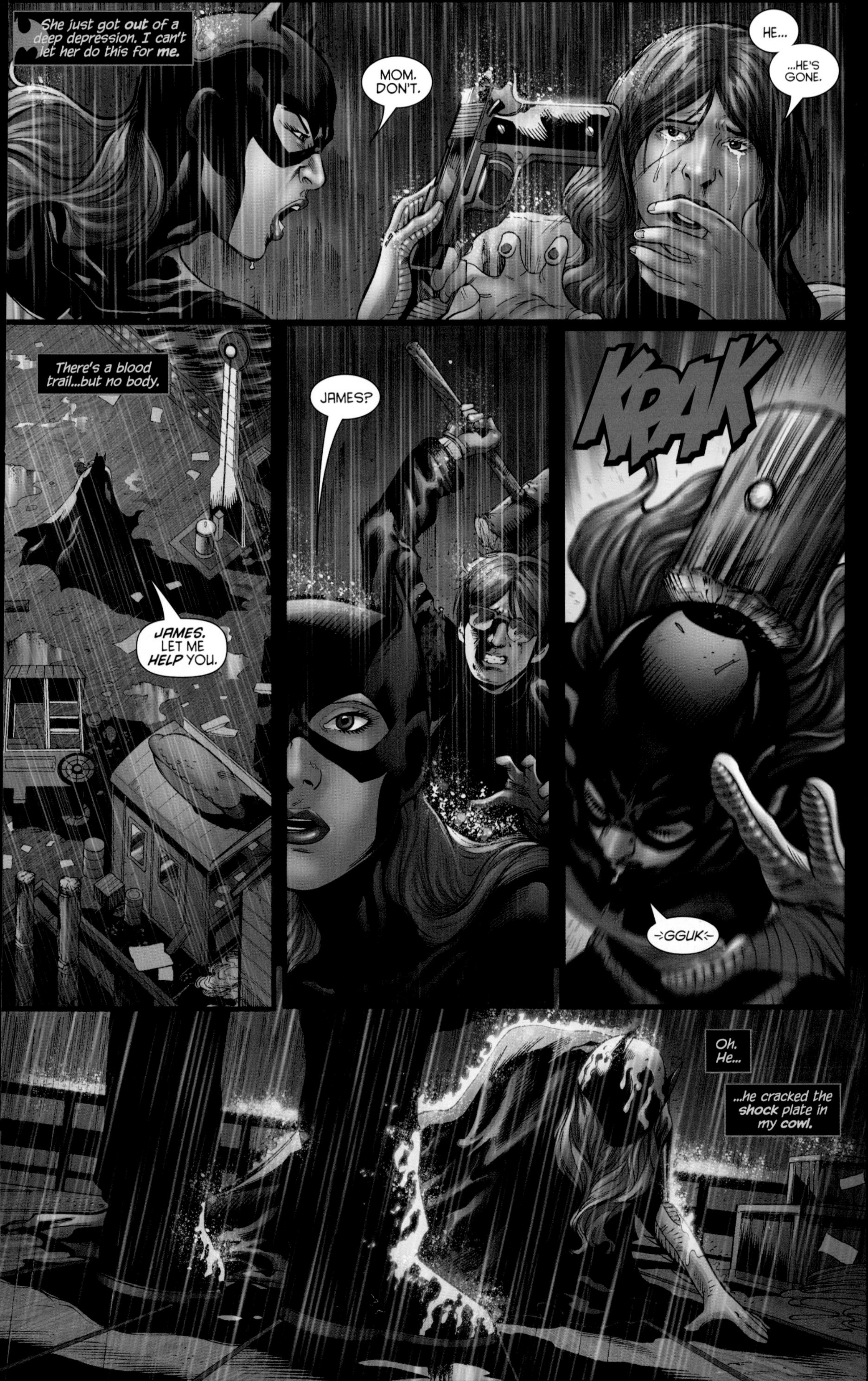
She just got out of a deep depression. I can't let her do this for me.
MOM. DON'T.
HE...
...HE'S GONE.
There's a blood trail...but no body.
JAMES. LET ME HELP YOU.
JAMES?
KRAK
GGUK
Oh. He...
...he cracked the shock plate in my cowl.

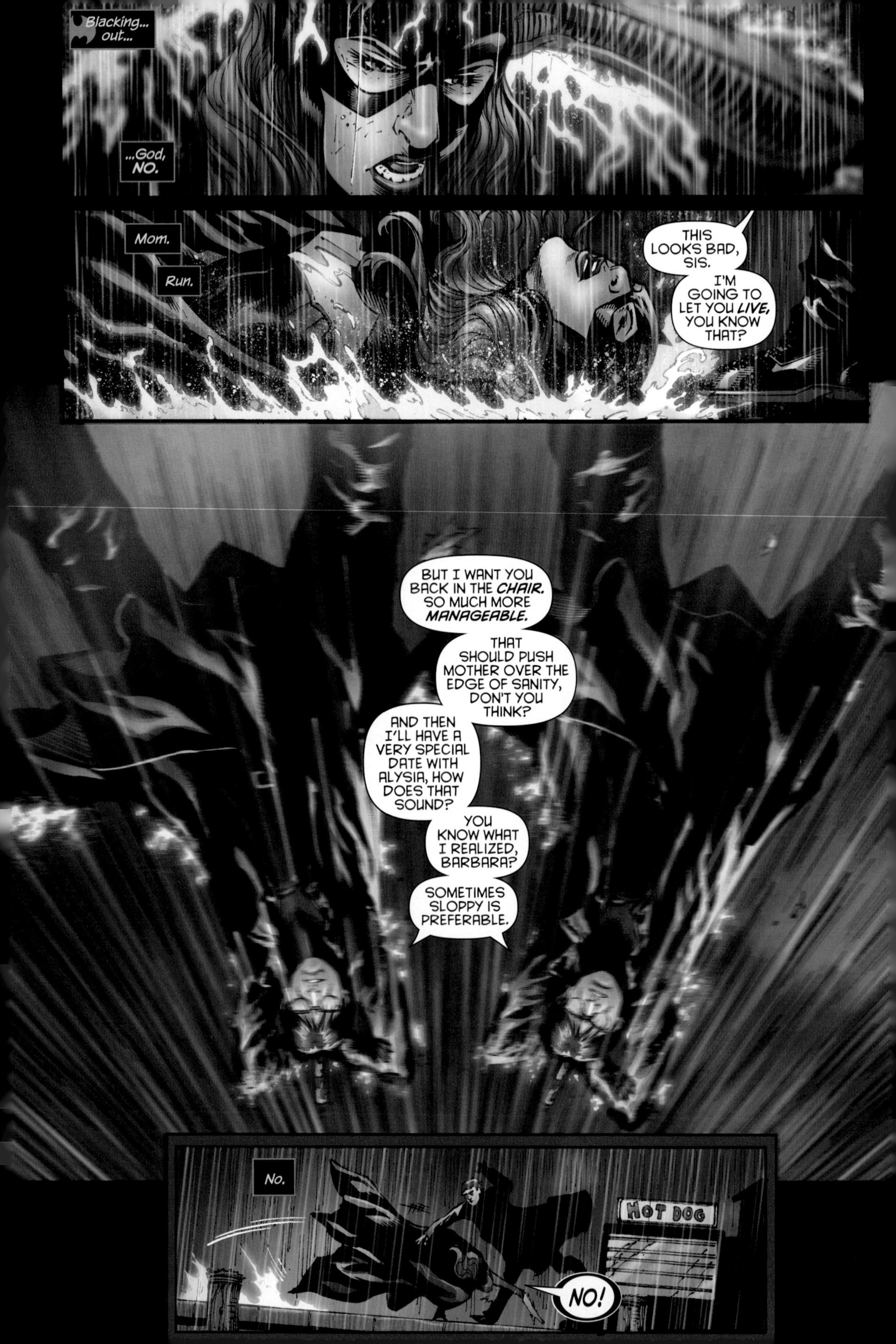
Blacking... out...
...God, NO.
Mom.
Run.
THIS LOOKS BAD, SIS.
I'M GOING TO LET YOU LIVE, YOU KNOW THAT?
BUT I WANT YOU BACK IN THE CHAIR. SO MUCH MORE MANAGEABLE.
THAT SHOULD PUSH MOTHER OVER THE EDGE OF SANITY, DON'T YOU THINK?
AND THEN I'LL HAVE A VERY SPECIAL DATE WITH ALYSIA, HOW DOES THAT SOUND?
YOU KNOW WHAT I REALIZED, BARBARA?
SOMETIMES SLOPPY IS PREFERABLE.
No.
HOT DOG
NO!

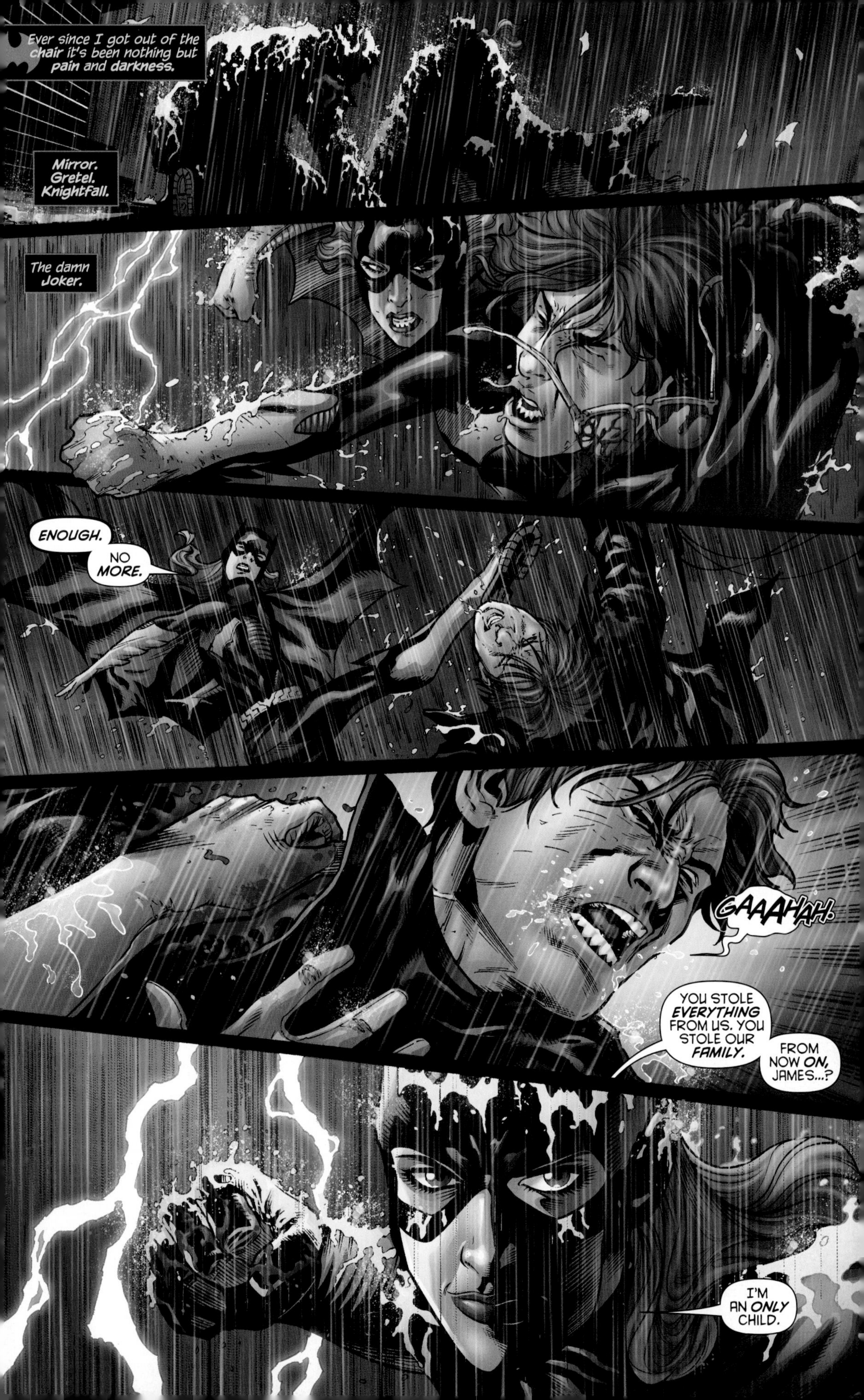
Ever since I got out of the chair it's been nothing but pain and darkness.
Mirror. Gretel. Knightfall.
The damn Joker.
ENOUGH.
NO MORE.
GAAAHAH.
YOU STOLE EVERYTHING FROM US. YOU STOLE OUR FAMILY.
FROM NOW ON, JAMES...?
I'M AN ONLY CHILD.

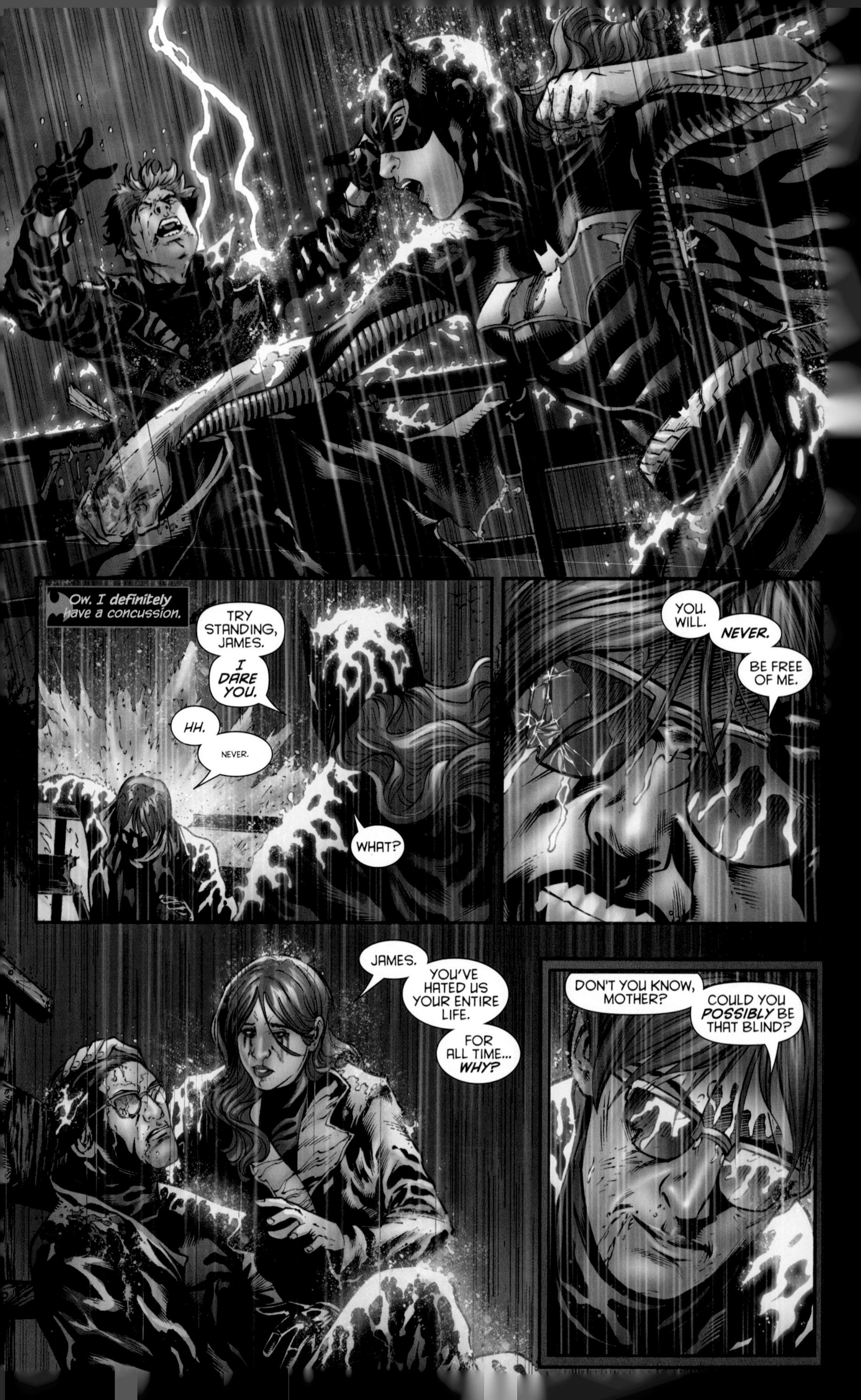
Ow. I definitely have a concussion.
TRY STANDING, JAMES.
I DARE YOU.
HH.
NEVER.
WHAT?
YOU.
WILL.
NEVER.
BE FREE OF ME.
JAMES.
YOU'VE HATED US YOUR ENTIRE LIFE.
FOR ALL TIME... WHY?
DON'T YOU KNOW, MOTHER?
COULD YOU POSSIBLY BE THAT BLIND?

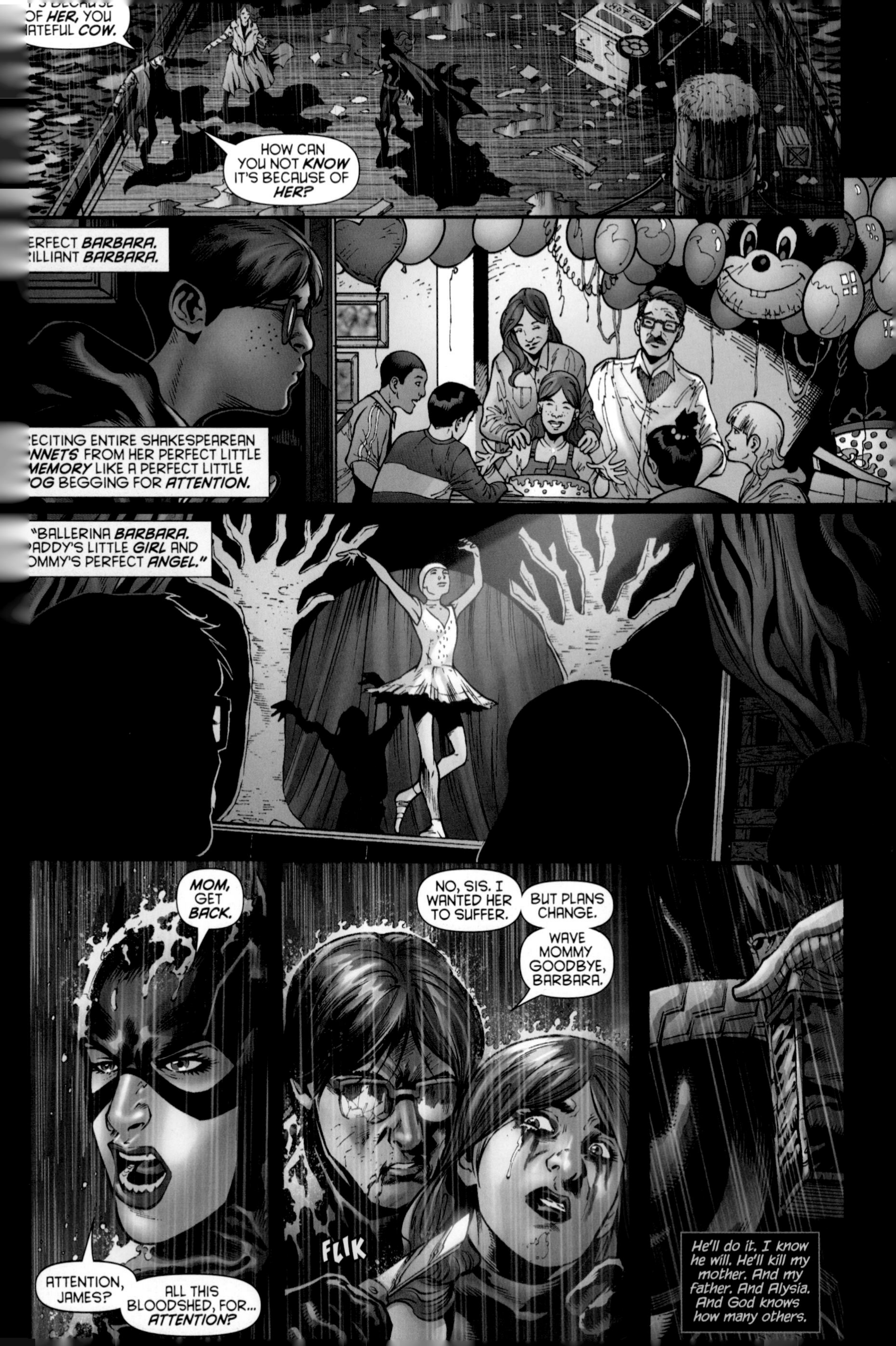

OF HER, YOU ATEFUL COW.
HOW CAN YOU NOT KNOW IT'S BECAUSE OF HER?
ERFECT BARBARA. RILLIANT BARBARA.
RECITING ENTIRE SHAKESPEAREAN NNETS FROM HER PERFECT LITTLE MEMORY LIKE A PERFECT LITTLE OG BEGGING FOR ATTENTION.
"BALLERINA BARBARA. ADDY'S LITTLE GIRL AND OMMY'S PERFECT ANGEL."
MOM, GET BACK.
ATTENTION, JAMES?
ALL THIS BLOODSHED, FOR... ATTENTION?
NO, SIS. I WANTED HER TO SUFFER.
BUT PLANS CHANGE.
WAVE MOMMY GOODBYE, BARBARA.
FLIK
He'll do it. I know he will. He'll kill my mother. And my father. And Alysia. And God knows how many others.

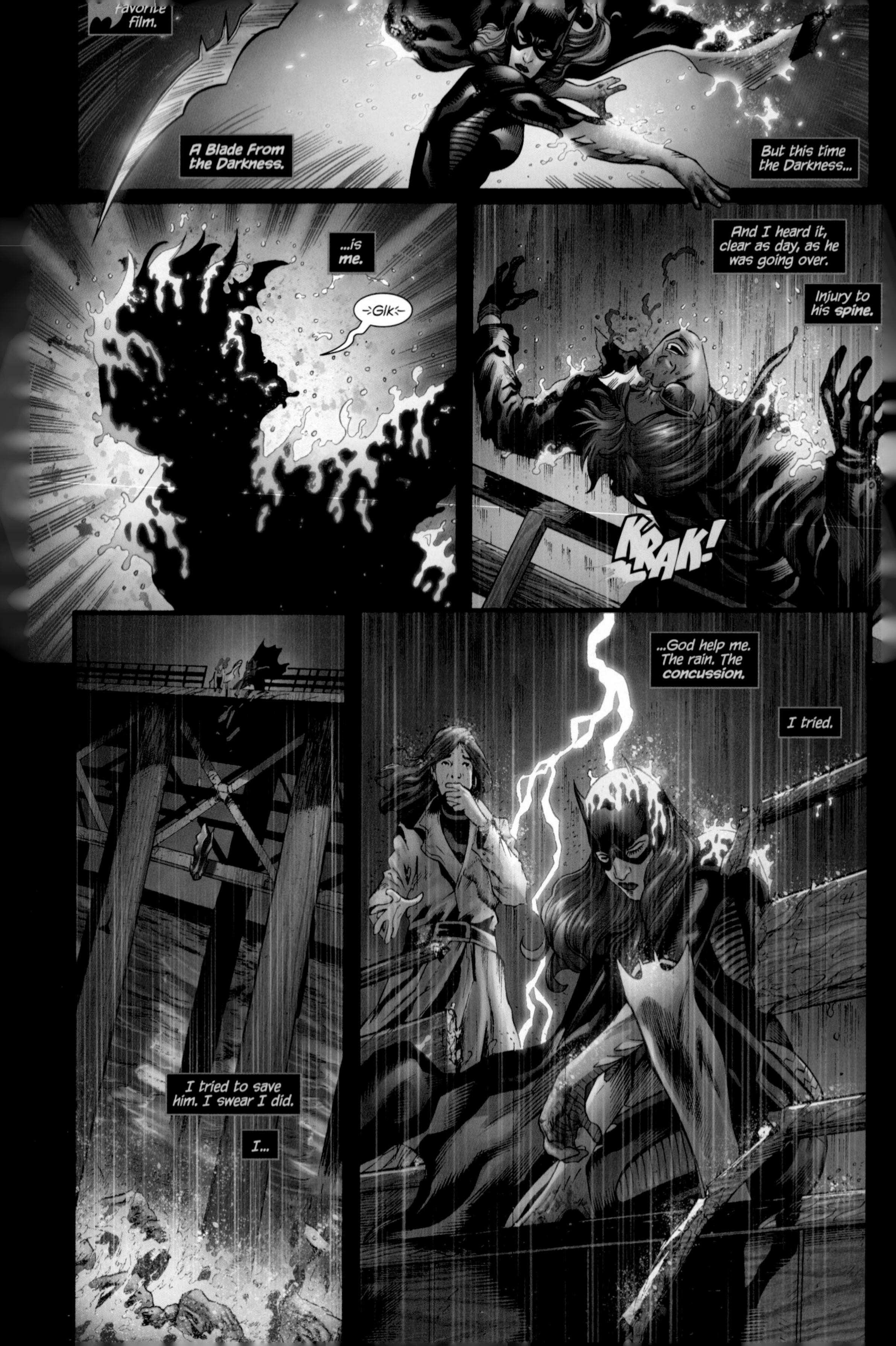
favorite film.
A Blade From the Darkness.
But this time the Darkness...
...is me.
-Glk-
And I heard it, clear as day, as he was going over.
Injury to his spine.
KRAK!
I tried to save him. I swear I did.
I...
...God help me. The rain. The concussion.
I tried.

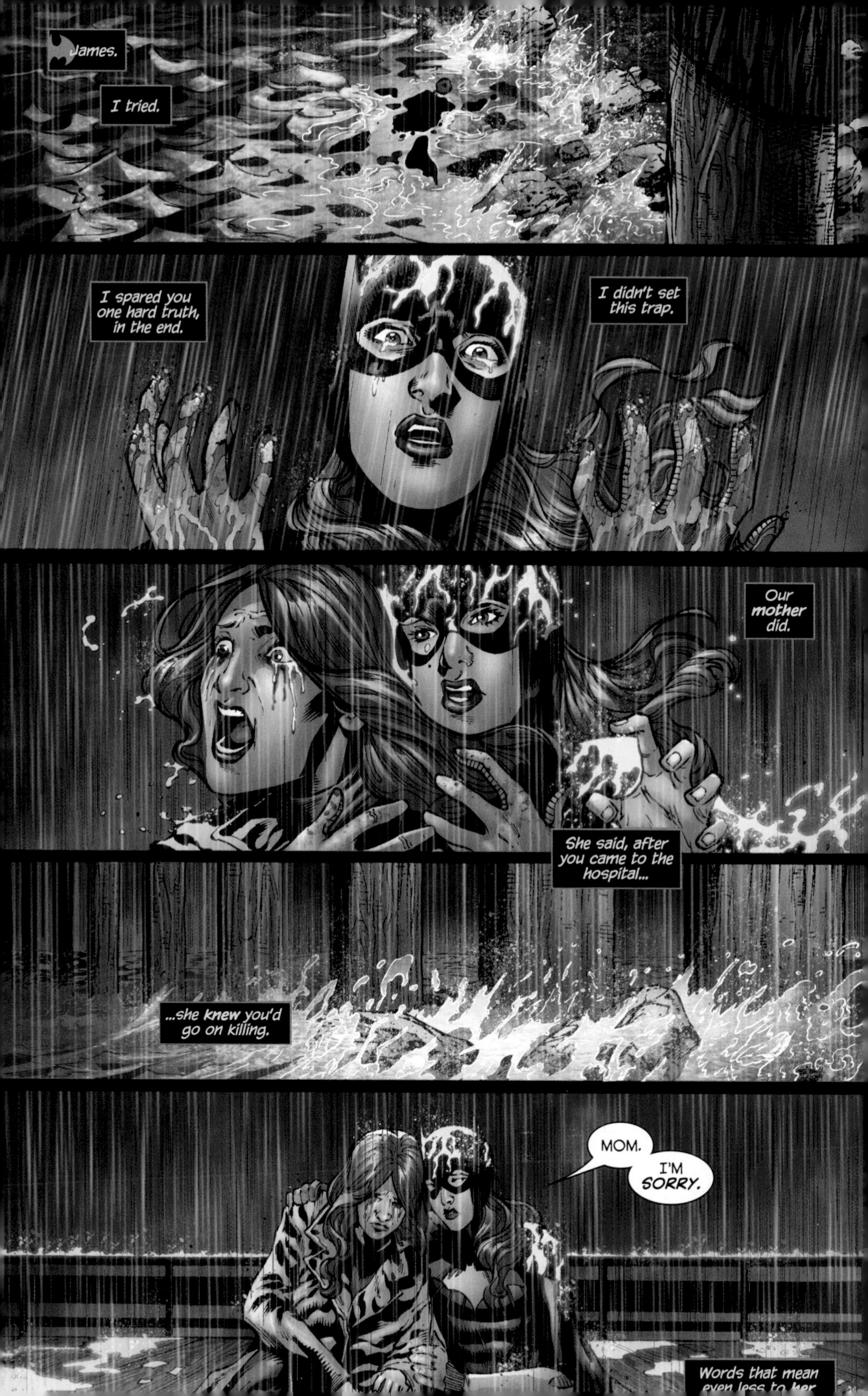
James.
I tried.
I spared you one hard truth, in the end.
I didn't set this trap.
Our mother did.
She said, after you came to the hospital...
...she knew you'd go on killing.
MOM.
I'M SORRY.
Words that mean

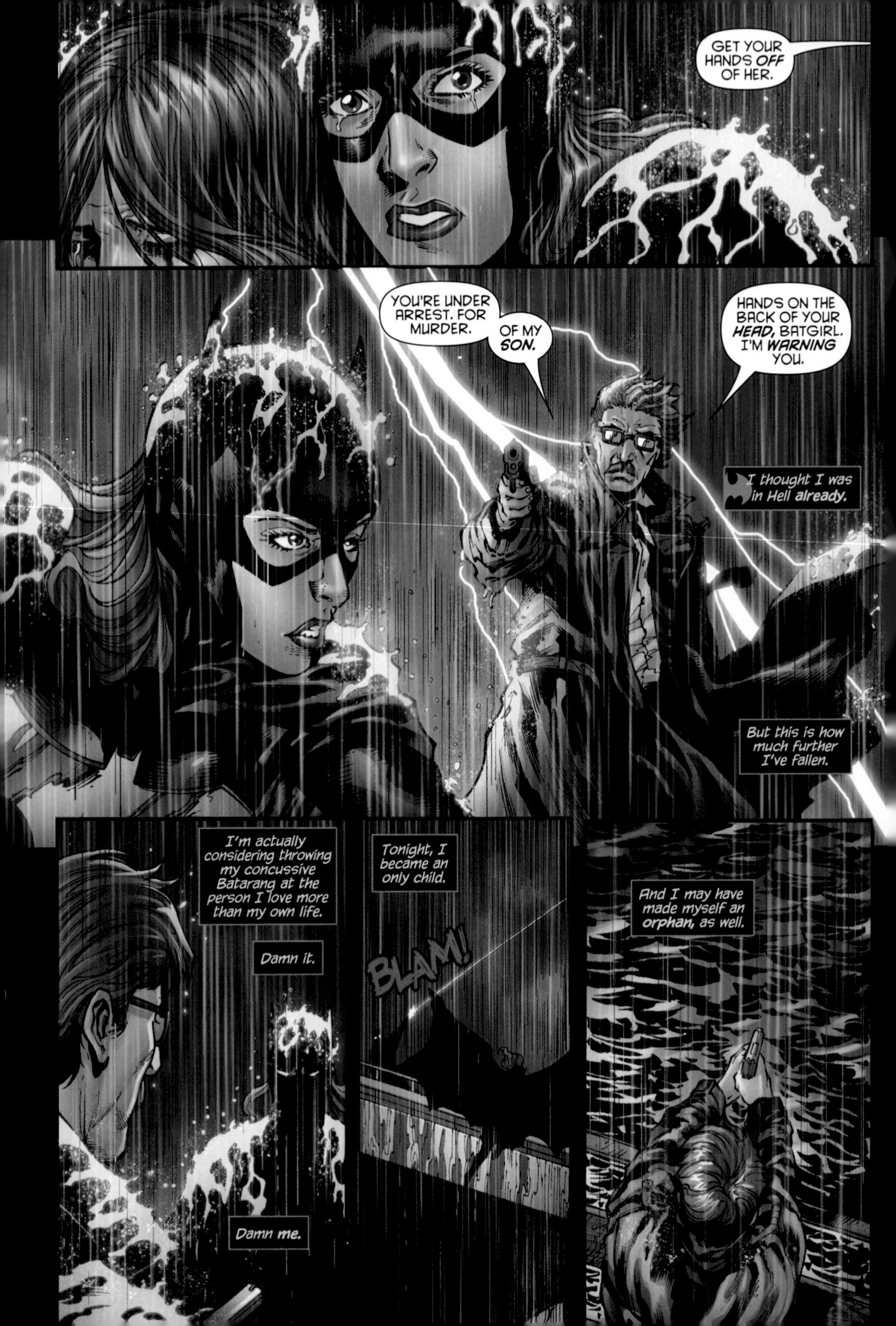
GET YOUR HANDS *OFF* OF HER.
YOU'RE UNDER ARREST. FOR MURDER.
OF MY *SON.*
HANDS ON THE BACK OF YOUR *HEAD,* BATGIRL. I'M *WARNING* YOU.
I thought I was in Hell *already.*
But this is how much further I've fallen.
I'm actually considering throwing my concussive Batarang at the person I love more than my own life.
Damn it.
Damn *me.*
Tonight, I became an only child.
BLAM!
And I may have made myself an *orphan,* as well.

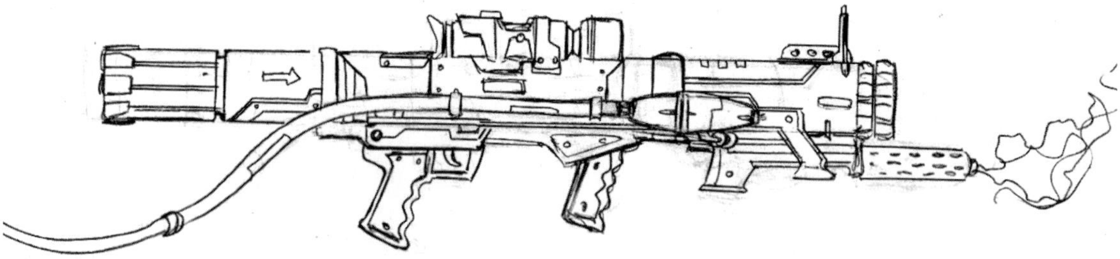

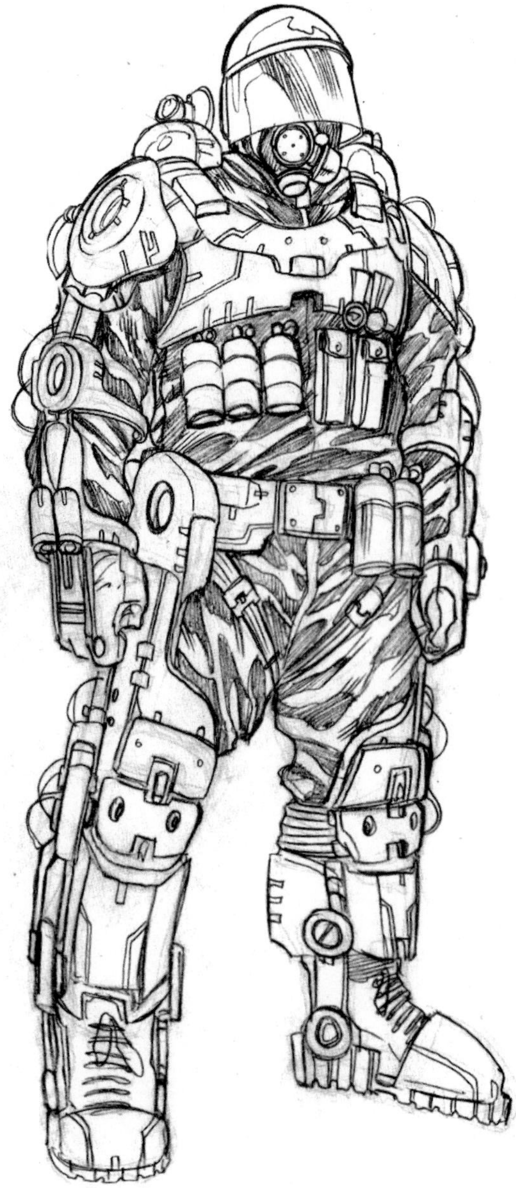

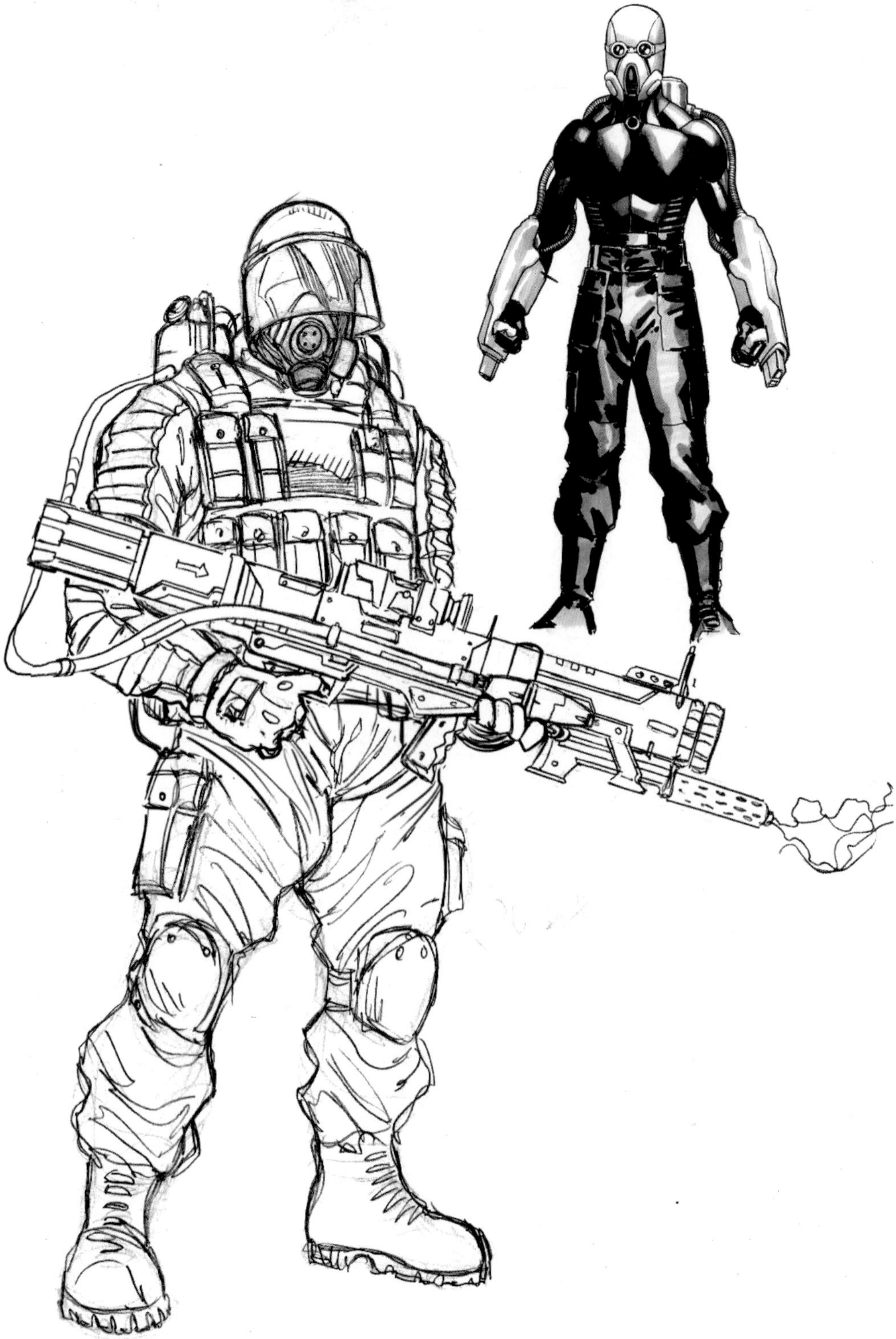

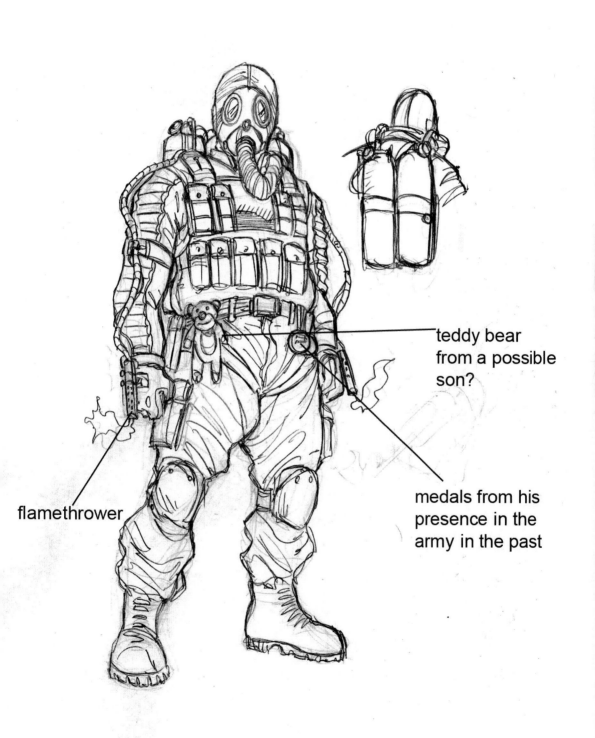

teddy bear
from a possible
son?

flamethrower

medals from his
presence in the
army in the past

"Simone and artist Ardian Syaf not only do justice to Babs' legacy, but build in a new complexity that is the starting point for a future full of new storytelling possibilities. A hell of a ride."
—IGN

START AT THE BEGINNING!

BATGIRL VOLUME 1: THE DARKEST REFLECTION

BATWOMAN VOLUME 1: HYDROLOGY

RED HOOD AND THE OUTLAWS VOLUME 1: REDEMPTION

BATWING VOLUME 1: THE LOST KINGDOM

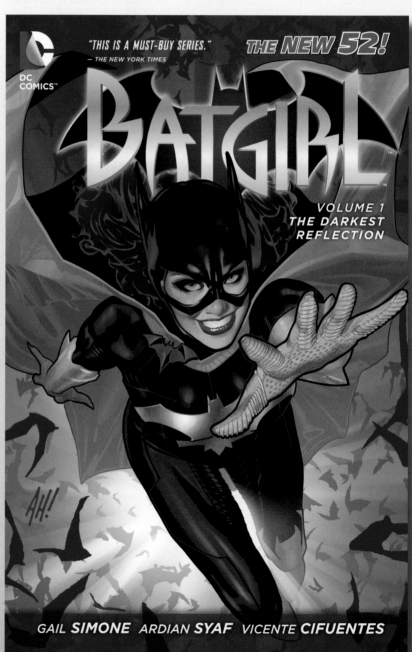

GAIL **SIMONE** ARDIAN **SYAF** VICENTE **CIFUENTES**

START AT THE BEGINNING!

BATMAN VOLUME 1: THE COURT OF OWLS

BATMAN & ROBIN VOLUME 1: BORN TO KILL

BATMAN: DETECTIVE COMICS VOLUME 1: FACES OF DEATH

BATMAN: THE DARK KNIGHT VOLUME 1: KNIGHT TERRORS

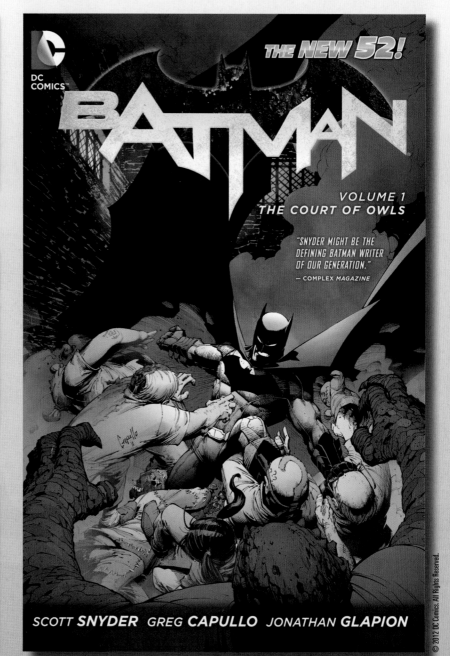

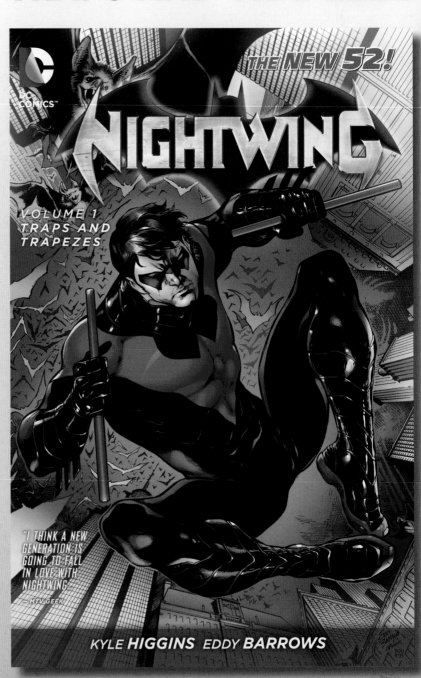